Nationalism and Power Politics in Japan's Relations with China

Despite flourishing economic interactions and deepening interdependence, the current political and diplomatic relationship between Japan and China remains lukewarm at best. Indeed, bilateral relations reached an unprecedented nadir during the spring of 2005, and again more recently in autumn 2012, as massive anti-Japanese demonstrations across Chinese cities elicited corresponding incidents of popular anti-Chinese reprisal in Japan.

This book systematically explores the complex dynamics that shape contemporary Japanese–Chinese relations. In particular, it analyses the so-called 'revival' of nationalism in post-Cold War Japan, its causality in redefining Japan's external policy orientations and its impact on the atmosphere of the bilateral relationship. Further, by adopting a neoclassical realist model of state behaviour and preferences, Lai Yew Meng examines two highly visible bilateral case studies: the Japanese–Chinese debacle over prime ministerial visits to Yasukuni Shrine, and the multi-dimensional dispute in the East China Sea which comprises the Senkaku/Diaoyudao territorial row, alleged Chinese maritime incursions and bilateral competition for energy resources. Through these examples, this book explores whether nationalism really matters; when, and under what circumstances nationalism becomes most salient; and the extent to which the emotional dimensions of nationalism manifest most profoundly in Japanese state-elites' policy decision-making.

This timely book will be of great interest to students and scholars of both Japanese and Chinese politics, as well as those interested in international relations, nationalism, foreign policy and security studies more broadly.

LAI Yew Meng is Senior Lecturer in Politics and International Relations at the Centre for the Promotion of Knowledge and Language Learning (CPKLL), Universiti Malaysia Sabah.

Sheffield Centre for Japanese Studies / Routledge Series
Celebrating 50 Years of Japanese Studies at the University of Sheffield, 1963–2013
Series Editor: Glenn D. Hook
Professor of Japanese Studies, University of Sheffield

This series, published by Routledge in association with the Centre for Japanese Studies at the University of Sheffield, both makes available original research on a wide range of subjects dealing with Japan and provides introductory overviews of key topics in Japanese Studies.

Nationalism and Power Politics in Japan's Relations with China

A neoclassical realist interpretation

LAI Yew Meng

LONDON AND NEW YORK

First published 2014
by Routledge
2 Park Square, Milton Park, Abingdon, Oxon OX14 4RN

Simultaneously published in the USA and Canada
by Routledge
711 Third Avenue, New York, NY 10017

Routledge is an imprint of the Taylor & Francis Group, an informa business

British Library Cataloguing in Publication Data
A catalogue record for this book is available from the British Library

Library of Congress Cataloging in Publication Data
Lai, Yew Meng
Nationalism and power politics in Japan's relations with China : a
neoclassical realist interpretation / Yew Meng Lai.
        pages cm
  Includes bibliographical references and index.
  1. Japan–Relations–China. 2. China–Relations–Japan. 3. Nationalism–
Japan. I. Title.
  DS849.C6L25 2013
  327.5105209'051–dc23   2013002739

ISBN: 978-0-415-62911-9 (hbk)
ISBN: 978-0-203-10010-3 (ebk)

Typeset in Times New Roman
by HWA Text and Data Management, London

MIX
Paper from
responsible sources
FSC
www.fsc.org   FSC® C013604

Printed and bound by CPI Group (UK) Ltd, Croydon, CR0 4YY

For Maureen, Nathania and Nadia

Contents

Illustrations

Figures

Tables

Acknowledgements

I would like to express my deepest gratitude to the following people and institutions for their significant contributions to the production of this book. My heartfelt thanks go to Professor Christopher W. Hughes and Professor Shaun Breslin for their astute supervision and unyielding support, without which neither this book nor the doctoral thesis from which it is derived, would have been possible. I am especially grateful to Professor Hughes for introducing this work to the series editor and thus paving the way for its publication. I would also like to thank Universiti Malaysia Sabah (UMS) for funding my doctoral study, and to acknowledge my debt to the following Japanese institutions, the Japan Foundation London Office, the Japan Institute of International Affairs and the Keio University's Institute of East Asian Studies and Faculty of Law – all of which provided invaluable assistance during my stay in Japan. My sincere gratitude to Professor Kokubun Ryosei for being the perfect host, sharing his insight on Japanese–Chinese relations and for setting up personal introductions, many of which yielded informative interviews with key elites. I would also like to thank my UMS colleague, John Mark Storey for carefully proof-reading the manuscript and suggesting improvements, and Chia Yean, for her assistance in preparing the illustrations for the book. Likewise, my deepest appreciation to the series editor, Professor Glenn Hook, for granting this modest work the opportunity to see the light of day, and to the Routledge editorial team for their professional support during its production.

On a personal note, I am indebted to my family for their unconditional love, support and encouragement which have given me the strength to endure the demands of the academic profession. My profound gratitude goes to my parents and sister, and especially my wife, Maureen, and our lovely daughters, Nathania and Nadia, whose love, understanding and sacrifices have made it possible for me to juggle my professional and familial responsibilities throughout the years of study. Above all, I thank God for the blessings, hope and spiritual guidance, without which, the completion of this book would not have been possible.

The publishers and the author would like to thank the following for permission to reproduce their material: Universiti Malaysia Sabah (UMS), for kind permission to reproduce parts of articles from Lai Yew Meng, 'Nationalism and shifting security perceptions in contemporary Japan–China relations', in Saidatul Nornis and Asmiaty Amat (eds), *Setitik Dijadikan Laut, Sekepal dijadikan*

Gunung: Sebuah festschrift untuk Dr. Mohd. Sarim Hj. Mustajab (Kota Kinabalu: Penerbit UMS, 2012), pp. 123–58; and Lai Yew Meng (2009) 'Nationalism and the question of "history" in Sino-Japanese relations', *Jurnal Kinabalu*, 15 (2009): 81–106. Cambridge University Press for kind permission to quote from Gideon Rose, 'Neoclassical realism and theories of foreign policy', *World Politics*, 51/1 (1998): 144–72. The International Association of Computer Science & Information Technology (IACSIT) Press, Singapore, for kind permission to reproduce parts of an article by Lai Yew Meng, 'Resurgent nationalism and changing security perceptions in contemporary Japan-China relations', in Dong Lijuan (ed.) *The International Proceedings of Economic Development and Research: Humanities, Society and Culture*, 20 (2011): 114–20. Springer Science+Business Media B.V. for kind permission to adapt a table on Japanese public opinion regarding prime ministerial visits to Yasukuni from Phil Deans (2007) 'Diminishing returns? Prime Minister Koizumi's visits to the Yasukuni Shrine in the context of East Asian nationalisms', *East Asia*, 24 (2007): 269–94. Taylor & Francis Ltd. for kind permission to quote from Gavan McCormack, 'Nationalism and identity in post-cold war Japan', *Pacifica Review*, Vol.12(3) (2000): 247–63. Daiki Shibuichi, 'The Yasukuni Shrine dispute and the politics of identity in Japan: why all the fuss?', *Asian Survey,* 45/2 (March/April 2005): 197–215. (c) 2005 by the Regents of the University of California. Reprinted by permission of the University of California Press.

All Japanese and Chinese names appear in the book with family name first, in line with Japanese and Chinese conventions.

Abbreviations and glossary

AOAB	Asian and Oceanian Affairs Bureau
APEC	Asia Pacific Economic Cooperation
ARF	ASEAN Regional Forum
ASEAN	Association of Southeast Asian Nations
ASEM	Asia-Europe Meeting
CCP	Chinese Communist Party
CCS	Chief Cabinet Secretary
CSC	Continental Shelf Convention
DPJ	Democratic Party of Japan
ECS	East China Sea
EEZ	Exclusive Economic Zones
EU	European Union
FDI	Foreign Direct Investment
FM	Foreign Minister
FTA	Free Trade Agreement
G-7	Group of Seven
G-8	Group of Eight
GDP	Gross Domestic Product
GSDF	Ground Self-Defence Force
IR	International Relations
JCG	Japan Coast Guards
JCP	Japan Communist Party
JDA	Japan Defence Agency
J-MSA	Japan Maritime Safety Agency
JETRO	Japan External Trade Organisation
JSP	Japan Socialist Party
LDP	Liberal Democratic Party
METI	Ministry of Economy, Trade, and Industry
MEXT	Ministry of Education, Culture, Sports, Science and Technology
MFA	Ministry of Foreign Affairs (China)
MOD	Ministry of Defence
MOE	Ministry of Education

MOFA	Ministry of Foreign Affairs (Japan)
MSDF	Maritime Self-Defence Force
NCR	Neoclassical Realism
NDPG	National Defence Programme Guidelines
NGOs	Non-Governmental Organisations
NIDS	National Institute for Defense Studies, Japan
ODA	Official Development Assistance
OECD	Organisation for Economic Cooperation and Development
PARC	Policy Affairs Research Council
PFT	Peace and Friendship Treaty
PKO	Peacekeeping Operations
PLA	People's Liberation Army
PM	Prime Minister
PRC	People's Republic of China
ROC	Republic of China
SDF	Self-Defence Force
SDPJ	Socialist Democratic Party of Japan
SFPT	San Francisco Peace Treaty
SNG	Sub-national Government
TMD	Theatre Missile Defence
TWL	Territorial Waters Law
UN	United Nations
UNCLOS	United Nations Convention on the Law of the Sea
UNECAFE	United Nations Economic Commission for Asia and the Far East
UNSC	United Nations Security Council
US	United States (of America)
WTO	World Trade Organisation

Japanese terms

anime	Japanese cartoon
fushinsen	mystery or suspicious ship
gaiatsu	foreign pressure
gaiko-zoku	diplomatic tribes/caucuses
habatsu	factions
Hinomaru	Japan's national flag
jinja	shrine
Kantei	The Prime Minister's Office
Keidanren	Japan Business Federation
Keizai Doyukai	Japan Council for Economic Development
Kimigayo	Japan's national anthem
koenkai	constituency-based organisations
kuromaku	Informal political actors and 'power brokers' of Japanese politics (e.g. ex-senior bureaucrats or senior politicians)

manga	Japanese comic
Nihon Izokukai	Japan Association of War-Bereaved Families
Nihon Seinensha	Japan Youth Federation
nihonjinron	theories of the Japanese
Nippon Kaigi	Japan Conference (the biggest nationalist-rightwing organisation in Japan)
sakoku	isolationism
seikei bunri	separation of politics and economics
Seirankai	Blue Storm Group (an ultra-nationalist/rightwing organisation affiliated to the Liberal Democratic Party of Japan)
tenno gaiko	emperor diplomacy
Tsukurukai	Japan Society for History Textbook Reform
uyoku	ultra-nationalists and ultra-rightwing elements
yakuza	Japanese 'underworld' elements/Japanese mafia
zaikai	Japanese big business community
zoku	policy tribes/caucuses

Non-Japanese terms

Article 9	The article in Japan's Constitution that renounces war and the use of force
Aussenpolitik	Foreign policy, foreign affairs
Comfort women	Women coerced into sexual slavery/prostitution by the Imperial Japanese Army during World War II
Innenpolitik	Domestic policy, domestic affairs
irrendenta	A territory that is historically, culturally or ethnically related to one nation or political unit but is subject to foreign political control
'kowtow' diplomacy	Deferential diplomacy
Lebensraum	Living space or habitat
sui generis	Peculiar or unique
terra nullius	Nobody's land or territory belonging to no one
Unit 731	A clandestine bio-chemical warfare research and development unit of the Imperial Japanese Army that conducted human experimentation programmes during the Second Japanese-Chinese War (1937–1945)

Introduction

The relationship between Japan and China has long been a source of interest to scholars of International Relations (IR). It is perhaps a puzzle for those who expect that intensified economic relations during the last three decades would result in warmer political and diplomatic exchanges. However, developments since the mid-1990s demonstrate that, despite flourishing economic interactions and deepening interdependence, political ties remain, at best, lukewarm. Besides an increase in diplomatic friction arising from the frequent resurrection of unresolved bilateral issues, there has been a noted decline in mutual affection between the two societies. Indeed, bilateral relations reached an unprecedented nadir during the spring of 2005, and again in autumn 2012, in the wake of the outbreak of massive anti-Japanese demonstrations across Chinese cities that uncharacteristically elicited corresponding incidents of popular anti-Chinese reprisal in Japan. Although both governments endeavoured to repair their fragile relationship following the so-called 'April storm' during the 2005 episode, their efforts were eventually undermined by then-Japanese prime minister, Koizumi Junichiro's fifth pilgrimage to the controversial Yasukuni Shrine in October 2005. The visit resulted in a year-long suspension of bilateral summitries as Japanese–Chinese ties struggled to find traction against a potential free-fall.

Experts commonly opine that political, socio-economic and strategic transformations or 'structural changes' in both domestic and international realms have made post-Cold War Japanese–Chinese relations volatile (Self 2002; Kokubun 2006; Mori 2007). Apparently, the revival of nationalism as a product of these structural changes has become a potent force redefining their national interests and external orientations, which concomitantly affected their bilateral relationship. According to observers, the noticeable shifts in Japanese and Chinese foreign policies have been as much a strategic response to the structural transformations brought about by the Cold War's demise as a reflection of the ongoing domestic socio-political changes, where nationalism has become influential in shaping the public mood and domestic political debate. Media coverage of their bilateral affairs has been unrestrained in blaming nationalism as the major culprit, while informed Japan–China watchers have consistently associated their fragile relationship with strong nationalist undercurrents in both countries. Although few predict violent conflict between Japan and China, many contend that domestic nationalist pressure is increasingly constraining both governments' foreign policy options, especially when managing nationalist-nuanced issues that persistently haunt diplomatic relations.

Scholars like Whiting (2000), Rozman (2002), Gries (2004) and Tamamoto (2005b) argue that nationalism is responsible for cultivating increasingly negative mutual images, stereotypes and prejudices, and raising the stakes of competition for pride and prestige. Meanwhile, Austin and Harris (2001), Self (2002), and contributors to Heazle and Knight's (2007) edited volume highlight its role in perpetuating and widening the perceptual divides between the two governments and societies, all of which are contributory to one another's markedly assertive foreign policy and hardnosed attitude in recent handling of bilateral issues that underscore their deteriorating relationship. Heazle (2007: 181) construes that both the Chinese and Japanese people's 'strong sense of national pride and growing [mutual] indignation ... play a large part in the current pattern of blame-laying and accusations between the two countries'. Similarly, Roy (2005), Christensen (1999), Yahuda (2006), among others, share the opinion that reactive-confrontational nationalisms and clashing national identities are exacerbating mutual suspicions, mistrust and historical acrimony, which not only threaten to derail overall Japanese–Chinese relations, but also draw the two East Asian powers into potential rivalry and conflict. Simply put, the conventional wisdom recognises nationalism's efficacy in (re)defining contemporary Japanese–Chinese ties.

To be sure, both governments have thus far managed to maintain a relatively functional and pragmatic relationship, and kept bilateral tensions from spiralling out of rational control. They also appear to have the capacity to rein in domestic nationalist sentiment, to an extent, and prevent it from undermining their broader national interests in the context of the bilateral ties and the region as a whole. In fact, diplomatic exchanges have proceeded at various levels and channels, despite the 'political chill'. Similarly, both sides have demonstrated willingness to put aside differences to cooperate via multilateral platforms on key regional security issues, i.e. the Six-Party Talks on North Korea's denuclearisation, not mentioning the political will to seek mutual, albeit ad-hoc measures to manage their own periodic diplomatic crises arising from unresolved bilateral disputes. Moreover, both countries have seen their socio-economic linkages strengthened during the period of worsening politico-diplomatic relations. Burgeoning bilateral trade and investments have brought mutual benefits and deepened interdependence, with an economically vibrant China not only supplanting the United States (US) as Japan's top trading partner in 2004, but also widely recognised as the 'growth engine' responsible for lifting the sluggish Japanese economy out of its prolonged doldrums (Taniguchi 2005). Meanwhile, 'human diplomacy' or grassroots-level interactions between the two societies have increased significantly, exemplified by the growth in tourism, cultural and educational exchanges, as well as flourishing sub-national-level cooperation, i.e. sub-regional economic integration schemes between Japanese prefectures and Chinese provinces, and the mushrooming of sister cities (Jain 2006). The Chinese characterised this dichotomous trend as 'cold politics, hot economics' (*zhengleng, jingre*), a representation likewise shared by the Japanese media and commentators in describing the state of the bilateral relationship.[1]

Against the backdrop of flourishing domestic nationalist sentiment in both countries, such paradoxical trends and developments appear to contradict the conventional notion regarding nationalism's salience in shaping one another's foreign and security policy orientation, let alone becoming an overarching feature in recent Japanese–Chinese relations. It is undeniable that the negative dynamics of rising nationalism, historical animosity and changing power relations are fuelling mutual insecurity and working against the emancipation of a genuinely stable and progressive relationship. Yet, other factors in the external and domestic realms (e.g. deepening economic interdependence, Washington's role within the US–Japan–China 'triangular' relationship and the domestic political process) simultaneously affect foreign policy-making, and can mitigate (or exacerbate) nationalism's impact on policy behaviour/preferences. More importantly for this book, how nationalism interacts with these variables and how they are mediated by the intersubjective perception and calculation of state-elites, under specific conditions and time periods, are crucial questions that need to be addressed, to ascertain the extent to which it influences Japanese policy-making.

Considering these fundamental questions concerning nationalism's role and potency, this volume sets out to systematically explore the complex dynamics that shape contemporary Japanese–Chinese relations. Although not discounting the significance of external/structural–material factors, it aims to explicate the role of domestic–ideational determinants, namely 'nationalism' and its interactions with other external–internal variables in influencing state behaviour/preferences in the bilateral ties. More specifically, this book seeks to analyse the so-called 'revival' of nationalism in post-Cold War Japan, its causality in redefining Japan's external policy orientations and its impact on the atmosphere of the bilateral relationship. Interpreting from a neoclassical realist perspective, it offers a theoretically informed and novel examination about why, how, when and to what extent nationalism matters in Japan's China policy, arguing that nationalism can be salient for Japanese state-elites.

Nationalism in Japanese–Chinese relations: a theoretical conceptualisation

Nationalism/identity politics has been an ever-present determinant in Japanese–Chinese relations due to the complex interplay between their shared history and culture, and the evolving power dynamics that have shaped their past and present interactions. It is therefore common to find it mentioned and/or addressed, either explicitly or implicitly, in most studies that scrutinise the subject matter. There is a rich collection of IR and area studies literature on Japanese–Chinese diplomacy, which range from classic works by Newby (1988) and Whiting (1989), to more contemporary ones by Drifte (2003), Rose (2005), Wan (2006), and Heazle (2007). While this literature has dealt comprehensively with Japanese–Chinese relations from one angle or another, and notwithstanding their acknowledgement of 'nationalism' as a factor, most have dedicated limited treatment to understanding its impact on the bilateral ties, let alone how it affects the policy-making of each nation.

To be sure, there are several works drawing explicit attention to the question of rising nationalism in Japanese–Chinese relations. Both Downs and Saunders (1998–9) and Deans (2000) explore nationalism's role in the bilateral management of the Senkaku/Diaoyudao dispute during the 1990s. The former focuses on how the contradictory goals of promoting Chinese nationalism and economic development as a twin 'legitimisation' strategy affect Beijing's responses, while the latter emphasises the manipulation of nationalism during the periods of dispute by elites and domestic actors in China, Japan, and Taiwan to realise their respective political and diplomatic expedience. Meanwhile, Rose (2000: 169) examines the resurgence of state and cultural nationalisms in both countries, arguing that they are 'predominantly inward-responses to domestic and external changes', and, therefore, carry no serious implications for Japanese–Chinese ties. Conversely, Rozman (2002) found that nationalism, as a political tool and emotive sentiment, has contributed to their worsening mutual images, undermining both governments' political will to bring about a lasting thaw in bilateral ties. Likewise, He (2006), Satoh (2006a/b), Chan and Bridges (2006), and Heazle (2007) argued that clashing nationalisms, national myth-making and the advent of the politics of pride, history and identity, are central to understanding current Japanese–Chinese problems. Although emphasising the role of nationalism, these article-length analyses have neither incorporated clear theoretical frameworks to systematically assess the extent to which nationalism is responsible for their deteriorating ties, nor explicitly addressed questions regarding its salience vis-à-vis other external–domestic variables influencing Tokyo and Beijing's behaviour in the bilateral relationship. Also, with the exception of Downs and Saunders (1998–9), most have not thoroughly explored the role of other variables in mitigating or exacerbating domestic nationalist impulses, and their consequential impact on both governments' responses towards sensitive bilateral issues. Furthermore, the questions of how, in what manner and under what conditions nationalism affects the domestic political apparatus and foreign policy-making process are left unexplained in these studies.

That said, there are book-length analyses like those of Bong (2002) and Chung (2004) that apply existing analytical frameworks to nationalism's role in shaping Japan and/or China's territorial policies. The former introduces a 'legitimisation strategy model' (similar to Downs and Saunders (1998–9)), which is also akin to Robert Putnam's 'two-level game' theory utilised by the latter, in their respective inquiries into the 1992 and 1996 Japanese–Chinese disputes over Senkaku/Diaoyudao. However, both studies focus exclusively on one issue area (territorial dispute *per se*) and not on Japanese–Chinese relations over a variety of issue areas. Their analysis of the Senkaku/Diaoyudao dispute is also the only specific case involving Japanese–Chinese interactions among the several case studies employed, with Bong (2002) looking chiefly into island disputes between East Asian states, whereas Chung (2004) focuses predominantly on China's management of its neighbourhood territorial rows. Moreover, nationalism is not explicitly identified as their research theme, and the period of investigation is limited to the early post-Cold War years, without many contemporary references. This book aims to address these oversights.

Indeed, as important a factor as it is, there are few IR-oriented studies that pay specific attention to nationalism and identity politics in explaining Japanese–Chinese diplomacy, and Japan's China policy-making. Elaborated in the following chapter is the qualitative difference between contending analytical approaches or theoretical traditions in terms of their treatment of nationalism in international relations, with the arguments largely transpiring within the mainstream IR-versus-constructivism/area studies debate. The former, especially those of the mainstream realist and liberal genre, tend to under-appreciate nationalism, and generally, the role of domestic–ideational variables in constraining the policy behaviour that affects their bilateral affairs. This is inherently due to mainstream IR theories' preoccupation with structural–material variables and system-level analysis, which causes them to ignore ideational and domestic-level theorisation, and assume 'nationalism' and the likes to be unproblematic and *a priori* given (Tooze 1996). In contrast, nationalism and identity politics is central to constructivism/area studies' line of enquiry, which emphasises domestic-level analysis and cultural–ideational factors in explaining Japanese–Chinese relations. As one would expect, the subject matter has received most attention amongst constructivists and Japanese/Chinese studies specialists, but existing works also encounter analytical limitations that include the lack of discernible theoretical frameworks to operationalise nationalism, and over-dependence on using domestic/cultural-ideational factors to explain foreign policy and international outcomes, at the expense of external/structural–material imperatives.

To address such limitations, this book proposes neoclassical realism (NCR), a 'middle-ground' IR construct that emphasises external–domestic interaction and bridges mainstream IR-constructivist reasoning, to operationalise and systematically assess nationalism's role in Japanese–Chinese relations, with a specific emphasis on Japanese nationalism and Japan's China policy-making. First coined by Gideon Rose (1998: 146), NCR is a theory of state behaviour/ preferences within the broad realist research programme that generally shares the tradition's standard assumption that 'the scope and ambition of a country's foreign policy' is driven primarily by systemic pressures and its relative power position in the international system. However, it rejects neo-realism's 'ultra-parsimonious' 'privileging of systemic-structural variables over [unit-level-ideational] factors' (Roth 2006: 487). Neoclassical realists assume that the effects of systemic imperatives are indirect, complex and subjective, and that 'there is no immediate or perfect transmission belt linking [them] to foreign policy behaviour' (G. Rose 1998: 146–7). Instead, they must be filtered through, or mediated by peculiar domestic political process/actors, or unit-level 'intervening' variables, i.e. state-elites/decision-makers' perceptions, domestic political competition, nationalism, state institutions, all of which under specific conditions and time contexts stand to precipitate variations in states behaviour/preferences (Sterling-Folker

1997; Taliaferro 2006; Schweller 2004; Lobell *et al.* 2009). In other words, external constraints do not automatically induce states towards specific policy choices. 'Rather, states respond (or not) … in ways determined by both internal and external considerations of policy elites, who must reach consensus within an often decentralised and competitive political process' (Schweller 2004: 164).

Specifically in this study, NCR allows nationalism to be operationalised as a domestic, ideational (identity) and material (power) variable within its essentially realist-oriented framework. This variable interacts with the domestic political process and influences Japanese policy-makers/state-elites' perceptions, which then determine particular foreign policy options that either exacerbate, or alleviate bilateral problems vis-à-vis China. By problematising nationalism, the NCR model developed in Chapter 1 can systematically assess its impact, and helps explicate the conditions in which it does or does not prevail in Japanese (or Chinese) policy-making in their bilateral affairs. More significantly, it can promote a better understanding of other dynamics involved, while simultaneously answering pertinent questions regarding nationalism's role in Japanese–Chinese relations that previous works have not convincingly elucidated.

The NCR framework has been utilised in earlier studies to incorporate ideational explanations in specific areas of East Asian diplomacy, namely those by Cha (2000), and Sterling-Folker (2009). For example, Cha (2000) elucidates the role of historical animosity within an NCR model of 'quasi-alliances versus balance-of-threat' to address the concepts of abandonment and entrapment in the triangular alliance dynamics between the US, Japan, and South Korea during the Cold War. Meanwhile, Sterling-Folker (2009) introduces identity politics and domestic political competition as the 'intervening variable' to provide a neoclassical realist explanation on why cross-straits relations became more confrontational during the mid-1990s, despite deepening economic interdependence between China and Taiwan. Although both studies introduce variables that are partially symptomatic of and related to nationalism, it is not their explicit undertaking to examine and operationalise its role in explaining their respective dependent variables, let alone their superficial definition and conceptualisation of the national phenomenon, which differs from that espoused by this book. Indeed, apart from these article-length analyses, there is no existing literature that incorporates a clear, systematic NCR model to specifically address the question of nationalism in the Japanese–Chinese relationship and/or post-Cold War Japanese foreign policy-making.[2]

As mentioned, nationalism has been explicated in preceding studies that utilise liberal-oriented or other 'integrative' theoretical constructs to explain Japanese–Chinese management of territorial disputes, mainly from China's perspective. Considering their inherent characteristics, these 'mid-range' theories like NCR share relatively similar basic assumptions, which have lead to the deduction of comparable sets of hypotheses (see Bong 2002: 20–3). However, as argued in the next chapter, there exist discernible theoretical distinctions, mainly in the theoretical arguments/nuances, and the deductive and ontological emphasis between these frameworks and the 'NCR model of nationalism and state behaviour' incorporated in this volume, apart from differences in the conceptualisation of the analytical construct, research problem and the scope of investigation. This book is therefore a relatively novel undertaking, which can contribute in theory-building terms to enhancing realism's explanation of nationalism, not only in Japan–China ties and Japanese foreign policy, but also in the international relations of East Asia or other regions, where nationalist/identity politics thrive in interstate diplomacy.

Definitions, empirical scope and case studies

Nationalism is commonly described as a nebulous phenomenon, intrinsically psychological, socio-cultural and profoundly political in essence, as it is emotional and instrumental in disposition. Chan and Bridges (2006: 130) rightly observe that the meaning of nationalism 'changes with issue, time, space, and target or object', which explains the amount of jargon found in the literature on nationalism to define the various dimensions of its manifestation.[3] Considering its complexities and intersubjectivity, and for clarity and relevance, this book limits 'nationalism' to an amalgamation of three mutually embracing and reinforcing meanings:

1   'a state of mind' (Kohn 1965: 9), or psychological condition that cultivates sentiments of belonging, and unites a collective group of people (community/ nation), whose members perceive they share a common identity based on unique physical-territorial, socio-cultural, historical and emotional elements (Guibernau 1996: 47) ('Self') vis-à-vis the 'Others';
2   a political ideology/principle that identifies the nation with the state (Gellner 1983), and mobilises the political will of its population 'to decide upon [and realise] their common political destiny' (Guibernau 1996: 47, 62), domestically or internationally; and
3   a political instrument utilised by state/state-elites for mass mobilisation and other domestic political expediency (state/official nationalism), and by nationalist groups to apply political pressure on the governmental decision-making process (popular nationalism).

Deriving their essence from the classic definitions of Kohn (1965), Gellner (1983), Smith (1986) and Guibernau (1996), they represent nationalism's fundamental underpinnings and multi-dimensional characteristics. These meanings typically manifest two distinctive yet correlated and, at times, mutually embracing forms, namely state/official/elite-driven and popular/grassroots nationalism. Both are examined in this book, since state/state-elites and popular nationalists concurrently 'participate in nationalist politics' (Gries 2004: 87). Nationalism's rational-utility and emotional dispositions are equally taken into account, as both 'sense/passion' and 'sensibility/reason' matter when analysing international relations and foreign policy-making (Gries 2004: 20, 87–90). Taken together, such a conceptualisation that places emphasis on the 'top–down' and 'bottom–up' perspectives, as well as nationalism's political/instrumental and socio-psychological dimensions, helps generate more accurate interpretations of its role in shaping both state–society and interstate relations. It is especially applicable to Japan's contemporary relations with China, since Japanese nationalism professes most of these meanings and exhibits the suggested attributes.

This book primarily draws on the causal role of Japanese (neo-)nationalism in shaping Japan's China policy during the Koizumi administration (April 2001–September 2006), and the years immediately preceding it. Here, (neo-) nationalism's definition is limited to its 'normalcy-driven', 'anti-China' and 'dependent' manifestations.[4] Chinese nationalism is periodically, albeit briefly, addressed to elucidate its reactivity towards Japanese policy and propensity for triggering reactive, anti-Chinese nationalism within Japan that induces Tokyo's specific policy responses. State agency and state-to-state relations are the central focus, while non-state elements are explored to comprehend their influence on the intergovernmental relationship. This study utilises the 'state' or more specifically, 'state-elites' as the principal agent, since they ultimately make the foreign policy decisions. The definition of 'state-elites' is limited to a small cohort of central decision-makers/power-wielders within the Japanese state apparatus, comprising typically the Prime Minister (PM), Foreign Minister (FM), Chief Cabinet Secretary (CCS) and the heads of the Ministry of Economy, Trade and Industry (METI) and Japan Defence Agency (JDA), among others.[5] The PM and the Prime Minister's Office or *Kantei*, is afforded particular emphasis following their consolidation of power vis-à-vis the bureaucracy via the political and administrative reforms in 2001, not mentioning the advent of a dynamic yet allegedly 'unconventional' leadership and policy-making modus operandi under Koizumi Junichiro. Besides state-elites, this study also addresses the role of relevant Japanese bureaucracies as part of the state agency. Equally under scrutiny are other domestic agents, especially political parties, i.e. the ruling Liberal Democratic Party (LDP), its coalition partners and their political opponents. Within the LDP, attention is given to the influence of factions (*habatsu*), policy-tribes (*zoku*) and senior 'power-brokers' (*kuromaku* and 'China-Hands') on China policy-making. Meanwhile, the business community (*zaikai*), pressure groups and public opinion represent the non-state agency in this analysis.

Since nationalism manifests itself through both state and non-state agencies, an important aspect of this study is to observe the aforementioned actors' association with and participation in nationalist politics. Particularly under scrutiny are the politico-ideological dispositions and affiliations of state-elites, their dependence on nationalism as a power instrument, their inclination towards a nationalist or pragmatic foreign policy agenda, and their domestic political resolve vis-à-vis nationalist and moderate elements, to infer nationalism's salience in affecting their policy perceptions and calculations. Similarly, the role of key nationalist pressure groups highlighted in Chapter 3, as well as public opinion towards China, will be elucidated, since popular nationalism, when expressed via these civil society channels, can be a formidable domestic political constraint on the behaviour of the Japanese state.

Externally, the atmosphere of the US–Japan relationship, specifically Tokyo's perception of Washington's 'alliance commitment/resolve'[6] under their bilateral security alliance, will be examined in concurrence with the developments in

Japanese–Chinese ties to measure Japan's relative power position vis-à-vis China at a given time period.[7] Relative power position, as defined here, does not merely refer to the conventional material power capabilities that a state possesses (i.e. economic; military, including 'offensive-defensive' capabilities; and other typical material-based wherewithal), but equally concerns, if not more, the estimation of one's favourable/unfavourable overall position and politico-diplomatic resolve vis-à-vis the other during a specific period and context. The result may not necessarily reflect the actual power distribution between the interacting states, since information on the relevant indices of power position has to be translated through what Sterling-Folker (1997: 19) sees as the 'opaque filter' of state-elites' perception and other domestic actors/processes, in accordance to NCR's dictum. The analysis also accounts for other significant contextual factors and actors in the international environment that concurrently affect Japanese state-elites' perceptions and calculations in China policy-making.

This book introduces two highly visible bilateral issues as case studies to test the NCR model, namely the Japanese–Chinese debacle over prime ministerial visits to Yasukuni Shrine, and their multi-dimensional dispute in the East China Sea (ECS), which comprises the Senkaku/Diaoyudao territorial row, Chinese maritime incursions and bilateral competition for energy resources in the contested waters. The case studies are selected on criteria of relevancy and nature of dispute. First, both are highly relevant cases insofar as they are contemporary issues that strike the nationalist chord, and arouse strong nationalistic impulses within Japan and China. As shall be elaborated respectively in Chapters 5 and 6, the Yasukuni problem relates to their clashing national-historical identities, whereas the ECS dispute is reflective of their competing territorial nationalism and its correlation with the notion of sovereignty. Indeed, rising nationalism in both countries is widely perceived to have increased the stakes and retarded possible resolutions of both issues. Besides inciting unadulterated nationalistic passion and emotion, both issues also have the tendency to be instrumentalised by Japanese (and Chinese) state/state-elites and non-state actors (i.e. nationalist pressure groups/individuals, etc.) for domestic political and external expediency. Secondly, both were amongst the most visible and contested bilateral issues during the period of investigation. Indeed, Koizumi's annual Yasukuni visits during his premiership became arguably the single, most damaging problem affecting their diplomatic relations, while the ECS debacle constantly ratcheted up bilateral tension that equally contributed to the Koizumi era being labelled as one of the most debilitating periods in Japanese–Chinese ties since their diplomatic normalisation in 1972. Also, both case studies echo long-standing and unresolved quarrels over wider issue areas: Yasukuni reflecting the perennial 'history problem', whereas the ECS concerns maritime territorial sovereignty and geo-strategic/economic considerations.

In addition, the two case studies are qualitatively different; the former is predominantly a symbolic and 'soft' issue, whereas the latter represents a 'real/ tangible' and potentially explosive problem. In other words, the Yasukuni issue, like most other 'history' problems, is the kind of bilateral issue in

Japanese–Chinese relations that, although having the capacity to stir passionate popular and official nationalistic outbursts, is not likely on its own to manifest more potent forms of bilateral confrontation. Conversely, the ECS debacles are, to an extent, 'zero-sum' issues of national security and sovereignty/integrity, which have the propensity to galvanise nationalistically charged societal and governmental responses of a more belligerent nature. Last, but not least, one case study is primarily a single-actor/single-issue dispute, whereas the other is multi-actor/multi-issue. Specifically, Yasukuni is a 'history'-related, single-issue dispute, concerning only prime ministerial shrine visits, and mainly triggered by a single actor in former PM Koizumi's controversial decision to pay annual homage, during his time in office. In contrast, the ECS is a multi-dimensional dispute that involves not only rival sovereignty claims, but also competition for geo-economic and geo-strategic control over the contested area (namely the symbolic, economic and military-security dimensions of their bilateral ties). It is likewise a multi-actor issue involving the actions, management and coordination of multiple state/official actors (i.e. related ministries and agencies), as well as the direct provocative actions of non-state actors (i.e. related activities of popular nationalist groups and individuals).

The selection of these two relevant, yet qualitatively different case studies is intended to ensure that this volume can adequately address not only the fundamental question of whether nationalism matters, but equally to examine why, how, when and to what extent it matters in Japan's relations with China, especially when it comes to managing sensitive bilateral issues of nationalistic persuasions. Since both issues are highly visible, nationalistic disputes, they are primed to help explicate: (1) whether nationalism (domestic nationalist pressure and/or state-elites' personal nationalistic convictions) is important in shaping Japan's China policy, and if so (2) when, and under what circumstances nationalism becomes most salient, in relations to other external–domestic factors that concurrently affect Japanese policy-making; and (3) the conditions and the extent to which the emotional and/or instrumental dimensions of nationalism manifest most profoundly in Japanese state-elites' policy decision-making. In doing so, both issues, which were also amongst the most hotly and frequently contested during the period of investigation, allow this study to simultaneously elucidate on the much anticipated question of whether nationalism was, in fact, the primary driver of Japan's China policy-making during the Koizumi administration, and the major factor shaping their deteriorating ties. Likewise, the intention to select these qualitatively different case studies is mainly to promote a broader, yet more astute comprehension of Japanese policy-makers' perception, attitude and responses towards domestic nationalist pressure and/ or their personal nationalistic convictions over a variety of issue areas, which this book argues may not be necessarily consistent, despite occurring under similar conditions and time contexts. Finally, the advantages of having single-actor versus multi-actor case studies are that they not only allow this study to comprehensively capture the whole range of Japanese policy actors and the different levels of policy-making involved, but also shed light on the degree of policy-making leverage that different levels/categories of actors have, or can exude, when managing single- and multi-issue bilateral disputes of nationalistic orientation vis-à-vis China.

Overall, this book is a study of state behaviour and international outcomes between Japan and the People's Republic of China (PRC). Specifically, its analytical aim is to explain how, when, under what conditions and to what extent nationalism as a domestic determinant affects Japan's China policy and the bilateral relationship. This means that, despite the necessary references to China and Chinese nationalism, it is Japan and Japanese nationalism which are the primary objects of investigation. Yet, this is not a study of Japanese nationalism *per se* and, therefore, does not purport to meticulously explore from all angles the intersubjectivities of the 'national' phenomena in contemporary Japan, although its fundamental underpinnings, nature, manifestations and political/ external dynamics are adequately explicated for the purpose of this investigation. It is also neither a general analysis of Japanese foreign policy-making nor a 'bi-country' undertaking to understanding Japanese–Chinese relations from a multi-dimensional perspective, but principally, a study of the contemporary trend and development of their bilateral ties as effected by resurgent nationalistic forces on the workings of Japanese statecraft in Japan's China policy.

Design and aims of the book

This book is designed to address three research questions pertaining to the commonly perceived notion of nationalism as a driving force behind the decline in contemporary Japanese–Chinese relations, namely:

1   the manner, conditions and the extent to which domestic nationalist pressure/ sentiment in Japan is responsible for their problematic bilateral relationship;
2   its salience vis-à-vis other external-domestic factors constraining Japan's behaviour towards China over sensitive bilateral issues; and
3   whether these other factors exacerbate or mitigate nationalism, and the related impact on Japan's policy options, under specific conditions and time context.

This volume agrees with the conventional wisdom, but only to a qualified extent. Bearing in mind the plausible roles of other variables, it takes a 'middle-ground' position by hypothesising that nationalism matters in Japan's relations with China, albeit under specific external–domestic conditions and time context, as perceived by state-elites. It argues that, besides domestic nationalist pressure, Japanese state-elites need to consider other factors, which they may perceive, during specific periods and under particular conditions, as more crucial in determining their policy decisions, even when managing the most sensitive of bilateral disputes. Moreover, domestic nationalist pressure does not act in isolation, but interacts with these other policy determinants, which can exacerbate/mitigate its effects on external decision-making. This study contends that nationalism's salience in affecting foreign policy choices, i.e. choosing between assertive–nationalistic and moderate–conciliatory policy options, hinges on state-elites' perceptions of the conditions related to its interaction with other 'power' variables that concurrently affect foreign policy-making, namely Japan's relative power position vis-à-vis China, and state-elites' domestic political resolve vis-à-vis nationalist and moderate forces, at a given time period (see Bong 2002; Downs and Saunders 1998–9). It also depends on their ability to balance or 'trade-off' between achieving nationalist and pragmatic policy objectives.[8] Ideally, the Japanese government/state-elites would like to embrace the domestic nationalist agenda, while simultaneously seeking to realise Japan's broader national interests. However, their ability to advance narrow/nationalistic China policy goals is dependent primarily on the condition of a favourable relative power position vis-à-vis China. Conversely, an ambiguous or disadvantageous relative power position would require state-elites to either balance or trade-off between the two contradictory objectives. When the balancing becomes unmanageable, they may have to trade-off one for the other (see Downs and Saunders 1998–9; Bong 2002), during which decision-making (rational, or otherwise) may decisively hinge on the intersubjective perceptions and calculation of state-elites and the prevailing domestic political process (Sterling-Folker 1997; Schweller 2004). Such considerations underscore this study's NCR supposition regarding the primacy of power politics and the intervening function of domestic-ideational variables in affecting state behaviour and the conduct of interstate diplomacy.

The results of this academic enquiry are expected to address questions regarding nationalism's propensity in shaping Japan's contemporary relations with China. Indeed, depending on the condition and time period, nationalism may or may not necessarily prevail in Japan's actual policy options, even when managing discernible nationalist issues, like the Yasukuni Shrine and ECS disputes, although it may manifest via the symbolic/rhetorical dimension of their diplomatic responses. This book also aims to

1   promote a balanced interpretation of the background, driving forces, characteristics, and international orientations of contemporary Japanese nationalism (especially so-called neo-nationalism), and its role in domestic politics/foreign policy-making process;
2   comprehend the workings of domestic nationalist pressure and other external–domestic variables shaping Japan's China policy trends, and the regressive atmosphere of their post-Cold War bilateral relationship;
3   enrich the related body of literature by providing an assessment of nationalism in Japanese–Chinese ties via an 'integrative' IR framework that operationalises and systematically analyses its role in the case studies concerned; and
4   contribute to the progressiveness of IR realism, where NCR's hospitability to domestic–cultural–ideational theorising can promote interactions between and theoretically bridge mainstream IR and constructivist/area studies reasoning to advance a holistic, albeit realist understanding of Japan's foreign policy and international relations.

Methodology and book structure

This qualitative study employed documentary analysis, supplemented by elite interviewing, as the main research methods. The primary sources derived from publicly available official documents (i.e. official publications, annual reports and white papers from related ministries/agencies and think-tanks), and relevant information in various published forms (i.e. official declarations and press statements, and media reports/commentaries/debates via newspapers, magazines and news monitoring services). The latter, especially media coverage from major Japanese and Chinese as well as international and regional news agencies, were a crucial empirical source due to the contemporary nature of the study. Additionally, public opinion surveys conducted by both government and the media provided statistical data for the analysis and interpretation of popular sentiment on nationalism, Japanese–Chinese relations and Japanese perceptions, images and attitudes towards the Chinese government and people, and vice versa. Meanwhile, secondary sources from the related literature furnished the background information, contending theoretical approaches, substantive argumentations and critical perspectives that helped deepen the knowledge and understanding required to tackle the research problem.

Also, elite interviews were employed as a supplementary, albeit important source of information to overcome problems concerning restricted access to and the 'superficiality' (*tatemae*) of official Japanese (and Chinese) documents. The targeted interviewees comprised relevant government officials, academics, politicians, press members, public figures and other informed individuals. The selection of interviewees was principally based on identifying those with first-hand knowledge of Japan's China policy pertaining to the two case studies, preferably the protagonists of the diplomatic processes concerned (Hagstrom 2003: 92). Equally important were relevant members of the academic community and media, and opinion leaders knowledgeable on Japanese nationalism and foreign policy-making.

This volume is divided into six chapters. The first deals with the contending theoretical debates, and the framing of the NCR model for this study. Chapter 2 offers a background of the dynamics, trends and developments in Japanese–Chinese relations during the Cold War and post-Cold War periods. An insight into nationalism in post-war and contemporary Japan is the undertaking of the third chapter. Meanwhile, Chapter 4 provides an analysis of nationalism and Japanese foreign policy-making, followed by an overview of the interactions between and the reality of nationalism's salience vis-à-vis other variables in shaping Japan's China policy and the bilateral relationship. The subsequent two chapters are dedicated to the case studies of the Yasukuni Shrine and ECS disputes. A generalisation of the findings and a view of nationalism's implications for future Japanese–Chinese diplomacy constitute the concluding chapter.

1 Interpreting nationalism in Japanese–Chinese relations

Contending approaches and analytical frameworks

The study of Japanese–Chinese relations, like most analyses of interstate relationships and foreign policy-making, has largely transpired within a broad range of analytical frameworks that straddle along different approaches and contending theoretical paradigms. Depending on their respective choice of central variables and level of analysis, these approaches have yielded rich, but often diverse explanations of their complex, multi-dimensional ties, and the periodic variations in Japanese policy with regard to the Chinese, when managing their bilateral affairs. This chapter discusses the efficacies and fallacies of the contending approaches, paying particular attention to their treatment of nationalism in explaining the nature of post-Cold War Japanese–Chinese diplomacy. It assesses and questions the viability of their respective interpretations, offering instead a realist-oriented, 'hybrid' analytical framework that bridges the reasoning of the competing disciplines and theoretical traditions, to systematically assess nationalism's role in Japan's policy-making in the context of the bilateral relationship.

Area studies versus mainstream IR theories and alternative frameworks

The task of identifying a suitable approach and theoretical framework is no less daunting, as a literature survey on Japanese–Chinese relations and Japanese/ Chinese foreign policies not only points to the complexity of choosing between competing approaches (between IR and area studies approaches), but equally in opting for one theory over another within the IR theoretical divides (C. Rose 1998: 29).[1] According to Caroline Rose, previous studies have largely developed within the confines of the separate disciplines of IR and area studies. The key distinction between these two so-called 'mutually exclusive' approaches lies in their perennial debate regarding the prevalence of the 'general' and 'specific' features in understanding state behaviour and the nature of international politics. Whilst IR-oriented studies seek to establish 'universally applicable' explanations by privileging general over 'country-specific' attributes, area studies emphasise the understanding of foreign policy via a state's idiosyncratic or *sui generis* features (C. Rose 1998: 28). Rose (1998: 28) opines that although both approaches have produced quality research, their respective preoccupations expose them to criticisms; the IR approach for over-emphasising parsimony and 'denigrating factual detail', whereas area studies is guilty of 'amassing empirical data but [is] usually devoid of theoretical value' (cf. Brecher 1972: 1).

Adding to this conundrum has been the presence of effervescent debates between competing theoretical paradigms within the IR discipline itself, notably realism versus liberalism of the mainstream genre, and lately, between mainstream and alternative theories like constructivism (C. Rose 1998: 28–9). These contending IR theories can be fundamentally divided according to their respective emphasis on the 'level-of-analysis', and preoccupation with particular variables in explaining state behaviour/preferences and international outcomes (Singer 1961; Zakaria 1992; Desch 1998). Proponents of macro-level analysis or *Aussenpolitik* favour external determinants and systemic-level explanations, in contrast to their exponents at the opposite end of the theoretical divide, who privilege *Innenpolitik* or domestic, unit-level reasoning (Zakaria 1992: 179–80; G. Rose 1998: 146). There is, likewise, analytical distinction amongst theories within *Aussenpolitik* and *Innenpolitik*, based on their preferred analytical variables, with some privileging structural–material imperatives, while others stress cultural–ideational factors.[2] For example, conventional macro-level theories like neo-realism (Waltz 1979; Mearsheimer 2001) and neo-liberal institutionalism (Keohane and Nye 1977; Axelrod 1984; Keohane 1989) privilege structural–material explanations (i.e. neo-realists on systemic distribution of power and relative capabilities; neo-liberal institutionalists on the logic of economic interdependence, degree of cooperation and institutionalisation). Meanwhile, alternative discourses in the guise of Alexander Wendt's (1992) 'systemic-constructivism' rationalise the workings of international politics primarily on ideational and normative grounds.[3] On a similar note, there are *Innenpolitikers* that advocate structural–material arguments: classical realists implicitly press on state–society relations and human nature (Taliaferro 2006: 470; Morgenthau 1967; Aron 1966), while proponents of liberalism place premiums on domestic politics, institutions and regime types (Rosecrance and Stein 1993; Evangelista 1997), i.e. 'two-level game' and 'democratic peace' theses (Putnam 1988; Russett 1993), as opposed to ideational arguments – culture, norms, identity and interests (Lapid and Kratochwil 1996; Berger 1996, 2003; Katzenstein 1996) – championed by domestic-constructivists.

In a sense, this theoretical division within the IR approach reflects, and to an extent subsumes, the interdisciplinary divides between IR and area studies (C. Rose 1998: 29), considering the overlapping assumptions and exclusively domestic-centred analysis espoused by both *Innenpolitik* and area studies. To be sure, there are subtle differences between area studies and *Innenpolitik* theories, insofar as the former is country-specific in focus, targeting attributes peculiar to the country/area of study, whereas the latter, especially of the mainstream genre, is inclined towards generally applicable variables and explanations. Yet, hospitability to ideational variables, which are also inherently *sui generis*, puts area studies and IR constructivism well within the same analytical confines. The similarities and differences between these contending approaches and theories are defined in Table 1.1, based on the 'level-of-analysis' and 'choice-of-variables' criteria.

Table 1.1 Similarities and differences between contending approaches and theoretical paradigms

Level of analysis	Type of variable	
	Structural–material	*Cultural–ideational*
Macro-level (external)	1. Mainstream IR theories of *Aussenpolitik* (neo-realism/ neo-liberalism)	1. Systemic constructivism
	2. Integrated framework	2. Integrated framework
Micro-level (domestic)	1. Area studies	1. Area studies
	2. Mainstream IR theories of *Innenpolitik*	2. Domestic constructivism
	3. Integrated framework	3. Integrated framework

To overcome their inherent rigidity and weaknesses, not mentioning fastidious categorisations, scholars have embraced an 'intra/interdisciplinary' approach, developing frameworks that not only integrate macro- and micro-level analyses (i.e. Zhao 1996), but also IR and area studies to generate more comprehensive and accurate accounts of international relations and foreign policy-making (C. Rose 1998: 29; Katzenstein 2008). Indeed, all three mentioned approaches appear in the literature on Japanese–Chinese relations.

Area studies approach

The area studies approach, which is akin to the constructivist and *Innenpolitik* line of thinking, and emphasises the idiosyncratic features as well as prevalence of domestic–ideational factors in shaping a country's foreign policy, is traditionally popular in the analysis of Japanese/Chinese foreign policies and Japan–China ties. This approach explicitly targets the 'unique' internal attributes and processes of Japanese/Chinese foreign policy-making, highlighting the significance of political and strategic culture, history, identity, ideology, domestic political process and the roles of decision-makers' perceptions, bureaucratic/factional politics, etc., while paying little attention to the forces of the international system in shaping state behaviour (C. Rose 1998: 33).

According to its proponents, Japanese–Chinese relations can be best explained through culturally and historically specific lenses, which shape the distinctive nature of their bilateral ties. For instance, they have frequently cited historical–cultural legacies, i.e. the 'cultural affinity' and 'teacher–student complex' theses (Iriye 1992; Ijiri 1996; Gries 2004: 40), historical experiences and 'war-guilt' complex (Mendl 1995: 85; Kojima 2000; Gong 2001a/b), among others, as key to understanding what Drifte (2003: 6–7) defines as post-war Japan's 'deferential' policy towards China, or Japanese 'minimalist' foreign policy, for that matter (Miyashita 2002: 163). Others draw on political cultures, i.e. Japan's traditional culture, behavioural patterns and isolationist tendency (Sato 1977; Reischauer 1977), Sinocentrism, or China's 'middle-kingdom' mentality (Fairbank 1968) and cultural inclination towards elite/factional politics (Whiting 1989) to explain their foreign policy behaviour as reflected in the bilateral ties. There are also works that highlight peculiar characteristics of foreign policy-making. Zhao (1993) argues that 'behind-the-scenes policymaking mechanisms' or informal channels and practice, which are distinct features of Japanese domestic politics, have been traditionally influential in Japan's China policy-making. The unit-level and *sui generis* emphasis of this approach, however, as Singer (1961: 83) asserts, tends to 'overdifferentiate' states, while under-appreciating the constraints of the international system on their foreign policy orientations (C. Rose 1998: 31).

The IR approach: Aussenpolitik and Innenpolitik

Conversely, the IR approach, characterised by a lively intradisciplinary debate, has received favourable attention in studies of Japanese–Chinese diplomacy (C. Rose 1998: 30). Proponents of *Aussenpolitik* in the neo-realist and neo-liberal institutionalist moulds emphasise the salience of systemic imperatives, and the primacy of structural–material factors in shaping Japanese/Chinese state behaviour towards their bilateral ties. According to neo-realist studies, the contemporary trend in Japanese–Chinese relations can be primarily viewed as a reflection of rational manoeuvring by both states in response to the structural transformation of the international environment, and their changing power dynamics, which offer constraints and opportunities in augmenting their respective external goals and strategies. Kokubun (2006), Roy (2005), Mochizuki (2007) and Yahuda (2006), among others, argue that the demise of the Cold War security architecture, growing regional uncertainties and changing power equations between Japan and China are key to explaining the downturn in contemporary Japanese–Chinese relations. Both states are seen striving to readjust to these new dynamics in their relationship, competing strategically on the one hand, and cooperating economically on the other, while redefining and jockeying for the leadership position in the unravelling post-Cold War regional order. Glosserman (2006) argues that their problematic relationship is predictably shaped by the new 'geometry' of East Asia, with China 'the ascending dragon' and Japan 'the setting sun', locked in an asymmetrical triangular relationship with America, the sole superpower. In his assessment of the security dimension of Japanese–Chinese ties, Wu (2000: 304) notes this realist logic in Japanese post-Cold War external orientation, where 'concerns over balance of power, geopolitical competition, and military-strategic rivalry constantly inform Tokyo's thinking about the PRC'.

Similarly, analysis of Japan's changing foreign/security policies by Heginbotham and Samuels (1998), Singh (2002) and Kliman (2006), and specifically, its China policy by Green and Self (1996), Green (2001) and Choi (2003), came up with terminologies like 'normal country', 'mercantile realism', 'reluctant realism', 'creeping realism', 'transitional realism' and 'selective realism', to characterise what they saw as Japan's increasingly realist-oriented external/security orientations, and its inclination towards a containment-cum-engagement strategy or policy of hedging against China's rise in the fluid East Asian environment. A realist-oriented definition of engagement is partially employed by Drifte (2003) and Hughes (2005), who both see Japan as having chosen a policy that is 'based on providing China with economic and political incentives, hedged by military balancing through its own military force and the military alliance with the US' (Drifte 2003: 3). The conventional realist interpretation of Japan's post-Cold War relations with China is best summarised by Green's (2001: 6 and 9) observation that:

> Japanese foreign policy is increasingly being shaped by strategic considerations about the balance of power and influence in Northeast Asia, particularly vis-à-vis China … [where] [c]onfidence that Japanese economic leadership would integrate China on Japan's terms has ebbed and a new realism has emerged regarding the limits of Japanese economic influence and the growing power aspirations of Beijing.
>
> (cf. Murata 2006: 41)

Meanwhile, neo-liberals see Japanese–Chinese relations as having been fundamentally shaped by economic considerations. Both states place high premiums on maintaining a pragmatic and functional relationship via bilateral and multilateral engagements to reap the benefits of deepening economic interdependence, despite periodic tensions fuelled by issues in the politico-strategic dimension. Heazle (2007) and Taniguchi (2005) opine that flourishing economic cooperation and interdependence are salient in keeping Japanese–Chinese relations from serious degeneration, and in understanding the 'cold politics, hot economics' dichotomy, or 'cold peace' in their contemporary bilateral ties. Wan (2006: 3), likewise, suggests that dramatic growth in Japanese–Chinese economic interactions fuelled by the global market are 'providing a cooperative foundation for the overall bilateral relationship and moderating political and security tensions'. The powers of interdependence and economic imperatives in promoting a pragmatic and relatively stable bilateral relationship are also echoed by Tok (2005) and Sutter (2002) in their less pessimistic observations of the contemporary trend in Japanese–Chinese diplomacy.

Undoubtedly, both mainstream IR theories offer broad insights and persuasive explanations via their respective analytical foci. Nonetheless, their inherent over-emphasis on systemic–structural influences make these IR approaches relatively inhospitable to unit-level investigation, thus rendering them problematic to critics who consider domestic and ideational factors as equally if not more crucial to understanding the bilateral ties.

On the contrary, *Innenpolitikers* advocating an approach that scrutinises the contents of the domestic 'black box' argue that the trends in Japanese–Chinese diplomacy are often manifestations of internal decision-making processes and fierce domestic political competition, i.e. among state-elites, and between contending factions and ideological divides. Deriving mainly from the mainstream IR tradition, studies of this nature remain tied to understanding their bilateral policies and relationship via generally applicable, domestic, structural–material (i.e. political system, decision-making apparatus, level of development) and agent-based (decision-makers' perceptions, personality and idiosyncrasies, etc.) explanations (C. Rose 1998: 32). For instance, in his scrutiny of the domestic politics of the principal actors in Japanese policy-making, Tanaka (2000: 3) contends that 'critical foreign policy areas such as Sino-Japanese relations have long been dominant themes of manoeuvring among domestic actors in the Diet, in the interagency bureaucracy, and in the media'. Murata (2006: 37) also views highly complicated domestic politics as a major source of Japan's China policy, arguing that 'changes in Japanese political parties, bureaucracy, and public opinion', or more specifically, 'negative mass sentiments towards China, the lack of policy coordination among coalition parties in power, and the relative decline of MOFA and its "China school", have made the Japanese [China] policy-making process more complex, defused and fragmented'. These observations are echoed by Kojima (2000) and Sasajima (2002) in their respective analysis of the domestic determinants/institutions shaping Japan's China policy.

Similarly, Takamine (2005, 2006) explores the domestic political and bureaucratic interests motivating Tokyo's strategic use of foreign aid, which brought a 'new dynamism' to its security relationship with Beijing. Meanwhile, Tok (2005: 296) sees China's policy towards Japan as 'a contentious issue among the Chinese leadership', shaped by fierce political infighting between the competing factions in the ruling echelon, a view shared by Breslin (1990) and Whiting (1989, 2000), who develop understandings of Chinese foreign policy-making via the analysis of leadership politics and perceptions, bureaucratic structures, institutions, and policy processes.

Some of these studies have also partially derived their explanatory power from the liberal analytical tool of 'domestic political systems/regime type' to explain the degeneration in post-Cold War Japanese–Chinese ties. The most common argument refers to their different political systems (i.e. divergent political norms, institutions and values), magnified since the Tiananmen Incident and the Cold War's demise, which have widened the 'perception gap' between both governments and societies (Glosserman 2003; Takahara 2004). Such divergence, according to Tsang (1999) and Takagi (2006), is one reason driving Japanese closer to a democratising Taiwan, and increasingly turning the island into a point of contention between Japan and China. The 'Putnam-esque' 'two-level game' framework is, likewise, utilised to analyse Japanese–Chinese disputes, i.e. the study by Chung (2004) on China's management of the Senkaku/Diaoyudao dispute.

An alternative and increasingly popular line of domestic-focused investigation on Japanese–Chinese relations and their respective policy-making is constructivism, which draws specifically on the power of unit-level, albeit cultural-ideational variables similar to those identified by Japanese/Chinese studies scholars. Constructivist works by Katzenstein (1996) and Berger (1998) explore the norms and culture of anti-militarism in post-war Japanese society to account for Japan's pacifist-oriented foreign policy, which according to Drifte (2003: 6) is an important source in explaining 'Japan's inclination to deference and restraint in the bilateral relationship with China' that mainstream IR theories of realism and liberalism cannot fully grasp. Most popular in the constructivist vein of study has been the emphasis of 'historical memory' in shaping the perceptions and images, not mentioning identity and interests of Chinese and Japanese that underscore their problematic relationship since diplomatic normalisation in 1972. In his seminal work, Whiting (1989) draws on the salience of history in shaping Chinese images of Japan and their bilateral ties. Whiting contends that Japanese war legacies in China remain pivotal in influencing the external perceptions, attitudes and decision-making of China's revolutionary generation of leaders, as reflected in Beijing's hypersensitivity towards any shift in Tokyo's China policy orientation and its vitriolic responses when managing their bilateral disputes during the 1980s. Similarly, Okabe (2001), Yang (2002) and Rose (2005) highlight the problems concerning history, memory and historical reconciliation that periodically undermine their post-Cold War diplomatic exchanges, while He (2006) elucidates on the manipulation of historical memories by both sides to create national myths and revisionist discourse, which are responsible for fuelling contemporary Japanese–Chinese enmity. Another typical/regular constructivist line of reasoning is to be found in the 'clash-of-identities' and 'divergent nationalisms' theses, which are elaborated in the following section.

As described in Table 1.1, there are overlaps between constructivism, mainstream *Innenpolitik* theories and the area studies approach, in terms of their chosen 'level-of-analysis' and choice of analytical tools. Accordingly, constructivist explanations tend to be criticised in a similar way to *Innenpolitik* and area studies, based on an over-emphasis on domestic-level explanations while failing to adequately acknowledge and theorise systemic constraints on Japanese/Chinese external behaviour towards the bilateral ties. Additionally, constructivism is guilty of marginalising structural–material factors in favour of cultural–ideational attributes peculiar to, and/or shared by Japan and China, which hinders its ability to make systematic and generalised assessments of the bilateral relations.

The holistic/integrated approach

The third approach is one that favours a synthesis of IR and area studies assumptions. Advocates of this eclectic and holistic approach opine that a more accurate explanation of Japanese–Chinese relations and/or Japanese/Chinese foreign policy can be derived by integrating the micro- and macro-levels of analysis, and drawing on both structural–material and cultural–ideational variables. Works by Caroline Rose (1998), Austin and Harris (2001), Drifte (2003) and Wan (2006), among others, have utilised such a framework to explain both governments' policy responses when managing their bilateral relationship. Caroline Rose (1998: 37–9) asserts in her analysis of the history textbook issue that the incorporation of an organising framework explicating the interactions between international and domestic variables is useful in overcoming the shortcomings of 'standard explanations of conflict in Sino-Japanese relations'.

Meanwhile, Drifte (2003: 4) proposes 'a dynamic model of engagement ... based on elements of Realism, Liberalism and Constructivism', which he deems necessary to adequately comprehend Japan's common and unique behaviour, when managing its security relations with China. Drifte's opinion is shared by Katzenstein and Okawara (2001) in their espousal of analytical eclecticism that avoids unproductive 'paradigmatic clashes' while fostering a non-exclusive, 'problem-driven' approach to explaining Japan, China and Asia-Pacific security (cf. Katzenstein 2008: 9–10, 20–4, ch. 2). According to Katzenstein (2008: 9), '[e]clectic scholarship complements and utilises, rather than replaces scholarship produced by existing traditions'. It also promotes epistemological and ontological flexibility that helps avoid parsimonious and myopic assumptions based on a single paradigm (Katzenstein 2008: 46). By combining realist, liberal and constructivist-oriented analytical tools, and recognising the benefits of multi-level/multi-variable analysis, analytical eclecticism generates a fuller interpretation of the evolution of Japanese–Chinese relations, which in Katzenstein's (2008: 24) opinion 'will be shaped by a mixture of engagement and deterrence in their bilateral relations, by their competitive and complementary region-building practices in an East Asia that will resist domination by either country (Katzenstein 2006), and by the cultivation of their different strategic and economic links to the American imperium'. Wan (2006: 3) likewise concludes that 'the complex Sino-Japanese relationship has been affected by systemic, social, and emotional factors following multiple causal processes in political, military, economic, and socio-cultural dimensions', which underscore the necessity for an eclectic approach to reduce the 'analytical myopia' resulting from the parochial lines of argument (Berger 2000: 411).

Since this volume explores the causal role of domestic–ideational determinants, specifically nationalism and its interactions with other external–internal variables in redefining Japan's relations with China, it is commonsensical to pursue this 'third' line of inquiry as the basic organising framework. Indeed, nationalism's salience vis-à-vis other determinants affecting Japanese behaviour/policy preferences towards the Chinese can be systematically assessed by developing a 'hybrid' framework that utilises analytical tools from both mainstream IR and constructivism/area studies. Such 'middle-range' theories that depart from the analytical orthodoxy are presently available, with some claiming to be more hospitable to and deductive in incorporating external and internal variables than others in the analysis of foreign policy. However, these theories, notably those foregrounding realism, have been accused of 'reductionism' and 'degenerative' analysis, as much by their hardcore theoretical brethren as by exponents from the opposing sides of the theoretical divides, for sacrificing parsimony, coherence and compromising realism's fundamental premises (Lakatos 1970: 117–18; Vasquez 1997; Legro and Moravcsik 1999). Before ascertaining a viable analytical framework, it would be appropriate to gauge the treatment of nationalism, generally, and its role in Japanese–Chinese ties, specifically, through the discourse found in existing literature, which has largely transpired within the context of the mainstream IR versus constructivism/area studies debate.

Treatment of nationalism in mainstream IR theories: realism and liberalism

The orthodox IR theoretical traditions of realism and liberalism are generally 'rationalist' theories that privilege structural–material variables in the analysis of state behaviour and international outcomes. In their contemporary guise, both neo-realism and neo-liberalism foreground systemic over unit-level investigation. The former emphasises the overarching importance of the anarchic international system in defining states' interests and actions in terms of relative distribution and balance-of-power within it (Waltz 1979); while the latter conceives state behaviour/preferences in the light of complex interdependence and interstate cooperation (Keohane and Nye 1977). Both theories share the assumption that unit-level and ideational factors are *a priori*, 'self-evident and non-problematic' (Lapid and Kratochwil 1996: 6) in the analysis of world politics. According to critics, their fundamentally 'statist', 'rationalist-materialist' as well as Hobbesian-oriented 'ahistorical', 'asocial' and 'acultural' perspectives of international relations, not to mention, fixation with systemic-level theorising, make these mainstream IR theories analytically inhospitable to problematising non-material factors, like culture, identity, historical memories and ideology (Inayatullah and Blaney 1996: 66–7; Pasic 1996: 85; Tooze 1996). In fact, cultural–ideational variables are deemed trivial and of secondary importance to both neo-realism and neo-liberalism, and are conveniently 'relegated to the domestic realm, where they remain irrelevant to the workings of international relations' (Pasic 1996: 85).

Mainstream IR theories' 'analytical myopia' on nationalism

Understandably, mainstream IR theories have severe limitations in offering a comprehensive understanding of nationalism in international affairs, since the 'national' phenomenon is a social construct, domestic and non-material in essence, as well as subjective and intersubjective in meanings/nature (Tooze 1996: pp. xviii–xix; Lapid and Kratochwil 1996: 13). This inadvertently leads these theories, or the IR discipline for that matter, to conveniently ignore 'the problem of nationalism' (Judt 1994: 51; cf. Lapid and Kratochwil 1996: 105), despite its growing salience in the post-Cold War epoch. For instance, nationalism is often under-appreciated, if not trivialised or neglected altogether, by neo-realism, due to its rigid theoretical construct and underpinnings that view states as undifferentiated (like-units), unitary actors, whose behaviour is conditioned and governed primarily by structural attributes of international anarchy (Waltz 1979). Also, conventional realist thought is dominated by the 'primacy of foreign policy' notion, which according to Zakaria (1992: 179–80), can mean: (i) international relations are significant in affecting the domestic arrangements of states; and (ii) interstate politics is a realm separate from domestic politics, where state behaviour is prevalently influenced by systemic, rather than domestic factors/pressures. By treating nation-state as a given, conventional realists in the Waltzian tradition are prone to overlook unit-level and ideational-normative imperatives, i.e. issues concerning the character of states and the social construction of state identity, which are related and essential to comprehending nationalism. Indeed, neo-realism's dismissal of such factors, its excessive indulgence in parsimony (Roth 2006: 487), and overdependence on 'system-level', 'rationalist-centred' and 'structural-material'-driven explanations, among others, are fallacies that render it 'problematique' when encountering nationalism from a theoretical viewpoint (Lapid and Kratochwil 1996: 116; Copeland 2000).

Similarly, liberal analysts tend to undervalue nationalism's efficacy. To neo-liberals, the construction of political identity is 'assumed to be unproblematic' due to its state-centric position (Tooze 1996: p. xviii). Despite viewing it as more of a collective, the state remains the neo-liberal construct's central unit of analysis, which puts 'sub-state' variables, like nationalism and identity, beyond its investigation (Tooze 1996: p. xix).

Critics of mainstream IR theories are also quick to highlight their flaws in theorising and explaining developments in regions like East Asia, where the political climate and intra-regional relations are commonly characterised by rising nationalist impulses, which tend to promote irregular and irrational state behaviour that somewhat defies the conventional IR logic and assumptions (Berger 2000, 2003). Realistically, the politico-security instability occurring in contemporary North-East Asia is as much a reflection of confrontational nationalisms and identity-related predicaments as of the usual variables identified by mainstream IR theories that affect regional stability, e.g. structural transformation of the regional security architecture, profound shifts in the power balance, emergence of potential non-status quo/revisionist powers, asymmetrical distribution of relative capabilities between regional actors, insufficient levels of economic interdependence and underdevelopment of multilateral norms and institutions, to name a few (Christensen 1999: 49; Friedberg 1993–4; Betts 1993–4; Berger 2000). In fact, rising nationalism and duelling national identities are increasingly shaping bilateral relations between regional actors like China and Japan, Japan and Korea, and China and Taiwan, which are problematic to standard neo-realist, or neo-liberal explanations (Berger 2003).

To be sure, mainstream IR theories have made efforts to incorporate nationalism and other unit-level ideational variables to address the glaring anomalies found in their theorisations of interstate relations, especially in specific regions during the post-Cold War epoch. To stem the retrogression of IR realism, which has come under severe attack from constructivists for its theoretical inadequacies, contemporary realists, i.e. Mearsheimer (1990a), Posen (1993) and Van Evera (1994), have opened up to nationalism's role under a revised neo-realist construct. Lapid and Kratochwil (1996: 110–16) opine that, through 'inclusionary control', they seek to address major nationalism-related problems in international politics from essentially neo-realist premises, a position that reflects a departure from the typically narrow Waltzian tradition of 'exclusionary control'.

However, critics like Lapid and Kratochwil (1996: 112) argue that the treatment of nationalism by these variants of neo-realism appears more of a 'retrofitting' or juxtaposing of the elusive phenomenon to fit into the traditional neo-realist construct without proper theorisation. In their opinion, nationalism is treated as 'merely a reflection of the more "basic" forces – such as the security dilemma and power balancing among the preexisting "like units"', reducing it to what Mearsheimer (1990b: 32) deemed a '"second order" variable, [or] an epiphenomenon of the international system and its anarchical structure' (cf. Lapid and Kratochwil 1996: 112). In other words, nationalism is often invoked as an ancillary factor to supplement the inadequacy of the Waltzian logic, exogenously incorporated to explain away anomalies in their non-traditional case studies.

Neo-realism's under-appreciation of nationalism in Japanese–Chinese relations

Indeed, most IR-centred studies of Japanese–Chinese relations tend to take nationalism less seriously, providing assumptions and analyses that fall short of appreciating the extent of its influence on their contemporary bilateral affairs. From the conventional realist perspective, nationalism is mostly a sub-factor exacerbating the 'strategic conundrums' and shifting power distributions between Japan and China, which studies by Green and Self (1996), Zhao (2002), Self (2002), Taniguchi (2005), Calder (2006) and Yahuda (2006), among others, deem as the core determinant affecting their bilateral ties. According to Yahuda (2006: 162), 'the key to understanding the deterioration in Sino-Japanese relations is the structural change in the international politics of East Asia'. Induced by the Cold War's demise, Yahuda (2006: 162–3) believes this change 'has led to the repositioning of regional great powers and … an intensification of economic development' among East Asian states, which has helped transform 'the regional and international balance of power'. Compounding the structural change have been the renewed efforts by regional actors 'to redefine their domestic, regional, and international identities', which Yahuda (2006: 163) insists have engendered a revitalisation of assertive nationalisms in China and Japan that are developing divergently, with one cast as the other's 'putative adversary'.

On a similar note, Kokubun (2001, 2006, 2007) has consistently associated the degeneration in contemporary Japanese–Chinese relations and shift in Japanese strategic thinking with the structural transformation of the post-Cold War international context, which brought an end to what he calls the '1972 System' that held the bilateral ties amiably together since diplomatic normalisation. The ensuing 'power shift' that saw China rising, and Japan stagnating, economically, politically and militarily, has evoked negative Japanese images and perception of the Chinese, fostering nationalistic attitudes that are increasingly driving Japan towards a so-called 'psychological cold war' with China (Kokubun 2007: 146–54). Zhao (2002: 39) notes China's rise to a foreign policy that is 'more assertive' and 'sensitive' to domestic popular nationalist sentiment, which complicates Tokyo and Washington's strategic calculations, as the Chinese leadership becomes more vulnerable to nationalist demands to address sovereignty issues like Taiwan and Senkaku/Diaoyudao, and redress Japanese-inflicted historical legacies.

The opposite is true of Japan's regression vis-à-vis China, notably in economic terms, which Takagi (2006), among others, insists has triggered Japanese consternation, fuelling anti-Chinese sentiment that exacerbates their negative perceptions of the changing power balance. Yang (2006: 133) notes that, 'facing China's rise, Japan's nationalism prevents the country from perceiving itself as a second-rate power', compelling it to use the US–Japanese alliance 'to balance out Chinese development while defending or promoting Tokyo's own international status'. The 'power shift' argument is also emphasised in several other studies, although some identify the shift not in terms of 'diverging fortunes' (Pei and Swaine 2005), but from a 'strong China, strong Japan' standpoint (Jin 2002: 51; Rose 2005: 6). Nonetheless, they generally share the view that Japanese–Chinese enmity and rivalry are the offspring of changing power dynamics, accentuated by rising nationalism in both countries.

Nationalism as a 'factor' aggravating the confrontational forces spawned by the fluid international order is also a theme shared by Christensen (1999), Self (2002), Calder (2006: 130) and Tsunekawa (2006), in their observations of how the unravelling Japan–China power equation, coupled with resurgent nationalisms fed by historical legacies, ethnocentrism and xenophobia in both countries, is magnifying mutual security concerns and fuelling a potential security dilemma. In his analysis, Christensen (1999: 54–5) pessimistically suggests that even though nationalist emotion has yet to severely affect 'the practical, day-to-day management' of Japanese–Chinese relations, it does influence their longer-term threat assessment, which 'may be more important in fuelling the security dilemma than particular diplomatic policies in the present'. Meanwhile, Tsunekawa (2006: 14) sees Japan's 'dependent nationalism' as a product of and a source 'that has precipitated the [security] dilemma through action–reaction cycles aggravating perception gaps among major powers in the region', including China.

Another related, key external–structural variable in the realist observation is the role of the US, and the US–Japan alliance, which is in Zhao's (2002: 32) opinion 'the most significant external actor/factor' shaping the direction of Japanese–Chinese relations. Echoing this is Takahara (2004: 161–2), who sees the US–Japan alliance as 'the largest issue in Sino-Japanese ties in the 1990s'. Its salience is, likewise, noted in most of the works cited earlier, although opinions do diverge regarding the implications of its interaction with nationalism or the appreciation of nationalism's role in these works. Optimists view the US–Japan alliance as a countervailing force suppressing chauvinistic nationalism in Japan and China. For instance, Green (2001: 87–9) suggests that the reason for MOFA's insistence on 'an iron-clad defense commitment' from the US on Senkaku/Diaoyudao during the 1996 dispute was to curtail Japanese nationalist pressure for 'a unilateral military capability' to deal with the issue, which could have triggered a Japanese–Chinese confrontation. Meanwhile, despite its fierce rhetoric, Beijing has always been quietly confident of the US–Japan alliance in containing a resurgence of Japanese militarism, although such confidence has somewhat eroded in recent years. Conversely, pessimists tend to see Washington's 'lopsided' policy as facilitating Japanese nationalist aspirations, i.e. reinstating military force as a foreign policy instrument, and emboldening other 'revisionist' agendas (historical revisionism, Taiwan policy, etc.) that are bound to trigger reactive anti-Japanese nationalism in China (Tamamoto 2004).

Apart from limited theorisation, another standard realist misgiving of nationalism is the tendency to accentuate its malevolence (Lapid and Kratochwil 1996: 114), which the majority of the above-mentioned studies have exaggerated when explaining Japanese–Chinese competition, rivalry and conflict. Such an extreme interpretation of nationalism is to be expected, due to realism's preoccupation with the assumption that state behaviour is conditioned by the 'possibility of conflict', where states are pressured into making calculations based on a zero-sum, worst-case scenario (Brooks 1997).

Likewise, it is common for realists to over-emphasise nationalism's instrumentality as a political tool utilised by both governments for diplomatic and domestic expedience. Tsang (1999) sees realist calculations as leading the PRC to foster a kind of narrow-minded nationalism that targets Japan, as a means to undercut Tokyo's credibility and intention to seek a larger political role in the region, which could hinder its own long-term external goals of irredentism and leadership in the Asia-Pacific. Conversely, the Japanese government, increasingly dominated by hawks and shaped by *realpolitik*, is, according to Miller (2000), Tamamoto (2004) and Taniguchi (2005), seeking to rejuvenate nationalism to mobilise popular support for a broader Japanese security role that has China well within its radar.

Simply put, a conventional neo-realist perspective of Japanese–Chinese relations draws explanatory power mainly from structural–material imperatives, namely shifts in relative capabilities and the balance of power, and the role of other external factors/actors, i.e. the US, in explaining Japanese/Chinese behaviour vis-à-vis the bilateral ties. Meanwhile, nationalism and identity issues are generally treated as a given and incorporated 'atheoretically' as an auxiliary variable exacerbating the salience of the realist central variables (Tooze 1996).

Neo-liberalism's treatment of nationalism: a 'mirror-image' of neo-realism?

Similar to neo-realism, nationalism's treatment by neo-liberalism is, at best, marginal, and lacking in proper theorisation. The marginalisation is due to neo-liberalism's fixation with its own set of analytical tools, which are state-centric and structural–material in essence. Although there are liberal theories that draw on domestic-level explanations, their preference for structural–material variables makes them less appreciative of nationalism or any ideational factors.

Most research in the liberal vein tends to under-estimate nationalism's forces, with Sutter (2002) and Heazle (2007), among others, implying that deepening socio-economic interdependence and incremental political reforms in China's case would help mitigate virulent nationalist sentiments, and eventually foster a progressive bilateral relationship. Likewise, a higher degree of institutionalisation of diplomatic norms and functions, and participation in multilateral institutions, serves to suppress excessive nationalism, while promoting greater cooperation between the two countries. For example, Sutter agrees that rising nationalist impulses in China and Japan are fuelling potential Japanese–Chinese rivalry even in the economic realm, as reflected by increased frictions in bilateral trade and Official Development Assistance (ODA) arrangements, and competition to establish regional Free Trade Agreements (FTA). However, there are, in his opinion, 'countervailing factors' limiting the rivalry, 'the most important' of which 'is that both Japanese and Chinese governments are domestically focused on the economic development of their countries', and thus, understand the importance of fostering peaceful, stable and cooperative relationships with each other, and with their regional neighbours to realise this priority goal (Sutter 2002: 39). This is echoed by Pei and Swaine (2005: 4–6), who cited two critical factors mitigating the risk of a Japanese–Chinese 'cold war', namely 'the top policy agenda of domestic economic reform', and steadfast interest in 'maintaining their mutually beneficial commercial ties'.

Similarly, Whiting (2000: 30) believes that, against the prevailing negative factors (i.e. fragile domestic politics fuelled by rising nationalism and mutual negative images), pragmatic considerations of mutual benefits with economics playing the key role are 'likely to tip the balance in a positive direction'. Meanwhile, Chung (2004: 53) notes that assertive nationalism in China and Japan 'is held at bay by expectations of mutual economic gains through increased trade and investment, and fear of accidental military provocation', in his 'two-level-game' study of the Senkaku/Diaoyudao dispute. Heazle (2007: 200) also concludes his analysis by suggesting the salience of the 'hot' economic relationship, which would at least for the foreseeable future, provide both governments 'with enough motivation to contain their [mutual] political animosity ... and resist any temptation to cause the relationship to deteriorate any further', despite the nationalism conundrum in current Japanese–Chinese diplomacy.

Indeed, from the liberal perspective, economic relations have always provided stable foundation for Japanese–Chinese politico-diplomatic ties, as with their effectiveness in channelling discord in the said arena, and are thus expected to remain so, as argued in the above studies. Nonetheless, the logic of economic interdependence is critically questioned by Yahuda (2006), who concedes that deepening economic interactions and mutual dependence have not necessarily led to more sanguine mutual images and improved political ties in the Japanese–Chinese case. Furthermore, Hilpert and Katsuji (2002: 152) note that growing economic interdependence can become problematic in the event of increased Japanese–Chinese economic competition, and that 'economic relations may also be a reason and a trigger for bilateral conflict', besides their unresolved nationalist disputes and shifting power relations. Shi (2007: 7) best sums it up by concluding that 'economic interdependence is far from a sufficiently reliable "safety cushion" for China–Japan relations'.

Another common neo-liberal view refers to multilateralism's mitigating role, where participation in regional multilateral platforms, like the ASEAN-Plus-Three, ASEAN Regional Forum (ARF) and Asia-Pacific Economic Cooperation (APEC), not to mention the Six-Party Talks on North Korean denuclearisation, are deemed constructive in forging mutual interests and cultivating 'a habit of cooperation' (Lam 2006a: 18), while containing nationalism-inspired bilateral competition and rivalry. Meanwhile, from the domestic-centred liberal perspective, the 'democratic peace' thesis highlights the potential role of increased political reforms and democratisation in curtailing the forces of confrontational nationalisms between China and Japan, paving the way for the development of a mature relationship. To be sure, observers tend to see popular anti-Japanese nationalism becoming more salient in a democratised China, as the restraining hand of the pragmatic Chinese Communist Party (CCP) regime withers (Takamine 2006: 146-7). However, Yang (2002: 23) suggests that, although 'democracy is not a panacea', and that 'greater openness in China in the short term may unleash some more extreme ultranationalist forces, in the long run, greater openness and critical examination of its own history – by a robust intelligentsia and by journalists' will help towards realising a genuine Japanese–Chinese reconciliation (Yang 2002: 26).

Proponents of the sub-state/non-state level of analysis share equally sanguine views of Japanese–Chinese ties, emphasising the mitigating roles of non-government organisations (NGOs), local governments, business groups and intensified 'people-to-people diplomacy' in cushioning the debilitating impact of nationalism and state-centred, 'zero-sum politico-strategic competition' on bilateral relations (Lam 2006a: 12). In his study of Japanese–Chinese interaction at the sub-national government (SNG) level, Jain (2006) explores the dynamic role of Japanese SNGs in promoting grassroots linkages with their Chinese counterparts via the twinning of cities/prefectures/provinces, trade promotion and economic/technical cooperation, which he asserts, 'can do much – and sometimes more than the central government – in cultivating close and valuable ties with China' (cf. Lam 2006a: 13). Takahara (2006) also claims that the activities of Japanese NGOs have contributed to forging mutual trust and alleviating anti-Japanese sentiment amongst Chinese peasants, in his case study of a Chinese province, while Hook (2006) contends that the 'China threat' discourse brewing in Japan did little to hinder the micro-regional economic cooperation and integration between Kyushu and Dalian.

In sum, mainstream IR studies in the realist and liberal veins are predominantly focused on theorising their respective central variables in explaining Japanese/ Chinese behaviour in their contemporary bilateral ties. Although commonly cited in their analysis, most have not dedicated adequate treatment to nationalism's role. Such marginalisation is the result of their respective theoretical preoccupations, which cause them to under-appreciate nationalism, and this explains their limited and typically 'after-thought' analysis of how it affects Japanese/Chinese domestic politics and foreign policy-making. It also accounts for why nationalist pressure does or does not translate into 'nationalist' foreign policy, due to state responses to external and domestic constraints/opportunities.

Nationalism in constructivism and area studies

As an alternative theoretical paradigm, constructivism addresses key issues in international relations that mainstream IR theories fail to adequately comprehend and explain. Like area studies, constructivism derives its strength from a set of assumptions and variables that systemic-based IR theories tend to ignore and consider as trivial, and of secondary importance. Specifically, it emphasises the constitutive and discursive role of domestic, cultural–ideational imperatives in constructing world affairs, i.e. culture, nationalism and identity, precisely the kind of (non-material/*sui generis*) variables scorned generally by proponents of neo-realism and neo-liberalism.

According to Berger (2003: 390), constructivists draw attention to the 'ideational and cultural world' of their 'research subjects' to understand the intersubjective meanings that generate their behaviour and actions. Constructivism explicates the social processes that endow actors (states, societies and individuals, alike) with particular cognitive lenses which help define their identities and interests and give meaning to their preferences and actions (Berger 2000: 410; Hopf 1998: 174–5). International politics/relations is assumed to be an ever-changing social process, defined by the peculiar identities and interests of its constituents (states), which are themselves social constructs, shaped and reshaped by intersubjective social norms and practices of their subjects (i.e. society/groups/individuals) (Wendt 1995; Hopf 1998). The emphasis on the intersubjective nature of the international system, and of identity and interests, means that constructivists are opposed to the 'rational-actor' assumption that state identity and interests are unchangeable, and fixed to that of self-interested actor, driven purely by the distribution of material capabilities within the international system (Wendt 1995; Hopf 1998; Berger 2003). This helps explains why some states behave 'irrationally' in the conduct of international relations, which mainstream realism and liberalism cannot comprehend, and thus, classify it as anomalous in their respective analyses.

Nationalism, as an intersubjective, socially constructed and psychological–emotional rather than rational–material phenomenon, is a staple item on the constructivist analytical menu. Indeed, constructivism and, to some extent, area studies have (re)gained much of their explanatory power following the advent of nationalism and identity-related issues and conflicts during the post-Cold War epoch, which have imposed a redefinition of the state-centric and structural–material meanings of international politics espoused by mainstream IR theories. Contrary to IR orthodoxy, a constructivist analysis problematises nationalism, not as an 'epiphenomenon', but an independent and intangible variable that shapes state identity and interests, which then 'mediate the material world, [or structure] including features like the balance of power, or opportunities for trade and cooperation' (Berger 2003: 390). Also, unlike mainstream reasoning, constructivism stresses the discursive (not material) power of nationalism and identity to explain state behaviour. This requires an approach similar to area studies, where the researcher, in Berger's (2003: 392) opinion, needs 'to be sensitive towards, and engaged in a sustained investigation of the debates' surrounding the meanings of nationalism and identity 'within the community of relevant policymaking actors, and to place those debates in the context of the broader societal discourses in domestic and international politics'. This demonstrates constructivism/area studies favouring 'interpretivist'/empirically dense and *sui generis* analysis (Hopf 1998: 198) over the parsimonious and universal theorisation of the IR orthodoxies, which reflects their explanatory salience with regard to nationalism and other ideational/non-material factors.

Constructivism/area studies' understanding of nationalism in Japanese–Chinese relations

As mentioned, there is a rich collection of constructivist/area studies literature on Japanese–Chinese relations. Whilst studies of nationalism and identity have flourished in this analytical vein, most are dedicated to analysing Chinese or Japanese nationalism *per se*, placing moderate emphasis on its external role, but paying limited attention to its impact on foreign policy and diplomatic relations.

Indeed, research on Chinese nationalism has proliferated, with Zheng (1999), Gries (2004), Zhao (2000, 2005) and Hughes (2006) providing among the most extensive understandings of nationalism's role in shaping modern China's international relations. Post-war Japanese nationalism has, likewise, received adequate scholarly attention, although specific studies on its role in Japanese foreign policy-making are surprisingly limited, despite growing recognition of its contemporary efficacy. Besides Pyle's (1996) realist-inclined study on nationalism and post-Cold War Japan's newfound assertiveness, key works by Yoshino (1992), Stronach (1995), McCormack (2000), Nish (2000), McVeigh (2004) and Shimazu (2006) provide accounts of Japanese nationalism mainly from the constructivist/area studies perspective, delving into its historical, socio-cultural, ideological and political dimensions, giving only partial treatment of its influence on Japan's external orientations, and almost negligible on Japan's China policy and the bilateral relationship. Miller (2000) and Samuels (2007a/b) also stress how nationalism is reshaping Japanese attitudes towards security thinking, and its implications for Japanese foreign policy, without explicating its impact on China policy-making. That said, Rose (2000, 2005), Rozman (2002), Tamamoto (2001, 2005b), Shibuichi (2005), Satoh (2006a/b) and Deans (2007) did address the effects of Japanese nationalism and identity politics on their bilateral ties.

The most common constructivist explanation of nationalism in Japan's relations with China centres on the 'clash-of-identities' and 'identity politics' theses, which are persuasively argued in Rose (2000), Tamamoto (2001), Shibuichi (2005) and Satoh (2006a/b), among others. This line of reasoning links to the arguments on historical memories, and changing images and perceptions that are elaborated in some of the above studies, as well as those by Rozman (2002), He (2006) and Sasada (2006).

According to Rose (2000: 178–9), the resurgence of state and cultural nationalisms in Japan and China is a fundamental reaction and readjustment to the aforesaid international and domestic developments, which have reignited nationalist debates on the questions of history, culture and national identity, at both elite and popular levels. Although primarily meant for domestic consumption, these debates have occasionally spilt over into their bilateral relations, triggering diplomatic controversies over 'highly symbolic issues which struck at the heart of

Chinese and Japanese national consciousness, identity, and interests' (Rose 2000: 170). However, since they are 'overwhelmingly domestic debates with domestic aims' (Rose 2000: 179), Rose (2000: 170) contends that rising nationalist impulses have 'not necessarily translated into an aggressive foreign policy', and that state nationalism in China and Japan 'did not threaten to spill out to the extent that it would jeopardize the stability of Sino-Japanese relations'.

Similarly, Satoh (2006a) links the 'odd-couple' relationship between Japan and China to the rise of the politics of history and identity in both countries. She sees their contemporary bilateral relationship as no longer predominantly defined in terms of material interest, but increasingly by expressions of identity, especially in Japan's case. The redefinition of foreign policy based on one's identity in relation to the other is fundamental to the worsening bilateral ties, as their identities and nationalisms are apparently at odds with one another (Satoh 2006a). Whilst modern Chinese nationalism is very much defined by historical memories of Imperial Japan's exploits in China, Satoh sees Japanese seeking either to distance themselves from or to reinterpret such memories positively, in their quest to reinvent a more prideful national identity. This 'clash of identities' is, in Satoh's (2006a: 5–7) opinion, 'an obvious recipe for disaster', when translated into their mutual bilateral policies.

Tamamoto (2001) and Shibuichi (2005) also make a similar argument in their studies of the Yasukuni Shrine dispute. According to Tamamoto (2001: 36), 'there is discontinuity in the Japanese [psyche] between the prewar and postwar states', with the 15 August 1945 surrender date marking the break and becoming 'the defining moment of a new postwar Japanese national identity'. As such, it is common for Japanese to be somewhat ambivalent regarding the pre-war and wartime eras, as reflected in their lackadaisical attitude towards war apology and Chinese (and Korean) sensitivities surrounding prime ministerial Yasukuni visits and historical revisionism, a sentiment which the Chinese find repulsive (Tamamoto 2001: 36). Meanwhile, Shibuichi (2005: 213) sees a clash of irreconcilable identities as 'the essence' of the Yasukuni dispute. According to him, the disputants (China, and Japanese leftists and rightists) hold contending images of Yasukuni that correspond to their respective historical identities; the Chinese perceive the shrine as a symbol of unrepentant Japanese militarism, while many Japanese, notwithstanding the leftists, view it as honouring fellow countrymen who sacrificed their lives for the betterment of the Japanese nation (Shibuichi 2005: 199, 213). Such divergent identities and symbolisms, Shibuchi (2005: 199) insists, leave the contending parties with little choice but to either oppose or support Yasukuni, triggering competing politico-diplomatic pressures on Japanese premiers' decisions regarding shrine visits.

Undoubtedly, the formation of confrontational national identities has much to do with conflicting interpretations of history and the evolving nationalist narratives in both countries, which have accentuated the perennial 'history problem', making it a major thorn in contemporary Japanese–Chinese relations. This line of inquiry is found in most constructivist-oriented analysis and specifically elaborated in Okabe (2001), Yang (2002), Gries (2005a/b), Rose (2005) and He (2006).

According to Rose (2005: 6), '[t]he history problem centres on an inability to agree on a shared version of history (both within Japan and between Japan and China)', a conundrum that has brought ramifications on other areas of the bilateral ties, which makes a genuine Japanese–Chinese reconciliation difficult, if not impossible to achieve. This is echoed by Satoh, who sees both countries holding particular and incompatible views on national history, especially of the Second World War; the Japanese war narrative has a narrower scope that generally begins with the Pearl Harbor attack, compared to the Chinese version of a protracted war starting with the 1931 Manchurian Incident. The widely perceived Japanese 'collective amnesia' over this 'obscured' war episode is pivotal to understanding the Japanese–Chinese 'history problem' (Satoh 2006b: 6).

The conflicting interpretation also stems from the so-called 'victor-victim' genres that evolved in their nationalist historical narratives. While Gries (2005a: 9) attributes Chinese indignation towards Japan to the emergence of a popular 'victimisation' narrative 'that blames "the West"', including Japan, for China's suffering', besides the official Maoist 'heroic' or 'victor' national narrative, Fujiwara (2001), Miller (2002) and Kingston (2004) see an enduring Japanese 'victim consciousness' as justifying a 'self-vindicating', revisionist history in Japan that contradicts Chinese interpretations. Indeed, He (2006) identifies such 'national mythmaking' triggered by domestic nationalist politics as fundamental to comprehending their current diplomatic problems. Specifically, she blames 'elite historical mythmaking' in both countries for the flourishing of 'flagrantly nationalistic historical myths', which created divergent national memories that 'perpetuated and reinforced the problems of history' in Japanese–Chinese relations (He 2006: 69). That said, Seaton (2007) claims that, despite the stereotypical images of the Japanese being in collective denial over their war history, Japan's war memories are not oxymoronic and dominated by the narrow elite-led nationalist narrative, but are probably 'the most contested memories of any of the major WWII combatant nations'. However, 'this perspective does not seem to matter in China and Korea where the "orthodoxy" of an unrepentant Japan in denial goes unchallenged' (cf. Kingston 2007).

There are also those who view different cultural responses to history as a basis for understanding their divergent treatment of the past. Whereas it is the Chinese cultural norm to reflect on history, Austin and Harris (2001: 61) opine that the Japanese 'cultural tradition of letting bygones be bygones' makes them comparatively less receptive to the past. Whiting (1989: 187) similarly notes a 'professed proclivity of the Japanese to live in the present with little interest in the past, particularly if it reflects unfavourably on the nation'. Yang (2002: 18–19) also shares the notion of cultural differences in creating misunderstandings that exacerbate the history row between China and Japan, such as those caused by their culturally rooted interpretations and usage of lexicons/terms to describe sensitive events of their shared history.

Another closely related argument refers to changing mutual images and perceptions, fuelled by growing fear/vulnerability and the 'superiority-inferiority' complexes inherent in both nations. As mentioned, Whiting (1989) links the shift in Japanese–Chinese ties during the 1980s to changing Chinese images of Japan that were fuelled by nationalism-induced historical memories of Japanese war exploits. Indeed, the correlations between nationalism and images and perceptions have become salient in shaping their post-Cold War relationship. According to Rozman (2002), nationalist emotions in Japan and China, coupled with a lack of political will from both sides to overcome mutual distrust and contain the intensity of public emotions, were responsible for the major deterioration in mutual images, and the downturn in bilateral ties between 1989 and 2001. Sasada (2006) also relates the rise of emotional, anti-Chinese nationalism in Japan, notably amongst youth, to deteriorating images and perceptions of China, which have been exacerbated by the 'China threat perception' and the proliferation of nationalist narratives via various media sources (i.e. *manga*, *anime*, internet, etc.), in light of the 'conservatisation' of the Japanese media and intelligentsia. Meanwhile, Yang (2006: 136) sees China and Japan as having both 'superiority and inferiority complexes' resulting from their 'mixed histories of being the most powerful East Asian countries and also being humiliated and marginalized', which makes nationalism much more salient in Japanese–Chinese relations. The psychological–emotional dimension that generates nationalist-flavoured sentiments of supremacy and fear, pride and prejudice, and power competition in their bilateral interactions are, likewise, argued in Matthews (2003), Tamamoto (2005b) and Tsunekawa (2006).

Undoubtedly, constructivism is helpful in explaining nationalism. In contrast to conventional IR approaches, which commonly ignore cultural–ideational and identity-related variables, constructivism explicitly identifies them in formulating its analytical underpinnings. Indeed, constructivism provides a useful platform for analysing nationalism in Japanese–Chinese ties that are significantly affected by history, culture and identity-related issues. However, limitations of the constructivist/area studies literature include their prevailing tendencies to not incorporate explicit analytical frameworks to operationalise nationalism, and to overstate the *sui generis* features of Japanese–Chinese relations and policy-making. And if mainstream IR studies marginalise cultural-ideational factors, i.e. nationalism and identity, constructivism/area studies often exaggerate their importance, while failing to adequately acknowledge the effects of the external environment and structural–material variables on state behaviour/preferences.

Bridging the divides: a neoclassical realist perspective

In view of the highlighted limitations, this study advocates Neoclassical Realism (NCR), which is hospitable to both mainstream and constructivist variables, as the central analytical framework. As declared, NCR's 'middle-ground' position of favouring domestic-level/constructivist reasoning allows this study to problematise nationalism as a variable that mediates the external environment, and influences the domestic political process and perceptions of Japanese policy-makers, which in turn, shape particular foreign policy behaviour that either exacerbates or alleviates bilateral problems vis-à-vis China.

NCR is a variant of IR realism that posits the role of domestic politics in international relations and foreign policy analysis. Emerging in the 1990s, NCR has gained relative ground as a realist theory of foreign policy that generally shares the fundamental tenets of the realist theoretical tradition, but separates itself from its systemic-focused brethren by explicitly underlining and theorising the 'intervening' role of domestic variables in producing foreign policy behaviour.

Indeed, contemporary realists have begun 'paying more attention to interactions between international and domestic politics', and 'integrating domestic political concerns into the *realpolitik* framework' (Sterling-Folker 1997: 3) to enhance realism's explanatory power. Major neoclassical realist works (Christensen 1996; Zakaria 1998; Cha 2000; Taliaferro 2006; Schweller 2006; Lobell *et al*. 2009) all illustrate the significance of what Schweller (2004: 164) deems as the 'peculiar domestic structures and political situations' of states as 'intervening' variables that partially affect their behaviour and response to the external environment. Beginning with the assumption that systemic and domestic-level theorising is potentially compatible, neoclassical realists distance themselves from the orthodoxy of the Waltzian tradition that invariably views realism as *a priori* systemic theory, which is 'deductively inhospitable to domestic-level theorizing' (Sterling-Folker 1997: 3). According to Roth (2006: 487), neoclassical realists reject neo-realism's ultra-parsimonious 'privileging of systemic-structural variables over second-image factors – those at the level of individual state – and first-image variables – those at the level of individual human beings'. This means that NCR does not deny the primacy of systemic-level analysis, but believes that unit-level impetuses are equally responsible for affecting state interests and policy choices, and thus ought to be incorporated to account for actor behaviour in interstate relations. Unlike most structural-realists, NCR adherents like Gideon Rose (1998: 146–7) contend that there is no such thing as a clear and automated 'transmission belt' that directly translates systemic imperatives into foreign policy outcomes. Instead, constraints/ opportunities offered by the international system are defined and translated through the complex domestic political process that serves 'to channel, mediate, and (re) direct policy outputs' (Schweller 2004: 164) in response to such external forces.

In other words, neoclassical realists agree that the parameters of a state's foreign policy and external interests are driven primarily by systemic pressures, i.e. relative power distribution of states within the international system. However, the definition and causality of such imperatives is 'indirect and complex, because [they] must be translated through intervening variables [such as state-elites] at the unit-level' (G. Rose 1998: 146). More specifically, they argue that constraints and opportunities thrown up by the anarchic international system are 'murky and difficult' to interpret (G. Rose 1998: 152), and have to be filtered through the fuzzy and intersubjective prism of foreign policy-makers or state-elites involved in the decision-making process, before being translated into policy outputs (Sterling-Folker 1997). State behaviour/actions are therefore dependent on the perception of those individuals or groups involved in foreign policy-making regarding the incentives/disincentives imposed by the international system, and their choosing of one option over others from the foreign policy menu (Taliaferro 2006: 485–6).[4]

Neoclassical realists have also earmarked other unit-level factors deemed important to the domestic political process, which include bureaucratic and factional politics, public opinion, media, political culture and state institutions, among others (Sterling-Folker 1997: 2; G. Rose 1998; Taliaferro 2006). From NCR's perspective, these variables have to be noted for their role as arbitrators between the international environment and state responses to it. They are treated as 'intervening' variables that affect a state's ability to respond effectively to systemic pressures, such as to explain what Desch (1998: 166) describes as 'the lag between structural change and alterations in state behaviour', and the 'irrationality' of some states that fail 'to adapt to the constraints of the international system'. The 'intervening' role posited to domestic variables is based on the conventional realist assumption that the level of pressure in the international system is always high, or what is defined as a 'structurally determinate condition' (Desch 1998: 169). As such, states' responses are expected to be primarily motivated by systemic pressure and failure for this to be the case is mainly due to domestic-level 'intervening' factors (Desch 1998).

However, some neoclassical realists suggest that domestic variables may have a more 'independent' impact on state behaviour, under specific structural conditions. According to those who assume that the international system is not always a constant state of malign power and security competition, domestic factors may be afforded 'greater independent explanatory power' (Desch 1998: 169) in foreign policy-making, under relatively benign and ambiguous external conditions (see also Sterling-Folker 1997: 22; Schweller 2004). This means that domestic variables can intervene most saliently under such conditions, during which they may even assume some independent functions. Here, the 'independent' notion refers more to flexibility in effecting policy variations rather than the propensity to 'operate independently of structural variables in shaping states' foreign policies' (Taliaferro 2006: 486), since such independence is still dependent on external–structural conditionalities. Generally, neoclassical realists share similar assumptions when describing the nature of the international environment and its impact on actor behaviour, as well as the function of the domestic political process in encouraging or preventing actors from effectively recognising and addressing structural–systemic imperatives.

A neoclassical realist framework of nationalism and state behaviour/preferences

How does nationalism affect the foreign policy of nation-states as an 'intervening' (with at times, 'independent' function) variable, and how best can it be incorporated into the NCR theoretical construct? NCR adherents have introduced domestic variables to supplement foreign policy analysis. The perception of state-elites, bureaucratic/factional politics, political culture, elite–mass linkage and the 'strong state–weak state' dichotomy are considered variables that potentially influence foreign policy direction (Schweller 2003; Taliaferro 2006). Notwithstanding the primacy of systemic imperatives in defining the parameters within which foreign policy choices are tailored, neoclassical realists argue that these domestic determinants are important and, depending on the particular time and situational contexts, may have the power to affect state interests and policy preferences via their 'intervening' properties. According to Schweller (2004: 164), 'Structural imperatives rarely ... compel leaders to adopt one policy over another'; rather, states respond to structural constraints and opportunities 'in ways determined by both internal and external considerations of policy elites, who must reach consensus within an often decentralized and competitive political process'. This suggests that state behaviour tends to be motivated by domestic rather than systemic-level factors (Schweller 2004: 164). Guided by NCR's dictum, this section aims to develop an analytical framework that incorporates and explicates nationalism's relationship with these domestic variables, along with its interactions with external determinants, to assess its salience in shaping Japan's post-Cold War relations with China.

The perceptions of decision-makers or state-elites responsible for foreign policy-making are deemed crucial and commonly utilised in NCR frameworks, since systemic pressures are assumed as having to be filtered through their 'opaque' cognitive lenses (Sterling-Folker 1997: 19). Without a direct link between system structure and actor behaviour, the incentives and constraints imposed by the structural environment are, at best, fuzzy, and have to be translated through the intersubjective understandings of 'flesh and blood officials' (G. Rose 1998: 158). This implies the need to account for policy-makers' perceptions, and scrutinise how these actors actually comprehend international pressures in particular situations, as it is such understandings that are then causally translated into foreign policy behaviours/outcomes (G. Rose 1998: 157–8). According to Gideon Rose, the introduction of perception as an 'intervening' variable marks a distinctive separation between hardcore structural-realists and their neoclassical brethrens, the latter offering a theoretical bridge that makes them relatively amenable to constructivists' reasoning.[5] It allows the theorisation of identity-related, cultural–psychological factors, including nationalism, that 'may serve to exacerbate, or mitigate the tendencies that are inherent in a system's structure' (Friedberg 1993–4: 11; cf. G. Rose 1998: 164), or more importantly, how they affect actors' perceptions of their own capabilities vis-à-vis others, and 'how such perceptions are translated into foreign policy' (G. Rose 1998: 168).

Indeed, neoclassical realists have called for the explicit incorporation of socio-psychological and cultural–ideational variables to elucidate how they inform state-elites' perceptions (G. Rose 1998: 168). Nationalism is one such variable, insofar as it derives its political character, meanings and power from these elements. How then, do nationalism and national identity affect perception? Perception is generally understood as one's intersubjective understanding of an object or situation derived from particular cognitive lenses (Jervis 1976). These cognitive lenses are developed by the socio-psychological, cultural and communicative processes that one is subjected to in life, which help define one's identity and interests, and inform choices about actions by 'mediating the material world or structure' (Berger 2003: 390). Nationalism, with its socio-psychological and cultural underpinnings, is one such cognitive lens that serves to: (i) imbue individuals or groups within the modern political community known as the nation with a collective identity, essentially defined as the 'national identity'; (ii) shape their perceptions; and (iii) inform their interests and preferences (Guibernau 1996). Since national identity is defined in the context of a society of nation-states, nationalism as its denominator essentially has direct causal effects on nation-state perceptions regarding its place in the objective, material world, and its relationship with other national actors (Guibernau 1996: 73). These perceptions, shaped by socio-psychological, cultural and communicative processes like shared historical memories, education, media and pre-existing cultural and belief systems, give meaning to and drive the forces of nationalism (Berger 2003; Guibernau 1996: Druckman 1994). Nationalism thus not only orientates the national consciousness, but also forges the perceptual lenses of both government and people in a nation-state.

In the NCR construct, nationalism affects state perceptions via state-elites/ central decision-makers. The perceptions of other elite and societal groups and the public are equally relevant in mediating the state's policy-making process (Taliaferro 2006: 485). For instance, in countries where factional politics is a dominant feature, rival elite groups' perceptions may at times influence policy choices. Likewise, the perceptions of pressure groups and the masses, when translated into public opinions, can have a strong policy-making impact, depending on the degree of elite–mass linkage. Specifically in foreign policy-making, nationalism may define central decision-makers' perceptions by evoking friendly or adversarial images of other countries, accentuating or reducing their mutual differences, not mentioning promoting confidence or scepticism of their place vis-à-vis other states in the international system (Druckman 1994). Moreover, in countries where the state is relatively susceptible to domestic politics and public opinion, nationalist sentiments that drive the domestic political debate and public perceptions may have a strong, albeit indirect arbitrary impact, insofar as they can pressure state-elites into adopting particular foreign policies that may or may not effectively address the constraints/opportunities imposed by the international system. In interstate relations, nationalism can widen or bridge mutual perceptual divides, leading to policies of appeasement or confrontation (Van Evera 1994).

Indeed, nationalism affects domestic politics, i.e. moulding the domestic political debate and influencing political competition, which may have a bearing on state foreign policy. In countries where nationalist elements dominate the political leadership and apparatus, the 'national interests' tend to reflect their parochial interests, and thus, the prevalence of policy preferences geared towards realising nationalist goals. Meanwhile, in countries where domestic power struggles between rival political parties/factions/bureaucracies/groups tend to affect governmental policy-making, nationalist pressure (i.e. from rightwing parties/factions, conservative politicians, military hardliners, etc.) may influence policy decisions and potentially undermine the pragmatic considerations of state-elites, when managing 'nationalist' issues. This is especially so in cases where state-elites are dependent on nationalist support to secure their domestic power position (Downs and Saunders 1998–9; Bong 2002).

Similarly, nationalism may be introduced into realist frameworks that draw attention to the 'strong state–weak state' dichotomy, or domestic mobilisation theories in explaining foreign policy-making. Both Zakaria (1998) and Christensen (1996) draw on the concepts of 'state power' and 'national political power' to emphasise the significance of the state's ability to control and mobilise domestic resources (human and material) in shaping its foreign/security policy initiatives. Such 'powers', according to them, underscore the relative effectiveness of state-elites in making unilateral decisions and dispensing strategies to meet international challenges or opportunities (cf. G. Rose 1998: 160–4; Taliaferro 2006).

Nationalism, when viewed as a political instrument, certainly has an 'intervening' role, and has been often utilised by state-elites for domestic mobilisation. Its utility function, in Taliaferro's (2006: 488, 491–2) opinion, is especially noticeable amongst 'weak states' (governments with limited powers of domestic extraction), where state-elites have a greater inclination towards manipulating nationalist sentiment to mobilise the political support of their citizenries for the adoption of particular domestic and/or external policy strategy. Conversely, domestic nationalist elements tend to stoke nationalism to undermine the efforts of pragmatic, but 'weak states' to mobilise national resources towards pragmatic policy considerations.

As presumed, nationalism can affect foreign policy-making to varying degrees via non-governmental pressure groups and public opinion. Although nationalism is generally associated with the state, popular nationalism may feature prominently in domestic nationalist discourse. Popular nationalism, in exerting its influence through civil society channels, can be a significant source of domestic political pressure on foreign policy-making, especially if strong elite–mass linkage characterises a state's political system, and when state-elites' domestic political resolve is dependent on nationalist support/patronage. Simply put, nationalism has the propensity to not only shape the perceptions, images and attitudes of state-elites, but also colour the domestic political debate (moderate-pragmatists versus ultra-rightists/revisionists), determine the adhesiveness and level of elite–mass linkages, and affect state capacity to mobilise domestic resources for national/ foreign policies, among others.

In view of its encompassing effect, this study develops an NCR analytical construct, with nationalism serving as a key variable possessing an 'intervening' (and sometimes 'independent') role that interacts with other unit-level and external factors to affect Japanese state-elites' policy choices that either exacerbate or mitigate the problems in Japanese–Chinese relations. For a start, the basic NCR framework comprises two sets of interactive variables (Figure 1.1). Whereas external factors are primarily 'independent' variables, domestic determinants serve as 'intervening' variables (sometimes with independent function) that mediate and interact with the former, and with one another to produce particular foreign policy options, or the 'dependent' variable. The external variables identified are: (1) the international security environment; (2) alliance commitment/resolve;[6] (3) diplomatic leverage vis-à-vis a disputant-state; and (4) interdependence (bilateral/ multilateral), which ascertain the parameter of Japan's China policy options.

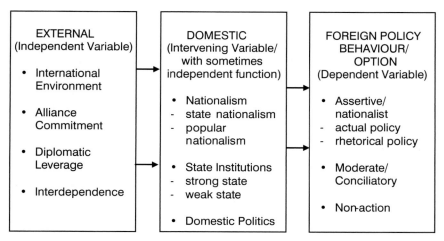

Figure 1.1 NCR framework of nationalism and state behaviour/preferences

Meanwhile, the domestic variables include: (1) nationalism (state/popular manifestations); (2) state institutions (strong/weak state); and (3) domestic politics (power competition between elites/factions/parties/bureaucracies). Specifically in this book, nationalism is assumed to interact with these other determinants in affecting Japanese state-elites' perceptions of external–domestic conditions, namely Japan's relative power position vis-à-vis China, and their domestic political resolve vis-à-vis 'nationalist' forces, which then define their specific policy options when dealing with the Chinese over the two case studies.

This framework requires the Japanese 'state', or more specifically, 'state-elites', to be the primary agent, since they ultimately dispense the foreign policy decisions. This necessitates identifying their political-ideological dispositions and affiliations, their dependence on nationalism as a power instrument, their inclination towards nationalist or pragmatic external agenda and their domestic political resolve vis-à-vis nationalist and moderate elements, to identify how far nationalism affects their perceptions/calculation. Also under scrutiny are other domestic agencies, namely the LDP and its coalition partners, bureaucracy (MOFA, JDA/MOD, METI, etc.), political oppositions and non-state actors (i.e. media, intelligentsia, nationalist/pacifist pressure groups, *zaikai* and public opinion). For external agencies, the responses of the Chinese government and society, and the US's role (within the US–Japan alliance, and as a salient actor in the US–Japan–China 'triangular' relationship) are considered together with other relevant contextual factors and actors in the international environment that simultaneously affects Japanese foreign policy-making.

Building on this modest framework, this section operationalises nationalism within an interactive 'macro–micro' model to explicate how, when and under what conditions it prevails in Japan's China policy-making. NCR stresses that domestic influence on foreign policy depends on the constraints imposed by the international system. This is coherent with the realist tradition's basic assumption, which emphasises the primacy of systemic imperatives in conditioning the environment in which nation-states function and operate. Nonetheless, NCR goes further by assuming that the environment primarily serves to limit, but not govern a state's specific foreign policy choices, leaving such processes to domestic factors/actors, i.e. nationalism and state-elites' perceptions (Sterling-Folker 1997; Dessler 1989). When international pressures are low, or when the probability of conflict is relatively obscure, NCR assumes that states can exercise a wider range of policy options, thus giving nationalism and other domestic factors a bigger impact on foreign policy-making (Desch 1998). Under such conditions where domestic political bargaining enjoys greater saliency in the decision-making process, nationalist pressures (i.e. nationalist politicians, popular nationalist sentiments, etc.) may prevail and force, or even encourage states to adopt nationalist over prudent foreign policy options. Likewise, state-elites who are dependent on nationalism for domestic political expediency may allow it a more effective role in engendering state behaviour, in a relatively low-pressure international environment. Conversely, when external pressures are high and the likelihood of threat becomes imminent, state preferences are bound to be curtailed, thus, reducing the leverage of domestic imperatives on foreign policy-making (Desch 1998). This implies that nationalist forces have lesser bargaining power in policy-making. Instead, state-elites as 'rational' actors are expected to respond to systemic imperatives, rather than domestic nationalist pressures or their nationalistic convictions, when determining policy options.[7]

NCR, however, does not exclude the possibility of domestic attributes superseding systemic imperatives, even in times of tremendous structural constraints, since international pressure does not directly translate into specific set of behaviour/preferences, but must be filtered through unit-level factors/ actors, namely state-elites' perceptions, which can 'intervene' and cause states to act contrary to systemic imperatives. According to Sterling-Folker, since state-elites perceive external pressures through the 'prism' of their own intersubjective processes, their evaluation of the situation may not necessarily be objective. Even in the pursuit of survival, their responses to those pressures 'remain grounded in the processes from which actor identities, interests and behaviours are derived' (Sterling-Folker 1997: 22). This assumption grants nationalism an 'intervening' role affecting state-elites' ability to dispense 'rational' policy options.[8] In sum, NCR prescribes nationalism with mostly 'intervening' and sometimes, 'independent' functions in foreign policy-making, depending on prevailing external conditions. Nationalism serves mainly as an 'intervening' variable under structurally determinate conditions, whereas under a low-pressure external environment it may develop concurrent independent functions in affecting actor behaviour/preferences (Sterling-Folker 1997: 22; Desch 1998: 168–9).

Superficially, NCR's incorporation of external and domestic-level theorisation looks similar to other middle-grounding frameworks deriving from both liberal and realist traditions. However, Sterling-Folker (1997: 22) argues that, unlike the liberal construct, both the systemic and the domestic can be deductively incorporated and function concurrently as 'independent variables in the [neoclassical] realist argument'. This is done by separating and juxtaposing both contexts under the 'environment–process' nexus, with the international system acting as the anarchic 'environment' that disposes a set of constraining conditions, while domestic factors serve as the internal 'process' through which systemic constraints are translated into policy outcomes (Sterling-Folker 1997: 4–8; Taliaffero 2006: 479–80; Dessler 1989). Ontologically, this 'environment–process' nexus separates NCR from the liberal-oriented 'two-level game' framework that incorporates both the systemic and domestic as process-based variables, which actually renders the latter deductively inconsistent and theoretically inhospitable to domestic-level theorising (Sterling-Folker 1997: 4).[9] NCR also differs from postclassical/defensive realism that purports to entertain domestic-level analysis (Brooks 1997). Unlike NCR, the latter variant is susceptible to charges of reductionism due to its tendency to over-depend on domestic-level rather than its 'first-order' systemic variables to account for much of the actual behaviour of states (G. Rose 1998: 150–1).

Last, but not least, NCR needs to be differentiated from analytical eclecticism (Katzenstein 2008; Katzenstein and Okawara 2001), despite their agreement on the importance of adopting a holistic approach that derives analytical tools from other theoretical traditions to comprehensively explain state behaviour and international outcomes. Unlike neoclassical realists, whose basic theoretical assumptions derive from IR realism (which explains their advocacy for the primacy of power politics and first-order systemic explanation, while not discounting other levels and types of variables of analysis), proponents of analytical eclecticism do not favour specific research traditions, but rather draw selectively on elements from multiple theoretical paradigms to generate their explanations. In doing so, they also totally eschew parsimony in preference for a non-'method-driven' analysis (Katzenstein 2008), which inevitably leads to an absence of clear, systematic analytical frameworks to produce theoretically informed understandings of foreign policy and interstate relations. Such differences and their incompatibility with this book's research objectives (i.e. to provide a systematic analysis via a discernible analytical construct, and to enhance IR realism's explanatory power and relevance) are the reasons why NCR is chosen ahead of analytical eclecticism, as the central analytical framework for this study.

Based on the stipulated assumptions, a modest NCR model can be generated by juxtaposing the external (independent) and the domestic (intervening/independent) variables in two separate axes, to represent their interactions, which produce foreign policy outcomes (dependent variable). Represented in Figure 1.2, the external variables identified earlier are incorporated into the model to measure Japan's relative power position vis-à-vis the disputant-state, China (as perceived by state-elites), along the Y-axis. Meanwhile, nationalism is factored with other domestic determinants to measure the domestic political resolve of state-elites, specifically against nationalist pressure, along the X-axis. Independently, both axes provide a measure of state-elites' perceptions/calculation in terms of the degree to which they feel confident or vulnerable to the pressure imposed by the respective set of variables, based on a 'favourable-to-unfavourable' continuum.

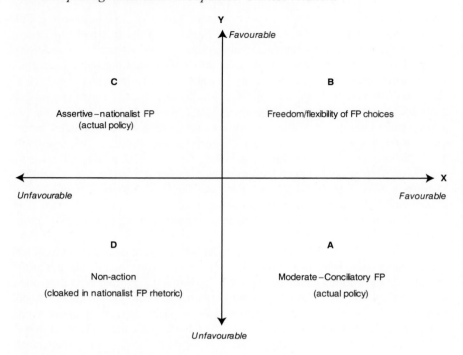

X = Domestic Political Resolve (vis-à-vis domestic nationalist pressure)

Y = Relative Power Position (vis-à-vis disputant state/China)

Figure 1.2 NCR model of nationalism and state behaviour/preferences

Ceteris paribus, each axis generates its respective hypothesis on the expected Japanese behaviour/policy option: (H1) by the Y-axis, and (H2), the X-axis. Essentially, the juxtaposition of X- and Y-axes would yield four more sub-hypotheses (H3–H6) representing the likely foreign policy options under specific external–internal conditions and time context (marked by Quadrant A to D; see Table 1.2).[10]

These policy options (H3–H6) are primarily hypothesised on the condition of the respective external–internal domains being either determinately favourable, or otherwise. In the event where state-elites face an ambiguous domestic political resolve, NCR's 'first-order' systemic argument assumes that the preferred policy option would largely depend on the perceived relative power position vis-à-vis the disputant-state. Conversely, an ambiguous relative power position would make a combination of assertive-cum-conciliatory measures the favoured policy option, irrespective of the prevailing domestic condition (Table 1.3).

By problematising nationalism, which under specific international and domestic conditions can cause variations in state behaviour/policy options, this NCR model enables its impact to be systematically assessed, and helps explicate the conditions in which it does or does not prevail in Japanese (or Chinese) policy-making, when

Table 1.2 NCR hypotheses on state behaviour/preferences

Hypothesis/ (quadrant)	External–domestic conditions and expected foreign policy options
*H*1	When the relative power position vis-à-vis the disputant state is decisively/determinately favourable (strategic environment + alliance commitment + diplomatic leverage + interdependence), a state tends to adopt assertive–nationalist foreign policies (domestic–ideational factors gain FP salience under low-pressure external–structural environment, hence the opportunity for state-elites to advance state/popular nationalist agendas to realise personal nationalist convictions and/or political expedience). Conversely, maintaining a moderate–conciliatory/ non-action policy is the likelihood, when a state faces unfavourable relative power position (state-elites expected to respond to external–structural constraints and suppress domestic–ideational goals).
*H*2	State-elites suffering from a decisively unfavourable domestic political resolve (vis-à-vis nationalist pressure) are compelled to adopt assertive–nationalist policies, when managing sensitive bilateral issues. Conversely, moderate–conciliatory policies are likely, when they enjoy favourable domestic political resolve (vis-à-vis nationalist pressure).
*H*3 (A)	When state-elites perceive a determinately unfavourable relative power position vis-à-vis the disputant state, but enjoy favourable domestic political resolve, the tendency is to adopt moderate–conciliatory policies.
*H*4 (B)	When the state encounters an advantageous relative power position vis-à-vis the disputant state, and the domestic political resolve of state-elites is favourable, they will enjoy flexibility/freedom in terms of policy choices.
*H*5 (C)	State-elites perceiving a favourable relative power position vis-à-vis the disputant states, but feeling vulnerable towards domestic nationalist pressure, may be inclined towards assertive–nationalist foreign policy option.
*H*6 (D)	State-elites perceiving their state's relative power position and domestic political resolve to be decisively disadvantageous are constrained to opt for non-action, cloaked in nationalist rhetoric/symbolic gesture, as a means to circumvent the problem of contradictory foreign policy goals posited by the international environment and domestic political process (external pressure supersedes domestic constraints).

Sources: Adapted and modified from Bong (2002: 20–3); Downs and Saunders (1998–9)

managing their bilateral affairs. More significantly, it can contribute to a better understanding of other dynamics involved, while simultaneously answering questions on nationalism's role in Japanese–Chinese ties that traditional IR theories and constructivism have not adequately explained.

Conclusion

There are contending approaches and theoretical constructs to explain Japanese–Chinese relations in general, and to assess nationalism's role in the

Table 1.3 Expected state behaviour/preferences

Domestic Political Resolve (vis-à-vis nationalist pressure)	Relative Power Position (vis-à-vis disputant state)		
	Favourable (H1)	*Ambiguous*	*Unfavourable (H1)*
Favourable (*H2*)	Flexible policy option (*H4*) (Quadrant B)	Assertive-cum-conciliatory policy options (between A & B)	Moderate–conciliatory policy option (*H3*) (Quadrant A)
Ambiguous	Assertive–nationalist policy options (between B & C)	Assertive-cum-conciliatory policy options	Moderate–conciliatory policy options (between A & D)
Unfavourable (*H2*)	Assertive–nationalist policy option (*H5*) (Quadrant C)	Assertive-cum-conciliatory policy options (between C & D)	Non-action (*H6*) (Quadrant D)

bilateral ties in particular. Notwithstanding their respective explanatory power, 'standard' theoretical approaches, from mainstream IR realism and liberalism to constructivism/area studies, tend to be ill-equipped to comprehensively address the subject. This 'analytical myopia' reflects their rigid analytical confines and limited tools, and leads to their respective over-emphasis on and/ or marginalisation of particular 'level-of-analysis' and 'type-of-variables'. In view of such limitations, this chapter proposes an NCR-oriented analytical framework to provide a better understanding of nationalism's role in Japan's China policy. The operationalisation of nationalism in the NCR model can help realise this book's objective of making a modest contribution to theory-building, specifically in enhancing IR realism's explication of nationalism in Japanese–Chinese relations. Indeed, NCR's underpinnings, as opposed to those of neo-realism, allow a degree of reciprocity with respect to non-realist/constructivist assumptions, which enhances realism's explanatory power of nationalism/ identity in the study of international relations. Although, neoclassical realists may be criticised by their hardcore brethren and non-realist exponents for failing to defend the tradition and integrity of IR realism (e.g. Legro and Moravcsik 1999),[11] many contemporary realists view such a reconstruction as necessary to enhance the 'progressive power of realism' (Walt 1997; Schweller 2003). What NCR offers is a level of flexibility not found in the narrow premises of the Waltzian construct, which opens the path for a deductive engagement with constructivism-inspired approaches, and a step towards alleviating some of the 'enduring dilemmas' of IR realism (Guzzini 2004: 558). The NCR model of nationalism and state behaviour/ preferences is operationalised in Chapters 5 and 6, to assess nationalism's salience in affecting Japan's policy options in the bilateral disputes over Yasukuni and the ECS. Preceding these are chapters that analyse the background of Japan–China ties, and Japanese nationalism and foreign/China policy-making.

2 The trends, developments and dynamics in Japanese–Chinese relations

The decline in recent Japanese–Chinese relations is hardly surprising, considering their tainted and hostile bilateral interactions throughout Asia's modern history. Japan's imperialistic transgressions on Chinese soil during two Japanese–Chinese wars that lasted until the end of the Second World War have set in motion and shaped the problematic nature of their bilateral exchanges thereafter. Although formal diplomatic ties resumed in 1972, and a progressive relationship ensued under the so-called 'peace-and-friendship' framework, it has remained fragile to date, and has yet to mature into one based on mutual trust and genuine amity. Instead, historical excesses continue to haunt the government and people of both countries, occasionally stifling and threatening to haul their contemporary relationship back to its confrontational past. Interpreting from a neoclassical realist perspective, what follows is an overview of the trends and developments, and the external and domestic dynamics (identified in the NCR framework), that shaped their bilateral ties throughout the Cold War and post-Cold War eras.

Bilateral relations during the Cold War: from confrontation to normalisation

Japanese–Chinese relations were largely adversarial during the Cold War, imposed mostly by ideological division and leanings on confrontational blocs that epitomised the rigid bipolar security order in East Asia. The physical and emotional–psychological 'wound' resulting from the second Japanese–Chinese war also made the Chinese Communist regime, whose legitimacy derived from its anti-Japanese resistance and heroics, cautious of post-war Japan. Since 1950, China had sought to align itself with the Soviet Union, following the US containment policy and threatening encroachment of its borders.[1] Conversely, the Cold War's advent saw Japan's post-war position strategically transformed from being an American-occupied territory to becoming Washington's 'junior partner' in the strategic calculus against the broadening Communist 'sphere-of-influence'. The 'policy reversal' saw Japan absorbed into the US-led alliance framework via the 1951 US–Japan Security Treaty. Correspondingly, its China policy was subordinated to the Cold War 'alliance logic', placing the Japanese directly in confrontation with their Chinese neighbour (Zhao 1997: 98–100).

The overarching alliance framework resulted in the absence of official diplomatic relations. However, it did not prevent both countries from maintaining unofficial economic ties, where bilateral trade proceeded, although at minimal levels.[2] Japan, led by the 'pragmatic' Yoshida administration, was reluctant to adopt an overtly confrontational posture, and thus did not sever all channels of interaction with China (Iriye 1996: 48). Beijing also sought to maintain unofficial interactions via 'people's diplomacy' or 'cultural diplomacy', aimed at wooing Japanese citizens as a strategy to detach Japan from its American ally (C. Rose 1998: 43). The pragmatism demonstrated by both governments propelled an expansion of non-governmental exchanges, and the conclusion of several joint statements and private trade agreements in the 1950s saw a gradual increase in Japanese–Chinese commercial relations. The 1962 semi-formal 'Liao-Takasaki' trade system, designed explicitly to help expand overall bilateral ties, with a view of ultimately realising diplomatic normalisation, also led to both sides enjoying a relatively congenial relationship, despite being technically at war (Taylor 1996: 3).[3]

That said, the 'unofficial' ties were intermittently undermined by developments in their respective domestic politics. For instance, most observers consider the 1958 'Nagasaki flag incident',[4] which led to China temporarily suspending relations with Japan, as a pretext for Beijing to display its discontentment over the reluctance of successive pro-US and pro-Taiwan administrations led by Hatoyama Ichiro and Kishi Nobusuke to reciprocate Chinese efforts to enhance unofficial relations (Lee 1976: 38).[5] Similarly, bilateral tension rose in the 1960s following the arrival of the Sato administration, whose purported 'anti-China' stance and overt leaning towards Taiwan and the US incensed Beijing, exacerbating an already delicate political situation stirred by earlier Chinese provocations (i.e. nuclear testing, and participation in the Vietnam War) that drew strong Japanese criticisms. Japanese–Chinese ties also suffered during the Cultural Revolution. Political friction ratcheted up to extreme levels, while trade activities were stifled by China's 'inward-looking' policy of self-sufficiency and overwhelming ideological considerations (Iriye 1996: 55), not to mention the escalation of anti-Japanese rhetoric and pressure on Japanese companies to meet Chinese political demands.

Japanese–Chinese diplomacy unravelled during the late 1960s as profound developments in the PRC's 'strategic-triangle' relationship with the two superpowers saw her distancing from the Soviet Union towards a confluence of strategic interests with the US. Beginning with Henry Kissinger's diplomatic overtures to Beijing in 1971, Sino-US rapprochement led to China rejoining the international community as a fully fledged United Nations (UN) member state, before culminating in President Nixon's visit in February 1972 (Yahuda 1996: 80). Japan was caught off-guard by the dramatic shift in Sino-US relations and the 'Nixon Shock' (Zhao 1997: 133), but convergence of economic and, increasingly, security interests over a growing Soviet threat enabled Tokyo to rapidly respond to the shift in Western attitudes to normalise relations with Beijing. Without structural constraints, Japan and China formally established diplomatic ties on 29 September 1972. Obviously, the 'normalisation' would have had been impossible without Washington's consent (Kokubun 2001: 10), as Tokyo had always subordinated and calibrated its China policy with its senior partner's grand strategy. It would have also been unfeasible without Chinese forbearance of the US–Japan alliance which, while initially perceived as threatening, was eventually appreciated as a means to constrain Soviet expansionism and underpin East Asia's strategic stability (Yahuda 1996: 84).

That said, domestic developments also laid the groundwork for a smooth normalisation process. Along with earlier efforts to maintain unofficial economic relations as a harbinger of full diplomatic ties, the ebbing of the Cultural Revolution and the emergence of a more pragmatic Chinese and Japanese leadership provided a conducive environment (Burns 2000: 40). Particularly, the arrival of a 'pro-China' Japanese administration under Tanaka Kakuei, whose diplomatic initiatives and skilful negotiations over problematic bilateral issues, ranging from Taiwan and Senkaku/Diaoyudao to war reparations, facilitated the swift establishment of diplomatic relations with Beijing, backed by strong encouragement from the *zaikai*, media and opposition parties (Drifte 2003: 22–3).[6]

Japanese–Chinese relations further strengthened following the signing of the 1978 Peace and Friendship Treaty (PFT). Preceding it were twelve other practical agreements covering various aspects of their engagement, including the Long-Term Trade Agreement, which established the legal framework for a progressive bilateral relationship under the 'peace-and-friendship' slogan. Although these earlier accords catapulted economic relations to new heights,[7] overall interactions remained limited primarily to bilateral matters, and were conducted almost entirely via government-to-government initiatives (Kokubun 2001: 11–12). It was the PFT which reconstituted Japanese–Chinese relations at the heart of East Asian international politics, especially with its tacit recognition of the Soviet 'threat' and *de facto* 'strategic alliance' with the US to contain its expansionism (Yahuda 1996: 85; Bedeski 1983). That said, the process towards concluding the PFT had its share of obstacles, characterised by protracted negotiations over the inclusion of the 'anti-hegemony clause', and the Senkaku/Diaoyudao dispute (Mochizuki 2007: 232–3).[8] Ultimately, both governments' pragmatic resolve facilitated the process, opening a new chapter in Japanese–Chinese ties.

Indeed, bilateral relations have flourished since 1978, underpinned by burgeoning economic interactions throughout the 1980s. The PFT, which coincided with the launching of China's economic modernisation programmes, facilitated a rush of Japanese firms into the Chinese market and the establishment of joint industrial plant projects during the so-called second 'China Boom' period (Kokubun 2003: 32). Most conspicuous was the financing of the Baoshan Iron and Steel by Nippon Steel Corporation, a product of intergovernmental initiative that became 'the flagship symbol of friendship between the two countries' (Kokubun 2003: 33). The Japanese business community's enthusiasm were, however, short-lived. Chinese firms, including Baoshan, started revoking their contracts following structural problems in the domestic economy that necessitated the implementation of an 'adjustment' policy (Howe 1996: 111). Japan was thus compelled to offer China ODA loans to help salvage these projects and alleviate the bilateral dilemma (Whiting 1989: 97).

The 'Baoshan' setback proved temporary as structural reforms and excess demands in China during the mid-1980s rejuvenated bilateral economic interactions. Especially, the decentralisation and 'marketisation' of the Chinese political economy saw market-driven decisions gradually replacing elite-inspired, intergovernmental initiatives, a new trade pattern that greatly facilitated the expansion of economic ties (Howe 1996: 15). By the latter half of the 1980s, more Japanese businesses began investing and moving their production facilities to China in search of cheap labour, pushed by the sharp rise of the Japanese yen and their desire to access the Chinese consumer market. Although the overall amount was insignificant throughout the 1980s, constituting less than 1 per cent of Japan's annual global Foreign Direct Investment (FDI) figures, Japanese investment started to soar following the signing of the 1988 Investment Protection Pact and Deng Xiaoping's symbolic 'southern tour' in 1992, which affirmed China's commitment towards economic liberalisation and reforms (Austin and Harris 2001: 207, 209–11, 226).

Equally boosting the bilateral relationship was the generous amount of Japanese aid to China. Beginning with the first package in December 1979, Japanese ODA[9] has become a symbol of Japan–China 'friendship' ties (Takamine 2005). Not only was Japan the pioneer distributor of ODA to China, it also became the single largest provider of bilateral loans to the Chinese, through four major assistance packages amounting to more than US$13 billion (Burns 2000: 45; Mori 2007: 30–2).[10] China emerged as the largest recipient in 1987, and remained amongst the leading destinations of Japanese ODA throughout the 1990s (Soderberg 2002: 120). Likewise, bilateral trade grew exponentially, especially with the opening of China's coastal provinces to international trade in the 1980s. Geographical proximity and mutual trade complementarities saw two-way trade figures surpassing US$19 billion in 1988 from just over US$5 billion, a decade before (Taylor 1996: 124). The flourishing trade ties especially benefited Japan, which gained a large trade surplus throughout the 1980s as Japanese goods dominated the Chinese market, prompting discontentment and concerns over a Japanese 'economic invasion' (Hook *et al.* 2005: 195). Nonetheless, the diversification of China's foreign economic relations and gradual transformation of its trade composition saw the surplus pattern swinging in its favour in 1988, and a Japanese trade deficit has since become an annual trend in their bilateral trade statistics (Zhang 2000: 53–68). By the early 1990s, Japan became China's largest trading partner, while the Chinese rose steadily in the Japanese list of largest trading nations (Taylor 1996: 122), epitomising their deepening economic interdependence.

Japan was also at the forefront of promoting China's integration into the international community. Besides helping China attain 'developing country' status in the Organisation for Economic Cooperation and Development (OECD) to facilitate ODA disbursement, Japan proactively supported Chinese membership in international institutions, from the World Bank to the World Trade Organisation (WTO), and also admission into regional multilateral fora, like the APEC in 1991 (Deng 1997: 375, 383; Burns 2000: 48). Tokyo also played a key role persuading other Group-of-Seven (G-7) member states to lift their economic sanctions on China, not long after the 1989 Tiananmen Incident (Whiting 1992: 46).

Similarly, mutual dependence has deepened via significant increases in grassroots-level exchanges. From tourists and students to industrial and business personnel, the number of Japanese entering China multiplied from 54,000 in 1979 to approximately 1.47 million in 2000. Reciprocally, Chinese entering Japan rose unprecedentedly since the 1980s, besides the influx of illegal entrants (Kokubun 2006: 27). Beginning in 1982, the 'twin/sister-cities' concept was introduced to commemorate the tenth anniversary of diplomatic normalisation (C. Rose 1998: 55), and this has since become a common practice in promoting greater socio-cultural exchanges. Favourable mutual societal images reflected in public surveys also depicted the generally amiable mood. Japanese affections towards the Chinese peaked at 78.6 per cent in 1980, based on the annual Cabinet Office opinion poll, and the affinity ratings remained high throughout the decade, hovering between the upper 60 per cent to lower 70 per cent range (Kokubun 2001: 9; see Figure 2.1).

On the diplomatic front, Japanese–Chinese ties recorded remarkable progress. The upbeat political climate was typified by the numerous high-ranking exchanges under the 'Japan–China friendship' banner, making the 1980s amongst the most conducive and friendly period (Takagi 1999). In May 1982, Chinese Premier Zhao Ziyang travelled to Japan to commemorate the tenth anniversary of diplomatic normalisation. Japan reciprocated with a visit in September by PM Suzuki Zenko. The CCP Secretary Hu Yaobang visited Tokyo in 1983, and this was followed by official visits from the new Japanese premier, Nakasone Yasuhiro, in 1984 and 1986. The amicable atmosphere continued with visits by Nakasone's successor, Takeshita Noburo and Chinese Premier Li Peng, in August 1988 and April 1989, respectively (Takagi 1999: 22–3). These state visits were usually accompanied by new ideas to enhance overall bilateral ties, and on Japan's part, economic incentives and loan/investment packages to cajole the Chinese (Deng 1997).

The bilateral relationship had its share of problems, the superficially positive trend notwithstanding. Specifically, unresolved 'history' problems and rising nationalism in Japan during the 1980s saw the Chinese dampening diplomatic relations temporarily, only to resume after obtaining Japanese concessions on negotiations over a variety of other issues. A case in point was the 1982 Japanese school history textbook controversy that coincided with the tenth anniversary of diplomatic normalisation. In what was originally a domestic affair, in which Japan's Ministry of Education (MOE) was 'falsely reported' by the leftwing media for 'diluting' Japanese wartime actions in a school textbook screening exercise, the issue became 'internationalised' and developed into a major diplomatic row with China (Ijiri 1996: 65; Yang 2001: 181). The event triggered a spate of 'Japan bashing' rhetoric by the Chinese leadership and media, who not only accused Japan of trying to 'sanitise' its war history by downplaying and omitting sensitive facts on Japanese brutality in China and Asia, but also charged Tokyo with abetting the revival of Japanese militarism. The controversy was eventually contained, after the Japanese government yielded and took measures to appease the Chinese. Observers see the incident as a classic example of how China skilfully manipulates 'history' to put Japan on the defensive, and in the process, draws Japanese concessions on other bilateral issues (C. Rose 1998).

Following the textbook incident, Japanese–Chinese ties returned to the superficial 'friendship' mood that signified the third 'China boom' phase (Ijiri 1996: 69). The goodwill eventually ebbed and bilateral relations suffered another temporary setback, when Japanese PM Nakasone made an official visit to the controversy-laden Yasukuni Shrine on 15 August 1985. The untimely homage, coinciding with the fortieth anniversary of Japan's Second World War surrender, triggered popular indignation across China (Whiting 1992: 45–6). Beijing's vehement criticisms and student-led anti-Japanese demonstrations in Chinese cities saw the Japanese government again buckling to Chinese pressure (Shibuichi 2005: 207). The trend repeated itself in the 1987 'Kokaryo' issue, where a Japanese high court ruling, recognising Taiwanese jurisdiction over an old Chinese student dormitory in Kyoto, sparked yet another diplomatic row that saw Beijing pressuring and Tokyo 'kowtowing' in the usual diplomatic fashion. Both issues were subsequently settled, following Tokyo's conciliatory measures, which further entrenched the asymmetrical trend governing their bilateral ties (Ijiri 1996: 73).

There were other bilateral irritants throughout the 1980s, ranging from the 1984 and 1986 sequels of the textbook issue, and Japanese politicians' controversial remarks on war history, to bilateral trade imbalances that escalated political tensions. Bilateral relations also suffered temporary interruption following the 'Tiananmen Incident' of June 1989,[11] when Japan and other industrialised nations imposed sanctions on China for alleged serious human rights violations by the Chinese authorities in suppressing the pro-democracy demonstrations. That said, Japan was initially reluctant to openly reprimand China, and was prudently managing the issue, due to its own dubious moral position and blemished wartime record, and the potentially negative repercussions of isolating the Chinese (Shambaugh 1996: 85–6). Indeed, Japan was the first G-7 member state to lift sanctions and resume diplomatic ties with China. However, it is widely believed that the Tiananmen Incident severely damaged Japanese perceptions and images of China, generating stark awareness and magnifying differences regarding the norms and values shared by the two governments and societies (Takagi 1999: 23). Most analysts view it as another watershed in Japanese–Chinese relations which, compounded by transformations in the international and domestic realms, propelled a declining trend throughout the remainder of the twentieth century.

Post-Cold War relations: 'cold politics, hot economics'?

The 'boom–bust' trend and political frictions not only persisted, but rose exponentially during the post-Cold War period, following 'structural changes' in the traditional framework of Japanese–Chinese relations (Kokubun 2001: 10). Externally, the Cold War's demise rendered the tacit US–Japan–China 'strategic triangle' meaningless, bringing a strategic transformation to the international order that affected bilateral relations to the core (Kokubun 2003: 37). Conversely, deepening socio-economic interdependence has spawned problems that were non-existent during the period of superficial relations, while generational shifts in leadership and masses, and changing tunes in domestic politics amid rising nationalism, have spun what Self (2002: 80) described as 'new social threads and political dynamics' that continually expose the limitations of the 'friendship framework'. Indeed, their vibrant economic interactions have not, contrary to some expectations, engendered closer politico-security relations. Diplomatic ties have reached a nadir in recent years, reflecting the so-called 'cold politics, hot economics' dialectic, or what some observers deemed as 'cold peace' (Taniguchi 2005), making Japanese–Chinese relations increasingly fluid and enigmatic (Heazle 2005: 6).

As mentioned, Tokyo's commitment to engaging and not isolating China following the Tiananmen Incident led to the speedy resumption of bilateral ties in 1991, marked by PM Kaifu's August visit to Beijing (Takagi 1999: 24). A year later, diplomatic relations reached a new milestone, when Emperor Akihito made an official visit to China, in what was considered 'an act of emperor diplomacy' (*tenno gaiko*) (Hook *et al.* 2005: 196). The historic 'first ever' visit by a Japanese monarch was laden with symbolism, given Imperial Japan's war legacy in China (Shambaugh 1996: 87). Although drawing protest from Japanese ultra-nationalist elements, the event proceeded without incident. Indeed, the generally positive reception in Japan and China had both governments reckoning on a 'new episode' in Japanese–Chinese relations (Jin 2002: 106), which ironically, turned out to be one that was eventually marred by persistent deterioration until late 2006.

Japanese–Chinese diplomacy progressed following reciprocal top-level visits by then-CCP General Secretary, Jiang Zemin, and the first non-LDP Japanese premier, Hosokawa, in 1993 and 1994, respectively, heralding a 'distinct warming in relations' (Shambaugh 1996: 87) that boosted expectations of a genuine reconciliation. The Japanese leadership has, on its part, offered varying degrees/ expressions of war apology during such summits, with the Emperor offering his 'deep remorse' statement in 1992 (Okabe 2001: 59), followed by Hosokawa's 'landmark' apology during his visit, where the term 'aggression' was used for the first time to refer to Japanese wartime actions (Austin and Harris 2001: 56). Since then, successive Japanese premiers, from Muruyama to Koizumi, have in almost ritualistic fashion professed different levels of apology on meeting their Chinese counterparts. Despite several 'history'-related problems, i.e. the discovery of 'Unit 731', 'comfort women', Chinese civil demands for war reparations, and insensitive statements made by Japanese elites regarding the 'Nanjing massacre' and the Japanese–Chinese war, diplomatic ties remained generally positive. China's pragmatism in securing Japanese goodwill and support during the post-Tiananmen period saw the 1990 diplomatic row over Senkaku/Diaoyudao quickly subsiding without much of the usual Chinese rhetorical display. Japan's moderately independent China policy, exemplified by the Hosokawa administration's acquiescence of the Chinese, or generally 'Asianist', stance on human rights, also facilitated warm relations (Hook *et al.* 2005: 197).

Meanwhile, economic relations remained robust. Bilateral trade reached US$39 billion in 1993, before escalating to US$57.5 billion in 1995 (Shambaugh 1996: 88–9; Hilpert 2002: 44–6). Paralleling this trend was the expansion of Japanese FDI, which soared 84 per cent to US$1.07 billion in 1992 alone, making Japan the fourth largest investor in China, with investment totalling US$3.39 billion (Shambaugh 1996: 89; Taylor 1996: 58; Burns 2000: 46). Another three-fold increase saw annual FDI reaching US$4.32 billion in 1995 (Austin and Harris 2001: 212). Likewise, Japanese ODA to China increased, despite the introduction of more stringent guidelines,[12] with annual figures surpassing US$1 billion, between 1992 and 1995 (Austin and Harris 2001: 164).

Nevertheless, mutual security developments have had both countries re-evaluating and raising concerns regarding their respective strategic ambitions in the transiting post-Cold War order. China's double-digit increase in annual defence spending since 1989, and modernisation efforts that focused on enhancing the People's Liberation Army's (PLA) power-projection capabilities (Bitzinger 2003), not mentioning the resumption of nuclear tests, began to worry Japanese security planners (Drifte 2003: 43). By 1993–4, growing anxiety over China's security development was being publicly expressed in both the Japanese and foreign media, leading to explicit concern from successive Japanese administrations (Shambaugh 1996: 93).[13] Conversely, a shift in Chinese strategic perception/thinking saw Japan emerging as a major rival and potential nemesis in the uncertain future regional order (Shambaugh 1994: 6). Exacerbating this mainstream Chinese perception and distrust of Japan was the groundbreaking, albeit gradual expansion in Japanese security policies, especially after 1992, along with the Self-Defence Force's (SDF) growing military capabilities and comparatively huge budget (Hughes 2005).[14] Their changing mutual security perceptions and developments proved to be a principal factor affecting their bilateral relationship.

As was the traditional tendency, their 'good-neighbourly' relations proved ephemeral. Diplomatic goodwill started receding from the mid-1990s onwards as structural transformation inevitably forced both countries to manoeuvre and readjust to the changing international and domestic environments. Their growing asymmetries and changing relative strategic and economic positions began to develop into a pertinent source of mutual discomfort. With China's economy growing annually at spectacular rates, matched by sustained military augmentation, concerns over a perceived 'Chinese threat' began to echo not only in the West, but also among Japan's 'China' watchers, and within the 'corridors-of-power' in Kasumigaseki and Nagata-cho (Drifte 2003: 80–3). Japan's protracted 'post-bubble' recession further accentuated the asymmetries and fuelled Japanese insecurity. Conversely, Tokyo's expanding international role and increasingly assertive foreign/security policy orientation generated unease in Beijing. Compounded by domestic developments, namely generational change and rising nationalism fuelled by historical enmity, Japan–China relations deteriorated amid a flurry of diplomatic clashes.

Bilateral tension was ratcheted up in March 1996, when China took belligerent measures to deter Taiwan from contemplating unilateral independence during the prelude to the Taiwanese presidential election. The PLA conducted full-scale naval exercises and missile tests in the Taiwan Strait, precipitating a dangerous escalation of hostility that saw two US Navy aircraft-carrier battle groups deployed to the narrow sea-lane to check Chinese intentions (Garver 1997: ch. 6). Although the crisis did not result in a military confrontation, it heightened Japanese awareness regarding their own (in)security vis-à-vis the Chinese, prompting Tokyo to freeze grant aid to China (Wang 2000: 361–2). In fact, the Diet had rallied for a similar punitive action the year before, in response to Chinese nuclear weapons testing (Green 2001: 78).

Not surprisingly, Taiwan has re-emerged a contentious issue, with the fragility of Japanese–Chinese diplomacy aggravated by the shift in Japanese attitudes towards Taipei (Wang 2000: 358). Although officially committed to the 'One-China' policy, Tokyo has become increasingly flexible, especially in granting Taiwanese state-elites permission for official/semi-official visits to Japan since 1994,[15] while the Japanese public image of Taiwan improved favourably vis-à-vis China, much to Beijing's chagrin (Takahara 2004: 161).

Similarly, Japan has begun reviewing its security policy in conjunction with the US, including the view of maintaining the status quo of Taiwan and its surrounding areas/sea-lanes that are strategically vital to Japan (Roy 2005: 200). The Clinton–Hashimoto joint declaration for the revision of the 1978 Guidelines for US–Japan Security Cooperation, soon after the Taiwan Strait crisis, reflected such intentions, along with the alliance's strategic interests in hedging against future Chinese power, as advocated in the 'Nye Initiative' (Drifte 2003: 89–93). Under the revised Guidelines, Japan agreed to provide 'logistical and rear-area support' for American operations covering military contingencies in 'areas surrounding Japan' (Johnstone 2000: 132). Despite both allies' reiteration regarding the non-inclusion of Taiwan, and the 'situational' rather than 'geographical' nature of the definition, Beijing remained unconvinced, perceiving it to be none other than a US–Japanese grand strategy to contain and intervene in China's domestic affairs. Tokyo's reluctance to renounce any involvement in a Taiwan contingency, and subsequent participation in the US-sponsored Theatre Missile Defence (TMD) programme, further persuaded the Chinese of Japan's support for a US-led intervention to derail their reunification aspirations. Roy (2003: 9) sees Chinese observers perceiving Japan's 'North Korean threat' excuse as a 'smokescreen' for a TMD project, ultimately aimed at negating China's missile capabilities (Wu 2000: 299–300). Besides advancing Japanese strategic interests, they fear its deployment on Aegis destroyers could effectively nullify the potency of a Chinese missile threat to Taiwan, and inevitably reinforce Taipei's secessionist tendencies (Yahuda 2006: 167).

The mid-1990s onwards also witnessed the eruption of territorial disputes and 'history'-related problems that failed to dissipate, despite earlier reconciliation efforts. The changing domestic political dynamics, and resurgent nationalism fuelled by a new generation of leaders and masses, have made these issues highly 'visible' and increasingly difficult to manage. Besides PM Hashimoto's July visit to Yasukuni, the Senkaku/Diaoyudao dispute resurfaced in 1996, when popular nationalist actions dragged both governments into a diplomatic stand-off, characterised by mutual high posturing and assertive rhetorical exchanges (Deans 2000). Although subsequently calmed through the usual ad-hoc diplomatic manoeuvres and statecraft, the incident underscored nationalism's growing constraints on both sides' ability to effectively resolve the territorial issue. More significantly, it highlights Tokyo's departure from its 'deferential' attitude in dealing with Beijing (Drifte 2003), signifying a 'new realism' and assertiveness in Japan's China policy (Green 2001).

Japanese–Chinese diplomacy worsened following Jiang Zemin's 1998 state visit to Japan that was marred by the Chinese head-of-state's excessive 'history' mongering. It was widely reported that Jiang had tenaciously sought the insertion of a formal apology statement from Japan in the Japanese–Chinese joint declaration during the visit, partly due to Tokyo's recent similar offering to South Korea's Kim Dae-jung, and domestic political pressure that ostensibly compelled him to forthrightly address the 'history' problem (Gong 2001b: 50–1). PM Obuchi's refusal to oblige[16] prompted the Chinese leader to lecture his Japanese hosts on their failure to appropriately redress 'history', a proven manoeuvre in pressuring Tokyo to satisfy Chinese demands (Roy 2005: 195). Japanese 'war-guilt and apology fatigue' set in on this occasion, with Jiang's actions triggering strong media and public indignation (Takagi 1999: 36). The visit ended disappointingly for both sides. It also reinforced the negative images of and hardened attitude in Japan towards China that would bring longer term repercussions to their relationship.

'History' festered as the Obuchi administration tackled significant post-war taboos, a development the Chinese deemed as counterproductive to the bilateral relationship. The 1999 legislation to expand the SDF's role alarmed Beijing, while the re-enactment of *Hinomaru* and *Kimigayo* brought more Chinese consternation about resurgent Japanese nationalism that put further strain on their relationship (Itoh 2001). That said, Premier Zhu Rongji's diplomatic finesse during his Japan visit in October 2000 proved successful in mending relations that were gravely affected following the mentioned bilateral impasses. According to Rozman (2002: 113), the Chinese 'charm offensive' under the so-called 'smile diplomacy' was a remedial step to address the badly damaged Japanese images of China and safeguard their vital economic interests.

The ambience of Japanese–Chinese relations failed to improve as the new millennium dawned. Despite general progress, bilateral ties remained bedevilled by 'history'-related quarrels that undermined mutual efforts to move the relationship forward. The Koizumi administration's assertive China policy did not help matters. Koizumi's contentious visits to Yasukuni-*jinja*, and his explicitly pro-Washington posture and unprecedented efforts to transform Japan into a 'normal state' made him amongst the most unpopular Japanese leaders in China. Apart from its alleged acquiescence in historical revisionism, the Koizumi administration's espousal of constitutional reform of Article 9, incremental policy shifts via legislation that extended the parameters of Japanese security activities abroad, and the strengthening of military relations with the US in the post-'9/11' era, have caused considerable Chinese unease. In certain respects, China would prefer the retention of the US–Japan alliance as a constraint on independent Japanese remilitarisation, but such a perception has become fuzzy following a renewal of 'alliance commitment' under the 'Armitage Doctrine',[17] with Taiwan imminently re-emerging in the US–Japan strategic calculus. Japan's decision to jointly declare Taiwan as a 'common strategic objective' during the US–Japan Security Consultative Committee (or 'Two-plus-Two' Talks) in February 2005 aggravated Chinese suspicions regarding Tokyo's shifting posture and, more significantly, the realness of the alliance's hedging strategy against China's rising power (Lam 2005: 280–2). The JDA's identification of China as a potential security concern in the 2005 National Defence Program Guidelines (NDPG) further fuelled Chinese apprehensions (van Kemenade 2006: 55).

Exacerbating Japanese–Chinese tension were several 'history'-related incidents, ranging from accidents involving chemical weapons abandoned in China by the Imperial Japanese Army to Tokyo's endorsement of 'revisionist' history textbooks. Diplomatic squabbles had also risen from recurrences of their maritime territorial disputes in the ECS, namely their rivalling claims over Senkaku/Diaoyudao, the demarcation of its maritime resource boundaries and contested jurisdictions regarding gas exploration rights. Another related issue was the alleged intrusions of Chinese vessels into Japanese territorial waters, under the pretext of conducting maritime research, but perceived as Chinese attempts to collect military data/ intelligence for eventual submarine operations (Takamine 2006: 129). Compounded by steady increases in Chinese naval capabilities, these incidents have heightened Japanese concerns over China's destabilising actions in maritime affairs.

Other notable diplomatic discords included the storming of the Japanese consulate in Shenyang by Chinese authorities in September 2002, the 'fracas' following China's defeat to Japan in the 2004 Asian Cup final and Chinese Vice-Premier Wu Yi's abrupt cancellation of a scheduled meeting with Koizumi in May 2005. Bilateral ties were also undermined by the all-out Chinese efforts to block Japan's intensified bid for a permanent United Nations Security Council (UNSC) seat in 2005, which sparked a popular Chinese internet petition campaign that garnered 44 million signatures (Calder 2006: 133), whilst Beijing covertly lobbied against Tokyo's bid. To be sure, there were positive expectations in 2002–3 that the new 'fourth generation' Chinese leadership under the technocratic 'Hu-Wen' administration would embrace a 'new thinking' on Japanese–Chinese relations,[18] and pursue a more pragmatism-oriented Japan policy. However, such optimism remained elusive as diplomatic relations reached an unprecedented nadir following massive anti-Japanese demonstrations across Chinese cities in April 2005.

Deepening socio-economic interdependence has also begun manifesting problems. Indeed, rather than bearing the expected fruit, enhanced people-to-people interactions have unwittingly accentuated their stereotypically negative mutual perceptions and images (Yahuda 2006: 162). Recent public opinion surveys illustrate a dramatic decline in mutual affection between the two societies. In Japan, the Cabinet Office annual polls reveal a regressive trend, with the percentage of respondents feeling no affinity to China gradually increasing,

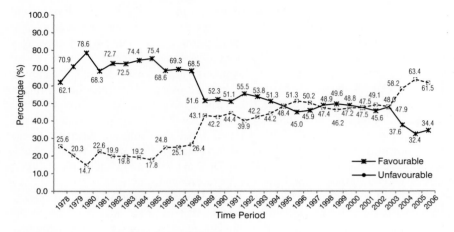

Figure 2.1 Japanese public image of/affinity towards China

Source: Cabinet Office, Japan, Public opinion survey on diplomacy. Available online at http//:www8. cao.go.jp/survey/[various years] (accessed March 2007)

and reaching unparalleled highs in 2005–6, while figures for those with positive responses plummeted from the surreal highs of over 70 per cent during the early 1980s, to less than 50 per cent (Figure 2.1). Conversely, Chinese polls in 2002 recorded a dismal 5.9 per cent of respondents suggesting Japan as 'friendly', while 43.3 per cent expressed the opposite view, and that escalated to 63 per cent in 2005 (cf. Yang 2003: 306; BBC 24 Aug. 2005). As Self (2002: 81) argues, the premise that intensified personal contact increases mutual affection between peoples has yet to be proven in the case of Japanese–Chinese relations.

On the economic front, the Japanese have become acutely aware of and concerned about China's growing challenge and the shifting balance in Japanese– Chinese economic interdependence. Notwithstanding the trade deficits, the spectre of Japan's manufacturing sector 'hollowing out' following mass relocation of manufacturing firms to China (*Nikkei* 19 Aug. 2002) to exploit Chinese comparative incentives and lower production costs raised fears of a Chinese economic threat. The 2001 trade dispute that saw both sides invoking protectionist measures to curtail mutual imports of certain products illustrates the drawbacks of deepening economic interdependence, which adds to their conventional bilateral impasses (Hilpert 2002: 46–7). Also, their contest to offer separate FTAs to ASEAN member states and competing ideas of East Asian regionalism, have enlivened the prospects of Japanese–Chinese economic competition and regional rivalry (Terada 2006).

That said, both governments have resolutely rallied behind their deepening economic interdependence to effectively buffer against serious erosions of diplomatic relations throughout the last decade. Japan, on her part, has maintained her policy of economic engagement and actively supported China's enmeshment in the global economy, i.e. China's accession into the WTO, where Japan was the first nation-state to conclude bilateral negotiations with China over WTO entry (Hook *et al.* 2005: 197). Similarly, China's 'third' and 'fourth' generation leadership has continuously promoted economic ties with Japan as the vehicle towards realising economic modernisation. Hence, the 'cold politics, hot economics' dialectic in Japanese–Chinese ties is not surprising, considering the continued emphasis on the economic dimension as the foundation of overall bilateral relations, despite their disagreements in the politico-diplomatic realm.

Bilateral trade surpassed US$100 billion in 2002 (MOFA 2003: 28), with China set to overtake the US as Japan's largest trading partner. This feat was duly achieved in 2004, with trade volume reaching US$214.6 billion (cf. Tok 2005: 299) as China accounted for 20.1 per cent of Japan's total trade, surpassing the US at 18.6 per cent (cf. Lam 2005: 289). Indeed, China's phenomenal economic performance served as the 'growth engine' that successfully alleviated the protracted Japanese recession. The reversal of economic fortune and awareness of China's importance to Japan's economic health saw 'Sinophobic' attitudes abating by 2003, as the *zaikai* appeared to increasingly 'tie its fate with the Chinese economy' (Taniguchi 2005: 445–6). With China maintaining its outstanding economic growth, a renewed sense of optimism accelerated Japanese FDI inflows into the Chinese mainland. According to Kokubun (2003: 34), Japan experienced its 'fifth China boom', with the rate of Japanese commercial investments in China rising exponentially since 2000, and totalling nearly US$40 billion by 2003 (Yahuda 2006: 164). Even the spectre of rising anti-Japanese nationalism during the April 2005 demonstrations failed to deter the buoyant mood of Japanese firms, with some 54.8 per cent enunciating commitments to expand their investments and presence in China soon after (Tok 2005: 299).

Overall, post-Cold War relations have expanded, but the fragility that has surrounded their bilateral ties since 1972 does not suggest the likelihood of a genuine Japanese–Chinese reconciliation. According to Yang (2003: 308), contemporary Japan–China relations are still very much 'in the shadow of the past'. Historical residue remains a chief source of mutual prejudice and distrust amongst policy-makers and the public, undermining their political will to seek resolution to both endemic and new bilateral issues. Self (2002: 77–8) argues that their over-reliance on the existing mechanism of 'friendship diplomacy' to mediate problems and preserve 'a mirage of good relations' has thus far 'accomplished no more than a façade of friendship'. Furthermore, structural changes in both international and domestic environments, and rising nationalism, have magnified divisions between the two countries. Although elements to promote a more sanguine outlook exist, the negative by-products of such changes are 'crowding out the positive aspects of bilateral ties' (Self 2002: 77).

External and domestic dynamics shaping Japanese–Chinese relations

The overview of the two defining eras reveals the shaping of Japanese–Chinese affairs by both external and domestic dynamics. Whilst the constraints imposed by the international system and their relative material and discursive capabilities have largely established the parameters of bilateral interaction, the overview also highlights the salience of domestic determinants that periodically influenced and dominated their foreign policy behaviour. This reflects NCR's dictum of the primacy of external/structural-material variables in limiting the boundaries of state behaviour, and the intervening role of domestic variables in dispensing the specific preference-of-action. Japan's relations with China are therefore comprehensible, when both sets of variables are systematically analysed via the NCR framework, to explicate their functions and dynamic interplay in shaping its China policy and bilateral trends.

External dynamics

Japanese–Chinese relations have always been and will continue to be shaped by external circumstances, which define the parameters of both governments' policy behaviour and responses in their mutual relations. The above overview shows that the external dynamics are similar to those identified as the 'independent' external variable in the NCR framework, namely the international environment, one's diplomatic leverage vis-à-vis the other, the US–Japan alliance commitment/ resolve and the correlating US–Japan–China triangular politics, and economic interdependence. As described, the post-1945 international system spawned constraints and opportunities that facilitated as well as impeded bilateral ties. In particular, the rigid bipolarity of the nascent Cold War system and 'alliance commitments' hindered opportunities for an early Japanese–Chinese reconciliation, insofar as both countries, being 'proxy states' in adversarial camps, had to subordinate their respective foreign policies to the overarching bipolar international order. Whilst the US–Japan security treaty restricted Japan's China policy, the Chinese were constrained by their alliance with the USSR, which impeded formal diplomatic interactions in the 1950s and 1960s.

Interestingly, bilateral interactions remained manageable at the height of the Cold War, despite the given context of regional bipolar hostility. The prospects of a renewed Japanese–Chinese conflict did not materialise in the form of direct military engagements, other than the episodic tensions caused by the indirect impact of Sino-American hostility during the Korean War, Taiwan Strait crises and Vietnam War, where Japan was implicated by 'alliance commitment' to help contain communist expansionism. Indeed, rather than totally subordinating the bilateral relationship to the logic of confrontation and non-engagement, pragmatism and mutual interests saw both states nurturing limited economic engagements at the unofficial level. Considering the Cold War's structural determinacy, such deviating state behaviour indicates NCR's assumption regarding the mitigating role of economic interdependence, and plausible intervention of domestic political and economic imperatives/actors in Japanese (and Chinese) policy-making.

Nonetheless, it should be noted that both countries' prerogative to partially circumvent the structural imperatives, i.e. evading direct military confrontations and keeping informal channels of economic interaction open amidst sporadic regional conflagrations, was abetted by the tacit acquiescence of the US and, to a lesser extent, the USSR. Indeed, their informal trade relations were dependent on American approval of the Japanese proposition of the 'separation of politics from economics' formula (*seikei bunri*), which allowed Japan to promote economic interactions with China in the absence of formal political ties (Iriye 1996: 53). Even then, Japanese–Chinese commerce was negligible, partly due to export restrictions imposed by their respective economic blocs.[19] Systemic pressures appeared more salient in the political realm, where persistent Chinese overtures to resume formal diplomatic interactions were matched by enduring resistance from successive post-war Japanese administrations from Yoshida to Sato, presumably the outcome of intense American *gaiatsu*.

Conversely, the deepening Sino-Soviet rift, and eventual fallout following their border skirmishes in the late 1960s, engendered a strategic transformation in the regional security architecture that ultimately provided a window of opportunity for Japan and China to normalise diplomatic relations. Specifically, it brought a confluence of strategic interests that provided the impetus for a Sino-American rapprochement (Zhao 1997: 132). This strategic shift correspondingly nullified the major constraint in Japan's China policy and saw Tokyo outdoing its American ally to establish official relations with Beijing. Developments in the international environment equally facilitated the signing of the PFT. On China's part, the threat of Soviet expansionism and the urgent need to incorporate Japan into a tacit strategic alliance against the USSR saw Beijing pushing for its early conclusion, and the inclusion of the 'anti-hegemony' clause. Japan's signing of the PFT, despite 'domestic' reservations, was also dynamically influenced by external considerations. These included Japanese concerns over a possible drawdown in US military presence under Carter's regional disengagement policy, Soviet hard-line policy on the Northern Territory impasse, and more significantly, the intention to harmonise with US diplomatic trends, following Washington's overtures towards normalising relations with Beijing (Bedeski 1983: 4, 40).

The decline in contemporary bilateral relations also reflects their manoeuvring and policy responses to the post-Cold War international environment. The Cold War's demise has immensely transformed the East Asian strategic landscape, and Japanese–Chinese ties have been duly affected by the fluidity and new configuration of power relations in the region. Not only did it render the US–Japan–China 'strategic-triangle' obsolete, the post-Cold War order precipitated the emergence of a relatively low-pressure or ambivalent external environment which, according to NCR's interpretation, gave both Japan and China newfound foreign policy flexibility, not to mention domestic leverage in policy-making. The period also saw their relative power positions undergoing significant shifts. 'Diverging fortunes' since the early 1990s – China's rapid economic growth against the protracted 'post-bubble' recession suffered by Japan – have altered the regional power balance (Pei and Swaine 2005). Compounded by China's strength and Japan's ambivalence in the politico-security realm, these asymmetrical developments in their relative strategic and economic positions have created considerable unease, leading to mutual policy readjustments that have contributed to a renewal of Japanese–Chinese animosities (Pei and Swaine 2005: 3).

In the security dimension, their respective policy shifts, undertaken as much in response to the fluid international strategic environment as to their changing relative security perceptions, have aggravated mutual insecurities. The incremental shifts in Japan's security policy have been partly a response to the international community's call for a more substantial Japanese contribution following the first Gulf War, where Tokyo was heavily criticised for 'free-riding' and overly depending on its 'cheque-book diplomacy' (Miller 2000: 5). Notwithstanding North Korea's mounting security threat – i.e. the Taepodong missile test, *fushinsen* (mystery ship) incursion and abduction of Japanese citizens – sustained Chinese military build-up and occasional belligerence in managing regional security issues equally encouraged a thorough review of Japan's post-Cold War security policy. Furthermore, the fundamentality of the US–Japan alliance to Japanese conception of security required Tokyo to continue calibrating its national defence guidelines to complement its ally. Such developments have concomitantly influenced China's strategic perceptions and sense of insecurity in a largely American-dominated 'unipolar' international system. With US foreign policy becoming increasingly unilateral in approach, and Sino-US relations deteriorating amid a series of impasses, from human rights to Taiwan, Japan's newfound assertiveness and renewal of 'alliance commitment' have heightened Chinese anxiety regarding Japanese security ambitions, specifically its remilitarisation under American auspices, in a perceived, joint effort to hedge China's rise (Christensen 1999: 59–63; Wu 2000: 301).

Indeed, Washington's shifting position in the context of the US–Japan–China 'triangularity' (Soerensen 2006) has profoundly affected Japanese–Chinese diplomacy. Zhao (2002: 32) rightly observes that the US is 'the most significant external actor/factor, and has had a tremendous influence on the direction of Sino-Japanese relations' ever since the PRC's establishment. In particular, developments in the US–Japan alliance have prevalently affected Japan's China policy and general trends in the Japanese–Chinese relationship. Most noticeable are the downturns throughout the two defining epochs, which have coincided with the periods of strengthened US–Japan relations and renewed Japanese obligations towards the American-led security arrangement. The nadirs in pre-1972 relations occurred when Tokyo sought to redefine the US–Japan security treaty, despite vociferous objections from Beijing and domestic pacifist forces within Japan. Likewise, the deterioration in post-Cold War diplomacy reflects China's apprehensions about Japan's decision to enhance US–Japan security cooperation, and uneasiness regarding the non-equidistant nature of the 'triangular relationship' that increasingly portrays China as the target, in a 'two-against-one' context, especially since the mid-1990s (Zhao 2002: 47). Complicating matters is 'Taiwan', a dilemma in Japan's relations with China due to Tokyo's alliance commitment that connotes an obligation to support US military intervention, in the event of a Chinese 'forceful reunification' of the island. Tokyo's cautious attitude towards Taiwan, exemplified by its measured response to the 1996 Taiwan Strait crisis, and what Drifte (2003: 97) sees as Japan's 'interpretational somersaults', or preferred ambiguity regarding the scope of the revised US–Japan Guidelines,[20] has been diluted by its subsequent participation in TMD development, and its 2005 joint declaration with Washington on Taiwan's future security. Such mixed signals have made Beijing ever more suspicious of Tokyo and Washington's commitment to the 'One-China' principle. China's passing of the Anti-Secession Law in March 2005 underscores such concerns, a move which further complicates the 'Taiwan question' in the US–Japan–China relationship.

In addition, the general atmosphere governing Japanese–Chinese interactions has been affected by the diplomatic leverage enjoyed by one party over the other during specific external conditions and time periods, their relative material capabilities notwithstanding. Although somewhat ambivalent during the pre- and immediate normalisation period, their Cold War ties recorded superficial progress in the decade following the PFT's conclusion, regardless of sporadic problems concerning war history and continuous political recriminations and manipulation of related issues by Chinese leaders to draw economic concessions from their Japanese counterparts. This generally upbeat political climate was partly facilitated by external–structural pressures that necessitated mutual efforts and political will to consciously promote warmer ties and subordinate bilateral differences for their common strategic interests in containing the Soviets. It was also largely fostered by what scholars deemed as Japan's 'deference' to a structured and asymmetrical pattern in their post-normalisation relationship that saw China consistently adopting a 'high-posture', while the Japanese, due to their war-guilt and moral inferiority complexes, always responded with the 'low-posture' attitude of mollifying the Chinese (Ijiri 1996: 61, 69; Drifte 2003: 18).[21] Barring the 'logic-of-reassurance' thesis (Midford 2002), this so-called 'friendship framework', which operated on tacit understanding and on an impromptu basis of removing 'immediate obstacles' to promote continuous 'superficial friendship' (Ijiri 1996: 64), was responsible for skewing the perceptions of diplomatic leverage towards each other that affected the lopsided management of bilateral issues during the 1970s and 1980s.

Conversely, the unfavourable ambience governing their post-Cold War relations reflects the change in perceptions of diplomatic leverage, especially in Japan's case. Underpinning this climate has been the emergence of a low-pressure, ambiguous international strategic environment that has encouraged the expansion of foreign/security policy scope and ambition, which, compounded by shifting power relations, has aggravated mutual insecurities. Together with domestic political developments, i.e. generational shifts in the leadership and masses, and changing political moods amid rising nationalism, these dynamics have instigated a shift in Japanese attitudes and perceptions of diplomatic leverage vis-à-vis the Chinese. Specifically, attitudes have hardened, bringing Japanese perception to more 'realistic' levels that have led to the abandonment of 'kowtow' diplomacy, when managing their bilateral affairs.

Economic interdependence is another bilateral dynamic that serves as a key mitigating factor in the international context, and vanguard of amiable Japanese–Chinese relations. Economic considerations provided the basis for unofficial relations during the early Cold War decades, laying the groundwork for the normalisation of political relations in 1972. Since then, their flourishing economic interactions and deepening interdependence have become a significant constraint on politically induced deterioration in overall ties. Drifte (2002: 62) contends that Japan's economic interaction with China 'has had a soothing influence on bilateral disputes'. Both governments have been acutely cognisant of its benefits, not only in boosting the performance of their respective national economies, but also in promoting a positive 'spill-over' effect into other dimensions of their relationship (Yahuda 2006: 166). According to experts, Japan has vigorously used its economic strength as a key China policy instrument, in view of its 'global civilian power' status (Drifte 2003: 28). Successive Japanese administrations have expanded trade and investments with China as well as disbursement of ODA to precipitate post-war reconciliation, and serve Japan's own economic interests. Pledges to promote economic ties are thus the favoured official intergovernmental rhetoric, and are considered fundamental to the realisation of a durable relationship.

As political ties suffer in the post-Cold War period, economic interdependence has become ever more critical in preventing a free-fall in overall bilateral relations. With their economies increasingly intertwined, one can reasonably argue that both governments have shown remarkable resilience in sustaining a working relationship, despite intensified diplomatic altercations, to safeguard their mutual economic interests. Like their predecessors, the 'Hu-Wen' leadership continued prioritising China's modernisation and development, and a robust economic relationship with Japan remains fundamental to realising such aspirations. Similarly, the Koizumi administration, despite its unparalleled assertiveness towards China, equally calibrated its engagement policies to avoid alienating its neighbour, considering the intractable importance of Chinese commerce to Japan's own economic vitality (Lam 2005: 286–9). Although interdependence has brought new problems, with signs of friction already apparent, it remains a strong rallying point for stable relations. Interestingly, as Japan and China find themselves 'uneasy bedfellows' (Zhang and Drysdale 2000) in the contemporary 'cold politics, hot economics' scenario, a sense of déjà vu reminiscent to the *seikei bunri* era can be felt, as both governments strive to prevent their politico-diplomatic differences from festering in the economic realm. Nonetheless, as Yahuda (2006) noted, the restraining effects of economic interdependence and globalisation remain questionable under thriving domestic socio-political dynamics that also shape their bilateral affairs.

Domestic dynamics

The above description highlights the external dynamics that define the parameters of the bilateral interactions between Japan and China. However, NCR also stipulates the salience of domestic dynamics, which have consistently affected Japanese–Chinese diplomacy, with variables from domestic political competition to nationalism having, to varying degrees, determined the policy and management of bilateral problems. Domestic determinants have especially become efficacious in the post-Cold War period, following the lessening of structural pressures and corresponding emergence of a fluid international environment. The rekindling and frequency of the aforementioned bilateral disputes underscores NCR's assumption regarding the potency of domestic variables in foreign policy-making under such external circumstances.

In particular, domestic political imperatives have incessantly influenced one side's policy towards the other, leading to the 'highs-and-lows' in Japanese–Chinese relations. Kojima (2000: 41) rightly observes that Japan's China policy has become 'intertwined' with Japanese domestic politics, especially since 1972, following the domestication of diplomatic issues by contending political factions, divided by their 'pro-Beijing' and 'pro-Taipei' sentiments. Indeed, scholars commonly agree that one cannot adequately explain many bilateral issues that have inflamed their relationship without referring to domestic political competition (Kojima 2000; Whiting 1989; Ijiri 1996). Some were primarily domestic-centred issues, only to be internationalised owing to political pressure and elite manipulations for domestic political expediency. Besides territorial disputes and Taiwan, the constant resurrection of 'history'-related problems needs to be understood in the context of internal political dynamics, which have occasionally forced Japanese and Chinese leaders to take assertive stances to bolster their power positions and political incumbency. From history textbooks to Yasukuni, the periodic diplomatic rows over 'history' in the 1980s coincided with key developments in domestic politics, and were linked to elite power competition (Kojima 2000: 41).[22] Its contemporary rekindling in similar circumstances, underscores NCR's assumption regarding the linkage between and 'intervening' function of domestic politics on external relations.

Japanese–Chinese relations have been similarly affected by correlated domestic political developments, i.e. shifting political terrain, and leadership transition/change-of-administration. Evidently, the 'highs-and-lows' coincided with the waxing and waning of political elites and parties that held favourable perceptions of each other, and were principally committed to promoting friendly relations. Especially in Japan, the emergence of 'China-friendly' administrations since 1972 (i.e. Tanaka, Ohira, Takeshita, Hosokawa) precipitated periods of remarkably affable relations (Murata 2006). Likewise, 'China school' MOFA bureaucrats (Drifte 2003: 19), and 'pro-China' politicians who hailed from the influential LDP's Keisei-kai faction, and generally, the 'normalisation' generation, with few exceptions, played important roles in cementing the 'friendship framework' (Self 2002) that governed bilateral ties until the early 1990s. Despite the occasional challenges from 'pro-Taiwan' and hawkish elements, the dominant sentiment within Japanese political circles had arguably been geared towards appeasing and enhancing ties with China, partly because of their war-guilt complex and sense of moral debt, and also due to pragmatic considerations. Moreover, the formidable leftwing/pacifist presence, i.e. the Japan Communist Party (JCP) and Japan Socialist Party (JSP – now the Socialist Democratic Party of Japan, SDPJ), during the Cold War, successfully neutralised ultra-nationalist-rightwing and 'anti-China' influences within the Japanese political arena, whilst exerting political pressures on successive LDP administrations to improve ties with Beijing.

However, domestic political transformations since mid-1990s, marked by generational change in leadership and the weakening of leftist/pacifist institutions, have begun to negatively affect Japanese–Chinese relations. Specifically, these 'structural changes' have altered the power balance and affected the customary competition between 'pro-Beijing' and 'pro-Taipei' forces in China policy-making. According to Drifte (2002: 53), powerful 'pro-China' politicians and bureaucrats responsible for mustering political support for warmer bilateral ties were replaced by a new generation of more independent, assertive and less 'China-sympathetic' leaders. The increased political frictions in recent times suggest the reluctance of contemporary Japanese state-elites to placate China, notably on traditionally sensitive issues. Unlike their predecessors, leaders like Obuchi and, particularly, Koizumi, were more defiant and willing to challenge and 'offend the Chinese, if necessary' (Self 2002: 80; Soerensen 2006: 114). Obuchi's disregard of the Chinese 'war apology' demand during Jiang's visit, and the obstinate posture adopted by Koizumi and his Cabinet members on the Yasukuni and textbook issues, are noteworthy elucidations of this domestic 'wind of change' in Japan's China policy-making.

The arrival of Koizumi Junichiro, a dynamic, but allegedly nationalistic Japanese PM, is of particular significance to this study. According to Lam (2005: 275), the 'Koizumi factor' (referring to his 'combative' personality and assertive policy), contributed immensely to the 'abysmal state of relations between the two neighbours'.[23] Indeed, Koizumi's apparent abandonment of 'friendship diplomacy' proved to be a principal source of bilateral friction. Since his appointment in April 2001, Koizumi's reluctance to succumb to Chinese pressure provoked the contempt of China's leadership and masses. Particularly, his annual Yasukuni pilgrimages, and insistence on his right to go there, irked Beijing, who considered such thoughtless acts by Japanese leaders as tantamount to celebrating Japan's militaristic past. The worsening ties had also to do with Koizumi's Cabinet appointments and their politico-ideological affiliations, as these, according to Johnson (2005), comprised several 'hard-line, anti-Chinese, pro-Taiwanese politicians'. Lam (2005: 285 n. 21) shared Johnson's observation that no 'China-friendly' politicians were appointed to his Cabinets (prior to October 2005), after the firing of Tanaka Makiko, ex-FM and daughter of Tanaka Kakuei, in January 2002. Furthermore, Koizumi is said to have had marginalised not only Keisei-kai, but factional politics, as a whole, by personally determining his Cabinet line-up and not depending on factional patronage, but instead drew support 'directly from the LDP rank-and-file and Japanese public opinion' (Lam 2005: 285 n. 22; Park 2001: 458). Koizumi's political independence and popularity, coupled with political and administrative reforms in 2001 that enhanced the PM's authority at the expense of bureaucratic influence, provided his administration with greater leverage on China policy-making (Pei and Swaine 2005: 3–4).

Meanwhile, within the ruling LDP, the correlated decline of Keisei-kai, following corruption scandals and retirement of 'China-Hands' like Nonaka Hiromu, precipitated the ascendancy of the hawkish and 'China-sceptical' Seiwa-kai faction (Taniguchi 2005: 452–3).[24] Paralleling such developments have been the waning influence of leftist/pacifist opposition parties, and the concomitant shift of Japanese politics to the centre-right position (Yahuda 2006: 168). Altogether, these domestic transformations have hastened the meltdown of 'pro-China' political forces in Japan.

The negative impact of Japan's political transformation on Japanese–Chinese relations has a mitigating domestic factor in the *zaikai*, which has been traditionally influential in pressuring Tokyo to adjust its overall China policy to advance Japanese commercial interests in the Chinese mainland. It was the *zaikai* that provided dynamic input to the *seikei bunri* policy that facilitated informal economic links with China during the pre-normalisation period, and since 1972 has continued preserving the most prosperous dimension of Japanese–Chinese relationship, while keeping politico-diplomatic ties in check against serious erosion. It is true that the *zaikai*'s policy-making influence has somewhat diminished along with the demise of Japan's traditional 'pork-barrel' politics, following electoral reforms in 1994. Yet one should not underestimate its role in deterring the Koizumi Cabinet from overly intimidating Beijing, since economic considerations remain fundamental to Japan's overall China policy calculations.

Nonetheless, the effect of economic factors can be balanced by an equally pervasive, domestic, socio-political dynamic in nationalism. Evidently, nationalism did undermine Japanese–Chinese relations during the Cold War. On China's part, diplomatic tensions arising from Senkaku/Diaoyudao, history textbook and Yasukuni controversies, among others, were as much manifestations of domestic nationalist impulses as Beijing's political manipulations to obtain politico-economic concessions from Tokyo. Similarly, these issues gained salience in the Japanese domestic political discourse and agenda, following manipulations by elements from the political left and right in Japan, as well as the rise of 'confident nationalism' during the era of 'miraculous' economic growth in the 1970s and 1980s (Sasaki 2001). However, both governments' pragmatism in shelving the related disputes suggests the prevalence of the Cold War-imposed external-structural constraints in negating excessive domestic nationalist influence in the policy-making process.

Importantly for this study, nationalism has apparently (re)gained salience in post-Cold War Japanese–Chinese diplomacy. Indeed, resurgent nationalism in Japan and China in the 1990s has produced a political climate detrimental to their fragile relationship. Besides undermining their mutual societal images and attitude, flourishing domestic nationalist forces have, to various degrees, affected one another's policy orientation, contributing to the recent proliferation of diplomatic discords over a plethora of bilateral issues. For instance, the aforementioned 'history'-related problems were manifestations of nationalism in Japanese and Chinese politics that have arguably influenced their mutually assertive responses when managing these disputes. The rekindling of the ECS dispute and Taiwan, and their changing mutual security perceptions/policies that seemingly target each other as potential threats, underscore nationalism's impact on bilateral ties. Especially in Japan, thriving anti-Chinese nationalist sentiment, compounded by the other mentioned political developments, are partly responsible for reinventing contemporary Japanese–Chinese diplomacy.

Conclusion

The above overview of Japanese–Chinese affairs highlights a relationship persistently shaped by a compendium of structural-material and ideational dynamics, deriving from both external and domestic realms. It also illustrates the primacy of external imperatives in defining the scope of bilateral interactions, and salience of domestic factors in dispensing policy preferences. In the post-Cold War period, domestic variables, particularly nationalism, have seemingly emerged as a key foreign policy driver and contributed to the worsening relationship. This scenario has prompted the questions posed by this book, namely how, in what manner and conditions, and to what extent does nationalism affect foreign policy-making, particularly in the Japanese context, when managing issues endemic to their problematic ties. This warrants an analysis of Japanese nationalism, followed by an impact assessment of nationalism in shaping Japan's China policy and the bilateral relationship, and these are the themes of subsequent chapters.

3 Theories of nationalism and its manifestations in Japan

Transformations in the international and domestic realms have markedly affected contemporary Japanese–Chinese relations. Domestically, structural and ideational changes have triggered coalescing political shifts that saw nationalism apparently regaining salience in their domestic and external agendas. As highlighted in Chapter 2, domestic nationalist pressure constitutes a growing constraint that can affect and limit foreign policy options, especially when managing nationalist-nuanced bilateral issues. In Japan's case, the frequent diplomatic impasses with China, and their correlations with domestic nationalist politics, reflect this policy-making scenario. This chapter analyses nationalism and its so-called 'resurgence' in post-Cold War Japan. It begins with a discussion on the definitions, concepts and roles of nationalism in modern international relations. Next, the intricacies of Japanese nationalism are explored via a brief account of its genesis and historical development, followed by an examination of the driving forces and manifestations behind its contemporary revitalisation. Special attention is paid to defining state/ elite-driven and popular nationalisms. Questions regarding the 'state–popular' relationship, notably their points of convergence or divergence and correlated influence on state behaviour are addressed accordingly.

Defining and understanding nationalism

The term 'nationalism' is among the most difficult to define and clarify with accuracy. The plethora of definitions accompanying nationalism's extensive literature suggests the lack of an all-encompassing meaning for this nebulous phenomenon. Hans Kohn (1965: 9), one of the 'founding fathers' of the intellectual discourse on nationalism (Kemilainen 1964) defines it as 'a state of mind, in which the supreme loyalty of the individual is felt to be due to the nation-state'. Ernest Gellner (1983: 1), another prominent scholar of nationalism, sees it as 'primarily a political principle, which holds that the political (state) and national (nation) unit should be congruent'. Meanwhile, Anthony Smith (1991: 73) contends that nationalism is 'an ideological movement for attaining and maintaining autonomy, unity and identity on behalf of a population deemed by some of its members to constitute an actual or potential nation'. These 'textbook' definitions exemplify nationalism's multi-dimensional nature – it is political, socio-cultural and psychological – making it a powerful and pervasive, yet enigmatic force in the modern world.

Predominantly viewed as a product of modernity emanating from eighteenth-century European history, nationalism is synonymous with and inseparable from the concepts of 'nation', 'nation-state' and 'national identity' (Baycroft 1998: 3). Nationalism fundamentally concerns the 'nation', another enigmatic term to define, due to its ambiguous relationship with other kindred concepts, i.e. race and ethnicity (Ozkirimli 2000: 58), and its tendency to be widely, but mistakenly equated with the concept of 'state' (Connor 1994: 92). Evidently, there is a marked distinction between the terms 'nation' and 'state',[1] as argued by scholars like Waldron (1985: 417), Kellas (1998: 3) and Ozkirimli (2000: 58), who saw the former espousing a socio-cultural and psychological dimension the latter does not possess, namely the objective features of language, culture, religion and common descent that form the basis of a collective identity, and the subjective element of consciousness, passion and affection towards the perceived shared identity (cf. Zheng 1999: p. x).

Nationalism also coexists with the 'nation-state' concept. Modernist views on the genesis of nationalism highlight political, economic and socio-cultural transformations, and the state's role in engendering nationalism and the formation of nation. Hobsbawm and Ranger (1983) see nation and nationalism as 'invented traditions', a product of 'social engineering' by states, while Gellner (1983) associates the formation of 'high culture' in industrial societies with the consequent emergence of nations through state fostering of nationalist sentiments via mass education and communication. Both perspectives, Guibernau (1996: 59) asserts, emphasise the state's utilisation of nationalism to create a nation-state that is 'coextensive' and identifies with it, where state–society/citizen/nation relations are not merely a political association, but also 'an expression of the multidimensional relation which derives from the idea of nation formation'. Moreover, according to Zheng (1999: p. x), nationalism comprises 'institution' and 'identity', two crucial components of the nation-state. Zheng argues that nationalism is not prominent when expressed by individuals in its raw and disorganised form, especially in the context of international relations. It becomes credible only after it is organised and expressed collectively by institutions. In modern international society, nationalism is successfully expressed through the 'state', the foremost institution in the Westphalian world order (Young 1976: 72; cf. Zheng 1999: p. x).

Nationalism also emphasises the individuality and distinctiveness of a nation-state, specifically its 'national identity'. Identity, by definition, refers to 'an interpretation of the self that establishes what and where the person is in both social and psychological terms' (Guibernau 1996: 72). Guibernau (1996: 72) construes that 'when one has identity one is situated', and that 'identities exist only in societies, which define and organize them', and it exists and defines only in relation to other identities. At the individual level, identity reflects 'the need to belong to a community', and in the modern world where 'nation' is one such community, 'national identity is its product' (Guibernau 1996: 72–3). National identity thus refers to the collective sentiment shared by members of a perceived nation, or an 'imagined community' (Anderson 1991) that distinguishes and situates them from other national communities. As the 'creator' of national identity (Guibernau 1996), nationalism situates a nation-state vis-à-vis other national actors within modern international society.

National identity usually derives its essence from more basic forms of identity. It is typical for nation-states with near homogeneous societies to forge national identity based on elements like shared culture and common descent. Conversely, such primordial features tend to be divisive and obstructive to its formation in nation-states with heterogeneous and polarised societies. However, 'national identity' can transcend these objective-cum-divisive features, if they are superseded by the intersubjectivity of what Kellas (1998: 3) describes as a people's consciousness of and devotion/affection for its nationality, and sense of belonging to the nation-state. This is where the symbolic-mythical content of nationalism, fundamentally the use of myths, symbols and rituals, becomes essential in national identity creation, serving as 'markers' to cloak internal differences, while highlighting commonalities within a nation, and differentiating members of one nation from others (Guibernau 1996: 80–2; Van Evera 1994: 30). Guibernau (1996: 83) concurs that these 'markers' are able to generate within individuals a feeling of extraordinary emotional intensity that emanates from their identification with the nation, a transcending entity that provides a sentiment of belonging, from which they derive 'strength and resilience', and under whose name they participate in 'heroic as well as barbaric actions' to defend its interests. Young (1976: 71), therefore, credibly asserts that nationalism is 'an ideological formulation of identity', of which the nation is stipulated as 'a terminal community' with 'transcendent moral sanction and authority', to whom 'active obligation' is mandatory, and 'ultimate loyalty is owned' (cf. Zheng 1999: p. x). In its radical manifestation, nationalism is '"the supreme loyalty" for people who are prepared to die for their nation' (Kellas 1998: 3).

In the international context, nationalism legitimises the Westphalian 'society of nation-states' doctrine, where the 'state', as the sovereign authority, represents and links nation to the international system (Zheng 1999: p. xi). According to Mayall (1990: 19–20), the principles of national self-determination and sovereignty espoused by nationalism recognise nation-states as independent, equal and separate political entities that interact on the basis of acknowledging each other's: (i) sovereignty, (ii) autonomy and monopoly of jurisdiction within their own political boundaries, (iii) territorial integrity and (iv) non-interference in domestic affairs. Indeed, its 'particularistic' feature of defining the 'self' from the 'other' drives nations towards 'the political notion of territorial self-determination, the cultural notion of national identity, and the moral notion of national self-defense in an anarchical [nation-state system]' (Zhao 2000: 3). Interestingly, these principles mirror the realist conception of the anarchic condition of the modern international system, which underscores 'survival' as the overarching goal of nation-states, and the plausible utility of force/war to realise the national interests that are primarily defined in terms of national survival (Mayall 1990).

Nationalism is inherently 'Janus-faced' (Guibernau 1996: 45). Depending on expression, it 'can be either a powerfully constructive or destructive force' (Nester 1995: 74). Nationalism has been effervescent throughout modern history, playing a fundamentally positive role in the decolonisation and nation-building processes, and domestic economic development (Posen 1993: 80). Then again, its malevolent nature has often prevailed, fuelling numerous international conflicts and 'human tragedies' (Zhao 2000: 1). Presumably, its promotion of 'particularism' tends to invoke ultra-nationalism, xenophobia and chauvinism that become the driving force behind such belligerent behaviour (Zhao 2000: 3; Van Evera 1994).[2] As history has repeated itself on many occasions, nationalism, when not prudently managed, always perpetuates violent outcomes.

To summarise, nationalism, as a 'modern' phenomenon with perennial roots attached to primordial elements (Smith 1986), is a profound force. It is socio-psychological and political, in both form and essence. Deriving intrinsically from members of particular social groupings who (perceive they) share a distinctive disposition, heritage and sentiments of belonging towards their collective identities, nationalism can be organised and emphatically expressed via the state to realise political ends. Its 'particularism' and advocacy of the principles of self-determination, sovereignty and equality between nations underscore the basis of modern international relations. Meanwhile, its instrumental value allows state/elite manipulation for popular mobilisation towards various political goals, both domestic and international. Yet, nationalism, for all its instrumentality, is unpredictable, and has the tendency to undermine the agencies that promote it.

As stipulated in the Introduction, this book's triple-pronged definition of nationalism represents its fundamental premises and multi-dimensional characteristics. The first definition reflects the cultural–ideational dimension, one which emphasises the socio-cultural and psychological attributes that intrinsically drive most, if not all forms of nationalist sentiments, and imbues the nation and its members with a 'national identity'.[3] Focusing on grassroots-level national consciousness, this definition suggests a 'bottom–up' view of nationalism that emphasises the role of ordinary people, non-state actors and populist emotions/passion in shaping the nationalist discourse and agenda of a nation-state (Gries 2004: 20). Conversely, the second and third meanings draw on the political notion and state-centric character of nationalism. As mentioned, nationalism is essentially political and generally associated with the state. From its basic form, represented by individual and popular sentiment, nationalism can be remarkably political, when expressed through the state and its apparatuses. The second definition underscores the correlation between 'nation' and 'state', where socio-cultural identity intertwines with political identity. Here, a 'top–down' perspective of nationalism is emphasised, whereby the state, viewed as the embodiment and political representation of the nation, has the power to mould although not dictate the content of domestic nationalist discourse (Gries 2004). Meanwhile, the third definition represents nationalism's instrumental value that encourages its utilisation for political expediency. To reiterate, nationalism's utility is not limited to the state/state-elites, as commonly but narrowly understood in mainstream IR literature. Non-state actors, namely nationalist pressure groups and the masses, also politicise it to influence governmental policies and decision-making (Gries 2004).

Altogether, these definitions classify nationalism commonly into two distinctive yet correlated, and at times, mutually embracing typologies, namely official/state/ elite-driven nationalism and popular nationalism. Although nationalism is largely seen as state-engendered and under the government's purview, the state does not necessarily monopolise the domestic nationalist agenda (Gries 2004; Seckington 2005). In nationalistically effervescent countries, popular/mass-oriented nationalism may feature prominently in the domestic nationalist discourse. State nationalism tends to be pragmatic, rational, affirmative and instrumental. It is also moderate, national interest-driven (based on the state's calculation of costs and benefits), and reactive rather than proactive (Zhao 2000: 2). Meanwhile, popular nationalism is generally more diversified, robust, emotional, spontaneous and potentially virulent, xenophobic and aggressive (Seckington 2005). It is driven by the collective consciousness of individuals, who identify themselves as members of a nation, under whose name they seek to defend its interests and champion its causes. It draws strength from nationalism's intrinsic values, possesses a more critical intellectual debate (Seckington 2005: 27), is largely independent of and 'should not be conflated with … official nationalism' (Gries 2004: 20).

That said, popular nationalism is, to an extent, abetted by state nationalism, which arguably provides a conducive environment for it to flourish (Rose 2000: 174). Also, popular nationalist discourse does overlap with official rhetoric and identifies with the state, when there exists a confluence of interests, such as advocating for dynamic and assertive foreign policies, and calling for more decisive action in defence of the national interests (Seckington 2005: 27), or against perceived external pressure and/or threats. Both types of nationalism may share certain objectives, while diverging in others. Popular nationalism forms the bulwark of support for the state's nationalist agenda, when their objectives are mutually complementary. However, competition for dominance over the domestic nationalist agenda may prevail, if conflicting interests and nationalist goals arise between these two domains. 'Popular nationalism can be critical of official policy' (Seckington 2005: 27), especially when the state is perceived as having failed to live up to its nationalist credentials. As previously stated, popular nationalist pressure emanating from pressure groups and public opinion can effectively constrain state behaviour. It can be especially salient if state-elites are politically dependent on nationalism, and strong elite–mass linkage characterises the domestic political system.

The incorporation of these definitions and typologies generates better understanding, compared to the conventional, mono-dimensional perspective that views nationalism as predominantly state-led, and merely a power instrument/ political tool to bolster social cohesion and political legitimacy. Gries (2004: 18–20, 87–90) argues that this view is only partially correct, as it cannot fully grasp the depth of nationalism and the significance of 'emotion and passion' in nationalist politics, which is by no means under the state's exclusive control or controlled by purely rational pursuit of national interests. Moreover, one should understand nationalism via a combination of definitions, and view it from both 'top–down' and 'bottom–up' perspectives, since state-elites and popular nationalists 'participate in nationalist politics, and both emotional and instrumental concerns drive their behaviour' (Gries 2004: 87). Simply put, nationalism's rational-utility and emotive dispositions should be simultaneously considered, since both 'sense/passion' and 'sensibility/reason' matter in international relations and foreign policy-making (Gries 2004). Most importantly, these classifications are relevant to interpreting nationalism in Japan, and its impact on contemporary Japanese–Chinese ties. The following section demonstrates that Japanese nationalism professes most of these meanings, and exhibits the stipulated attributes.

The genesis, evolution and meanings of nationalism in Japan

The Cold War's passing and the burst of Japan's 'economic bubble' triggered socio-economic and political malaise that deepened 'the crisis of national identity and purpose' amongst Japanese in the so-called 'Lost Decade' of the 1990s (McCormack 2000: 247). Against this backdrop, the desire for 'national regeneration' has led to a series of socio-political developments that is symptomatic of a new national mood in Japan (McCormack 2000: 247–8), with nationalism apparently regaining currency after being a 'taboo' for decades, following its dreadful manifestation in the Second World War (Rose 2000). Understandably, nationalistic endeavours and expressions in recent times have raised both international and domestic concerns. Debates regarding its future direction have generated contrasting opinions; pessimists within and outside Japan perceive it as representing the potential resurrection of pre-war ultra-nationalism, whereas optimists denounce such observations as misunderstandings born out of ignorance, viewing the so-called 'neo-nationalism' as simply a benign and inevitable development as Japan seeks to re-establish a 'normal' nation-state identity. An overview of pre-war and post-war Japanese nationalism is thus necessary to comprehend the contending debate as much as the driving forces, characteristics and international orientations of its contemporary manifestations.

Overview of pre-war nationalism

Generally, most scholars identify the roots of Japanese nationalism with the Meiji epoch, during which its reform-minded oligarchs borrowed the Western concepts of nationalism and nation-state, together with their institutional and technological efficacies, to rebuild feudal Japan into a modern nation-state. They also largely agree that the essence of nationalism and national identity derived primarily from Japanese traditional culture and symbols, and perceived common ethno-religious bonds that Meiji state-elites reinvented to inculcate the nationalist ideology via education, media, military conscriptions and other state apparatuses, under a centralised polity (Gluck 1985: 17–23; Pyle 1971: 11). There were, indeed, 'nativist-based', pre-modern nationalistic expressions throughout

Japan's medieval history, i.e. 'elitist-proto-nationalism' (McVeigh 2004: 42), and the semblance of a centralised political system under the Tokugawa Shogunate. However, nationalism, as an organised socio-political movement espousing national identity and nation-statehood, was, in Conroy's (1955: 821) opinion, non-existent in pre-1868 Japan, due to traditionally divisive 'horizontal (feudal classes) and vertical [forces] (the fiefs)' that impeded its development.[4] That said, these nascent expressions laid the ideological groundwork for modern Japanese nationalism.

Scholars generally acknowledge that Japanese national consciousness was fostered by external factors, namely China's 'Opium War' experiences, and Japan's very own encounter with foreign pressures after two centuries of isolationism (*sakoku*) (Matsumoto 1971: 51), beginning with the arrival of Commodore Perry's 'black ships' (1853), and the subsequent imposition of 'unequal treaties' and Western powers' bombardment of Kagoshima (1863) and Shimonoseki (1864) (Hasegawa 1985; Nish 2000: 82). Before this, Japanese had held an ethnocentric, Confucian-based 'culturalist' worldview that regarded Japan as a culturally and morally superior entity, while dismissing the West as barbaric and culturally inept (Matsumoto 1971: 51). This worldview was discredited in the wake of Western imperialism in East Asia, which saw the Japanese re-evaluating and acknowledging their backwardness compared to the politically and militarily advanced Western nations (Matsumoto 1971: 51). According to Stronach (1995: 32–4), unlike the Chinese, who got 'suffocated by the weight' of their great civilisation, the Japanese were more flexible in adopting foreign ideas, due to their past tradition of borrowing from other cultures (especially from China). Japan therefore had less problems opening to and vigorously learning from the West. The fear of succumbing to Western 'gunboat diplomacy' motivated the Meiji government to embark on an expansive modernisation-cum-westernisation programme to reinvent the Japanese state and nation. During the initial stages, campaigns to eradicate Japanese feudal traditions were launched by Meiji oligarchs committed to the wholesale emulation of Western ideals, institutions and know-how. Whilst nationalism and nation-state-building of the Western genre were officially sanctioned, 'culturalism' was vilified as the source of degeneration, and an obstacle to reinventing a modern Japan. A centralised bureaucracy in Tokyo, and the use of state instruments, i.e. national education system, military services, communication/transportation networks, an influential media and bureaucratically controlled local organisations, facilitated the mass-level penetration of the nationalist ideology (Conroy 1955: 823; Pyle 1971: 11).

However, the intensive state-led policy provoked a 'nativist' reaction, as rising internal tension between Western-centred modernisation and nativist traditions created deep social fissures and identity crises. Meanwhile, externally, continuous Western pressure and unequal treatment, despite Japan's achievement of modern nation-statehood, meant many within Japanese society were disenchanted. Calls by intellectual groups and conservative elites for the revival of Japanese traditions and culture in the face of Western onslaught stirred popular discontent. This prompted the embattled Meiji state-elites to instrumentally recreate the cultural component of the nationalist ideology, based upon key traditional symbols and myths, namely the 'State-Shinto' religion and *tennosei* (emperor) system,[5] while simultaneously sustaining the modernisation agenda as the basis for Japan's national renewal (McVeigh 2004: 42–3; Stronach 1995: 40; Tamamoto 2001).[6]

Imperial Japan's successful initial experiments with expansionism, notably in the Japanese–Chinese and Russo-Japanese wars, boosted Japanese nationalism, and national pride and confidence considerably (Nish 2000: 84). National consciousness was also heightened by the disproportionate recognition and increased external pressures from Western powers that accompanied the resulting peace treaties' negotiations, namely the Triple Intervention in 1895 and the 'lopsided' US-negotiated peace accord in the aftermath of the Russo-Japanese conflict (Pyle 1971: 8). According to Stronach (1995: 42, 49–50), the Western powers' persistent disregard of Japan on equal terms aggravated popular anti-Western and anti-government sentiments, propagating the 'siege mentality' and 'nativist' resurgence in Japanese nationalist discourse. These attributes were further strengthened by the outcomes of international events following the end of the First World War, where Japan was again pressured into accepting unequal terms under the Treaty of Versailles and several other international disarmament accords during the interwar years. The continuous perception of external bullying played a significant role in mobilising national loyalty under an increasingly parochial Japanese state, and encouraging the rise of militarist ultra-nationalism (Stronach 1995: 43).

Ultra-nationalism in the 1930s was, likewise, driven by the radicalisation of the nationalist discourse in response to growing domestic socio-economic discontentment. Ultra-nationalists deplored the Western liberal-democratic values that corrupted the traditional mores of Japanese society, and were critical of the government's incompetence in alleviating economic suffering and reducing urban–rural disparities, besides its failure to tackle corruption in the Japanese political economy and bureaucracy (Stronach 1995: 43–4). Perceiving these trends as signs of a Japanese nation in peril, radical ideologues and nationalist groups called for 'a second revolutionary renovation, a "Showa Renovation"' (McVeigh 2004: 46), reminiscent of the all-encompassing Meiji reforms, to reconstruct the domestic order and unshackle Japan from its malaise. Yet, unlike the Meiji nationalists, they were more fundamentalist and unabashedly xenophobic. McVeigh (2004: 46–7) saw these so-called 'Showa patriots' revolting against the maligned political and socio-economic status quo, and advocating the return to 'direct imperial rule' in place of democracy, and 'a militarily-based, spiritual revival'. As ultra-nationalism brewed in domestic politics, political *coups* were staged, culminating in the 1936 'February 26 Incident' that saw the beleaguered Japanese state succumbing to ultra-nationalist pressure, where parochial ideals were eventually incorporated, and radical figures like Araki Sadao and Tojo Hideki embraced as part of the 'new bureaucracy' (Conroy 1955: 828; McVeigh 2004: 47).

With the militarists/ultra-nationalists gaining political power, greater emphasis was placed on promoting national solidarity and reinforcing state–society linkage, as well as securing nationwide support for official political, economic and military objectives, under the domestic-centred 'New Order Movement'. Externally, the state promoted Japanese–led Pan-Asianism under the 'East Asia New Order', which subsequently metamorphosed into the 'Greater East Asia Co-Prosperity Sphere' (McVeigh 2004: 47). Whether truly liberationist or expansionist in essence, this external policy led the Japanese state to mobilise the populace under the aegis of an official nationalism that was skewed towards militarism. Japan's colonisation of Manchuria and subsequent invasions of China and French Indo-China provoked serious Western retributions that exacerbated the Japanese 'siege-mentality' and anti-Western sentiment (Stronach 1995: 44). It also led to the launching of the National Spiritual Mobilisation Campaign and the autocratic Imperial Rule Assistance Association (McVeigh 2004: 108), as Japan geared itself for general mobilisation towards its ill-conceived involvement in the Second World War.

In sum, nationalism in pre-war Japan was primarily elite-inspired, fostered in reaction to *gaiatsu*, and manifested in the form of state-sponsored nationalism that aspired to national renewal and a unified, strong and prideful Japanese nation. Nationalism was also inculcated to create a unique national identity, and enhance Japan's competitiveness and survival in the international system. Although state nationalism was predominant, popular nationalist sentiment was equally effervescent. As Gluck (1985: 9–10) suggests, 'the strongest views – the hard line – often came from outside the government, from the *minkan* (people)'. Popular nationalist discourse and activities were influential in constraining and, at times, even shaping the official nationalist agenda. Yet, these populist movements were not genuinely grassroots, but elite-driven, often by individuals of noble descent (*samurai*), the intelligentsia, journalists and public personalities (Gluck 1985: 10; McVeigh 2004: 48). Another noted element of pre-war nationalism was its inclination towards militarism and expansionism. These characteristics were driven by Japan's fear of foreign oppression that, according to Matsumoto (1971: 53), made the 'preservation of national polity' through 'self-perpetuation and self-expansion' the ultimate national mission, and by the wellspring of popular disaffection that saw state-elites advocating expansionist-cum-diversionary policies as a solution to domestic discontentment.

The persistence and evolution of nationalism in post-war Japan

Japan's traumatic Second World War experience altered the Japanese view of nationalism and national identity. According to Sasaki (2001), nationalism was blamed for precipitating the war, and Japan's defeat saw a temporary hiatus in its development, only to subsequently reappear in distorted forms, as post-war Japanese struggled to re-embrace nationalism in a 'natural', open and forthright manner. The common observation was that the Japanese were facing an acute identity crisis, since the symbols and institutions they ardently identified with and held dear, were no longer a source of national pride. Apparently, along with the rejection of pre-war institutions, the traditional notions of nation-state also dissipated following the war defeat, American occupation, disarmament and the embrace of pacifism, democracy and Westernisation/Americanisation (Matsumoto 1971: 55; Stronach 1995: 45). However, nationalism did not totally disappear, but chose to re-emerge in different and mostly 'banal' forms (Billig 1995), i.e. cultural, economic and peace nationalisms, among others (McVeigh 2004; Rose 2000). Even pre-war ultra-nationalism has survived, manifesting itself in a number of fringe, non-official, ultra-rightwing movements that draw limited mass appeal (McVeigh 2001). Other notable characteristics of post-war nationalism include the perpetuation of discourses that sought national renewal and independence via different strategies, and its depoliticisation that saw the weakening of state-sponsored nationalism and state–society linkage, and the rise of political apathy (McVeigh 2004; Stronach 1995; Matsumoto 1971).

Scholars commonly divide post-war nationalism into three defining periods; (i) the early Cold War decades; (ii) between the 1960s and 1980s, when Japan enjoyed miraculous economic growth; and (iii) 'post-bubble' malaise from the early 1990s till the present (Sasaki 2001; McVeigh 2004). Interestingly, these periods coincided with the aforementioned structural shifts in the international system that affected Japan's foreign policy directions and Japanese–Chinese diplomacy, suggesting the influence of external imperatives on nationalism's manifestations. Like Gao (1997), Sasaki (2001) contends there were two diverging expressions of nationalism during the first phase (1945–60); the first being the restoration of 'official' nationalism and a conservative, rightwing-oriented polity that sought alliance with the Americans, while simultaneously seeking the reinstallation of Japan's defence capabilities and diplomatic autonomy. The second came in the form of promoting military pacifism, and an independent, neutralist position that opposed the subordination of Japan into the Western bloc, advocated mainly by the political left/centre-left and popularly embraced by Japanese society.

The reinstatement of official nationalism amid attempts to disengage Japan from its nationalistic-cum-militaristic past was indirectly the result of what is described in Chapter 2 as the emerging Cold War security architecture that saw post-war Japan gaining strategic importance in Washington's regional containment policy. Fearing the communist threat from within and outside Japan, the US ended its occupation and encouraged the re-establishment of a conservative, rightwing Japanese government that was incorporated into its alliance framework to fight a common enemy (Kingston 2004). Not only did it hamper the pacification process, the American policy shift sponsored the restoration of pre-war nationalistic elements, which included, among others, an 'Emperor-system democracy' (Dower 1999), the military, albeit under a US-sponsored limited self-defence framework, an entrenched bureaucracy and wartime figures, convicted but eventually released and encouraged to revive their political careers within mainstream politics (Berger 2007: 191). The establishment of the 'conservative-rightwing' LDP in 1955 reflected the influence of rehabilitated ex-wartime politicians and bureaucrats, like Hatoyama Ichiro and Kishi Nobusuke (Pyle 1996: 57–8), whose respective appointments to the premiership position indicated not only the continuities of pre-war nationalism in post-war Japanese politics, but also the budding of an official nationalism that was 'dependent' on American encouragement and acquiescence.[7] Indeed, Washington was behind Kishi's attempt to remilitarise Japan via a revision of Article 9, and his resolve to renew the US–Japan security treaty in 1960, despite a severe public backlash (Miyazawa 1997: 12).

Conversely, leftwing political organisations, i.e. the JSP and JCP, promoted a so-called 'peace nationalism' that sought to distance Japan from the Western bloc, and kept vigil against ultra-nationalism resurrecting within the Diet, considering the ominous presence of far-right LDP elements that intermittently wielded their influence in post-war politics (Orr 2001). Peace nationalism became influential and synonymous with non-official nationalism embraced by post-war Japanese society, which was generally suspicious of 'official' nationalism, owing to the popular notion that the Japanese state was responsible for the war, and that the people were victims of its nationalist-cum-expansionist policies (McVeigh 2004: 77, 207). Despite the apparent official–popular dichotomy, there was a confluence between popular and state nationalism via depoliticised expressions, namely economic and cultural, which characterised Japanese nationalism between the 1960s and 1980s.

The second phase coincided with the period that saw a reduction of bipolar hostility and an acceleration in Japan's economic growth (Sasaki 2001). A 'new consensus' on a nationalist discourse centred on economic endeavours and culturalism rather than defence and foreign policies, led to the convergence of state/official and popular nationalisms, and public acquiescence to state-sponsored nationalist agendas to promote economic advancement and inculcate ideas of 'Japanese-ness' (Sasaki 2001; McVeigh 2004: ch. 6). Post-war economic nationalism has its roots in pre-war ideals of building a strong Japanese nation-state via national mobilisation, and the implementation of state-guided 'developmentalist' policies and economic projects, to amass economic power for national self-preservation (McVeigh 2001). During the early post-war period, similar nationalist agendas and practices became the catalyst for post-war recovery, as official nationalism was purposefully redirected towards the reconstruction of Japan (McVeigh 2004: 110). With the US–Japan security framework guaranteeing national security, Dower (1993: 31) saw the Japanese state concentrating its efforts on economic development, 'mobilizing [the national] population and resources resolutely behind productivity and economic nationalism', to transform a defeated nation-state into an economic powerhouse. Predictably, the mutually reinforcing effect of state developmentalism and nationalism became the driving force catapulting the Japanese economy to miraculous heights in the 1960s–1980s (Gao 1997: 296). Japan not only emerged relatively unscathed from the global oil crises and economic recession, its admission into the G-7 epitomised the success of economic-centred nationalism that helped revitalise Japanese national pride and identity (Sasaki 2001). This so-called 'GNP nationalism' (McVeigh 2001) peaked in the 1980s, when Japan gained economic superpower status, while the Japanese 'developmental state' model was popularly adapted and applied in the developing world (Hook *et al.* 2005: 234–8; Vogel 1986).

This brand of confident economic nationalism also facilitated the development of ethno-cultural nationalist discourses, where a mounting desire existed to associate Japan's economic achievements with Japanese cultural uniqueness and their social system (Yoshino 1992: 189). The proliferation of the *nihonjinron* (theories of Japanese) discourse in the 1970s–1980s clearly reflected this buoyant national mood, where the notions of cultural 'exceptionalism' and homogeneity were popularly contrived to as much define Japanese identity as explain Japan's economic success (Chan and Bridges 2006: 136). Like economic nationalism, *nihonjinron* nationalism has roots in pre-war Japan, where the bureaucratic state and intellectual elites employed Japanese traditions and cultural distinctiveness to 'reconstruct national identity [that was] threatened by Westernisation and rapid industrialisation' (Yoshino 1992: 186; Befu 1992). And, like pre-war *nihonjinron*, its popular-oriented, post-war manifestation was duly appropriated and enmeshed into the national cultural policy by the Japanese state, to promote sentiments of community and the myth of common descent among its citizenry, for the purpose of motivating post-war society towards realising national objectives (McVeigh 2004: 194).

Indeed, cultural nationalism thrived at the height of Japan's economic prowess in the 1980s. Scholars like Befu (1992) and Yoshino (1992: 187) claim that national confidence and pride drove the Japanese to challenge the hegemony of Western/American culture and lifestyle that has significantly penetrated both 'public' and 'private' domains of the post-war society, by reaffirming the essence of Japanese identity through their supposedly unique 'culture, society and national character'. Economic affluence also stimulated political nationalism that saw the Nakasone administration advocating a review of Japan's political and military roles commensurate with its economic strength (Pyle 1996: 101–3). Nonetheless, strong domestic anti-revisionist forces in the Diet, together with public apprehension and external pressures from Japan's neighbours, stymied the agenda.

The confident nationalism underpinning post-war Japanese identity and pride permeated the 'bubble economy' period. However, when the 'bubble' burst in early 1990s, the Japanese economy collapsed into a protracted recession. Post-war nationalism met a similar fate, since it derived its vitality from Japan's economic success. Facing serious structural problems, the public again queried the Japanese-style political economy and bureaucratic-state system that symbolised the uniqueness of cultural traditions and societal norms, basically, the very tenets that personified Japan's post-war national identity (Sasaki 2001). The dramatic 'reversal of fortune' saw Japanese society suffering a general loss of confidence and bearing, leading to mass soul-searching for a renewal of the national 'self'.

Contemporary Japanese nationalism: driving forces and manifestations

Driving forces

The rise of 'neo-nationalism' in contemporary Japan, in many respects, reflects the need to address the deepening national identity crisis as socio-economic malaise and persistent political helplessness have fed a desire for national renewal (McCormack 2000: 247; Fujiwara 2001: 40). For one, the debilitating conditions in the decade following the end of the 'economic miracle' have had a demoralising impact on the Japanese psyche. Annual GDP growth throughout the 'post-bubble' period staggered with recessionary rates, the Nikkei stock exchange suffered from prolonged lean spells, while corporate insolvencies and unemployment reached unprecedented levels (Matthews 2003: 80; Kingston 2004: 242–3). Public debts were the highest amongst industrialised nations following the cumulative effects of mismanagement of public funds, government bailouts and spending to bolster structural reforms and public works packages (McCormack 2007: 45; Bix 2001). The economic depression also aggravated social problems,[8] and endemic corruption was 'eroding confidence in government and business alike' (McCormack 2000: 248). Domestic political stability suffered from public disaffection, underscored by the rapid succession of state leaders, and the temporary loss of political power by the LDP, which had dominated Japanese politics since 1955 (Jameson 1997: 1).[9]

The so-called 'Lost Decade' not only saw Japan losing economic prosperity and political cohesion, but also its international status. In the politico-diplomatic dimension, the 1991 Gulf War 'humiliation' reinforced its reputation as a 'political dwarf' (Miyashita 2002: 144–5). Meanwhile, continuous subordination to the US has had Japan yielding to American pressure on various policy matters, besides being marginalised on international issues (McCormack 2000: 248), and increasingly subjected to 'Japan bashing' and 'Japan passing' by its 'senior partner' and neighbours alike (Shibata 1995). Furthermore, despite being a leading donor to international organisations, and having contributed substantially to East Asia's economic dynamism through foreign investments and aid, Japan has rarely been accorded the level of international recognition and agenda-setting influence commensurate with its contribution, a status that has further dissipated with the recession-induced contraction of its economic resources (Matthews 2003: 80–3). The domestic morass and fading international prestige have inevitably prompted calls for national regeneration (Cronin 2007). Neo-nationalism is thus, principally, a reflection of the popular mood and state/elite responses to alleviate the 'psychological-emotional' distress of perceived Japanese weakness, and to reinvigorate national pride and reaffirm Japanese identity (Sasaki 2001; Kase 2001). According to Kingston (2004: 229), it also reflects dissatisfaction with Japan's 'prolonged subordination' and 'deferential adherence to the US', and the desire to establish a more independent policy stance, if not a symmetrical US–Japan relationship. Such responses are equally directed against China, to whom Japan has accorded deferential treatment in its 'kowtow' diplomacy since the normalisation of their diplomatic relations. Likewise, the neo-nationalist agendas for rearmament and international proactivism are steadily accepted by the Japanese public as viable solutions to accrue the international respect that has thus far eluded their country (Matthews 2003: 83).

Historical grievances, and their impact on Japanese pride and identity, are another factor fundamentally related to the flourishing neo-nationalist discourse. During the 1990s, Japanese were hounded by the excesses of war history, as information and records pertaining to atrocities and abuses committed by Imperial Japan were revealed by the archives, ex-servicemen and the MOE/MEXT via more 'open' history treatment, following the demise of Emperor Showa (Kingston 2004: 231; Benfell 2002). Compounding the revelation of this 'national shame' was the sustained external pressure for the redress and proper accounting of Japan's war responsibility, along with renewed domestic political efforts, i.e. by state-elites like Kono Yohei and PM Muruyama, to acknowledge, express remorse, and seek judicial resolution for war-related issues (Kingston 2004: 231; McCormack 2000: 250). The sudden disclosures disconcerted many Japanese who, due to a 'diluted' and 'victim-oriented' post-war history education, were largely unaware of the true extent of Japan's disreputable wartime record (Benfell 2002). This unflattering past further dented national pride and identity, which were already undermined by socio-economic gloom. Neo-nationalism's related agenda for historical revisionism is thus another nationalist response to restore national pride through the promotion of a 'less-masochistic' view of history (Mori 2007: 57–8), and to engender a sense of unity and strength against perceived national vulnerability and foreign pressure.

The neo-nationalist appeal is also closely associated with public perceptions regarding national insecurities, generational change and the related domestic political transformations mentioned in Chapter 2 that have significantly affected Japanese–Chinese relations. Indeed, looming security concerns and 'threat perceptions' vis-à-vis China and North Korea have fuelled Japanese public support for a more assertive foreign/security policy. They have led to Japan's gradual remilitarisation and enhanced security cooperation with the US, and openness about the nuclear armament debate (McCormack 2007: ch. 8), all of which were previously considered 'taboo' issues, but which are now publicly accepted and regularly debated in the Japanese media (Sasada 2006: 115–16). Specific to this study, China's rise has contributed significantly to Japan's growing insecurity. The Japanese are aware of the shifting power distribution and economic fortunes between the two countries since the mid-1990s. Resentment of this power shift, coupled with strategic tensions and concerns over sustained Chinese military build-up, have exacerbated the 'China threat' perception. Meanwhile, passionate history quarrels and anti-Japanese-flavoured Chinese nationalism have triggered a nationalist backlash within Japan that fuelled negative perceptions, images and attitudes towards China in recent years (Kaneko 2005). This shift in the Japanese national psyche reflects a growing realism about national security in a fluid post-Cold War external environment (Green 2001; Tsunekawa 2006), a shift which is interestingly facilitated by Washington's encouragement, under the pretext of strengthening the US–Japan alliance.

Back at the domestic front, demographic and generational changes have subtly altered Japanese expressions of nationalism. As noted, nationalism became 'taboo' after 1945 (Rose 2000: 171), emerging in distorted forms and unrealistic expressions due to apprehension of the post-war generation. According to Matthews (2003: 76), 'nationalism was relegated to the fringes of Japan's popular debate', as post-war Japanese society suffered from the so-called 'fear of itself' syndrome, namely the fear that nationalism may again mislead the nation towards militarism. The war generation's passing has since diluted such apprehension, and together with it the fear of nationalism's perils (Matthews 2003: 80). The present generation, raised in the era of economic success, is prideful and less encumbered by war-guilt, and hence more prepared to express nationalist sentiment without fear or favour. Contributing to the 'aloofness' has been their superficial knowledge of Japan's militaristic past, deriving from history education whose content was subject to revisions and alleged 'sanitisation' (Kingston 2004: 230). To be fair, many Japanese are not ignorant or in denial of the war history, an awareness deriving as much from education as the periodic reminders by Japan's neighbours and war victims. Yet they also long for closure, and to become normal citizens who can freely express devotion to and identify with their national state and symbols.

In the political realm, younger leaders more comfortable on the world stage and less backward-looking on the national past have emerged, inspiring foreign/ security policy shifts that are geared towards national interests and enhancing Japan's role in the international community. These leaders also espouse a different external posture from that of their predecessors, when dealing with problematic interstate relationships. As previously described, Japan's diplomacy was passive, characterised by 'deference' towards neighbours like China and Korea (Drifte 2003; Ijiri 1996), a posture criticised by nationalists as humiliating and lacking national self-assertion (Sasaki 2001). Today, however, the transfer of power to a generation spared the traumas of history has led to present leaders being assertive and less tolerant, especially towards foreign criticism of Japan's imperial legacies, perceiving this as a ploy 'to unsettle the Japanese' (Sasaki 2001; Self 2002). The attitudinal change reflecting this new wisdom in Japanese society is also apparent amongst ordinary folks, who are increasingly resentful towards *gaiatsu* and foreign interference on issues they consider to be Japan's domestic affairs.

Another correlating factor is the decline of pacifist-leftwing forces in Japanese politics, which had previously constrained and neutralised nationalistic-rightwing overtures that periodically challenged the post-war pacifist norms. The change in national mood has seen pressure groups like Nikkyoso[10] fading, and the popularity of the JSP/SDPJ and JCP concurrently diminishing in their Diet representation since the mid-1990s. These so-called 'neutralising forces' have not only weakened, but also suffered a loss of political will and direction that even saw the JSP/SDPJ accepting a 'political marriage of convenience' with the LDP in 1994 (Miyashita 2002: 154), and relocating to the 'centre-right' on previously divisive issues (Sasada 2006: 117–18). Consistently dismal election results marginalised their influence, as these leftwing parties failed to muster sufficient political support to prevent what McCormack (2000: 262) sees as 'the drift towards accommodation with the right on an axis of nationalism, or neo-nationalism'.

Lastly, according to Sasada (2006), the 'conservatisation' of Japan's mainstream media and intellectual community, together with the emerging popularity of alternative channels to foster and disseminate the neo-nationalist message, i.e. internet, *manga*, and international sporting events, have contributed to rising nationalism, especially among Japanese youth (see also Tanamichi 2005:

33–4).[11] Indeed, most observers, including senior Japanese officials, see Japan's ideologically slanted media as a driver of nationalistic sentiments, especially via biased and/or sensationalised reporting, and sustained criticisms on 'nationalist' issues that fuel preconceived (mis)perceptions and stereotypical images vis-à-vis states like China and North Korea (Johnston 2007). These factors have shaped political views that are facilitating Japan's contemporary ideological shift from pacifism towards nationalism.

Fault-lines and manifestations of the neo-nationalist discourse

Changes are evident as Japan inches towards a more 'normal' and 'nationalistic' outlook. Most notable has been the drift of the political debate and public consensus to the right, and growing support for the neo-nationalist cause (Kingston 2004; Kaneko 2005). Observers generally agree that the fault-lines of Japanese nationalism have remained relatively unchanged, although the power balance has shifted (Samuels 2007b: 112). The contemporary nationalist discourse on history and security has drifted according to the prevalent trend, where the leftist-oriented, 'peace' nationalism's advocacy of historical responsibility and military pacifism is being gradually overshadowed by the neo-nationalist's revisionist history and remilitarisation agenda. Samuels (2007a/b) argues that agenda-setting within the neo-nationalist camp is shaped by the 'neo-autonomist' (ultra-nationalist) versus 'normal nation-alist' debate that generally converges on historical revisionism and the reintroduction of the 'use of force' as a foreign policy instrument, but which diverges on their support for the US–Japan alliance. Neo-autonomists like politician Ishihara Shintaro, academics Nishibe Susumu and Nakanishi Terumasa, and *manga*-artist Kobayashi Yoshinori, among others, advocate a remilitarisation independent from the US, while 'normal nation-alists' prefer one that remains under a strengthened US–Japan alliance (Samuels 2007a: 128–9, 138). Samuels, however, sees a split between 'realists' and 'neo-conservatives' within the 'normal nation-alist' camp regarding 'history'; leading realists like ex-premier Nakasone, politicians Ishiba Shigeru and Ozawa Ichiro, and opinion leader Okazaki Hisahiko, espouse a moderate-pragmatic view aimed at reconciliation with neighbours to advance Japan's broader national interests. Meanwhile, Koizumi's cabinet members, namely Abe Shinzo, Aso Taro, Hiranuma Takeo, Nakagawa Shoichi, Machimura Nobutaka and Koizumi himself, to an unclear extent, are amongst 'mainstream' neo-conservatives, who are more ideologically/revisionist-inclined, and less apologetic about history (Samuels 2007a: 144–5; Taniguchi 2005: 451).

Several of my Japanese interviewees, who seem to equate nationalists with ultra-rightwing personalities, have questioned Koizumi's nationalistic disposition. They see Koizumi as a progressive, and believe that his Yasukuni policy was due to personal convictions, political gamesmanship, and disinterest in diplomacy, rather than nationalism.[12] Conversely, Gilbert Rozman opined that, although Koizumi may be less nationalistic compared to the ultra-nationalists, his actions and policies actually made him no different from them, since he was a protagonist who helped advance the 'revisionist/nationalist' agenda in Japan.[13] This study shares Samuels's (2007a/b) categorisation of Koizumi as a 'normal nationalist', but locates him in between the 'realist' and 'neo-conservative' camps because of his ambiguous and non-committal stance on the more hardcore 'history' issues.[14]

Indeed, the neo-conservatives and Koizumi have consistently provoked controversy with their nationalistic posture, exemplified by their support for Yasukuni pilgrimage, acquiescence to historical revisionism and advocacy for constitutional reform of Article 9. Their political influence has broadened under his premiership, seen in attitudinal and policy shifts that have affected Japan's regional relations. The Koizumi administration definitely unnerved Japan's neighbours, particularly China, with its assertive stance on nationalist-flavoured bilateral issues, and its efforts to redefine the Japanese security outlook has had many observers citing this administration as among the most nationalistic since pre-war Japan (Kaneko 2005; Matthews 2003). Their brand of 'revisionist-ideological nationalism' (Cronin 2007; Deans 2007) has become more overt under the administration led by Koizumi's protégé, Abe Shinzo. Renowned for his nationalistic disposition, Abe's pledge to create 'a beautiful Japan' by restoring patriotism during his first premiership (Cronin 2007: 1), and the agenda he has to offer in his second stint as PM, will indubitably help advance the neo-nationalist cause.

Neo-nationalism has also gained support within the National Diet, resulting in efforts to reinterpret history, promote constitutional, educational and security policy reforms, and restore national pride and prestige based on the archetypal Japanese identity (McCormack 2000: 251–3). Japan watchers note that Diet support for the neo-nationalist cause has flourished under groups like the Diet-members League for a Bright Japan and the Diet-members League for Passing on Correct History (McCormack 2007: 10). Meanwhile, over 200 Diet-members were affiliated to the influential rightwing-nationalist 'umbrella' organisation, Nippon Kaigi, via the Japan Council Diet-members Group, established in 1997 to promote these agendas (Rose 2006: 139). Their active presence and support have influenced the course of events seeing post-war taboos gradually lifted, laws enacted and national symbols reinstated, all without the usual Diet encumbrances (Itoh 2001). One can infer the neo-nationalist influence from the quick passage of defence bills to expand Japan's security role, and overwhelming support for the official sanctioning of the *Hinomaru* and *Kimigayo* in July 1999, both 'taboo' issues that could have previously 'paralysed the Diet' (Itoh 2001). Yet, McCormack (2000: 248) claims that these legislations were 'bulldozed' through with other 'apparently innocuous' bills that 'subtly shifted the boundaries of private and public, individual and state, in favour of the state', not mentioning the reinstatement of constitutional reforms on the political agenda. Similarly, bi-partisan support and solidarity among Diet-members on Yasukuni visits underscore this nationalistic drift.

Outside the Diet, nationalist forces have reorganised from a primarily fringe pressure group movement to becoming popular-based in recent years, as the neo-nationalist cause has gained the interest and support of the professional middle class, intellectuals, artists, business elites and even powerful corporate and media groups (McCormack 2000: 251–2). During the post-war period, nationalist causes were championed by rightwing organisations, like Jinja honcho (National Shrine Association), Nihon Izokukai (Japan Association of War-Bereaved Families), Shinto seiji renmei, Seicho no ie (McCormack 2000: 251; 2007: 10–11; Shibuichi 2005: 200), Seirankai (Blue-Storm Group), and Nihon Seinensha (Japan Youth Federation) (Chung 2004: 36–41), among others. Most *uyoku* (ultra-right) outfits also overlapped with the *yakuza* (Japanese mafia) (Shibuichi 2005: 201), and were allegedly connected to political elites and LDP factions, through which their influence was imposed, and interests advocated in mainstream Japanese politics (McNeill 2001: 4). However, since the mid-1990s, a more articulate, ideologically driven and politically committed movement has flourished, represented by the likes of Tsukurukai and Nippon Kaigi that draws strength from popular resentment towards the relentless external vilification of Japan's wartime record, and Tokyo's 'apology diplomacy' which entertains such 'Japan bashing' (McCormack 2000: 251; McNeill 2005). It also taps into the deep-rooted, popular fear of a waning Japanese state and debilitating national economy, and is driven by 'nostalgia for a strong Japan' (McCormack 2000: 252). The movement enjoys corporate sponsorship and endorsement from leading Japanese companies, while major media groups, like Yomiuri, Fuji-Sankei, Bungei Shunju, and media/internet sources, i.e. *Shokun!*, *Seiron*, *Sapio*, *Spa*, *Brutus*, *Channel-2*, *Channel-Sakura*, among others, actively promote its causes (McCormack 2000: 252; Rose 2000: 175; Johnston 2007: 113–15). Interestingly, a confluence of interests in promoting 'healthy' nationalism and the 'national cause' also saw some Japanese liberal/progressive intelligentsia acquiescing to the neo-nationalist discourse (McCormack 2000: 253).[15]

The 'nationalistic' drift in public mood is equally conspicuous, albeit one that is more emotionally reactive-defensive rather than ideologically driven. This is observable from public reaction towards perceived external threats, pressure and slights, which arouse their defensive attitude towards the 'perpetrators', and encourage acquiescence towards neo-nationalist agendas concerning Japanese identity and national security. For example, despite the controversy surrounding their symbolism and meanings, Koizumi's visits to Yasukuni-*jinja* received favourable public support, not for his or Yasukuni's ideological convictions, but predominantly a defensive-reaction against external/Chinese pressure. The prevailing mood has also stimulated interest in and facilitated the circulation of 'revisionist' publications/media/internet sources that project neo-nationalist views to the ordinary Japanese (McNeill 2005).

Public pacifism has likewise eroded on national security matters. In 1999, Japan launched its first-ever 'unilateral exercise of force' against a North Korean *fushinsen*, a constitutionally infringing action that ironically received popular approval of over 80 per cent (Midford 2002: 13; McCormack 2007: 59). The repeat of a similar incident in 2001 ultimately led to the Japan Coast Guard's (JCG) historic sinking of a foreign vessel (Samuels 2007–8: 96). Similarly, there was a distinct lack of public uproar over the gradual expansion of Japan's security role via legislation in 1999 and the aftermath of '9/11' that saw Maritime-

SDF (MSDF) ships sent to foreign waters on active duty for the first time since 1945, and peacekeepers to Iraq in the US-led war on terrorism (Samuel 2007b: 119). The public was also relatively mute on other defence-related issues, i.e. controversial debates over a nuclear-armed Japan, the right of pre-emptive attack, plausible revision of Article 9 and the JDA's upgrading to ministry status. These developments suggest that neo-nationalism has become a pervasive force, which appears to receive support from both left and right in Japanese politics (McCormack 2000: 256), and which is embraced by a broad spectrum of society. Interestingly reminiscent of the 1950s, its contemporary manifestation is again dependent on and facilitated by American acquiescence of such an agenda, following their mutual need to strengthen the alliance in anticipation of the fluid external security environment. Some observers have come to define this as Japan's 'dependent nationalism' (McCormack 2007; Tsunekawa 2006).

More importantly for this study, the neo-nationalist discourse brewing in Japan has an essentially 'anti-China' manifestation (Samuels 2007a: 133; Tamamoto 2005b), shaped as much by Japanese desire for national self-assertion as their pride and prejudices over the changing power relations vis-à-vis China, and indignation towards perceived Chinese arrogance, bullying and pressure. Elaborated in Chapter 4, these dynamics have triggered a perceptual and attitudinal shift towards China, which enhances nationalism's efficacy in Japan's China policy-making.

State and popular nationalism in contemporary Japan

The above analysis highlights Japanese nationalism's state/elite-centric nature and the populist drive behind its discourse, agenda and manifestations. State-oriented nationalism, discredited since 1945, may be 'the weakest form of nationalism in Japan' (Stronach 1995: 166), whilst popular modes of nationalism have flourished. Indeed, the 'official' nationalist discourse no longer exudes the kind of 'pre-war' popular influence, and the state does not appear to dictate the highly diffused nationalist forces in post-war Japan (McVeigh 2004: 10). Yet it is also evident that state nationalism has continued to subtly permeate and indirectly affect Japanese daily life via innocuous state/society channels. McVeigh (2004: 84) argues that, although the state does not determine popular modes of nationalism, 'it certainly has enough institutional points of contact with them [to challenge] the nation/state dichotomy' in contemporary Japan. This suggests the Japanese state's persistence as the 'primary agent' behind nationalism's omnipresence (McVeigh 2004: 180). It also illustrates the 'state–popular' axis, as the former remains stealthily influential in abetting the popular nationalist discourse through education, ethno-cultural-historical mythmaking, 'media cartelisation' and 'developmentalist' economic policies, among others (McVeigh 2004: 90–1, chs 6–7). Conversely, popular nationalism, while appearing to be either apolitical and/or periodically anti-state, does find a convergence of interests and identify with the official nationalist aspirations on the agenda of national renaissance (McVeigh 2004; Rose 2000).

Contemporary state/elite-inspired nationalism is pragmatic, national interest-driven, instrumental, and meant for domestic consumption.[16] Similar to the Meiji and post-war eras, the present official nationalist discourse has been pragmatically centred on the neo-nationalist agenda of rebuilding a strong, affluent nation-state, and reinstating the Japanese identity, amid denigrating internal adversities and mounting external pressure. Core to these aspirations is none other than a return to 'normal' statehood after decades of post-war identity discrepancies. Externally, state nationalism has a reactive, assertive, yet adaptive international orientation geared towards defending and maximising the broader national interest (Zhao 2000; Matthews 2003). Whilst Japan has begun projecting a more reactive-cum-assertive external disposition, diplomatic and decision-making prudence remains, generally, the *modus vivendi* of Japanese foreign policy, especially when managing bilateral quandaries with key regional states like China and both Koreas. Tokyo has also sought to redefine the national security outlook and expand Japan's international role, albeit under the US–Japan alliance framework. Overall, the official nationalist discourse remains moderate, while steadfastly advocating the assertion of a prideful Japanese history and identity, constitutional revision and the rearmament of Japan (McCormack 2000: 262). Undoubtedly, the quest for national security, 'healthy' nationalism and the possession of an indigenously crafted constitution to resurrect a 'normal state' identity, belie the Japanese state's/ state-elites' cajoling of these neo-nationalist causes (Tamamoto 2001: 39).

State nationalism is instrumental. Like its predecessors, the contemporary Japanese state has promoted nationalism as the unifying and motivational force behind the public support for its implementation of demanding structural reforms to revive the country's ailing economy. This is also meant to provide psychological-emotional support, or what Kingston (2004) calls 'feelgood nationalism' for the Japanese nation during such testing times. Likewise, nationalism functions as a tool to bolster the legitimacy of and restore public confidence towards the Japanese bureaucratic state, eroded by endemic corruption, inefficiency and malpractices. Its instrumentality is equally represented by state manipulation of its fluid content, where state-elites have sought to reinstate the military and past national symbols, and acquiesce in the neo-nationalist advocacy of a 'revisionist' history, to facilitate the restoration of national pride and prestige. Its utility function is, perhaps, most vividly reflected in Japanese state-elites' manipulation of its symbolism for personal political expediency.

Popular nationalism identifies with the official nationalist discourse on key national goals, although they may differ in the approaches to realise them. The diversity of popular expressions, from 'peace' and 'cultural' nationalisms to ultra-rightwing and contemporary neo-nationalist discourses, means that some forms are bound to dovetail with the official line, while others are critical of the state on nationalistic issues. However, McVeigh (2004: 53) sees most non-official nationalist movements as having linkage with, and the support of, officialdom through various state–society channels. These popular-based organisations also seek to exert pressure and political influence by providing financial backing to established 'power-cliques' and state-elites. Notwithstanding their differences on specific issues, this intricate matrix concurs with Rose's (2000: 174) assertion of the 'symbiotic relationship' between state-oriented and popular nationalisms; the former attempts to establish common grounds by appropriating the richness of the popular discourse for mass mobilisation behind state endeavours; the latter finds the state a 'vehicle' to channel its manifestations and institutionalise its causes. The 'neo-nationalist' undercurrent highlights this state-official/popular-non-official linkage, where common interests have seen both nationalisms mutually reinforcing each other.

That said, popular neo-nationalist discourse, passionately driven by an enduring sense of 'victimhood', indignation about external pressures and a longing for independence, prestige and international recognition, can be critical of the Japanese state's pragmatic convictions. Popular 'neo-autonomists' have often chastised the state's inability to sever its post-war dependency on the US, while others have been critical of its inadequate responses to defending Japanese interests pertaining to territorial, history and other nationalist-flavoured issues, particularly when dealing with China (Samuels 2007a/b; Fujiwara 2001). Although not incessantly radical in their views, these neo-nationalists have demanded an autonomous and more forceful foreign policy that runs counter to Tokyo's calculated considerations. Similarly, the Japanese government has been 'reluctantly' dragged into occasional diplomatic disputes vis-à-vis China over Senkaku/Diaoyudao by the provocative actions of ultra-nationalist groups. However, the evolving domestic power dynamics and political ascendancy of mainstream neo-nationalists, e.g. neo-conservatives/realists, suggest that the state may remain pragmatic yet more willing to pander to nationalist ideals (Samuels 2007a/b), and thus increasingly constrained by related pressures to embrace a nationalistic–assertive external orientation, albeit under American auspices. This aforementioned mainstream manifestation of 'dependent nationalism' is theoretically consistent with the NCR dictum espoused by this book, whereby nationalism's salience in Japan's China policy is dependent on state-elites' perceptions/calculation of a favourable 'alliance commitment/resolve' via the US–Japan alliance.

Conclusion

Nationalism remains a salient force manifesting itself in various, albeit atypical forms in post-war Japan. The advent of neo-nationalism is largely seen as the re-embracing of a more orthodox nationalism, where after decades of self-doubting behaviour a broad consensus has determined that Japan should reassert her national interests and priorities, and move from her past to embrace the future as a 'normal' nation-state (Muto 2001: 187). The present manifestations have not exuded the malevolence that typified pre-war nationalism, and appear unlikely to do so, considering the different external–domestic conditions that perpetuated them. Besides her ageing demographics, Japan's embrace of liberal democracy, in many respects, has made her a transparent, liberal and civil society, which, in principle, does not warrant overreactions, unscrupulous decision-making or indiscriminate actions on the part of the Japanese state, when handling nationalistic issues. Finally, the US–Japan alliance and economic interdependence remain the major external constraints against the rise of chauvinistic-aggressive nationalism, although both may encourage the current mainstream manifestations.

Nonetheless, this 'neo-nationalist' renaissance has generated unease. Internationally, the efforts of Japanese state-elites and popular nationalists alike to foster nationalism by encouraging historical revisionism and reviving past national symbols, as well as advancing a more assertive external orientation, are driving a wedge between Japan and its Asian neighbours (McCormack 2000: 263). This division has been compounded by resurgent nationalism in countries like China and Korea, where Japan is a key influence on their nationalistic sentiments. The deteriorating Japanese–Chinese ties are a particular case in point. Specifically, both state and popular nationalisms are reinventing Japan's policy behaviour towards China. Against the backdrop of rising Chinese nationalism, this apparent 'clash of nationalisms' (Chan and Bridges 2006) has magnified their differences, perpetuating mutual animosity and mistrust that threatens to destabilise the bilateral relationship. The crucial questions of how, when and to what extent nationalism affects Japan's China policy and Japanese–Chinese ties are, therefore, the undertakings of the following chapters.

4 Nationalism, Japan's China policy-making and Japanese–Chinese relations

Resurgent nationalism has ostensibly contributed to Japan's increasingly assertive external behaviour, especially when managing problematic bilateral ties and nationalist issues. Japanese–Chinese diplomacy is undoubtedly among the most affected, given the burden of their unsettled past, unresolved disputes and unrelenting mutual enmity that have periodically undermined relations. This chapter explicates nationalism's causal role in defining Japan's China policy via a neoclassical realist perspective. It undertakes to shed light on whether rising nationalism necessarily indicates a nationalistic policy towards China, and how, and under what conditions, it affects Japanese policy-making. An examination of how nationalism exacerbates the problems of perceptions, images and attitudes, and the corresponding impact on the bilateral relationship, sets the tone of the chapter. This is followed by an overview of Japanese foreign policy-making, the actors and processes involved, with emphasis given to exploring the linkage between domestic nationalist pressure and the policy-making apparatus/actors. The chapter concludes with a general observation about nationalism's impact on Japanese attitudes towards China concerning 'history' and security, and Tokyo's policy orientations which have affected Japanese–Chinese diplomacy.

Nationalism and the problems of perceptions, images and attitudes in Japanese–Chinese relations

As previously elaborated, nationalism has seemingly reoriented Japan's China policy to underscore their declining bilateral relations. This unfavourable development is to be expected, since nationalism accentuates a clash of identities, and the kind of nationalism evolving in Japan is reactive and driven by popular angst and threat perceptions (Stronach 1995). Furthermore, nationalism tends to invoke xenophobia and/or chauvinism that target other nations (Zhao 2000). Such nationalistic expressions, compounded by the 'demonising' of the 'other', not only widen the perceptual chasm and aggravate distrust, but also reinforce stereotypically negative images and unconstructive attitudes (Druckman 1994: 50–2) that may detrimentally affect their mutual policies. If the policy is perceived to be provocative, a vicious cycle of reactive nationalism could manifest responses that may escalate and ultimately cause bilateral tension to spiral out of control (Druckman 1994: 53). Simply put, nationalism commonly aggravates the problems of perception, images and attitudes that can undermine international relations.

Although the 'burden of history' (Miller 2002) has not prevented a functional relationship from materialising, contemporary Japanese–Chinese ties appear to have worsened at a time when nationalism is regaining currency in Japan (and China). Diplomatic rows have become frequent amid nationalism's debilitating impact on how they perceive each other. At the grassroots level, opinion polls cited in Chapter 2 suggest that nationalism has adversely affected the mutual images and attitudes of both citizenries. The statistical trend largely reflects nationalism's influence on the changing public mood that is reinventing their intergovernmental ties. Especially in Japan, generational change and the appeal to nationalism to redefine a national identity that typifies a 'normal state' have gradually altered Japanese perceptions regarding their relationship with neighbouring states, and their role as citizens of the international community (Wan 2006: 161). It has undoubtedly affected Japanese public opinion of China, which has swung from a superficial and over-enthusiastic outlook, to a more cautious view over the last decade. Also, 'Sinophobia' is permeating the contemporary Japanese psyche, with the conservative-rightwing media and neo-nationalists 'demonising' China amid fears of a Chinese economic and security 'threat' to Japan (Clark 2006; Johnston 2007). Indeed, Self (2002: 80) argues that 'agitated reporting' about China's military modernisation, maritime encroachments and anti-Japanese education, coupled with concerns over Chinese triads and illegal workers operating in Japan at the expense of public security, 'have collectively produced a tinderbox of irritation'. Recent anti-Japanese demonstrations in Chinese cities have further damaged Japanese public opinion, fuelling the rise of reactive, popular anti-Chinese nationalism to unprecedented levels. Since neo-nationalism derives its strength in reaction to perceived internal weaknesses and external bullying, such unfavourable public images and attitudes are likely to proliferate as China continues to outpace Japan politically, militarily and economically, whilst maintaining its anti-Japanese attitude.

Meanwhile, the aforementioned generational change in Japan's leadership saw the so-called 'friendship' generation replaced by a more nationalistic cohort of state-elites, who are less willing to appease China. These leaders, including Koizumi and some of his cabinet members, presumably suffer from 'apology and kowtow diplomacy' fatigue, and detest the Chinese government for insisting on Japan's continuous deference (Miller 2005–6: 41). Indeed, the revelation from a former Japanese ambassador to China that Koizumi had personally told him that Japan 'has to do something … and cannot always say "yes" to China',[1] indicates this prevalent attitude, shaped by changing images of the Chinese. There are also opinion leaders, (e.g. ex-Tokyo Governor Ishihara) who are unabashedly anti-Chinese in their outlook (Samuels 2007a/b; Hood 1999).[2] Although most Japanese may not share their extreme sentiments, the rhetorical antics of these outspoken public figures during a time of depleting goodwill tend to fuel popular 'Sinophobia'.

There are observations that the recent shift in Japanese perceptions of China reflects the restoration of a 'normal' mode of viewing the Chinese. It is arguable that past Japanese public affection ratings were unrealistic due to limited grassroots-level interaction. Such favourable perceptions were partly the product of intergovernmental efforts to promote 'friendship', and Japan's over-exuberance in embracing the so-called 'China-boom' sentiments (Kokubun 2003). It was also plausibly a manifestation of the Japanese war-guilt complex, which prompted the war generation to be more sympathetic and receptive towards the Chinese. However, the generational shift and intensified popular-level exchanges have produced new dynamics that expose this flawed image. Nationalism has cultivated awareness amongst the current generation of Japanese regarding the need to redeem national pride and self-assertion when dealing with the Chinese. This 'return to normalcy' has inevitably brought Japanese opinion of China back to more 'realistic' levels. Unfortunately, this 'new realism' in Japanese perceptions has led to worsening images of China. According to Self (2002: 78), 'stronger warning signals have emerged in Japanese political circles and popular opinion than they have in China, but shifts on both sides indicate that change – more likely for the worse – is building'.

With Japan becoming less responsive towards China's demands, it has made the Chinese even more forthright in professing their instinctively anti-Japanese sentiment. This 'perceptual readjustment' has been further complicated by what observers labelled as 'the burden of double-expectations' (Glosserman 2003; Konishi 2003). Because of their socio-cultural similarities, both the Chinese and the Japanese expect to be overcompensated by the other for the differences that emerge, and when that fails to materialise, the sense of indignation becomes deeper (Glosserman 2003). According to Glosserman (2003), Chinese over-expectations that Japan will continue to assuage their demands as a form of 'moral redemption' have made them incensed about perceived Japanese insensitivities. Meanwhile, Japan's over-expectation that the Chinese will 'exorcise the ghost' of its past aggression has made Japanese weary and annoyed over perceived Chinese ungratefulness, and their taking advantage of Japan's previously obliging attitude. Their lack of '"intersubjectively shared" ideas, norms and values' (Yang 2005: 7) is another drawback, which has prevented a confluence of understanding that could help bridge differences. Most obvious is their contrasting political norms and culture, with Japan largely a liberal democracy and China an authoritarian state. This 'ideological gulf' has obstructed the promotion of mutual trust (Glosserman 2003). It has also seemingly encouraged an ideologically centred superiority complex amongst ordinary Japanese that has made them reluctant to trust or comprehend the Chinese, let alone negotiate with them (Wan 2006: 163).

Ultimately, the clashing nationalisms evolving in Japan and China are widening differences in the interpretations of their past, present and future. According to Gong (2001a: 41), 'divergence between domestic pressure for Japan to establish itself as a "normal country" and domestic pressures for China to replace a faded ideology with rising nationalism' that targets Japan, is fostering a potentially destabilising scenario. Since Beijing has fanned anti-Japanese sentiment as a partial strategy to sustain political legitimacy, Chinese nationalism is bound to react to shifts in Japan's China policy. The Chinese would prefer to deal with the Japan that was 'penitent over the war and basically distrustful of itself' (Self 2002: 82). However, neo-nationalism that calls for a prideful national identity has had the Japanese distancing themselves from their self-imposed, post-war pacifism and deferential attitude, a development that runs counter to Chinese hopes and expectations. Hence, an assertive and less remorseful Japan is bound to fuel Chinese nationalism. Conversely, a 'wounded' Japanese nationalism is reactive and apprehensive about a rapidly rising China, whose rejuvenated national confidence has made the Chinese more nationalistic and feisty in advancing their national interests, some of which are at Japan's expense (Self 2002: 82). Their 'diverging fortunes' (Pei and Swaine 2005) have certainly accentuated Japanese insecurity and distrust which, against the backdrop of such 'reactive-confrontational' nationalisms, are widely believed to be straining recent bilateral relations.

This study therefore raises important questions regarding the extent to which nationalism, real or perceived, is shaping their deteriorating relationship, notably from the Japanese side, and also how, in what manner and under what conditions domestic nationalist pressure affects Japanese foreign policy-making. This warrants an analysis of the actors and process, and an examination of the linkage between nationalism and policy-making, as well as the constraints and opportunities arising from domestic nationalist sentiment and other external–internal restrictions that concomitantly influence Japan's policy options pertaining to Japanese–Chinese relations.

Japanese foreign policy-making: an overview

This section provides a general idea of Japanese foreign policy-making, focusing particularly on the basic framework for Japan's China policy, and the actors involved in the decision-making process during the period of investigation (2001–6). This includes an analysis of the connection between nationalism and policy-making, notably the manner and conditions in which it exerts influence in the presence of other variables that equally matter to Japanese state-elites' perceptions/calculation.

Actors and process[3]

Japanese foreign policy-making is commonly noted for the 'elitist' (Johnson 1995) and/or 'pluralist' (Zhao 1993) nature of the principal actors and structures involved. Although different terminologies have been coined to describe the Japanese model, scholars tend to identify a similar cohort of principal actors constituting a 'tripartite' policy-making structure, and share a common description of their interwoven relationships, which illustrates a network of interdependent and generally collaborative ties between these actors, namely the central bureaucracy, incumbent ruling party (predominantly the LDP) and the *zaikai* (Tanaka 2000; Hook *et al.* 2005). Earlier studies mostly portray Japanese policy-making as inherently elitist, monolithic and coherent, while contemporary works seem to highlight its pluralistic and fragmented features, where decision-making is subjected to not only intense competition amongst policy-making elites, but also pressure from other relevant domestic and external actors/factors as well as informal policy-making mechanisms (Zhao 1993; Hughes 1999: 161–2). Also, Japan's policy-making regime has been deemed 'enigmatic', 'highly diffuse' and indeterminable, in terms of power distribution and actor dominance in decision-making (van Wolferen 1993; Drifte 1996: 5, 28; cf. Hagstrom 2003: 84–5).

Regardless of this debate, it remains credible to view contemporary Japanese foreign policy-making as essentially 'elite-led', yet 'increasingly pluralistic, with various groups exercising different degrees of influence' (Hughes 1999: 162), depending on the specific time context and issue addressed (Hook *et al.* 2005: 46). Hence, present analytical models should simultaneously account for a compendium of political actors and determinants that directly or indirectly influence the policy-making process.

The following is a description of the principal actors and mechanisms identified as influential, to varying degrees, in Japanese foreign and, specifically, China policy-making during Koizumi's premiership. As stipulated, the 'bureaucracy–LDP–*zaikai*' tripartite model forms the core of the general policy-making structure. However, a specific analysis of the executive roles of the PM, *Kantei* and the Cabinet, which are intertwined with the bureaucracy and ruling LDP, serves as an important starting point in addressing a key question regarding the prevalence of state-elites' (central decision-makers) domestic political resolve and nationalistic disposition in shaping foreign policy choices.

Prime Minister, Kantei, and the Cabinet

As the head of government, the PM wields significant foreign policy influence, though 'executive power' is constitutionally 'vested in the Cabinet', which is 'collectively responsible to the Diet' (Tanaka 2000: 4). Theoretically, the PM has the authority to determine the Cabinet line-up, allowing him the prerogative to form an executive branch that unanimously, or at least, in principle, agrees with his policy directions (Tanaka 2001: 4). Yet, in practice, there are structural limitations that tend to curtail the power of a Japanese premier (Mulgan 2004: 7). These include, among others, the traditionally entrenched and divisive ruling party politics that usually makes him comparatively weaker than his counterparts in exerting influence over party members in the Diet, and the organisational constraint of a relatively small support staff under the *Kantei*, often seconded from key ministries (Tanaka 2000: 4–6; Hook *et al.* 2005: 54). Another related and well-known shortcoming is the rapid premiership changes that undermine 'continuity in executive leadership in Japan's international relations' (Stockwin 1998, cf. Hook *et al.* 2005: 54). These politico-institutional constraints and their ambiguous power position suggest that Japanese PMs tend to put more emphasis on domestic politics – securing domestic political support often outweighs their interest in foreign policy-making (Hook *et al.* 2005: 54).

Despite such limitations, Tanaka (2000: 7) sees the PM wielding enough power to channel bureaucratic resources for national goals, and officially serving under the cabinet's auspices as the final arbiter of policy decisions, making him 'the single most important player in the game that is Japan's domestic politics, and particularly in the [two-level] games of complex domestic/foreign policy interaction'. This is especially so when managing key bilateral relationships and/ or foreign policy crises, during which the PM's role becomes paramount (NCR's assumption), a position in which he can 'make a difference both positively and negatively' (Tanaka 2000: 7). Perhaps, crucially, Japanese premiers also command what Hook *et al.* (2005: 54) call sufficient 'moral authority', which enables them to mobilise the domestic political apparatus and the public towards specific foreign policy objectives. Moreover, prime ministerial powers have grown since the 2001 administrative reforms, enabling him to circumvent cumbersome bureaucratic constraints in decision-making.[4] The reforms also enhance the *Kantei's* ability to deal with, coordinate and respond proactively to 'complex foreign policy and crisis issues' (Hook *et al.* 2005: 56). Indeed, Shinoda (2007: 83) sees a 'power shift' taking place since 2001, with the *Kantei* becoming central in foreign policy-making. Together with key *Kantei* officials, Hagstrom (2003: 86, n. 191), in citing Tanaka (1991: 191), sees the PM playing a central role with regard to the formulation of Japan's China policy, where 'no important decision is taken, and no substantial policy is implemented, without his consent'. Sasajima (2002: 83) shares a similar view, suggesting that political decision-making at the PM level has 'tremendous influence on diplomacy with China', especially under the leadership of strong-willed premiers, such as Tanaka, Nakasone, Takeshita and Koizumi.[5]

Next, Cabinet members, specifically the FM, and others to varying extent, affect decision-making at the apex. As part of the *Kantei*, the Cabinet Secretariat also plays an increasingly important, albeit mostly supportive and coordinating role in policy-making (Shinoda 2007). Among the protagonists are the CCS[6] and his deputies, who serve as higher level mechanisms of foreign policy coordination and decision-making, notably when the process is stifled by unresolved disputes and inter-ministerial 'turf battles' (Ahn 1998: 53). The Cabinet Councilors' Office for External Affairs and the Cabinet Security Affairs Office, established in 1986 to improve foreign and security policy coordination between the Cabinet and ministries, also exert credible influence (Hook *et al.* 2005: 54). Apparently, the former plays a key role in China policy-making; the unit head, together with the MOFA, is responsible for furnishing the PM with information on China (Sasajima 2002: 83). Moreover, officials previously appointed to that position were mostly from the so-called 'China school' cohort, and usually former director-generals of the MOFA's Asian and Oceanian Affairs Bureau (AOAB) (Sasajima 2002: 83), giving their information and advice much credibility. However, ex-North American Affairs Bureau (NAAB) officials seemingly took over these offices during Koizumi's premiership, which explains his administration's increasingly 'pro-US' policy direction, at the expense of Japanese–Chinese ties.[7]

Bureaucracy

The bureaucracy, comprising ministries (*sho*) and agencies (*cho*), is traditionally influential, and remains crucial in the formulation and implementation of contemporary Japanese foreign policy, despite its subordinate position to the Cabinet, and the LDP's growing role in policy-making (Hagstrom 2003: 85; Hughes 1999: 162). The MOFA is the chief bureaucratic protagonist responsible for Japan's foreign policy-making and diplomatic affairs, while other regular actors include the METI, the Ministry of Finance and the JDA/MOD. Among others that occasionally get involved over specific issues in China policy-making are the MOE/MEXT and the JCG.[8] Within the MOFA framework, the AOAB and the China and Mongolia Division are central in the formulation of China policy. Both sections are traditionally headed and/or dominated by 'China school' bureaucrats who staunchly believe in 'good-neighbourly friendship' (Sasajima 2003: 83), and advocate a policy of appeasement and low posturing when dealing with China (Takamine 2006: 79). However, a younger generation of less-partisan (or pro-US) officials[9] now forms the MOFA core, bringing an inevitable shift to its China policy orientation that prioritises Japan's (pro-American) national interests (Sasajima 2002: 83; Murata 2006: 45). Furthermore, the MOFA's China policy-making influence has been gradually eroded by the ruling LDP since mid-1990s, following 'structural-functional' adjustments that shifted the power balance in policy-making between the two actors, not mentioning the latter's enhanced foreign policy expertise (Takamine 2006: 80).

Generally, the key bureaucratic-level personnel in China policy-making are the China Division director and the AOAB's director-general, both of whom can make decisions that 'directly influence the course of policy' (Sasajima 2002: 83). However, decisions over specific/major bilateral issues may require the deliberations of higher-ranking 'political' actors, i.e. the MOFA vice-minister, and Cabinet members, such as the CCS, FM, and ultimately, the PM, during which policy-making assumes a more 'top–down' orientation (Tanaka 1991: 196, cf. Hagstrom 2003: 86; Sasajima 2002: 83). This means that MOFA bureaucrats exercise more independent decision-making on routine and general affairs, but their influence becomes restricted, when critical bilateral issues arise (Hagstrom 2003: 86). Even so, policy decision-making at the highest level remains relatively dependent on information derived from the MOFA, or other ministries (Tanaka 1991: 192, cf. Hagstrom 2003: 86–7), underscoring the bureaucracy's fundamental role in the overall policy-making structure.

Political parties and Diet

The LDP, the largest and most dominant political party in post-war Japan, has been a principal foreign policy actor, owing to its political control over the executive and legislature during its time in power. Previous studies have asserted the influential role of LDP politicians in the policy-making process, in view of growing (foreign) policy expertise deriving from the Policy Affairs Research

Council (PARC) and other intra-party committees (Takamine 2006: 83), as well as the LDP's dominance in Japan's political system (Hook *et al.* 2005: 57). Despite a temporary loss of power between 1993 and 1994, the LDP survived, rebounded and restored its political clout through power-sharing and decisive electoral majorities, notably during Koizumi's premiership, until its electoral defeat in 2009. The party regained control of the government after emerging victorious in the 2012 elections.

The LDP foreign policy-making initiative is engendered by formal and informal actors. The president,[10] secretary-general and chairpersons of PARC and the Executive Council, respectively, constitute the former; whereas the latter comprises top-level *kuromaku* (i.e. ex-senior bureaucrats/politicians), *habatsu* (party factions),[11] *zoku* (policy tribes/caucuses with specialised interests in particular issue areas), and *koenkai* (constituency-based organisations) (Hagstrom 2003: 86–7; Hiwatari 2005: 35). These internal decision-making mechanisms are particularly influential when the LDP commands comfortable majorities in both Houses of the Diet, notably on important foreign policy initiatives and management of controversial issues (Tanaka 2000: 11).

The deliberations within the LDP have a profound bearing on Japan's China policy.[12] There exists an intra-party polarisation of interests and attitudes towards China, along the line of the so-called 'pro-China' and 'pro-Taiwan' groups (Zhao 1993: 67). Membership within these contending groups derives from across political factions and apparently does not coincide with factional politics, making *habatsu*'s influence on China policy, or foreign policy, in general, negligible (Hagstrom 2003:87). Similarly, informal actors, i.e. *zoku* and *koenkai*, tend to focus predominantly on domestic issues, hence their presumed limited interests in external affairs, especially before the 1990s (Takamine 2006: 84). However, such presumptions are deceptive since Japanese–Chinese relations have been quintessentially shaped by domestic issues, suggesting an under-estimation of these informal actors' influence on China policy-making. In fact, certain factions, i.e. Keisei-kai and Kochi-kai, have exhibited influence in promoting good relations with China, although their clout is presently diminishing. Conversely, the Seiwa-kai that Koizumi headed before his premiership appointment has been traditionally sympathetic to Taiwan. Its political ascendancy is not unrelated to the decline in Japanese–Chinese ties, thus, challenging suggestions regarding *habatsu's* negligible influence. Also, the rise of *gaiko-zoku* (diplomatic caucuses), whose membership includes ex-MOFA elites deeply knowledgeable on Japanese–Chinese relations, underscores its prominence in China policy-making (Takamine 2006: 84).[13] It is, nonetheless, commonly agreed that *kuromaku*'s 'behind-the-scenes' role has been traditionally vital, especially in mediating and seeking diplomatic resolutions via informal/personal channels during crisis periods (Sasajima 2002: 84; Zhao 1993). Taken together, these LDP policy-making actors can profoundly influence China policy direction, especially considering the bi-partisan split and overall hardening of attitudes towards China. Since the mid-1990s, 'anti-China' LDP hardliners have often criticised the government and MOFA's 'soft' policy towards China, and successfully pressured Tokyo for more assertive management of their bilateral affairs (Sasajima 2002: 85).

The foreign policy-making influence of other political parties has been noted, especially in exerting domestic political pressure and *gaiatsu* on the government via unofficial and personal diplomatic channels to improve relations with specific countries. Relations with China have traditionally received significant attention from Japanese political parties, whereby the likes of the JSP/SDPJ, JCP and notably, Komeito (presently called Shin-Komeito) played key roles in Japanese–Chinese normalisation (Hughes 1999: 163). Although the transformation of Japan's political landscape in the 1990s weakened their political convictions and influence (as indicated by their acquiescence to the general drift to the right), these parties together with then-opposition DPJ remain important mediators in Japanese–Chinese relations. That said, bi-partisan treatment of China also exists within the opposition, specifically amongst DPJ members, and indeed, across the Diet. At the Diet level, the Japan–China Parliamentarians' Friendship League, whose members span party divides, are advocates for amicable Japanese–Chinese ties, while 'pro-Taiwan' organisations established by both LDP and DPJ members, serve to sway Diet influence on China policy (Sasajima 2002: 86). Although the Diet's foreign policy-making role is generally passive, considering Japan's parliamentary system, where the PM theoretically enjoys majority support (Tanaka 2000: 11), ongoing power shifts have raised its profile, notably in directing policy towards major powers and issues, including China policy (Cooney 2007: 95, 181–3).

Zaikai

The *zaikai* comprises Keidanren (Japan Business Federation), Nissho (Japan Chamber of Commerce and Industry) and Keizai Doyukai (Council for Economic Development). Amongst the most influential of non-governmental entities, *zaikai* is renowned for its informal foreign policy-making role, and even conducts its own diplomacy (Hagstrom 2003: 88). Lobbying is essentially its *modus operandi* to affect the Japanese state's foreign policy direction, although *zaikai* also commonly utilise informal channels of communication to promote relations with foreign states. According to Tanaka (2000: 13–14), Keidanren, especially, has long been influential due to its 'close formal and informal relations with political leaders' and its function as 'a conduit for the distribution of funds to political parties'. Similarly, Doyukai has become vocal on foreign policy issues under the stewardship of Ushio Jiro and Kobayashi Yotaro (Tanaka 2000: 14). In the era of economic interdependence, they assume an important role in mediating Tokyo's foreign policy, and mitigating relations with countries like China to protect Japanese business interests. Chapter 2 has described the *zaikai*'s historically crucial roles in advancing Japanese–Chinese relations. During Koizumi's premiership, it pressured against prime ministerial Yasukuni visits, and helped sustain the informal channels of economic diplomacy with China in the face of the decline in political relations.

Other actors

There are other actors in the domestic context who influence policy-making, albeit mostly indirectly, through 'agenda-setting and/or participation in various formal and informal settings' (Hagstrom 2003: 88). They include, among others, the mass media, academic community and think-tanks, SNGs, pressure groups and public opinion (see Hook *et al.* 2005: 67–72).

The mass media significantly influence the domestic discourse on and the agenda of Japanese foreign policy, due to the avid consumption of newspapers and other media products by domestic society (Hook *et al.* 2005: 67; Johnston 2007: 113). However, its influence on the policy-making process is limited by the exclusive and heavily regulated *kisha* system (press club), which challenges the impartiality of the news information provided (Takahara 2007).[14] In general, the major national newspapers are politically opinionated and lopsided to a degree, with the *Yomiuri, Sankei,* and *Nikkei* holding the pro-establishment, conservative and nationalistic line, while the *Asahi* and *Mainichi* tend to align with discourse from the opposite side of the political divide (Tanaka 2000: 14). With regard to media opinion towards China, the latter two are generally more sympathetic and pro-China, while the former group, especially *Sankei,* has been 'poisoning the atmosphere' with its vocal criticisms of the Chinese and Tokyo's generally conciliatory policy towards Beijing (Johnston 2007).

Additionally, government/non-government think-tanks and the academic community also affect foreign policy-making, notably through the furnishing of information and expertise, as well as by generating general debates and on specific issue areas. Prominent scholars sitting on the government's special advisory committees are especially well positioned to exert influence through policy briefings and advice to policy-makers (Hook *et al.* 2005: 69). For instance, the joint research efforts of Japanese intellectuals within the New Japan–China Friendship Committee for the Twenty-First Century play a crucial role in seeking a reconciliation of their bilateral history.[15] Meanwhile, SNGs are considered emerging foreign policy actors, through their external relations and activities with counterparts abroad (Jain 2000). In the realm of Japanese–Chinese ties, Japanese SNGs are actively promoting economic cooperation zones, sister-city programmes and other cultural exchanges with their Chinese counterparts, which are beneficial in improving overall bilateral relations (see Hook 2006; Jain 2006). Conversely, their actions can challenge the national government's diplomatic position and undermine ties, for example, strident criticisms and 'anti-China' remarks by the ex-Tokyo governor, Ishihara Shintaro, intermittently dented bilateral goodwill (Jain 2000: 26).[16]

Pressure groups, or NGOs, are another credible civil society channel in exerting political pressure on the government's foreign policy position, especially on specific issue areas that overlap with domestic interests (Hook *et al.* 2005: 70). Among the issue areas that draw their interests include agriculture, fisheries and the environment, as well as the more contentious issues of anti-militarism, constitutional revision and nationalist education reforms. In China policy-making, some NGOs are capable of exerting political pressure on a range of domestic issues that remain as barriers to genuine improvement in Japanese–Chinese ties. From Yasukuni to textbook rows, 'nationalist' groups like Izokukai, Tsukurukai, and Nippon Kaigi have relentlessly pursued the rewriting of a 'positive' national history, venerating the war dead and rebuilding a 'normal' Japan. Similarly, Nihon Seinensha has actively exerted Japan's claims over Senkaku/Diaoyudao that periodically trigger diplomatic rows with China. The occasionally uncompromising stance exhibited by recent Japanese administrations on these issue areas, imply the salient, albeit indirect influence of such pressure groups on the policy-making apparatus.

Lastly, public opinion on foreign policy issues is regularly gauged via surveys conducted by government agencies and the mass media, i.e. the related Cabinet Office annual polls. Public opinion reflects the interests of the Japanese people, which the democratic government of Japan is required to take into consideration in policy-making. Indeed, public opinion has been significant in shaping what Miyashita (2002: 155) calls the 'core values' or 'opinion moods' that define the parameters within which post-war Japanese policy-makers have operated, such as Japan's pacifist, anti-militarist stance in international and security affairs. However, its influence is essentially indirect and restricted to establishing 'the general background against which policy-making agents reach decisions' on foreign policy issues (Hook *et al.* 2005: 72). As described, the shift in Japanese public opinion of China has concurred with shifts in Japan's China policy and the overall mood of their bilateral relations, reflecting its 'ambience-setting' role in China policy-making.

Nationalism and foreign policy-making

The above description identifies areas where nationalism can intersect and influence Japanese policy-making. For a start, nationalism can influence top-level decision-making through the cohort of state-elites, namely the Cabinet headed by the PM. Since they act as the final arbiter of policy decision-making, the personalities and political dispositions/affiliations and perceptions of these key elites, especially the PM, tend to shape their policy preferences and influence their decisions. As stated earlier, generational change has seen the arrival of more 'nationalistic' Japanese leaders, who are eager and prepared to pursue domestic and external policies that further Japan's national interests, even at the cost of aggravating traditionally sensitive bilateral relations. Post-Cold War Japanese premiers, i.e. Hashimoto, Obuchi, Koizumi and especially, Abe, have shown nationalistic dispositions, and their alleged political affiliations with nationalist groups within and outside the government, not to mention the LDP's conservative slant, underscore nationalism's potential salience in affecting decision-making at the apex of Japanese foreign policy apparatus (Shibuichi 2005: 200–1). Concomitantly, nationalism's influence pervades the LDP-dominated Cabinets, whose membership would have derived from related factions, and/or shared the ideological/political outlook and interests of the presiding premier.[17] Moreover, nationalism was able to exert its influence during Koizumi's premiership through *habatsu, zoku* and increasingly, the new group of non-faction legislators dubbed the 'Koizumi Children', which emerged dominant in the LDP following the 2005 election (Hiwatari 2005: 34). Notwithstanding their personal political preferences, nationalism's salience in top-level policy-making is also determined by the domestic political resolve of these principal elites vis-à-vis nationalist and moderate forces in domestic politics, where increased dependence on either side for political power and survival could plausibly lead to lopsided decision-making.[18]

At the bureaucratic level, nationalism can, in similar ways, affect policy-making via power-wielding individuals and related institutional interests. At the MOFA, the new generation of bureaucrats is, expectedly, more confident in their external outlook, and in advancing Japan's national interests in the international arena. Although MOFA's policy direction has traditionally been moderate rather than nationalistic, its assertive diplomatic posturing in recent times suggests nationalism's gradual redefinition of its policy-making structure and process. Institutionally, the MOFA's operational behaviour is essentially pragmatic and 'rational-utility'-oriented when managing Japan's diplomacy. However, its jurisdiction tends to be affected by the political affiliation/disposition of the presiding FM, apart from decision-making at the higher level, as demonstrated by the overarching *Kantei*, which may ultimately determine its diplomatic options.

Likewise, the JDA/MOD, JCG, METI and MOE/MEXT, among others, may share a more nationalistic outlook owing to similar impetus as well as their respective institutional interests, which are national security in the case of the first two, and national economic interests and patriotic society-building through education for METI and MOE/MEXT. Despite their domestic-oriented interests, these institutions have occasionally found themselves entangled in foreign policy-making due to the 'internationalisation' of related issues, and thus have been required to advance their interests within the policy-making framework. Understandably, it would be in the interests of the JDA/MOD and MOE/MEXT to support neo-nationalist goals, e.g. constitutional revision of Article 9, and the promotion of revisionist history, two domestic issues that constantly impinge on Japan's foreign policy towards neighbour-states generally, and China specifically. Moreover, in the JDA/MOD's case, strong nationalist pressure in foreign policy-making would conceivably transpire as a result of its institutional interests in defending Japanese sovereignty and territorial integrity. Other correlated interests would be competition for policy-making influence on security matters vis-à-vis MOFA, and justification for a larger budgetary allocation.

Domestic nationalist pressure can equally affect foreign policy-making via the non-state actors described earlier. The key protagonists are the nationalist-oriented mass media, pressure groups, intellectuals and the public. The intimate ties between nationalist-rightwing groups and the ruling LDP, where their 'patron–client' relationship serves to secure political support for the latter, and where group/party membership tends to overlap, underscore their capacity to affect the LDP government's external policy related to domestic nationalist concerns (Shibuichi 2005: 200–1). Meanwhile, the media sources mentioned in Chapter 3 are convenient 'mouthpieces' and advocates of neo-nationalist goals, who, together with 'revisionist' intellectual support, can set the nationalist discourse and agenda for Japan's international relations. Similarly, nationalism's influence has been exerted through the activities and *modus operandi* of the aforementioned pressure groups, while the general drift in public opinion towards the right is another avenue which has to be accounted for in Japanese policy-making. In fact, both the media and public opinion have gained extended policy-making influence under recent Japanese administrations, as contemporary leaders, especially Koizumi, and Abe to a lesser extent, were widely perceived to be 'populist' and 'image-dependent', making them responsive to media and public pressure (Iida 2003).

Other variables in foreign policy-making

The above section infers the plausible agency connecting nationalism and foreign policy-making. However, nationalism is just one of the several key variables influencing Japan's China policy-making. In Chapter 2, it is argued that contemporary Japanese–Chinese relations have been consistently defined by a combination of interrelated, external–domestic determinants. Besides factoring into the key policy-makers' calculation, these variables are also areas that connect with the interests of other mentioned actors, who can exert their moderating influence on domestic nationalist forces in foreign policy-making. For instance, the significance of interdependence in Japan's economic agenda means that Japanese policy-makers are inclined to demonstrate pragmatism and restraint in managing their difficult relationship with China, to safeguard their economic ties. To this end, domestic pressures from *zaikai* could constrain Japan's China policy. Moreover, the purported 'politics–business linkage' also possibly influences state-elites' decision-making pertaining to advancing their vested interests in the bilateral relationship. Meanwhile, 'moderate' forces participating in domestic politics, i.e. opposition parties, pacifist pressure groups like Heiwa izokukai zenkoku renrakukai (National Organisation of Pacifist Bereaved Families), and leftwing media, i.e. *Asahi Shimbun, Shukan Kinyobi* and *Sekai*, may curtail nationalistic tendencies within the foreign policy decision-making circle (Shibuichi 2005: 203–4). Externally, powerful levers like the US and the US–Japan alliance can pressure Japan (and China) into adopting moderate policy options, although US policies can equally exacerbate nationalist impulses. Simply put, nationalism's policy-making salience is mediated by and dependent on its interactions with other determinants.

Hence, the extent to which nationalism becomes dominant in Japan's China policy-making generally boils down to conditions related to state-elites' domestic political resolve against nationalist and moderate forces, and Japan's relative power position vis-à-vis China, as perceived/calculated at a particular time context. Subscribing to this book's NCR framework, domestic nationalist pressure may influence Japan's China policy-making under conditions of relatively favourable or ambiguous structural/external pressure, or be suppressed, when Japanese state-elites perceive the external conditions to be unfavourable. In particular, nationalist–assertive policy options could prevail, when Japan enjoys favourable 'alliance commitment/resolve' (US support) and diplomatic leverage vis-à-vis China. Conversely, a Japanese state suffering from relatively unfavourable power position may opt for a moderate–conciliatory or non-action policy option, when managing nationalist-flavoured bilateral disputes. By the same token, nationalism may manifest itself under the condition where state-elites, weak in domestic political resolve and susceptible to nationalist pressure, find it necessary to adopt nationalist–assertive policy options to enhance political standing. Then again, nationalism is less significant when state-elites enjoy favourable domestic political resolve which allows them to risk moderate–conciliatory policies without fearing the brunt of domestic nationalist backlashes. In sum, although not discounting the potential irrationality of nationalist passion, these assumptions are based on: (i) the 'rationality' of Japanese state-elites' perception of the external–domestic nexus, within a specific time context, and (ii) Schweller's (2004: 164) aforesaid NCR notion that states respond (or not) to constraints/opportunities in ways determined by state-elites' consideration of this nexus, against the backdrop of a dynamic, competitive and decentralised political process.

Balancing nationalist and pragmatic goals in contemporary Japanese–Chinese diplomacy

The analysis of Japanese policy-making highlights the linkage between domestic nationalist pressure and foreign policy behaviour. It emphasises nationalism's interaction with other external and domestic imperatives in the decision-making process, which the policy-makers have to consider when managing Japan's problematic relations with China. In particular, their political dispositions/affiliations and outlook towards nationalist and pragmatic foreign policy goals, their domestic political resolve vis-à-vis nationalist/moderate elements, and dependence on nationalism as a power instrument, not mentioning the 'alliance' factor and Japan's diplomatic position vis-à-vis China, all serve to formulate, to various degrees, their policy options. This raises the question of whether rising nationalism necessarily leads to a distinctively nationalistic China policy, and the consequential impact on Japanese–Chinese affairs.

The following overview of the manner in which Japan has thus far managed 'history' and security-related issues generates a somewhat different impression from that of the conventional wisdom regarding nationalism's efficacy in post-Cold War Japanese–Chinese diplomacy. Nationalism has certainly prevailed in 'sensitising' and engendering the diplomatic ambience that has made the resolution of such issues difficult. It has also prevailed under less deterministic conditions, and mainly on symbolic issues, to satisfy domestic passion and safeguard state-elites' political incumbency and parochial interests. Yet pragmatic consideration of their deepening economic interdependence, the mitigating roles of moderate elements in both government and private spheres, and external pressures from Washington, have appeared to carry equal if not more weight in determining Japan's actual foreign policy options. Such an impression concurs with this book's central arguments, which state that nationalism's salience in affecting foreign policy choices, i.e. choosing between assertive–nationalistic or moderate–conciliatory policy options, is dependent on state-elites' perceptions/ calculation of its interaction with other 'power' variables that concurrently affect foreign policy-making, in a given time and context. It also depends on their ability to strike a balance, or trade-off between achieving nationalist and pragmatic goals (Bong 2002).

Nationalism and the 'history' problem

'History' has become a major irritant in Japanese–Chinese relations, against the backdrop of rejuvenated nationalism and 'elite historical mythmaking' (He 2006: 69). According to Gong (2001a/b), the 'selective remembering and forgetting' of the war history has as much reinforced nationalism as the conscious efforts to foster nationalist sentiment have made 'history' an intractable bilateral impasse. Undoubtedly, Japan's flourishing neo-nationalist movement for historical revisionism has contributed to magnifying differences and intensifying the 'history' row since the mid-1990s. Notable disputes over 'war apology' and sequels of the history textbook and Yasukuni debacles, as well as a series of unresolved war legacies, were related to and partly perpetuated by neo-nationalism's influence on Japanese changing attitudes towards history, and their relations with China. This has resulted in Beijing frequently reprimanding Tokyo for allegedly acquiescing in the revisionist agenda, and chastising neo-nationalists, especially those of neo-autonomist and neo-conservative leanings (Samuels 2007a/b), for their reluctance to accept the war judgement, and their downplaying of Japan's military role in China and Asia.

The fundamental problem concerning history is that both countries appear to promote contending interpretations of what happened in the past. Underlying this conundrum in contemporary Japan has been the popularisation and gradual mainstreaming of the (neo-) nationalist war history discourse that exacerbates what Morris-Suzuki (2005) deems 'the unresolved problems of historical responsibility' (cf. Samuels 2007b: 113). According to Samuels (2007b: 121–7), neo-autonomists and, to an extent, normal-nationalists have shown disdain for the so-called 'victor justice' handed by the Tokyo War Crimes Tribunal (He 2006: 77). Such sentiments underscore their contestation of the conventional wisdom regarding Japan's war responsibilities found in the 'victor narrative' subscribed to by the Chinese, and their resultant agenda for historical revisionism. Neo-nationalists generally share the view that Japan was fighting a war of liberation, on behalf of the colonised Asian nations, to free them from the yoke of Western imperialism. They also contend that the 'Pacific War'[19] was essentially a war in which the Japanese were compelled to fight for national survival against ominous US/Western encroachment in the Asia-Pacific, where Japan was the victim, and America, the perpetrator (Hasegawa 1985). Hence many refuse to internalise or acknowledge Japan's war-guilt, which explains their unwillingness to apologise to countries like China, and their sentimentalism towards what their Asian/Chinese neighbours deem as 'whitewashing' or 'glorification' of Japan's war past. Although previously marginalised, this 'revisionist' view has regained currency under the auspices of neo-nationalism, and the political empowerment of mainstream neo-conservative elites.

Another related problem is their conflicting interests in and treatment of war history. Austin and Harris (2001: 61) argue that China, for various reasons, prefers to remember and draw an apology and/or other concessions from Japan. Conversely, the Japanese, for reasons of national pride and identity, yearn for closure, and look to the present and future. Japanese 'cultural traditions/norms' are also cited as reasons, although the neo-nationalist agenda for a prideful national history appears to be the driving force behind the 'selective amnesia' and revisionist treatment of Japan's war history (Rose 2005; Samuels 2007a/b). Furthermore, the current generation of Japanese tend to view the (re)interpretation of history from one's national perspective as normal, and in accordance with Japan's national interests and sovereign rights (Miller 2002: 3). Indeed, 'revisionist' neo-nationalism has partly made them feel less responsible for and more detached from their country's past conduct, leading Drifte (2003: 16) to comment on their 'astonishing degree of insensitivity and ignorance about the [increasingly distant] past'. Inevitably, such developments have led to Chinese accusations of Japan's enduring reluctance to face history squarely, her insincerity in acknowledging historical responsibility, and her failure to atone for past atrocities in China. Conversely, the Japanese perceive China's obsession with history as amounting to self-indulgence, and a self-serving attempt to unsettle them (van Kemenade 2006: 42). Moreover, Japan's leaders are acutely aware of and no longer willing to play to China's 'history card', although they themselves manipulate it for domestic expediency (Soerensen 2006: 114).

Additionally, major nationalist-rightwing pressure groups have wielded indirect influence over LDP policy-makers, through a complex nexus of politico-business funding and networking that helps keep such nationalist agendas alive. Others resort to activities ranging from booming martial anthems/nationalist rhetoric on *gaisensha* (sound trucks) around Tokyo to more extreme measures like political intimidation and violence, which are the *uyoku's* quintessential *modus operandi* (McNeill 2001; Prideaux 2006). Although ultra-nationalism remains unappealing to many Japanese, McNeill (2001) finds extremist political violence in Japan displaying distinctive features, including high-profile intimidations of political figures,[20] and the alleged connections of these *uyoku* groups with the 'underworld' (*yakuza*) and power-brokers. McNeill (2001) even suggested that 'the relationship between the *yakuza-uyoku*, the neo-nationalists, and established political figures is a complex matrix of financial, political, and personal ties, with conflicting and contradictory elements', while Stronach (1995: 101) identifies this 'special relationship' as the 'Black Nexus'. Such activities and linkages, together with an obliging media sympathetic to neo-nationalist causes, undoubtedly contribute to the persistence of historical revisionism, and the enduring reluctance of some quarters in Japan to reconcile with the conventional interpretation of war history, let alone accept China's 'moral judgement' (Austin and Harris 2001: 65).

The 'war apology' issue offers a sterling example of nationalism's propensity to undermine Japanese–Chinese historical reconciliation. When diplomatic relations resumed in 1972, the 'Tanaka–Zhou' joint communiqué noted a statement from Japan expressing responsibility and remorse for its role in the Japanese–Chinese war (Kawashima 2005: 17). Since then, the Japanese government has conveyed numerous expressions of 'apology' to promote reconciliation, but to no avail, as the Chinese continue to demand a more 'sincere apology', which in their opinion has yet to be offered by Japan (Shambaugh 1996: 91). However, the arrival of nationalistically motivated Japanese leaders has made it difficult for Beijing to keep drawing the 'history card' as a lever in bilateral negotiations, let alone to demand more apologies. Contemporary Japanese political elites are decreasingly prepared to subscribe to the conventional wisdom of Japan's war responsibilities, as they feel less burdened by the need to apologise. For instance, Abe Shinzo and other Koizumi allies staged a walk-out from the Diet chamber in 1995, in protest against the issuance of what critics deemed as a 'diluted' apology to Japan's neighbours, in conjunction with the sixtieth anniversary of the end of the Second World War[21] (Samuels 2007a: 145). Furthermore, these neo-conservative elites have gone on to dominate the apex of Japanese policy-making, which explains the salience of nationalism and history in Japan–China diplomacy. Apart from the power wielders, politicians championing the 'just war' perspective and firmly opposing 'apology diplomacy' derive from the Diet-groups mentioned earlier.

Other related reasons for the reluctance to apologise to China include the view that Japan's behaviour resembles that of other imperialist powers of that era, and that the atrocities committed were 'collateral damage' resulting from a protracted campaign in China (Austin and Harris 2001: 53), which were obscured in post-war Japan's narrative of the Pacific War (Satoh 2006a: 7–8). Likewise, the Japanese have reason to believe that 'history' is often manipulated for political purposes (Nakanishi 2005). For instance, both Japanese and Chinese see each other adjusting with the China war casualty statistics, particularly and most contentiously in the case of the Nanjing Massacre, where the variances in their reported figures have hindered any realistic judgement on the issue (Austin and Harris 2001: 54). Although an anticipated norm in such politicised issues, nationalism has more often than not transformed such distortions into national myths that have subverted reconciliation (He 2006). The commonly held view that 'history' is simply an instrument the Chinese government uses to exert pressure on Japan has not only made Japanese decreasingly sympathetic and unsupportive of any concessions to their neighbour (Austin and Harris 2001: 55), but has also induced a nationalist backlash regarding the apology issue, and the war history in general (Miller 2002: 8).

Neo-nationalism's influence on the shifting Japanese discourse on history is, likewise, responsible for the outbreak of other 'history' issues and related rhetorical *faux pas* by political elites that have marred contemporary Japanese–Chinese diplomacy. These controversies include history textbook revisions that allegedly 'sanitised' Imperial Japan's wartime actions. The first such allegation triggered the 1982 textbook row mentioned in Chapter 2. The subsequent incident in 1986 saw the high-school Japanese history textbook, *Shinpen Nihonshi*, edited by the rightwing group Nihon o Mamoru Kokumin Kaigi (National Conference for Defending Japan) passing the MOE/MEXT textbook screening to become the first such publication in post-war Japan (Rose 2005: 56). The controversy re-emerged in April 2001, when China accused Tsukurukai's *Atarashii rekishi kyokasho* (New History Textbook) of portraying Japanese imperialism as a liberating force in Asia. Especially inflammatory was the original draft's attempt to downscale the Nanjing Massacre by defining it as an 'incident' not amounting to a holocaust, which infuriated the Chinese (BBC 3 April 2001). Although the MOE/MEXT-approved version referred to the 'Massacre', the textbook's content doubted its reality and the validity of the Tokyo Tribunal's verdict (Yang 2001: 182). Beijing responded by seeking specific changes to the textbook. The Koizumi administration, however, refused to bow to Chinese (and Korean) pressure, prompting the Chinese MFA to express 'regrets and strong outrage', and denounce Tokyo's position as 'unacceptable' (BBC 10 July 2001). In 2005, the MOE/MEXT's passing of a revised edition of Tsukurukai's textbook reignited the controversy.[22]

Undoubtedly, the textbook issue occurred against the backdrop of rising nationalism in Japan. The first two incidents were unmistakably an outgrowth of the undercurrents of confident economic nationalism during the 1980s. Meanwhile, Tsukurukai's textbook reflects the contemporary neo-nationalists' revisionist agenda, which has surfaced in a variety of other media, including films, *manga* and magazines. Not surprisingly, its publication triggered Chinese outrage. Although China probably used it to manipulate Japanese politics and foreign policy, its criticism of Japan's attitude towards history has also much if not more to do with nationalistic impulses in Chinese domestic politics (Miller 2002: 8).

Further dampening relations are the prime ministerial visits to Yasukuni, which will be studied in the following chapter, the biochemical warfare research of Unit 731 and the Imperial Japanese Army's abandoned weapons, 'comfort women' and the Nanjing Massacre. Likewise, one-off incidents related to the war legacy include the alleged Zhuhai sex-orgy involving Japanese tourists, and the insulting play by Japanese exchange students in Xian, in 2003. This chapter will not discuss each of these incidents, but rather extrapolate the complexity and sensitivity of history in Japanese–Chinese relations, and the reality of nationalism turning such incidents into diplomatic impasses. Indeed, 'history' may continue to subvert a genuine reconciliation between the two governments and societies, despite mutual efforts to subordinate war memories for more wide-ranging goals of peaceful cooperation (Austin and Harris 2001: 64). With nationalism gaining currency, it is equally hard to see mutual public opinion reconciling over history. Rather more obviously, it reveals the 'vulnerability to nationalist pressures of any attempt at a comprehensive settlement of the history quarrel' (Miller 2002: 8).

The perpetuation of 'history' disputes in post-Cold War Japanese–Chinese diplomacy reflects the NCR assumption regarding domestic variables gaining salience in foreign policy-making, especially under low-pressure or ambiguous external–structural conditions. The Cold War's demise induced such an environment, permitting the domestic political calculus to feature more prominently in Japan's (and China's) external decision-making; hence the constant resurrection of nationalism's exacerbating role in the 'history' quarrel. Also, internal pressures, namely the need to foster nationalism for domestic objectives and the parochial motivations of nationalistic elites and/or institutions, appear to have greater leverage in shaping Japanese external behaviour. Since Japanese–Chinese relations have been traditionally most affected by domestic issues (Tanaka 2000: 3), the deteriorating trend is to be anticipated, in light of rising domestic nationalist pressure and the prevailing external–structural conditions.

However, nationalism's impact on the 'history' problem, though intermittently triggering bilateral tensions, has not totally derailed overall ties. According to Wang (2002: 116), the history quarrel 'has seldom caused substantial damages to the relationship since 1972. While both sides could be quite emotional and vocal on the issue, in practical policy, they rarely let the animosity over history carry the day.' It is true that 'history' has affectively dented politico-diplomatic ties. Yet the 'cold politics, hot economics' dialectic suggests that there are other determinants, besides nationalistic considerations, which 'rational' policy-makers in Tokyo have to consider, when managing their bilateral affairs. More importantly, rising domestic nationalist pressure does not necessarily translate into a nationalist foreign policy *per se*, where 'sense and passion' override 'sensibility and reason' (Gries 2004) in the pursuit of Japan's broader national interests.

Indeed, Japan's overall management of the aforementioned 'history'-related disputes offers an indication of how substantial nationalism is, or otherwise, in shaping its China policy, despite the hard-line posture and rhetoric that dominated the initial stages of the controversies. For instance, Japanese nationalism's manifestation in both the war apology and textbook debacles is indisputable, and Tokyo's obstinacy in not mollifying Chinese demands may well have the makings of a nationalist–assertive China policy. Yet, it has not prevented Japanese leaders from exercising 'post-crisis damage control' to stabilise the bilateral relationship (Roy 2005: 191). Typical of these initiatives were PM Obuchi's July 1999 summit meeting in Beijing with China's leaders, and Premier Zhu Rongji's Japan visit in 2000, where mutual efforts to bring about a diplomatic thaw were apparent after the 1998 'war apology' fiasco. They included the planned establishment of a leadership hotline, bilateral security exchanges, elaborate celebrations to commemorate the thirtieth anniversary of diplomatic normalisation, and the use of 'partnership' to describe the new direction of Japanese–Chinese relations, with the Chinese going even further by unilaterally advancing the term 'strategic partnership' to emphasise their fresh approach towards bilateral ties (Rozman 2002: 117).

Similarly, the Koizumi administration's defiance over the textbook and Yasukuni rows that undermined China's 'smile diplomacy' (Rozman 2002) were arguably offset by Koizumi's subsequent efforts to revive communication between the two countries (Wang 2002). This demonstrates Tokyo's balancing act between realising nationalist and pragmatic goals under perceived external–internal conditions, and the plausibility of both leaderships' tolerance and willingness to make allowances for each other's domestic nationalist agenda. The empirical study of Japan's management of the Yasukuni controversy in the following chapter allows an assessment of nationalism's impact vis-à-vis other determinants in shaping its policy options, when managing this highly symbolic 'history' issue in Japanese–Chinese affairs.

Nationalism and shifting security perceptions and policies

Nationalism's saliency can likewise be seen in how Japan manages its security relations with China. Amid shifting power dynamics, rising nationalism has prompted a mutual re-evaluation of strategic perceptions and security concerns in recent years. Specifically, Japan's neo-nationalist agenda for a 'normal nation', which 'stripped to its essence ... simply means a "nation that can go to war"' (Samuels 2007b: 111), has fuelled Chinese concerns about Japan's ever-expanding security role, and occasional paranoia regarding the revival of Japanese militarism. Conversely, neo-nationalism, born out of feelings of insecurity, has made Japan wary of China's spectacular economic and military development, with Japanese defence planners increasingly echoing, albeit subtly, the 'China threat' notion, popularly contrived by their hawkish Western counterparts, media and commentators (see Bernstein and Munro 1997; Gertz 2000). One can argue that China's military modernisation plausibly reflects vigilance and counter-balancing against Japan's evolving security agenda, while Japanese security policy shifts are partly driven by growing concerns over the emerging Chinese security challenge. Compounding their caginess are the unresolved ECS dispute, the 'Taiwan' dilemma in US–Japanese security arrangements, and nationalism's exacerbation of mutual mistrust. Regionally, their rising defence budgets and renewed rivalry are increasing the stakes in East Asian security, as they could undesirably escalate into a Japanese–Chinese arms race (Christensen 1999: 69–71). As Green (2001: 93) noted, these are 'ingredients for a classic defense dilemma' between Japan and China.

Again, such developments echo NCR's assumption that domestic-ideational variables, i.e. historical grievances and nationalism, have the potency to aggravate security dilemmas under changing relative power dynamics and a fluid external environment, such as in the case of Japan's post-Cold War relations with China (Christensen 1999). As highlighted, neo-nationalism's impact on Japanese security discourse and policies has led to a reconceptualisation of mainstream Chinese strategic thinking, whereby Japan is perceived as China's chief future security concern (Shambaugh 1994: 6). Indeed, the Chinese are aware that contemporary Japan has become more powerful and militarily prepared than it outwardly appears to be, despite the constitutional constraints. This includes having among the world's largest military budgets, notwithstanding the SDF's disposition as a strictly self-defence force, and its reputation as a modern, highly sophisticated military boasting top-of-the-range hardware that technically allows Japan to project power far beyond its constitutional rights[23] (Yang 2003: 308; Wang 2002:

110–11). As mentioned in Chapter 2, the SDF's continuous redefinition under a strengthened US–Japanese security alliance has aggravated Chinese suspicions regarding Japan's intention to resurrect its military power status (Wang 2002: 110). The Chinese also saw the US 'war on terror'[24] as an event that has facilitated Japan's rearmament and pursuance of a 'normal state' identity (Yang 2003: 309). They perceive Japan's rising security profile, and the recent joint restructuring of US–Japanese forces as a move that ultimately targets China, with Tokyo becoming what Yu (1999: 10) contends is the fulcrum of Washington's 'containment by stealth' policy and grand strategy in East Asia via their revitalised alliance.

Conversely, the Japanese saw their renewed security orientation as inevitable in view of the challenges imposed by the fluid post-Cold War environment. From the more immediate North Korean 'threat' factor[25] and global terrorism, to growing concerns regarding China's military development and related ambitions in the Taiwan Strait and ECS, these uncertainties have driven Japan to rethink its national security, besides the relentless 'allied' pressure to assume a more prominent international security role (Soerensen 2006: 111). In addition, Japan seeks to become a 'normal state' not only because of the need to be able to act normally in defending its national security interests, but also due to domestic nationalist pressure to redress national identity and international prestige, which has galvanised the transformation of the Japanese security agenda towards 'normalisation' (Singh 2002: 88; Tamamoto 2005b). However, the issue is not so much about Japan becoming a 'normal state', but more whether China can accept a 'normal', rearmed and internationally proactive Japan that would directly challenge its emerging regional influence, and possibly lead to power competition and rivalry for regional dominance. Some Chinese observers even perceive Japan's drive towards 'normalcy' as a nationalist pretext for reviving Japanese militarism (Roy 2003: 4). Ideally, the Chinese would prefer Japan to be continuously 'abnormal', or as Yahuda (2006: 169) observes, a Japan that is 'politically and strategically quiescent until such time as presumably it would be overshadowed by China'.

While Beijing worries about a nationalistic and assertive Japan, Japanese security analysts are wary of China's rise and emergence as a key security concern of the twenty-first century (JFIR 1995). Tokyo's interest, according to observers, is in devising an adequate strategy to manage a rising, but unpredictable China. This includes developing durable ties, and helping the Chinese avert potential domestic instability that could be detrimental to Japan's own security (Roy 2003). Indeed, the 'China threat' to Japan is as much about China becoming a strong military, anti-status quo power as a weak China spawning regional instability.[26] Hence, Japan's contemporary China policy has been to engage, while maintaining sufficient hedging measures to facilitate its emergence as a responsible power and stakeholder in regional security (Drifte 2003).

Nonetheless, domestic support for a policy of engagement has weakened, following the worsening of Japanese perceptions and attitudes towards China resulting from rising nationalism, and apprehensions regarding emerging Chinese capabilities and intentions. Specifically, heightened anxiety over Chinese power, influence and ambitions has elicited vocal complaints from nationalists regarding Japan's overly accommodative posture, and decreased Japanese confidence in the logic of economic interdependence engendering improved politico-security relations with the Chinese (Roy 2003: 3; Yahuda 2006). According to Samuels (2007a: 146), Japanese neo-nationalists of all hues commonly view China as a 'potential threat'; the realists focusing on the PLA's rising military challenge, whereas the neo-conservatives and neo-autonomists spice up the debate with a distinctively anti-Chinese flavour. Underpinning their security concerns have been the steady augmentation of Chinese military capabilities, marked by sustained double-digit annual defence expenditure,[27] and the related lack of transparency in military decision-making and the tendency to under-report actual spending. Bitzinger (2003: 1) notes that most US assessments share the view that 'China's official defense budget greatly under-represents actual military expenditure by a factor of two to three'.[28] The Chinese argue that their defence budget is comparatively lower than that of other developed countries, including Japan, and that the annual increase is mainly for the replacement of outdated hardware, and to cover the basic operating expenditure for its sizeable standing army (*PD* 5 March 2006). However, Japanese and US defence planners alike are aware that China is gradually shifting the military balance with its mass purchasing of sophisticated, power-projection weaponry and defence technologies from Russia, ranging from fighter-aircrafts to submarines and destroyers, besides the development of indigenous defence production capacity (Drifte 2003: 41–8; NIDS 2003). Complemented by the world's third largest nuclear arsenal and a rapidly advancing aerospace industry, China's defence spending trajectories have raised concerns regarding its intentions, as consistently noted in Japanese defence white papers (JDA 2004, 2005, 2006). Ironically, Japanese concerns, as Drifte (2003: 43) contends, 'would have been much less pronounced', if not for China's rapid economic growth.

China's propensity to use force to advance its security interests, i.e. in Vietnam (1979), the South China Sea archipelagos of Paracel (1975) and Spratly (1995), and most glaringly, during the 1996 Taiwan Strait crisis, fuelled Japanese anxiety regarding potential Chinese belligerence when managing their maritime territorial dispute in the ECS. Beijing's forceful handling of the 2002 'Shenyang incident' further aggravated such concerns. Additionally, Japan is wary of China's intention to control sea-lanes crucial to its economic prosperity. The PLA-Navy's metamorphosis into a blue-water navy and increased naval activities indicate Chinese ambition to achieve operational capacity in the South and East China Seas, where it may be able 'to interdict shipping inbound to or outbound from Japanese ports' (Roy 2003: 3). Besides prioritising the development of its submarine force (Goldstein and Murray 2004), the PLA-Navy's repeated vessel incursions into Japanese territorial waters for oceanographic research and alleged naval intelligence gathering operations since the late 1990s are plausibly related to such ambitions (Roy 2003: 3; Drifte 2003: 56–7). Japan's security transformation is, therefore, as much a response to alleviate anxieties about the strategic uncertainties posed by China as to counter North Korea's cavalier attitude

(Funabashi 2000: 136). Japanese nationalists are also drumming up the 'China threat' to justify remilitarisation, and even the prospects of a nuclear-armed Japan to counter Chinese security challenges (Samuels 2007b: 122–3).

Equally fuelling Japanese unease is the brazenly anti-Japanese nationalism flourishing in China. Tokyo is aware of Beijing's conspicuous promotion of anti-Japanese sentiment through education (Kawashima 2005: 19–21) and other propaganda channels for domestic political expedience. Although the Chinese regime is prudent and pragmatic in stoking nationalism, and has had occasionally reined in popular sentiments, the decades of indoctrination and reminders of Japanese misdeeds have cultivated virulent anti-Japanese passion among China's younger generation. Such sentiment has transpired in popular anti-Japanese discourse and demonstrations like those in April 2005 and September–October 2012. Indeed, contemporary Chinese public opinion reflects a zealously nationalistic generation, whose frustrations are predominantly directed against Japan (Shirk 2007: 151–2), exacerbating Japanese concerns regarding the perils of unrestrained Chinese nationalism and Beijing's ability to maintain a pragmatic Japan policy. It is rather ironic that contemporary Japanese insecurity vis-à-vis the Chinese mirrors that of the Chinese towards their neighbour. While the Japanese are concerned about the potential security challenges of resurgent Chinese nationalism and a militarily powerful China, the Chinese are paranoid about the revived threats of Japanese nationalism and remilitarisation to their security interests (Roy 2003).

The Chinese have taken measures to soothe Japanese and neighbouring concerns, especially regarding the 'China threat' perception. Besides publishing defence white papers,[29] Beijing has actively recited the mantra of 'peaceful rise' to reassure neighbours of its intentions (Zheng 2005). Chinese officials and media have also fervently refuted Japanese perceptions, claiming that Japan's defence white papers are misleadingly portraying China as a source of regional instability by exaggerating its military strength/spending (*CD* 18 July 2001; *PD* 3 Aug. 2005). Many of China's 'Japan' commentators perceive the Japanese intention as to sidetrack international attention and provide excuses for their own military development. They also place the blame for the Japanese fixation with the 'China threat' notion mostly on the workings of nationalists (*CD* 18 July 2001). There is an element of truth in such claims, as Japanese nationalists have sought to exploit worsening images of China in Japan to advance their agendas (Rozman 2002), and contemporary Japanese nationalism is indeed directed mainly at China. Such developments have undoubtedly encouraged a policy shift vis-à-vis China 'from commercial liberalism to reluctant realism' (Green and Self 1996: 36).

The above analysis demonstrates nationalism's aggravation of mutual security (mis)perceptions and concerns that encourage the reassessment of one another's security policy and accentuate mutual suspicion and tension. However, it has not led Tokyo (and Beijing) to ruthlessly pursue narrow, nationalist-oriented security goals irrespective of the broader national interests, or at the expense of the bilateral relationship. Moreover, in the age of interdependence, the traditional notions of security have broadened to include more holistic definitions, i.e. economic and environmental security, both of which are crucial to their respective conceptualisation of comprehensive national security (Drifte 1990: 29–31; SCIO 2004).

Japan, specifically, has sought to promote Chinese confidence regarding its shifting security orientation. Although domestic nationalist demands have made Japan's transformation into a 'normal' state inevitable, rational Japanese policy-makers are cautious about letting nationalist agendas dominate their foreign/security policy deliberations, to the detriment of Japanese–Chinese ties. Understandably, pragmatic considerations about Japan's economic vitality, China's moderate posturing in the regional security equation, and cooperation in both conventional and non-traditional security issues (i.e. environmental security), are high on Japanese comprehensive security calculus (Drifte 2003: 70–6). Additionally, domestic pacifist forces, though relatively weakened, remain sound in moderating ultra-nationalist tendencies within the government. Furthermore, despite their apparent nationalistic dispositions, Japanese state-elites have exhibited the political will to balance and maintain a degree of pragmatism in their management of sensitive bilateral security issues. Lastly, Japanese security policies remain constrained by the US–Japan alliance and Washington's overarching security agenda, a position that Beijing is, perhaps, more willing to countenance than one involving a unilateral Japanese remilitarisation. Hence, Japan has been treading cautiously, pushing the national security reform agenda incrementally, while simultaneously reassuring China of its intentions. Tokyo has also been prudent in its official statements regarding China's security developments, and has not openly subscribed to the 'China threat' notion, as reflected in the 'non-committal/carefully-worded' texts found in Japanese defence documents. Indeed, notwithstanding longer term concerns, the overall Japanese perception of China is more of caution than actual fear, and security assessments consider the prospect of conflict with China as '"entirely unlikely" in the immediate future' (Austin and Harris 2001: 94).

Japan's cautious optimism, however, does not render the negative implications of domestic nationalist pressure on Japanese–Chinese impasses baseless, especially when it comes to the ECS dispute, and more so regarding Taiwan. It is also uncertain as to how long such pragmatism can last against the backdrop of confrontational nationalisms that are expected to widen differences in their security interpretations, perceptions, and interests.

Conclusion

This chapter has highlighted the impact of rising nationalist impulses in Japan (and China) on mutual perceptions, images and attitudes that correspondingly affect bilateral relations. It has also exhibited the 'nationalism and foreign policy-making' linkage by identifying the principal policy-makers and other actors who provide nationalism with the agency to influence Japan's China policy. However, nationalism's salience is mediated by other variables that Japanese state-elites have to account for, under particular external–domestic environs and processes, which reflects the NCR schema. Japan's overall management of the issues of history and security vis-à-vis China reveals a plausible fallacy in the conventional wisdom regarding nationalism's efficacy in shaping its actual policy responses and their worsening relationship. Notwithstanding the reality of nationalism's influence on Japanese attitudes, Tokyo's apparent balancing act and noted efforts to ameliorate ties following periodic diplomatic rows highlight the propensity of other determinants to be equally and at times more prevalent in affecting Japanese decision-making pertaining to the bilateral ties. By utilising the NCR framework, nationalism's salience vis-à-vis other external–domestic imperatives will be systematically assessed, via the Yasukuni-*jinja* and ECS disputes, in the following chapters.

5 Case study I

The Yasukuni Shrine dispute

The decline in post-Cold War Japanese–Chinese relations has been associated with rising nationalism, which has exacerbated mutual enmity over 'history' and undermined efforts to seek a genuine reconciliation of their shared past. Amongst the history-related grievances, prime ministerial visits to Yasukuni-*jinja* have become a major impasse, perpetuating as much domestic popular indignation in China as debate in contemporary Japan regarding the need to address crucial questions concerning Japanese national identity and wartime history. The debacle has raised concerns regarding nationalism's salience in undermining a fragile and historically tainted relationship, as Japan seeks to reconcile her national past with her present aspirations to become a 'normal' state and fully fledged player in international politics. Yet, as pointed out in Chapter 4, Tokyo's ability to maintain a functional relationship, seeking timely and calculated diplomatic measures to prevent a free-fall in overall bilateral ties, while promoting dynamic economic interactions, suggest the potential of other factors than nationalism affecting Japanese–Chinese diplomacy and Japan's China policy-making.

This chapter draws on the diplomatic dispute over Yasukuni visits by Japanese premiers, against the backdrop of rising domestic nationalist undercurrents, particularly during the Koizumi administration. A brief background of the contentious shrine and the origins of the dispute are outlined before we look at Koizumi's annual pilgrimages, which sent Japanese–Chinese political relations to arguably their lowest point since 1972. The following sections delve into the bilateral dynamics involved during the periods of contention, paying particular attention to the interactions between domestic nationalist pressure and other external–internal variables via the NCR framework, to assess the extent to which nationalism constrained Tokyo's management of the dispute, as well as the impact on its relationship with Beijing.

Background of the Yasukuni issue

Before examining the origins of the Yasukuni debacle, a brief exploration of the historical background, politico-religious meanings and pseudo-ideological connotations or the *raison d'être* of this institution is essential to understand the controversies it has courted, both domestically and internationally, for post-war Japan.

The origins of Yasukuni Shrine

Yasukuni-*jinja* is a Shinto establishment, located in Tokyo's Kudan district, near the vicinity of the Imperial Palace. Formerly known as *Tokyo Shokonsha*,[1] the shrine was founded in June 1869, under the auspices of the Imperial Meiji government, originally to commemorate 'patriots' who died serving the Emperor and the Imperial cause, during the tumultuous period of power transition from the Tokugawa *bakufu* to the Meiji Restoration of 1868 (Gardner 2002: 666–9; Tokita 2003: 48). The present name 'Yasukuni' was conferred by Emperor Meiji in June 1879, at which time the shrine gained its official designation as *bekkaku kampeisha* (Special Government Shrine) (Deans 2007: 271), and acquired its consequential role as the 'central custodian of national memory and mourning commemorating Japan's war dead' (Harootunian 1999: 144).[2] Prior to the Second World War, Yasukuni-*jinja* was a state institution, jointly managed by the Army, Navy, and Home ministries (Hashizume 2001: 55). As the official ritual epicentre of the State-Shinto ideology, the shrine, via the ministries' screening process, was responsible for enshrining fallen military personnel and citizens who died serving their country.[3] Following Japan's war surrender, the US Occupation forces abolished State-Shintoism and Yasukuni-*jinja* due to their ideological role in fostering militarism, but the latter was subsequently reinstated, albeit as a private, religious organisation under the new post-war Constitution (Deans 2007: 271).

It may seem ironic that 'Yasukuni', literally meaning 'for the country's peace' (Tokita 2003: 48), has unwittingly emerged as a major source of Japan's diplomatic contention with her East Asian neighbours. This predicament has much to do with the shrine's widely acknowledged pre-war function as a vital instrument of the Imperial Japanese state to foster nationalism for nation-building, and symbolic driving force behind national mobilisation for the propagation of its much maligned military 'adventurism' and 'empire-building in Asia' (Lam 2006b: 3: Wan 2006: 235–6). Even more controversial is the fact that Yasukuni's ideological disposition has remained relatively unchanged, not to mention its continuous linkage with and influence on domestic politics, despite the pacific transformation undertaken by post-war Japan, and the repudiation of its 'official' status under the constitutional provision regarding the separation of state and religion. It is such legalities, and its manifestation of elements of pre-war continuity that have politicised Yasukuni into becoming a domestic and diplomatic issue, where 'official visits' and patronage by Japanese heads of state are deemed unconstitutional and perceived as a beacon of Japan's unrepentant attitude towards its role in the Second World War. Simply put, the Yasukuni issue is intricate in that it represents what Mikuriya sees as a 'simultaneous equation' of correlated and conflicting problems, ranging from religion and ideology to perceptions of history, identity and foreign relations (Matsumoto *et al.* 2005: 3).

Nationalism and the politics of identity: the 'Yasukuni problem' defined

One needs to explore the 'sociology/genealogy' of Yasukuni (Breen 2004, 2007), its ideological disposition and their correlations with nationalism and Japanese identity to understand the 'Yasukuni problematique'. For a start, Yasukuni-*jinja* is primarily 'a ritual site', where the spirit of Japan's war dead rest, presumably based on the traditional Shinto practice of venerating the dead, the influence of which can be traced back to ancient Japanese, Buddhist and Confucianist customs (Breen 2004: 77–82; Yamaori 2003: 45). To date, it has enshrined approximately 2.47 million souls, the vast majority being fallen servicemen from the Pacific War (Tokita 2003: 49). Against such a religious and cultural backdrop, pilgrimage to and mourning the dead at Yasukuni would naturally be seen as normal and common practice to ordinary Japanese. As highlighted in Chapter 3, observations of such traditions and rituals are considered an integral part of the cultural uniqueness that forms the Japanese national identity, pre-war and post-war. Indeed, Yasukuni played a substantial role in promoting such traditions during the pre-war era. According to Harootunian (1999: 149), it was commonly acknowledged back then that Japanese soldiers went to battle believing that they would eventually be venerated and worshipped at the shrine as 'national gods of the ancestral land (*sokoku kuni*)', if they sacrificed their lives for the Emperor's cause. Meanwhile, family members were consoled by the belief that they would be reunited with their perished loved ones, who would be honoured as 'national heroes' at Yasukuni. Such beliefs are still held by war-bereaved families in contemporary Japan, and herein is one of the main issues concerning Yasukuni.

Additionally, the concept of a 'national war memorial' is a universally accepted norm, and as such, Yasukuni, according to its advocates, fulfils a similar role to the Arlington cemetery in the US and the Cenotaph in Britain (Tamamoto 2001: 34; McGreevy 2005). In this regard, an official shrine visit to commemorate the war dead is not only a cultural matter, but also a moral duty to be fulfilled by Japanese state leaders. According to the romantic views of Japanese nationalists, Yasukuni is, in Shibuichi's (2005: 199) words, as much an embodiment of Japanese tradition, religion and culture as a 'heartwarming symbol of self-sacrifice and patriotism' that represents the essence of 'Japan's historical identity as a modern nation-state'. Such quixotic perceptions are fundamentally behind their passionate calls for Japanese state-elites to pay tribute and recognise Yasukuni's position at the heart of Japanese national consciousness. Another reason for their unbridled support relates to Yasukuni's symbolism in Japan's war history. The 'revisionist' logic behind Japanese nationalists' unwillingness to compromise to the leftist and Chinese demands over Yasukuni is very similar to their reasons for rejecting the conventional interpretation of Japan's role in the Pacific War, namely the fear of undermining modern Japan's historical identity, and castigating their forebears as war criminals (Tamamoto 2001: 35; Shibuichi 2005: 200).[4]

Furthermore, some Japanese scholars argue that under the constitutional provision of Article 20, freedom of expression of one's religious beliefs should also be allowed to state leaders, and hence prime ministerial visits in a private capacity should not be defined as unconstitutional (Hashizume 2001: 51). Nationalist intellectuals also see Yasukuni as emblematic of Japan's national identity, which the Japanese people can and should rightfully assert, as befitting a sovereign nation (Hashizume 2001). Ultimately, ordinary Japanese regard the

Yasukuni issue as a domestic concern, and thus perceive the unrelenting emotional outbursts and diplomatic pressure by foreign governments, namely China and Korea, as tantamount to interfering in Japan's internal affairs.

Nonetheless, from the perspective of Japan's neighbours and war victims, as well as its own pacifist-oriented citizenry, Yasukuni remains a contentious institution, a remnant of the pre-war system that continues to exude an ideological aura and political influence in post-war Japanese society. According to Matsumoto, the problem with Yasukuni is that it 'still retains a distinct flavour of State-Shinto, the official cult of prewar Japan', and that 'the element of political ideology is too strong', which makes it 'inappropriate for a religious institution', even without strong external criticisms (Matsumoto *et al.* 2005: 25). Not only is it the symbol of militaristic nationalism synonymous with the 'belligerent' Japan of the pre-war and wartime eras, Yasukuni is controversial precisely because of its continuous propagation of such ideals, and its infallible advocacy of Imperial Japan's wartime actions as 'just' and 'divine'; notions that are backed by strong domestic political support, notably from the LDP (Harootunian 1999). This can be observed from the shrine's notorious role in eulogising Japan's war past, as reflected in its Yushukan 'war museum', and perhaps, even more so, by its decision to secretly enshrine fourteen Class-A war criminals in October 1978, allegedly with the tacit acquiescence of the Japanese authorities.[5] In fact, their enshrinement has become arguably the centrepiece of the Yasukuni debacle, since its revelation back in spring 1979.

There are also scholarly opinions that the 'unique' Yasukuni enshrinement rituals are not genuinely rooted in ancient Japanese traditions, as commonly and superficially understood by ordinary Japanese.[6] Instead, such practices were mostly an 'invented tradition' undertaken by the Meiji administration to cultivate nationalism through pseudo-religious beliefs, to meet the political needs of the modern Japanese state (Breen 2004, 2007). Fukuda and Yamaori (2004: 37–8) see the Yasukuni dispute as being 'inextricably caught up with the design of Japan's transformation … in the nineteenth century', where the Meiji oligarchs 'invented' the State-Shinto ideology, based on traditional folklore, beliefs and customs, to provide a spiritual foundation for the sustenance of Japanese identity, as they strove to transform Japan into a modern nation-state. Yasukuni thus unmistakably represents the essence of modern Japanese pre-war identity and nationalist ideology that was employed by the State to mobilise the Japanese people for war and conquests on the Asian continent. In this light, its conspicuous presence in post-war Japan, coupled with the official visits by Japanese leaders and senior government personnel, have drawn both domestic and international criticism, condemning such homage as inappropriate, due to the shrine's historical legacy and parochial ideals. Some critics associate such visits with the revival of chauvinistic nationalism and Japanese militarism, while others perceive them as a sign of 'historical amnesia' representing Japan's enduring inability to reflect on its wartime responsibility and actions (Dolven 2002: 60–1; Miller 2002; Shibuichi 2005).

The Yasukuni problem is double-edged in that it involves contending participants from both Japanese domestic politics and foreign relations, with the nationalist-rightists vying against their leftwing counterparts in the domestic arena, and China and the two Koreas as the external disputants (Wan 2006: 236). Domestically, the staunch supporters of prime ministerial visits derive mainly from three broad nationalist groupings, namely major nationalist-rightwing pressure groups, smaller *uyoku* organisations, and nationalist intelligentsia who disseminate their ideas via the mass media (Shibuichi 2005: 200–3). The first is commonly acknowledged as the most powerful and influential politically, with key organisations like Nihon Izokukai wielding financial and electoral clout via its sizeable membership (Shibuichi 2005: 200; Breen 2007: 5). Together with Jinja Honcho, Nippon Kaigi, Issuikai and veterans' associations like the Military Pension Federation (gunjin onkyu renmei), Association to Commemorate the Spirit of Fallen Heroes (Eirei ni kotaeru kai[7]) and the Yasukuni Worship and Tribute Society,[8] these 'nationalist' organisations have put sustained pressure on Japanese politicians to pay tribute at and restore state patronage of Yasukuni-*jinja* (Shibuichi 2005: 200; Breen 2004: 85–7; Harootunian 1999: 157). Shibuichi (2005: 200–1) observes that their political influence lies in the fact that these groupings have close ties and overlapping membership with the LDP, with some serving as LDP Diet-members, and senior LDP politicians often chair these organisations. Since the LDP is widely noted as a 'catchall party' for conservative/ ultra-nationalist groups and individual politicians, the intimate connection and dependence on electoral support compel LDP politicians/state-elites to satisfy the demands of these organisations (Shibuichi 2005: 200; Lam 2006b). Japanese premiers from the LDP are, like any LDP politicians, susceptible to domestic nationalist pressures to visit Yasukuni[9] (Shibuichi 2005: 201).

Conversely, domestic participants from the opposite end of the ideological spectrum comprise leftist political parties, i.e. JSP/SDPJ, JCP, and pacifist NGOs and the leftwing media mentioned in Chapter 4. The leftists/pacifists repudiate the idea of Yasukuni's relationship to Japanese identity, perceiving it as the symbol of a militaristic Imperial Japan responsible for the war sufferings of its neighbours and its own people, which was ultimately buried in the ashes of the Second World War defeat (Shibuichi 2005: 203). Meanwhile, China and Korea represent the key external disputants. From the viewpoint of the Chinese government and people, specifically, Yasukuni-*jinja* induces memories of past humiliations and sufferings under the yoke of Japanese imperialism and military aggression, which provoke popular resentment and official displeasure towards the shrine (Deans 2007: 285–9). With a nationalistic Chinese population fed on decades of patriotic education of distinctly anti-Japanese colouration, and the CCP state's dependence on nationalism as a legitimisation tool, one would expect popular Chinese indignation accompanied by strong diplomatic protests from Beijing, in reaction to Japanese prime ministerial visits to Yasukuni.[10]

Obviously, Yasukuni evokes contending meanings and images for those involved in the dispute. With each disputant's identity defined by the respective image and meaning held by them of this shrine, Shibuichi (2005: 199) concurs that Yasukuni unavoidably serves as a trigger for a clash of identities, which is fundamental to understanding the problem itself. Scholars also stress the need to consider the shrine's instrumentality in the context of domestic ideological and political competition, and worth as a diplomatic card in Japan's relations with the disputant-states (Rose 2007; Deans 2007). As will be demonstrated, the Yasukuni debacle in Japanese–Chinese ties is not merely the case of clashing nationalisms/identities, but also utilised by state-elites for domestic political and diplomatic expediency. It illustrates the manifestation of the psychological/ emotional and political/instrumental properties of nationalism, where state-elites' external perceptions and calculations are influenced by sense/passion as much by sensibility/reason, with one prevailing over the other, depending on the time and conditions.

Yasukuni Shrine as a domestic issue

Domestically, Yasukuni Shrine first emerged as a political issue in the early 1950s, when Nihon Izokukai[11] staunchly advocated its (re)nationalisation, as a means of securing state tribute to the war dead and pension for the bereaved families (Breen 2004: 86). Its cause was championed by the LDP, which on five occasions between 1969 and 1974 sought, albeit unsuccessfully, to submit bills to the Diet calling for Yasukuni to be granted special status and placed under state patronage (Tokita 2003: 48). Strong resistance from leftwing bodies eventually forced the LDP to abandon the nationalisation bill, compelling the shrine's proponents to recalibrate their focus towards realising official visits by Japanese premiers and Cabinet members as their major political agenda (Tokita 2003: 49; Rose 2007: 26). In fact, the term 'official' has since become diluted to simply being 'prime ministerial visits' (Tanaka 2003). Interestingly, prime ministerial visits never elicited much contention before 1975, with most post-war premiers, from Shidehara Kijuro onwards, having paid homage, while annual visits by the Emperor[12] during auspicious festivals were considered a norm. However, the declaration of the 'private nature' of the April 1975 visit by then-PM Miki Takeo (Deans 2007: 272), triggered a fierce, 'left-versus-right' debate within Japanese politics, in the context of the constitutional separation of religion and state, which has since transformed Yasukuni into a highly politicised domestic issue (Tokita 2003: 49). Core to the debate is the constitutionality of such visits in both private and official capacities, and the definition of and differences between them (Sono 2005). Previous homage by Japanese premiers had been largely interpreted as private, as indicated explicitly beforehand, or implicitly, by their quiet visitation and their eschewing of the use of any symbols of official trappings and subtle changes in ceremonial rituals during such visits (Wan 2006: 236–7). Nonetheless, critics argue that what constitutes 'official' or 'private' is subjective, ambiguous and tends to overlap, and that it is difficult to objectively distinguish the two categories (Sono 2005: 52). In view of such ambiguity, state leaders should thus refrain from visiting Yasukuni, to avoid the possibility of infringing the related constitutional provision.

The shrine courted more domestic controversy in 1979, when *Asahi Shimbun* revealed its secret enshrinement of Class-A war criminals the year before, sparking further debates on the legality of the decision, and possible government involvement and contravention of the related constitutional provision (Lam 2006b: 3). According to Tokita (2003: 49), the Yasukuni authorities defended their action, citing the 1953 Law for Relief of War Victims and Survivors as having granted equal status to the deceased war criminals, which allowed them to be treated like other war dead, and that their castigation was 'an act of arbitrary condemnation' of the vanquished, based on victor justice. Meanwhile, the Japanese state denied any involvement in the controversy. In responding to calls for the removal of the war criminals, the government stipulated that it had no legal authority to order the shrine to do so, given the provision in Article 20 of the Constitution (Lam 2006b: 3).

Internationalisation of the Yasukuni dispute

Notwithstanding the fervent Diet debates, Yasukuni remained essentially a domestic issue until the mid-1980s. Visits by Japanese premiers following the mentioned controversies did not provoke significant international criticism. In the context of Japanese–Chinese relations, the Chinese authorities had never taken offence at prime ministerial visits prior to 1985 (Deans 2007: 274–5). Although veiled protests were made in response to homage between 1982 and 1984, none escalated into a diplomatic standoff.[13]

However, the publicised 'official' visit by Nakasone Yasuhiro on 15 August 1985 unexpectedly triggered international opposition, mainly from China and South Korea. The Chinese took offence and vehemently protested at the visit, albeit unofficially, through state and popular channels (Rose 2007: 29–30). A self-professed nationalist, Nakasone declared the visit 'official', despite strong domestic protests from leftist/pacifist groups (Shibuichi 2005: 207). His decision was apparently based on an independent consultative committee's conclusion that 'an official visit would not be unconstitutional if carried out in a manner relatively free of religious elements' (cf. Tokita 2003: 49). The underlying reasons were both political and personal, namely strong pressure from Izokukai, and Nakasone's experience as a military officer during the Second World War (Shibuichi 2005: 206), which underscored his sentiment, and arguably, dependence on nationalist-based political support that required living up to his nationalist reputation. Nonetheless, the Chinese reaction forced Tokyo to seek remedial measures to pacify Beijing, and Nakasone to reconsider future shrine visits. Taking the Chinese protest seriously, he did not visit Yasukuni again during his premiership,[14] despite severe criticisms and character attacks from nationalist groups and rightwing intellectuals, as well as threats of assassination by *uyoku* for allegedly 'kowtowing' to Chinese pressure (*AS* 3 Aug. 2001 cf. Shibuichi 2005: 209). Nakasone's successors followed suit, establishing a temporary moratorium of prime ministerial visits, amid strong nationalist pressure, presumably to avoid further internationalisation of the dispute (Kingston 2004: 238; Shibuichi 2005: 209).

The Yasukuni issue remained dormant in Japanese–Chinese diplomacy throughout the early 1990s, but was resurrected in July 1996, by then-PM Hashimoto Ryutaro's 'private' visit.[15] Apparently, it was not Hashimoto, but Miyazawa Kiichi, who first broke the moratorium by secretly visiting Yasukuni during his tenure (*KN* 25 July 2001). China strongly protested against Hashimoto's pilgrimage, which coincided with the period of rising Chinese nationalism and worsening ties caused by bilateral problems highlighted in the preceding chapters. It is widely construed that Hashimoto made the visit to appease Izokukai, of which he was former chairperson before securing the PM position, ostensibly via Izokukai's clout in LDP politics. Nevertheless, like Nakasone, Beijing's protestation 'effectively prevented him from making another visit [during his premiership]' (Wan 2006: 237). Subsequent premiers, from Obuchi to Mori, avoided the debacle by keeping Yasukuni at arm's length. The Obuchi administration rekindled the call for the removal of Class-A war criminals and purging of Yasukuni's religious nuances, and even proposed the creation of an alternative site in 1999 (Breen 2004: 88).

However, the coming of Koizumi Junichiro in 2001 triggered what was to become the most debilitating period of Japanese–Chinese political relations since 1972, with his Yasukuni pilgrimages at the heart of their diplomatic conundrum. Koizumi became the first post-Cold War Japanese PM to visit the controversial shrine annually during his tenure. These visits were carried out despite fervent protests from China and Korea, and a chorus of international criticism, domestic consternations notwithstanding. In regard to Japanese–Chinese relations, Koizumi's visits forced the infuriated Chinese government to freeze leader summits and top-level exchanges, turning what was merely a symbolic issue into a '*diplomatic faux pas*' (Satoh 2006a: 2; Okazaki 2006).

Koizumi's nonchalance in relation to the Yasukuni issue distinguished him from his predecessors (e.g. Nakasone and Hashimoto), who unlike Koizumi had crumbled under staunch domestic and international pressure that saw them shying away from subsequent shrine visits. Interestingly, this distinction has been closely linked to resurgent Japanese nationalism, and the apparent national fatigue with Japan's 'kowtow diplomacy' and desire to establish a 'normal-cum-equal' relationship with China. This raises questions regarding the extent to which domestic nationalist pressure intervenes and affects Japanese leaders' perception and management of the Yasukuni dispute, and whether such assertiveness is directly induced by the emotional properties of nationalism and identity politics, and/or calculated responses for domestic and diplomatic expediency.

The Yasukuni problem in Japanese–Chinese diplomacy: nationalism and the external–domestic nexus in Japan's China policy-making

Yasukuni Shrine re-emerged as a serious point of contention in Japanese–Chinese ties during the Koizumi administration, at a time when nationalism and the question of identity resonated increasingly loudly within the Japanese domestic political debate and popular consciousness. It also coincided with the changing power relations between the two resident powers of East Asia, in a fluid post-Cold War international environment that has perpetuated a Japanese sense of insecurity, fuelled by China's rise and a flourishing nationalism that seemingly targeted Japan. The juxtaposition and interactions between nationalism and these shifting external–domestic dynamics were responsible for fuelling the 'China threat' perception, and redefining Japanese external behaviour when dealing with the Chinese, as illustrated by Tokyo's tough posturing over the Yasukuni issue.

The following sections examine the international and domestic environments, and the related processes that affected Japanese state-elites' perceptions and calculation, to explicate nationalism's salience vis-à-vis other variables in shaping Tokyo's policy options and diplomatic manoeuvres during Koizumi's shrine visits. Koizumi's defiance and Japan's diplomatic responses to Chinese challenges during each visit between 2001 and 2006 offer an opportunity to analyse the interaction between domestic nationalist pressure and foreign policy behaviour, under particular external–domestic conditions, as perceived/calculated by Japanese state-elites. Many Japanese observers share the opinion that Koizumi's stubbornness, maverick personality, and personal convictions (nationalistic or otherwise) are central to understanding his persistence in visiting Yasukuni.[16] However, a critical examination of the context leading to his shrine visits, and the manner in which they were carefully choreographed and executed, not to mention the diplomatic manoeuvring thereafter, suggest that shrewd calculations involving the use of nationalism for domestic political objectives, and its delicate balancing and trade-off with other factors, were also at play. Moreover, a comparative observation of the ambiguous position taken by Koizumi's successor, Abe Shinzo and his Cabinet on the issue, despite their overtly nationalistic disposition (Lam 2006c), implies that emotional nationalism and domestic nationalist pressure may not necessarily be the driver of Japan's China policy, or the overarching feature of Japanese–Chinese diplomacy after all.

Koizumi and the Yasukuni disputes (2001–2006)

Koizumi's rise to the apex of Japanese politics occurred amid the structural transformation in Japanese–Chinese relations, which saw both governments readjusting to the changing bilateral dynamics since the mid-1990s. His appointment also reflected the shift in Japan's domestic politics, where he became the first Japanese premier elected based on popularity and mass support, instead of the usual backroom negotiations between the LDP *habatsu* that saw relatively obscure politicians appointed to the office previously (Anderson 2004: 152). Against the milieu of rising domestic nationalist impulses, Koizumi would have been responsive to nationalist pressure during his premiership, particularly as he was a popularly elected leader who relied heavily on mass sentiment and media appeal (Iida 2003). In the context of Japan–China ties, his administration would have been reasonably vulnerable to pressures from the mentioned nationalist groups, conservative media coverage and an increasingly sceptical, anti-Chinese public opinion, especially when it came to dealing with Beijing over the Yasukuni problem. That said, mitigating domestic forces and pragmatism in maintaining friendly ties with China to facilitate Japan's broader national interests could have similarly affected Koizumi's policy considerations. This external–domestic nexus in foreign policy decision-making was apparent in the circumstances surrounding Koizumi's inaugural visit in August 2001.

Externally, Japanese–Chinese relations had shown signs of improvement since early 1999, as both governments took 'damage control' initiatives to improve ties, which had been undermined by a series of bilateral disputes culminating in the diplomatic fiasco during Jiang Zemin's 1998 visit. As elaborated, the Chinese leadership resorted to a diplomatic 'charm offensive' after realising the damage caused by their excessive manipulation of the 'history' issue and stoking of popular anti-Japanese nationalism, which had undermined Japanese–Chinese goodwill since the mid-1990s (Rozman 2002). The Obuchi and Mori governments reciprocated China's so-called 'smile diplomacy' (Rozman 2002), bringing a thaw in political ties that complemented their increasingly robust economic relationship. Despite the positive developments, Japan remained cautiously optimistic, adopting a so-called 'reluctant realist' policy of containment-cum-engagement to hedge against potential belligerence from a powerful China (Green 2001), as demonstrated by its incremental security policy shifts under the auspices of an enhanced US–Japan alliance.

The domestic environment in Japan was less sanguine, due to growing public scepticism regarding China's benign rise, and their unfavourable images and unabated resentment of the Chinese. Japanese nationalists and the media exploited this 'thriving' domestic condition, 'demonising' and fuelling the 'China threat' perception to advance their parochial agendas, with prime ministerial Yasukuni visits high on their priority list. Predictably, Yasukuni became a key issue during the run-up to the 2001 LDP presidential election, occupying the campaigns of the two leading candidates – Koizumi and Hashimoto. It was ironic that Hashimoto, the former Izokukai chief, and the most recent of ex-premiers to have visited Yasukuni during his time in office, declared that he would not be repeating the feat if elected again. Meanwhile, Koizumi pledged to pay annual homage on 15 August, and made this promise an integral part of his LDP presidential campaign manifesto. It is believed that he made the pledge on 15 April 2001 to Morita Tsuguo, Izokukai's vice-chairman (Yoshida 2005), in a calculated attempt to distinguish himself from, and cash in on Hashimoto's earlier decision.[17] This timely move, made a week before the election, would have given Koizumi the opportunity to undercut Hashimoto's power base within Izokukai, alienate the latter from other nationalist groups, and consequentially, benefit from their electoral support.[18] Koizumi's decision to woo nationalist support may have proven decisive, as he outpolled Hashimoto 51 per cent to 40 per cent at the parliamentary level, while gaining an 87 per cent to 11 per cent victory margin at the prefectural level (Anderson 2004: 153). Koizumi's pledge drew Chinese (and Korean) concerns, and his election and consequent anointment as PM saw the Japanese and Chinese governments locked in a protracted diplomatic 'tug-of-war' over the Yasukuni issue, culminating in his inaugural visit on 13 August 2001.

Retrospectively, Koizumi's Yasukuni pledge was ill-timed, as April 2001 also saw a resurrection of the history textbook controversy, Li Denghui's controversial visit to Japan,[19] and a trade dispute over agricultural produce,[20] factors which were already straining their relationship (Wan 2006: 237). On the day he assumed the LDP presidency, Koizumi reiterated his intention to fulfil his pledge, much to Beijing's dismay (*KN* 24 April 2001). The Chinese MFA immediately responded with a statement imploring the PM-elect to act responsibly to restore damaged ties and reconsider his plan to visit Yasukuni (Reuters 24 April 2001). This was followed by intensified Chinese pressure during the next few months to dissuade Koizumi from his shrine agenda. During his meeting with South Korea's ruling party delegation on 28 May, President Jiang Zemin criticised Koizumi over the Yasukuni issue, and his management of the textbook controversy (Jiji 28 May 2001). A Chinese MFA spokesperson kept up the pressure days later, by questioning Japan's commitment towards promoting friendly relations, stating that Koizumi would be sending a mixed signal to Japan's neighbours with his shrine visit (XNA 31 May 2001). On 25 June, the Chinese ambassador to Japan purportedly urged Koizumi to rethink his plan (Jiji 25 June 2001), while Jiang again expressed concern in a 10 July meeting with the secretaries-general of Japan's ruling coalition, during their visit to Beijing (*DY/YS* 11 July 2001). It was believed that this inaugural trip by Japan's new coalition government to China and South Korea came with a correlated errand to placate its hosts, and explain Japanese position concerning the history textbook and Yasukuni visit.[21] Predictably, the Chinese rebuffed such efforts and remained adamant that Japan should carefully manage the 'history' problem, conveying their displeasure at Koizumi's insensitivity towards both issues (*JT* 11 July 2001). Upon their return, Koizumi was briefed, and urged by the secretaries-general to carefully reconsider his plan (Wan 2006: 238), but the PM reaffirmed his resolve to visit during a pre-Upper House election debate with the opposition (*JT* 12 July 2001). China pressed on during the mid-July ASEAN-Plus-Three meeting in Hanoi, when Tanaka Makiko was told by China's FM, Tang Jiaxuan, that the visit 'must be cancelled' (Jiji 24 July 2001). The Japanese FM agreed to relay Chinese concerns, and advise Koizumi (*KN* 26 July 2001), while categorically expressing her personal opposition to the planned homage (*MDN* 31 July 2001). The Chinese leadership also relied on 'China Hand', Nonaka Hiromu, to intervene and persuade Koizumi to cancel his pilgrimage, during the LDP stalwart's trip to China in early August 2001 (*JT* 3 Aug. 2001).

Besides external pressures, Koizumi encountered domestic opposition from within and outside the LDP, and ambiguous public support towards his Yasukuni visit. All the opposition parties were against it, while moderate LDP lawmakers, i.e. current and ex-secretaries-general, Yamasaki Taku and Kato Koichi, urged Koizumi to be prudent and suggested changing the date of the visit (*KN* 7 Aug. 2001). In fact, during the cabinet meeting on 7 August, most members wanted the PM to exercise caution, while stating their own apprehension about visiting Yasukuni on the symbolic 15 August (Wan 2006: 240). However, Yamasaki had confirmed earlier that the pilgrimage would 'certainly be made', pending a decision on the date by Koizumi (*JT* 6 Aug. 2001). Public opinion surveys by *Asahi Shimbun* also revealed a shift towards a more cautious position by early August, in light of intense media scrutiny and debate on the issue, with those supporting the visit declining to 26 per cent from 42 per cent, a month before (Takashina 2001: 50).

Despite the opposition, Koizumi stood by his decision and visited Yasukuni, albeit two days earlier than the promised date. The visit received blanket international and domestic media coverage, with commentators associating it and other recent 'taboo-breaking' developments with rising nationalism in Japan. With regard to Japanese–Chinese ties, Koizumi's uncompromising posture towards Chinese demands suggests increasing domestic nationalist constraints on Japanese state-elites in China policy-making. That said, one could equally contend that the 'change-of-date' strategy represented a political compromise by Koizumi to appease the contending participants located at the opposite ends of the Yasukuni dispute. This brings us to question nationalism's salience vis-à-vis other factors/actors, and their roles in determining the particular policy option taken by the Koizumi administration.

Not surprisingly, Beijing issued a strongly worded official statement in protest at the visit (BBC 13 Aug. 2001). Stronger diplomatic reactions ensued, such as Chinese refusal to grant a bilateral summit with Koizumi, and Jiang's intention to cancel his meeting with the Japanese premier come October's APEC convention in Shanghai (*ST* 18 Aug. 2001). Conversely, the Japanese government was surprisingly keen to mend relations in the aftermath of the standoff, with Koizumi repeatedly indicating his desire to visit China before the APEC summit (*JT* 27 Aug. 2001, 5 Sept. 2001). Tokyo's 'fence-mending' efforts were subsequently, albeit ironically facilitated by the '9/11' incident, which dramatically altered 'the parameters of Sino-Japanese relations' (Wan 2006: 244). With both sides eager to shelve the Yasukuni issue to smoothen the path for cooperation in the US-led campaign against terrorism (Bezlova 2001), Koizumi seized this window of opportunity to make amends during his 8 October working visit to Beijing (AFP 8 Oct. 2001). His widely reported 'friendly' gestures during the trip drew favourable Chinese remarks, which helped lessen political tension (XNA 8 Oct. 2001). Japan–China ties regained traction following further cordial exchanges at the sidelines of regional multilateral fora. Despite these diplomatic efforts, and the 'benefit of the doubt' given to him by the Chinese government (Wan 2006: 245), Koizumi refused to rule out future Yasukuni visits, as demonstrated by his 'non-committal' press statements during his high-profile China trip (*JT* 9 Oct. 2001).

Beijing was clearly infuriated when Koizumi decided to make it a routine with his second Yasukuni trip on 21 April 2002. The 'Spring Festival' visit took the Chinese by surprise, for they probably did not expect Koizumi to be that indecorous after having only recently made positive remarks about Japan–China ties, during the Boao Forum in Hainan (*JT* 13 April 2002).[22] Moreover, both sides were planning an elaborate celebration in September to mark the thirtieth anniversary of diplomatic normalisation. The Chinese response was ritualistic, with the Vice-FM summoning the Japanese ambassador (XNA 21 April 2002), while the MFA swiftly issued an official statement denouncing the visit (AFP 21 April 2002). Beijing also postponed scheduled defence exchanges, namely the April visit to China by JDA chief, Nakatani Gen, and the inaugural port calling of a Chinese warship to Japan in mid-May 2002 (AFP 23 April 2002), but surprisingly, proceeded with senior CCP leader Zeng Qinghong's Japan visit (AFP

25 April 2002). Nonetheless, Chinese indignation ultimately saw the cancellation of Koizumi's state visit to China, and postponement of the summit scheduled to coincide with the anniversary celebration (*AS* 9 Aug. 2002).[23]

Koizumi appeared unfazed by the adverse impact his shrine visits had on the political atmosphere of the bilateral ties. With political relations worsening amid fresh Chinese protest over the disputed Senkaku/Diaoyudao in early January 2003, the 'maverick' premier paid another visit to Yasukuni on 14 January, making it his third in as many years. Again, the Chinese seemed unable to do anything more than lodge official protests (*JT* 15 Jan. 2003). However, it became clear by then that Koizumi was unwilling to yield to Chinese pressure, while the new Hu-Wen leadership was not in a favourable position, domestically, to compromise over the Yasukuni diplomatic *faux pas*, for fear of nationalist retribution. The Chinese government thus had to maintain an assertive stance, by repeatedly rejecting Japanese proposals for a bilateral summit between their state leaders, and by making a halt to Yasukuni visits the prerequisite for any top-level exchanges to materialise. China's hardened posture was demonstrated by FM Kawaguchi's repeated failures to arrange Koizumi a state visit to meet President Hu Jintao, during her trips to China, and Premier Wen Jiabao's lukewarm response to Koizumi's invitation to visit Japan (*KN* 7 April and 7 Oct. 2003). Indeed, Wan (2006: 249) thought it was probably Chinese intention to snub Koizumi by choosing Kan Naoto, the DPJ leader, for Hu's first meeting with Japanese political elites, in his capacity as China's new head of state. That said, Koizumi was able to meet Hu in St Petersburg on 31 May 2003, on the sidelines of the Russian city's tri-centennial celebration, where amiable exchanges transpired between the two leaders and foreign ministers (*Nikkei* 31 May 2003).

Whilst Hu's pragmatic approach towards Japan, ostensibly influenced by the so-called 'new thinking' on Japanese–Chinese relations discourse, provided opportunity to improve ties, it was Koizumi yet again who decided to rankle and second-guess the Chinese, by reiterating on 19 June that Yasukuni visits would remain on his agenda (*KN* 19 June 2003). The previously highlighted history-related quarrels during the second half of 2003 threatened to strain bilateral relations further. Despite that, China's new leadership appeared less emotional in its handling of these problems, possibly demonstrating eagerness to improve relations, in hope of a reciprocal response from the Koizumi administration over the Yasukuni issue. Beijing also utilised other levels of bilateral interaction, and meetings on the sidelines of multilateral platforms, like the 2003 ASEAN Summit in Bali, to continue to stress the need for Japan to manage 'history' carefully, and restore 'favourable' conditions to facilitate top-level exchanges, in a veiled attempt to pressure Koizumi against further Yasukuni visits (*JT* 8 Oct. 2003). To China's dismay, Koizumi remained adamant to the point of mocking Chinese efforts by insisting that they understood his intention, and that shrine visits would not damage bilateral relations (*KN* 13 Oct. 2003).

The Japanese PM kept to his words by paying his fourth Yasukuni homage on New Year's Day 2004, thwarting any realistic opportunity to improve relations with China that year. The Chinese MFA reacted with the usual diplomatic protests

(*MDN* 2 Jan. 2004), and again postponed the much awaited, mutual navy visit, despite it having only been recently set up again, during the resumption of high-level defence exchanges that saw JDA chief, Ishiba Shigeru, visiting Beijing in September 2003 (Jiji 9 Jan. 2004). Meanwhile, the LDP maintained its staunch support, stating that Yasukuni visits would be declared as part of its political platform, on 16 January 2004, together with constitutional revision and several other nationalist-oriented issues that were once considered taboo (*JT* 7 Jan. 2004).

The Yasukuni debacle continued unabated throughout 2004, compounded by bilateral grievances like the ECS maritime territorial dispute, anti-Japanese incidents during the July Asia Cup football tournament and the Chinese submarine incursion in November. Beijing, nonetheless, pragmatically maintained relations at other levels, while continuously shunning Koizumi, e.g. Wen 'cold-shouldered' Koizumi at the October Asia-Europe Meeting (ASEM) summit in Hanoi (*SCMP* 11 Oct. 2004). Conversely, Tokyo reaffirmed its willingness to improve ties, with Koizumi indicating keenness to meet the Chinese leaders, despite the Yasukuni conundrum (*JT* 11 Oct. 2004). On 21 November 2004, Koizumi met Hu at the APEC summit in Chile, where the latter, for the first time, explicitly mentioned Yasukuni as the major issue stifling Japanese–Chinese political ties, and reminded the Japanese premier of the sensitivity surrounding the year 2005, in an attempt to dissuade another visit by him (*MDN* 22 Nov. 2004). Premier Wen raised a similar concern with Koizumi at the ASEAN-Plus-Three summit in Laos on 30 November 2004 (BBC 30 Nov. 2004). Interestingly, unlike previous occasions, Koizumi did not rebuff the Chinese leaders when questioned by Japanese reporters after those meetings (Wan 2006: 255), but maintained public silence regarding his Yasukuni plan, although many expected him to continue his annual pilgrimage (*DY* 22 Dec. 2004).

With the shrine row still unresolved, the eruption of other contentious issues mentioned in Chapter 2 saw Japanese–Chinese ties sinking to a nadir in 2005. Bilateral tension ratcheted up when the Japanese government assumed ownership of the Seinensha-built lighthouse in Senkaku/Diaoyudao. Then Chinese concerns over the implications of the February 'Two-Plus-Two' meeting on Taiwan saw Beijing responding with the Anti-Secession Law a month later (Kokubun 2007: 145). Compounding the emerging Japanese–Chinese strategic rivalry was Japan's UNSC ambition, which triggered the noted internet petition in China in March. Tokyo's declaration of China's 'graduation' from Japanese ODA after the Beijing 2008 Olympic Games (*YS* 3 March 2005), also did not augur well with the Chinese. The MOE/MEXT's approval of a new edition of Tsukurukai's contentious textbook on 5 April drew further Chinese protests (Nakanishi 2005: 19). All these Chinese grievances resulted in popular anti-Japanese demonstrations across China's major cities that lasted almost three weeks (Kokubun 2007: 138–9). Tokyo demanded a formal apology and compensation for the damage inflicted upon Japanese companies and diplomatic missions, but Beijing refused to budge and instead blamed the Japanese government entirely for the popular outburst (Zhu 2005: 16).[24] Although both sides eventually sought to stabilise relations, Tokyo was clearly annoyed when Vice-Premier Wu Yi unceremoniously cancelled her scheduled 'fence-mending' meeting with Koizumi on 23 May 2005, apparently in reaction against the Japanese premier's 'untimely' reiteration of his Yasukuni resolve before the event[25] (*MDN* 24 May 2005).

As political tension escalated in the following months over the ECS gas dispute and China's indiscreet opposition to Japan's UNSC bid, there were growing calls for Koizumi to visit Yasukuni on 15 August, to show contempt and defiance towards the Chinese. Meanwhile, speculation was rife that Koizumi might utilise Yasukuni to rally support for the 11 September Lower House elections, which were crucial to his domestic reform agenda. Eventually, Koizumi did not turn it into an election issue, nor did he visit Yasukuni on 15 August. Instead, he made his fifth shrine visit during the Autumn Festival on 17 October, following the LDP's 'landslide' electoral victory, which provided the political mandate for him to do so, despite Chinese indignation (*JT* 18 Oct. 2005; Funabashi 2005). The timing of the visit was deemed 'a serious provocation' as it coincided with the success of China's second manned space flight (*KN* 18 Oct. 2005). Beijing instantly protested by summoning the Japanese ambassador, and then postponing senior official-level meetings scheduled later that week, which included FM Machimura's meeting with his Chinese counterpart (AFP 18 Oct. 2005). As if to add further insult to injury, a defiant Koizumi reshuffled his Cabinet on 31 October, appointing well-known 'anti-China hawks' and staunch Yasukuni supporters to key Cabinet positions. They were Abe Shinzo, the new CCS replacing the more moderate Fukuda, who was absent from the new line-up, and Aso Taro as FM (AFP 31 Oct. 2005). Interestingly, the 'moderate' Tanigaki Sadakazu was reappointed Finance Minister (*JT* 1 Nov. 2005). Clearly bemused by Koizumi's audacity, China's leaders ignored their Japanese counterparts at the November APEC summit in Pusan, and together with South Korea, suspended the tripartite meeting under the auspices of ASEAN-Plus-Three in December 2005, freezing all channels of high-level exchanges, including those at the fringes of multilateral foras, as Japanese–Chinese political relations worsened (Togo 2006: 5).

Aware of their powerlessness to change Koizumi's attitude, and realising his term would end in September 2006, the Chinese shifted their attention to and began applying pressure on the prospective LDP presidential/prime ministerial candidates by early 2006. During a meeting with the heads of seven Japan–China friendship organisations on 31 March 2006, President Hu 'extended an olive branch' by indicating his readiness to resume talks with Japanese leaders upon their clarification to halt future Yasukuni visits (*PD* 1 April 2006). However, the Japanese leadership hopefuls were quick to rebuff Beijing, with Abe criticising the Chinese for pinning the fate of their bilateral ties on a single issue, while Aso even labelled China a military threat (*JT* 3 April 2006; Lam 2006b). Abe also suggested that he would continue Koizumi's shrine legacy if elected (*KN* 12 Jan. 2006). Indeed, Abe was known for his nationalistic disposition, and hawkishness towards North Korea, while Aso was perhaps seeking to bolster popular and rightwing support for his presidential campaign by maintaining an anti-China stance, and harping on nationalistic issues, including calling for the Emperor to visit Yasukuni (Reuters 28 Jan. 2006). Conversely, Tanigaki was more prudent, espousing 'strategic ambiguity' on the Yasukuni issue (*KN* 12 Jan. 2006). Both former CCS Fukuda and ex-LDP Secretary-General Yamasaki, opposed prime ministerial visits, with Fukuda, as the 'dark horse' in the presidential race, proposing a secular war memorial as an alternative to Yasukuni (*DY* 11 Jan. 2006). Although Koizumi and Abe called for the exclusion of prime ministerial Yasukuni visits as an issue in the LDP polls (BBC 11 Jan. 2006), it became clear that its politicisation would be unavoidable, with the Japanese nation drawn into the debate.

Meanwhile, there were speculations that Koizumi would make his final visit on the symbolic 15 August, before stepping down. Pressure began to mount, both externally and domestically, with nationalist groups and opinion leaders pressing for a continuation, while moderate forces, including some conservatives, called for a moratorium on shrine visits by Koizumi's eventual successor (Satoh 2006b: 5). Externally, even the US, usually silent about the Yasukuni issue, weighed into the debate, as American expert opinion and media began calling for a review of Japan's Asia and China policies, with the halt to shrine visits presumably at the heart of the debate.[26] Apparently concerned about its ally's increasing political isolation in the region, which could undermine overall American interests, President Bush hinted that Koizumi should stop visiting Yasukuni (*MDN* 2 Jan. 2006).[27] Growing American opposition also ostensibly denied Koizumi the chance to address the US Congress, during his farewell tour of the US in June 2006.

Similarly, public support began to erode, as the average Japanese started questioning the wisdom of continuing such visits, in light of the searing images of massive Chinese, anti-Japanese demonstrations and widespread international criticisms that cost Japan dearly, in diplomatic terms (Satoh 2006b). A July 2006 *Mainichi* opinion poll recorded decreasing public support for Yasukuni visits, from 47 per cent in January to 33 per cent, while those opposing increased from 47 per cent to 54 per cent (cf. *PD* 28 July 2006). Even the rightwing *Sankei Shimbun*'s public opinion survey conducted several months earlier showed 52.6 per cent opposing against 36.2 per cent who supported the visit (*SS* 20 March 2006; cf. Lam 2006b: 10). The *zaikai* also voiced concerns over the potential negative impact of an antagonistic China policy on Japan's national interests, given the significance of their burgeoning economic ties in sustaining Japanese economic recovery. The Keizai Doyukai had, for the first time, explicitly called for a halt to prime ministerial Yasukuni visits, and officially proposed an alternative national memorial, in May 2006 (*DY* 10 May 2006). Meanwhile, Keidanren expressed hopes that the new premier would improve ties with China, and refrain from visiting Yasukuni, as reflected by its chairman, Mitarai Fujio's call for the PM to 'respect public opinion and use his political wisdom to solve the issue of the Yasukuni', and be 'prudent on the issue' (*PD* 29 July 2006).

Pressure mounted on Koizumi and the LDP leadership hopefuls on 19 July, following *Nikkei*'s revelation of a memoir by a former Imperial Palace aide containing information explaining Emperor Showa's sudden decision to stop visiting Yasukuni. The memoir cited the Emperor's displeasure over the enshrinement of the Class-A war criminals, which was, ironically, the very reason behind Chinese opposition towards Yasukuni visits (*MDN* 20 July 2006). Perhaps, most significantly, the intense international opposition and domestic commotion saw Yasukuni's staunchest advocate, Izokukai, uncharacteristically weighing to propose the separation of Class-A war criminals as a possible solution to the impasse (*MDN* 2 Aug. 2006).

Despite the unprecedented opposition, Koizumi made good his 2001 election promise by visiting Yasukuni on 15 August 2006. Many viewed his decision as an intention to defend his 'stubborn maverick' and 'reformer' image, which were key components of his popularity (Yoshida 2006). Although the Chinese protested, it is believed that they had anticipated and somewhat resigned themselves to the idea that Koizumi would pay his last visit as premier on 15 August, and thus, had concentrated on resuscitating the bilateral ties 'on a clean slate' with Koizumi's successor (Tang 2006). With the LDP leadership race revving up and the Yasukuni issue inextricably tied to the election agenda, the front runners – Abe, Aso and Tanigaki – were forced to declare their position under intense public scrutiny. Tanigaki made a concrete decision by declaring that he would not visit Yasukuni, if elected, while both Abe and Aso, interestingly, shifted their initially assertive pro-Yasukuni posture to a more prudent stance. Aso, who was uncharacteristically antagonistic towards China earlier in the year, decisively mellowed down his opinion by opting to visit only when Yasukuni's legal status was changed, while the hardliner, Abe, chose a position of 'strategic ambiguity' initially proposed by Tanigaki (Lam 2006c).

After fulfilling his 'Yasukuni obligation', Koizumi stepped down in September and was succeeded by his protégé, Abe, who emerged victorious in the LDP presidential election. The new PM wasted no time in mending Japanese–Chinese ties, choosing China, instead of the US, for his first official visit, shortly after his anointment in October 2006. This came as a surprise, since few expected a Japanese–Chinese reconciliation to materialise so early into Abe's premiership, especially in view of his previous 'anti-China' stance and nationalistic outlook. Whilst Beijing did not press him for a declaration on his Yasukuni policy, Abe maintained an ambiguous position and did not visit the shrine during his short-lived, first premiership stint. Abe did, however, pay a 'secret' visit in April 2006, months before his appointment, and made a 'sakaki' tree donation during the Spring Festival of 2007 (Nakata 2007).

Power politics versus nationalism and identity politics: a neoclassical realist assessment of Koizumi's Yasukuni policy

Why did Koizumi make those visits? Were they predominantly responses to domestic nationalist pressure, and/or based on his ideological disposition and personal convictions? More importantly, were they strategically calculated decisions and carefully choreographed actions based on accurate or skewed perceptions of domestic and international conditions that warranted an assertive-cum-conciliatory China policy, to fulfil both external and internal expediency, without damaging overall bilateral ties? In utilising the NCR model developed in Chapter 1, this section seeks to map the Koizumi administration's position during each Yasukuni visit within the four quadrants of the NCR diagram, via the assessment of the prevailing international–domestic conditions and actors/ factors, and their interactions, which influenced Japan's China policy-making. Besides the overarching international environment, Japan's perceptions of its allied commitment/resolve and diplomatic leverage towards China will be inferred along with the Koizumi administration's domestic political resolve vis-à-vis nationalist pressure and other domestic constraints, to determine the perceived conditions around the policy options for each visit.

The 13 August 2001 visit

The Koizumi administration came to power at a time when Japan was experiencing a relatively indeterminate post-Cold War international environment. With the exception of North Korea, the demise of the Soviet threat factor relieved Japan from any direct external security threat, strategically altering the regional power balance and rendering the 'China card' in the US–Japan–PRC 'strategic-triangle' relationship obsolete. Concomitantly, the changing international, bilateral and domestic dynamics have generated new challenges and opportunities for Japanese foreign policy-makers. This has brought a noticeable shift in Japan's China policy, from the traditional 'deferential' diplomacy to a more assertive, realist-oriented approach, especially when managing sensitive bilateral issues.

According to NCR assumptions, domestic considerations tend to have foreign policy-making salience under an ambiguous or benign external environment. As such, the obsolescence of China's strategic value in balancing against the USSR, coupled with the impact of resurgent nationalism on Japanese domestic politics, would be expected to affect Japan's China policy-making, and specifically, Tokyo's management of the Yasukuni dispute. The concurrence of these factors probably explains why Japanese PMs during the Cold War era, notably Nakasone and his successors, were 'more prudent and cautious' (Satoh 2006b: 5) about visiting Yasukuni, especially after the 1985 diplomatic row with China, while Koizumi and his post-Cold War predecessors, namely Miyazawa and Hashimoto, were comparatively undeterred by Chinese pressure, in proceeding with their pilgrimages (Shibuichi 2005: 212–13). For instance, it is believed that Nakasone gave priority to the 'de facto strategic alliance' with China, and was thus willing to incur domestic nationalist wrath to appease Chinese demands by terminating his shrine visits (Shibuichi 2005: 207–9). Given the structurally determinate external environment and significance of the 'China card', it was unsurprising that the remaining Cold War premiers – Takeshita, Uno, and Kaifu continued to observe the Yasukuni moratorium. Conversely, both Miyazawa and Hashimoto were more willing to risk damaging relations with China to satisfy domestic demands, in the relatively flexible international conditions produced by the Cold War's demise. The prevailing environment also possibly established the parameters for Koizumi's calculated decisions to make his Yasukuni visits, and advance a more assertive China policy during his tenure.[28]

Additionally, Japan could count on an increasingly favourable alliance commitment/resolve as a result of the enhancement of the US–Japan security alliance, from April 1996 onwards, which saw the Clinton–Hashimoto Declaration establishing new agendas for bilateral security cooperation, with a rising China ostensibly their key strategic consideration. Despite a period of uncertainty following Clinton's so-called 'Japan passing' in 1998 (Zhao 2002: 39), Tokyo would have had eventually taken comfort in Washington's hard-line posturing against Beijing that became conspicuous during the nascent period of the 'neo-conservative' Bush administration.[29] With the 'China threat' theory gaining ground in the US Congress from the mid-1990s, and against the rising diplomatic tensions in the wake of the Belgrade embassy bombing and the EP-3 spy-plane incidents, the Bush administration appeared to favour a 'containment-cum-engagement' policy towards China, with Japan serving as the fulcrum of the US grand strategy in Asia. The influential 'Armitage Report' of 2000 was well received in Tokyo and enthusiastically embraced by the incoming Koizumi government, which possibly foresaw opportunities to realise important foreign and domestic policy goals via a strengthened US–Japan security relationship. In the presence of a presumably hawkish and 'anti-China' US administration, it would not be an exaggeration to say that Koizumi's decision to embrace a pro-American, instead of pro-Asian, foreign policy provided Tokyo with the perception of a sanguine external environment, in terms of favourable alliance commitment/resolve, to seek a nationalistic, 'anti-status quo' China policy. Koizumi's resolute stance in visiting Yasukuni amid mounting Chinese pressure partly reflected this bold policy.

However, Yasukuni is not an exclusively Japanese–Chinese issue, as it also involves South Korea, another US ally in North-East Asia. With Japan identified as the hub of its Asia doctrine, it would not be in Washington's interest to see Tokyo damaging ties with Seoul over a symbolic issue, which could undermine its regional strategy (*KN* 3 Aug. 2001).[30] The decision to shift the date of Koizumi's first visit was believed to be partly influenced by such considerations, besides Tokyo's attempt to allay Chinese and domestic opposition. Indeed, it was reportedly engineered by CCS Fukuda, with the intention of minimising Seoul's response, and the visit's impact on Japan–Korea ties within the American-sponsored 'allied diplomacy' framework, among others (Wan 2006: 240).[31]

In the bilateral context, the Chinese 'smile diplomacy' adopted since 1999 provided 'cautious optimism' for the Japanese government to pursue a more normal-cum-equal relationship with Beijing. Anticipating diplomatic leverage vis-à-vis China, Koizumi could have estimated that a Yasukuni visit would not trigger an excessive Chinese response, in view of Beijing's recent efforts to tone down and reduce the use of 'history' as a diplomatic card. Indeed, a perceived Chinese concession over the 'war apology' issue after the 'Jiang fiasco' could have set a precedent for Tokyo to maintain its assertiveness over other 'history'-related problems. Japan's confidence was bolstered by unusually subdued Chinese reactions towards the history textbook row in April 2001, which were reportedly milder than those of the South Koreans (Yang 2001: 183). To Japanese policy-makers, China's response implied pragmatism in handling the 'history' issue.

Similarly, Beijing's postponement of Li Peng's Japan visit in May 2001 in protest against Tokyo's decision to allow Li Denghui to seek medical treatment in Japan was perceived by Japanese sources as a low-intensity reaction (Przystup 2001b: 97). In view of the timely displays of Chinese pragmatism, a shrine visit would probably trigger similar responses that would not adversely affect Japan–China relations. Also, Japanese policy-makers tend to perceive popular Chinese, 'anti-Japanese' nationalism to be predominantly state-abetted. Thus, popular Chinese protests against a Yasukuni visit would have been considered manageable. Moreover, flourishing trade ties and China's reliance on Japanese investments and ODA would have dampened potential Chinese blowback over an issue of merely symbolic significance.

Furthermore, the Chinese showed signs of tolerating a date change, while Tokyo calculated that Beijing would perhaps give Koizumi the 'benefit of the doubt', as it was his first visit (Wan 2006: 245). *Yomiuri Shimbun* reported that Beijing had indicated to the ruling coalition's secretaries-general in July that it would tolerate a shrine visit on a date other than 15 August (*YS* 8 Aug. 2001). A similar claim was later made by Koizumi's aide that Beijing had made a 'behind-the-scenes' concession by accepting Koizumi's visit, pending a change of date (*JT* 29 Dec. 2003). Koizumi's former political ally, Kato Koichi, ultimately confirmed this speculation, by revealing that a senior Chinese official acting as intermediary for the negotiations had personally conveyed Beijing's acquiescence before his crucial 'last-minute' meeting with Koizumi on 11 August.[32] Hence, despite explicit Chinese pressure against the visit, the prevailing bilateral conditions and mixed signals from Beijing would have had Tokyo perceiving an ambiguous diplomatic position vis-à-vis China.

On the domestic front, Japanese public sentiment towards China has deteriorated, while nationalist demands for an assertive China policy have grown, requiring Koizumi to adequately respond to public opinion. Besides nationalist pressure from within the LDP, generational change across the domestic political spectrum saw the emergence of more nationalistic politicians, who wanted to replace the traditional 'kowtow' diplomacy with a realistic and equidistant relationship with Beijing. According to Wan (2006: 6), 'Koizumi's insistence on visiting the shrine illustrates Japan's desire to reshape its relationship with China on its terms and highlights the transformation of the bilateral relations from a "special" one to a "normal" one at the top level'. Although it is difficult to pinpoint his nationalist convictions, observers have identified Koizumi as a moderate, 'normal-nationalist' (Samuels 2007a/b),[33] who, Tamamoto (2004: 13) insists, is like many in the political class who 'see Japan as ... a sort of "half-state"', and long for its return to 'normalcy'. Both Hashizume (2001) and Satoh (2006a) contend that Koizumi is a reformer who understood the need for Japan to resolve the 'history' impasse in its post-war politics, which is responsible for the long-standing Japanese identity crisis. By visiting Yasukuni, he confronted the 'history' problem straightforwardly, bringing it into scrutiny by exposing it to Chinese criticism (Satoh 2006a: 7), and in so doing, implicitly called on the Japanese to face up and seek reconciliation of their history and identity (Hashizume 2001: 54). Seen in this light, Koizumi's

Yasukuni policy was plausibly part of his agenda to reinstate Japan as a 'normal' state. It was also an indication of his resolve to realise other related moderate-nationalist/neo-conservative goals, namely a more dynamic and assertive, albeit pro-US external orientation, constitutional revision and the re-establishment of the military as an instrument of Japanese foreign policy. Objectively, Koizumi was an astute politician, who knew how to manipulate the symbolic and political values of Yasukuni to his political advantage, to advance his policy agendas.

Although attributing Koizumi's single-mindedness on Yasukuni to his nationalistic conviction is debatable, it is undeniable that he was under pressure from nationalist-rightwing groups to fulfil his electoral promise. However, one might query his decision to place himself in a politically vulnerable position, by making the initial deal with Izokukai, and undertaking the visit, despite commanding immense popular pre-election support and enjoying incredibly high approval ratings during the nascent months of his premiership.[34] Observers cited personal convictions, either nationalist or otherwise,[35] but a more objective answer lies in the anticipated political drawbacks of his unprecedented domestic reform agenda to transform Japan's cumbersome, 'developmental state' political economy. Koizumi's quest to eradicate the entrenched political and business culture, and in so doing, destroy the LDP's *modus operandi* and traditional pillars, especially Keisei-kai's dominance, created many political enemies and oppositions within the ruling party, and alienated *zoku* support from traditional business sectors (Shibuichi 2005: 210).[36] In this sense, Koizumi's Yasukuni pledge may be attributed to a perceived need to rely on Izokukai's political clout and rightwing support to gain an electoral edge over Keisei-kai's Hashimoto,[37] and then to ensure their continuous political backing for his domestic reforms.[38] According to a former Japanese ambassador to China, there was no nationalist pressure on Koizumi to make the Yasukuni pledge, but he did it out of political considerations. His decision to visit the shrine as much emboldened Japanese nationalist voices as fuelled Chinese nationalism, which, in turn, stimulated reactive popular anti-China sentiments in Japan.[39]

Moreover, unlike his predecessors, Koizumi encountered insignificant domestic political opposition over Yasukuni visits, following the weakening of the SDPJ, JCP and other leftist/pacifist bastions. Meanwhile, Japan's largest opposition party, the DPJ, is conceivably another 'catchall party' comprising as many progressive politicians as right-leaning Diet-members who supported shrine visits, whilst smaller parties like the Liberal Party, and the LDP coalition partners, Shin-Komeito and Hoshuto, although apprehensive, were not vocally influential. As such, the aforementioned domestic opposition, launched by the usually sympathetic and 'pro-China' voices of the Japanese progressives, was somewhat ineffective. Conversely, Koizumi received a timely boost when 105 lawmakers forged a non-partisan group to support his decision, and three ministers confirmed their intention to visit Yasukuni,[40] on the same day a majority of his Cabinet members expressed their wariness of his plan (*JT* 8 Aug. 2001).

Koizumi also enjoyed strong public support for his planned pilgrimage, based on *Mainichi Shimbun's* pre-visit opinion polls (Figure 5.1).[41] Although the support figures declined in the 4 August *Asahi Shimbun* poll, with only 26 per

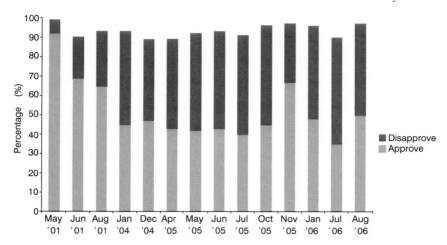

Figure 5.1 Japanese public approval of prime ministerial visits to Yasukuni (2001–2006)

Source: Mainichi Daily News/Mainichi Shimbun (various issues); adapted from Phil Deans, 'Diminishing returns? Prime Minister Koizumi's visits to the Yasukuni Shrine in the context of East Asian nationalisms', *East Asia*, 24 (Oct. 2007), 269–94, table 4 (with kind permission from Springer Science+Business Media B.V.)

cent supporting his visit 'positively', while 65 per cent wanted Koizumi to be 'cautious', the poll had apparently skewed the outcome by forcing respondents to choose between the two alternatives, thus encouraging 'neutral' or undecided respondents to opt in favour of 'caution' (cf. Takashina 2001: 50). Moreover, opinion polls by other broadcasting media agencies found the majority supporting the visit: Nippon Broadcasting System (3 August) found 76 per cent supporting a 15 August homage; TV Asahi (4 August) recorded a 59 per cent support rate; and Fuji Television Network (10 August) reported 48.8 per cent (cf. Takashina 2001: 50). These figures suggest most Japanese supported Koizumi's plan, giving him a favourable domestic climate for proceeding with the visit.

The *Kantei* also enjoyed decision-making leverage under the political and administrative reforms law mentioned in Chapter 4, which saw a corresponding reduction in MOFA's bureaucratic influence on foreign policy-making, generally, and its China Division's traditionally strong foothold in shaping Japan's China policy. Indeed, Wan (2006: 243) noted that the MOFA 'was not central to Koizumi's decision', as the PM appeared undeterred by bureaucratic opposition, including FM Tanaka's explicit disagreement over his planned visit. Apparently, the MOFA was in turmoil over scandals involving senior bureaucrats, and Tanaka's allegedly inept management style, which affected public confidence and created a rift between Koizumi and herself (Nabeshima 14 Aug. 2001). This chasm led Koizumi to bypass the MOFA on the Yasukuni issue, and Tanaka was not even informed of the decision to shift the date of the visit, as decision-making ostensibly centred around the *Kantei* (*YS* 14 Jan. 2001).[42] The PM was equally unfazed by Nonaka Hiromu's criticism, suggesting the waning influence of *kuromaku* in China policy-making (*KN* 5 Aug. 2001). Incidentally, Koizumi and Nonaka had previous disagreements over his domestic reform agenda, not to mention the latter being the 'deal-maker' for his LDP election rival, Hashimoto (*JT* 24 April 2001), which made Koizumi all the more dismissive of the old 'China Hand's' suggestions (*AS* 30 July 2001; cf. Wan 2006: 239).[43] Nonetheless, it was evident that internal pressure and advice from Cabinet members and trusted political allies did have an impact on Koizumi's decision-making, as his minimal 'date-changing' compromise suggests. Indeed, the decision transpired following the mentioned 'eleventh-hour', 'dinner-cum-discussion' with two of his closest political allies, Yamasaki Taku and Kato Koichi,[44] and CCS Fukuda Yasuo's advice (*KN* 11 Aug. 2001; *YS* 14 Aug. 2001). Koizumi also reportedly received the guidance and blessings of Izokukai's deputy president, Koga Makoto (ex-LDP secretary-general) (*YS* 17 Aug. 2001), which cleared a key domestic-nationalist obstacle for Koizumi to proceed with the altered arrangement.

Overall, it is fair to conclude that Koizumi's decision to visit was based on the perception/calculation of an ambiguous external environment (relative power position) shaped by favourable alliance commitment/resolve, but somewhat indeterminate diplomatic leverage vis-à-vis China, following mixed signals from Beijing. However, his administration did consider the potential repercussions of China's response, and had taken measures to seek Chinese understanding before and after the visit, which included the 'change-of-date' strategy, conciliatory pre-visit press statement[45] (BBC 13 Aug. 2001), feasibility studies for a secular war memorial (*JT* 19 Aug. 2001), and Koizumi's much publicised 'friendly' gesture during his October visit to China. Domestically, Koizumi would have perceived himself to be in a less favourable position, insofar as his dependence on nationalist-rightwing support made him vulnerable to nationalist demands, his personal conviction notwithstanding.[46] It could be that Koizumi felt he had no choice but to fulfil the promise, since his popularity depended on his reputation as a reformer and a strong-willed leader. Also, Koizumi could have anticipated the need to utilise Yasukuni as a 'litmus test' to demonstrate his resolve on domestic reform programmes (Taniguchi 2005: 449). Moreover, insignificant domestic opposition gave him political room to manoeuvre and make the visit, either for political expediency or nationalist conviction.

In view of the stipulated conditions, one could locate Koizumi's position between quadrant C and D in the NCR model (Figure 5.2). An ambiguous external environment, taken together with unfavourable domestic political resolve vis-à-vis nationalist pressure, required Koizumi to seek assertive–nationalist policy options (visiting Yasukuni) to satisfy nationalist demands, followed by visible, conciliatory measures to reduce the negative impact on bilateral ties.

The 21 April 2002 visit

In the NCR schematics, the international environment leading to the 2002 visit remained relatively favourable for the Japanese government to maintain a high posture towards China. For one, the '9/11' incident provided the basis for intensified

US–Japan security cooperation, and Japan took advantage of the growing public fear of international insecurity to answer its ally's call for a 'global war on terror'. The Afghanistan campaign not only provided the opportunity for Koizumi to strengthen US–Japan ties, but also gave Tokyo the necessary justification to augment its international security role, under the pretext of assisting its ally in the UN-sanctioned operation. The intensification of the US–Japan alliance would have had Tokyo feeling confident of a favourable allied commitment/resolve as it proceeded with the repositioning of its bilateral relationship with Beijing. Moreover, Washington's subsequent silence over the previous Yasukuni row, despite initial voices of concern, would have emboldened Koizumi's resolve to pursue his shrine routine (*KN* 14 Aug. 2001).

Concurrently, Japanese–Chinese ties were on the mend, and mutual efforts to forge constructive relations had gained momentum since '9/11'. Although a reluctant partner in the US 'war on terror', Beijing did not allow the speedy Diet passage of defence bills in October 2001 that expanded Japanese security activities to sidetrack the improvement of bilateral ties. Chinese pragmatism was also due to flourishing trade relations, and continued dependence on Japanese investment and aid to fuel economic development. It is reasonable to suggest that Beijing's keenness to improve relations was partly to facilitate the disbursement of Japanese ODA, which was delayed by strained ties over the 2001 Yasukuni debacle (*JT* 6 Aug. 2001). On Japan's part, Koizumi took full advantage of the 8 October visit to demonstrate his eagerness to reconcile with the Chinese. His symbolic gestures in visiting Luguoqiao and the nearby war memorial hall, and expressing his apology,[47] followed by meetings with Jiang Zemin and Zhu Rongji, managed to pacify and convince the Chinese of his intentions (Bezlova 2001). Indeed, a former Japanese ambassador who witnessed the events states that Jiang was 'very happy' and 'almost embraced Koizumi'.[48] Reportedly, a congenial atmosphere transpired following the 'fence-mending' rendezvous (Przystup 2002a: 90–1).

According to Japanese analysts, Koizumi's China trip was apparently timed to coincide with the US's first strike on Afghanistan, to put indirect pressure on the Chinese to reciprocate Japan's 'fence-mending' efforts and promote stable bilateral ties to facilitate cooperation with the US (Wan 2006: 244). The Japanese government maintained the thrust of reconciliation after the successful visit with bilateral summits at the fringes of the APEC and ASEAN-Plus-Three meetings. Beijing's responsiveness in improving ties also convinced Tokyo of Chinese pragmatism in managing their symbolic 'history' disputes, which included the Yasukuni issue. Koizumi could have, therefore, calculated that future shrine visits would not seriously impede Chinese will to maintain a functional relationship with Japan.

Nonetheless, the timing of the second Yasukuni visit was apparently calculated with China in the equation. China's Japan experts, like Wan Xinsheng and Lin Xiaoguang, considered the April visit to be propitious, as it would have allowed ample time for criticisms to subside by the fall of 2002, thereby minimising its harmful effects on their thirtieth anniversary celebration of diplomatic normalisation (cf. Wan 2006: 246). Also, Koizumi must have thought that his positive exploits at the Boao Asia Forum had won him sufficient Chinese goodwill to mitigate the impact of his visit.[49] Tokyo would have anticipated that Koizumi's remark on 'China as not a threat but an opportunity to Japan' made during the Forum (*JT* 13 April 2002) would undercut the magnitude of Chinese response towards his subsequent Yasukuni visit, since it would not be in China's interest to overreact and prove him wrong so soon. Indeed, Koizumi told reporters before the homage that 'it is the best timing' for a visit (*JT* 22 April 2002). Moreover, from a region-wide perspective, Koizumi's inaugural shrine trip did not trigger criticisms from ASEAN-states, whose officials were noticeably silent over the issue during Yamasaki Taku's diplomatic rendezvous to South-East Asia in the aftermath of the visit (*AS* 23 Aug. 2001; Wan 2006: 242). Notwithstanding Korean responses, the anticipated bilateral position and prevalent regional climate vis-à-vis China and the ASEAN-states would have given Tokyo confidence to press on with future shrine pilgrimages without being overly concerned about damaging Japan's regional interests.

Domestically, Koizumi may have continued to perceive the need to garner support from nationalist groups and maintain his 'reformer' image in the eyes of the Japanese public, in order to push forward his reform agenda. Since it was only his second year in office, and the reform programme had barely taken shape due to strong anti-reform forces, Koizumi knew he had to keep on portraying himself as a strong leader, different from his predecessors, as this endeared him to the public. In fact, Koizumi faced severe opposition from within the LDP regarding his postal privatisation policy during April 2002, and public scepticism began to mount about the prospect of and his resolve towards the reform programme (Anderson 2004: 176; Koizumi and Shiroyama 2002: 11). Compounding Koizumi's domestic problems was the scandal that hit his political ally, Kato Koichi, who was forced to resign briefly from the LDP and the Diet in April over improprieties involving his former aide (*YS* 9 March 2002). The incident was a major embarrassment that somewhat undermined public confidence regarding his administration's commitment toward political and economic reforms. Growing public scepticism saw Koizumi's personal approval ratings dropping 40 percentage points, a year after taking office (BBC 8 April 2002). He also probably lost some popular and political support after firing Tanaka Makiko in January 2002 (Murata 2006: 44).[50]

Feeling under pressure, the timing of the second Yasukuni trip possibly reflects Koizumi's calculated intention to bolster faltering domestic support.[51] By visiting Yasukuni annually, and not faltering under Chinese pressure, Koizumi intended to demonstrate unwavering commitment to his pledges, since action speaks louder than words. Moreover, maintaining an assertive China policy was in line with popular sentiment and appreciated by nationalists, both within and outside political circles. Koizumi was obviously emboldened to make another shrine visit, since the previous trip had not hurt him politically in the domestic arena, with the public largely supporting it. Furthermore, the 'change-of-date' strategy had not adversely affected his reputation in the eyes of Japanese nationalists. A *Mainichi Shimbun* opinion poll conducted soon after Koizumi's first visit revealed that 65 per cent supported his decision, with only 28 per cent opposing it (*MDN* 21 Aug. 2001).

The manner in which Koizumi made his second Yasukuni trip also indicates a calculated strategy for domestic political expediency. According to Tanaka (2003), although superficially appearing to be a 'surprise' and an 'unofficial' visit, the large media presence and coverage suggest that the PM had intended all along to utilise the event to impress nationalist groups and the general public. Tanaka noted that Koizumi reportedly arrived at Yasukuni much earlier on the day of visit. However, the apparent 'time wasting' by the usually 'schedule to the minute' premier before appearing at the main altar to perform the rituals was, in Tanaka's opinion, intentionally arranged to allow the media sufficient time to converge and cover the event, to make it look like a 'prime ministerial visit'.[52] Koizumi also signed the shrine's guestbook and presented a wreath in the name of the PM, which further confirms the observation (Tanaka 2003; *YS* 21 April 2002). By making a consecutive visit and making it appear 'official', Koizumi would have pleased nationalist organisations like Izokukai, which had long campaigned for 'official visits' by Japanese leaders (Tanaka 2003). Indeed, the second trip, made just after Izokukai established a new agenda to institutionalise prime ministerial visits, received warm appraisals from Izokukai's chief, Koga Makoto, who characterised it as a 'splendid and wonderful act' that 'represented a step forward toward regularisation of the visit' (cf. Tanaka 2003; *JT* 22 April 2002).

The external–internal conditions leading to Koizumi's second trip suggest the salience of domestic considerations over international constraints in shaping his policy choice. Enjoying a perceived favourable relative power position (external environment) in terms of allied commitment/resolve and diplomatic leverage vis-à-vis China, yet facing indeterminate domestic leverage, Koizumi's position would have been between Quadrant B and C, allowing the implementation of a nationalist–assertive policy option to facilitate domestic political objectives. Appeasing the nationalists would gain Koizumi much needed political support from certain LDP quarters to counter the 'anti-reform' forces within the ruling party itself. Furthermore, limited measures to appease China in the visit's aftermath highlight a calculated risk and trade-off by the Japanese government that saw domestic political expediency supplanting the maintenance of friendly ties with China as the immediate priority at the time.[53]

The 14 January 2003 visit

Japan continued to enjoy a relatively favourable external environment in the run-up to Koizumi's third shrine visit. In terms of allied commitment/resolve, the security alliance with the US became fundamentally stronger as the 'anti-terror' war progressed, with the Japanese enthusiastically providing 'rear support' to its ally. As Koizumi's foreign policy became indiscreetly pro-US, Washington further encouraged the rearmament and expansion of Japanese security policy, to the delight of normal-nationalists in Japan. The US also remained conspicuously mute about Yasukuni and its debilitating impact on Japan's Asia policy. Indeed, opinions abounded that 'the Koizumi style of nationalism is only possible with American encouragement' (Tamamoto 2005a: 16). It was believed to be Koizumi's grand strategy to seek intimate ties with the US and utilise the alliance to facilitate Japan's quest for normal statehood (Huo 2005). To this end, Koizumi's pro-US policy also gave Japan leverage over China in the US–Japan–China 'strategic triangularity' (Soerensen 2006), and boosted Tokyo's confidence in pursuing an assertive China policy.

Nevertheless, the North Korean nuclear proliferation and Japanese abduction issues meant that Japan needed both China and South Korea, together with the US and Russia, to deal with Pyongyang's belligerence. This would necessitate Tokyo prudently managing its souring relationship with Beijing and Seoul, especially concerning their diplomatic rows over Koizumi's shrine visits. In the Japanese–Chinese context, ties had deteriorated, underscored by visible Chinese protests against the second Yasukuni trip. The 'Shenyang Incident' in May 2002 that saw Chinese authorities storming the Japanese consulate to retrieve North Korean refugees, further tested their relationship (Kokubun 2007: 144). The worsening bilateral atmosphere led Koizumi to cancel his planned visit to China for the thirtieth anniversary celebration. Koizumi was, however, unperturbed by Chinese reaction, nor was he upset by Beijing's 'cold shoulder', at this stage.[54] Anyhow, the suspension of top-level visits had not prevented Koizumi from meeting China's leaders at the fringes of multilateral summits,[55] nor had it derailed other levels of bilateral exchange crucial for maintaining a functional, day-to-day relationship. Indeed, he believed that a third shrine visit would not damage Japanese–Chinese relations (*JT* 15 Jan. 2003).

Despite Koizumi's complacency, *Yomiuri*'s editorial suggested his third visit was apparently timed to avoid potential diplomatic clashes with the new leadership in Beijing and Seoul (*DY* 15 Jan. 2003).[56] Tokyo may have been optimistic about the coming of China's 'fourth generation' leadership, perceived as more pragmatic, less consumed by 'history', and certainly not tainted by personal experiences of Japanese war occupation (Pryzstup 2003a: 105). As mentioned, indications of a 'new thinking on Japan' by the Hu-Wen leadership were apparent from Ma Licheng's December 2002 article, which triggered fierce debates in China, but which was welcomed by the Japanese intellectual and foreign policy communities, and Japan's rightwing press (Lam 2004: 10; Kokubun 2006: 30).[57] Since Koizumi intended to visit Yasukuni annually, an early trip before Hu Jintao's official anointment would have taken it out of the list of annual bilateral grievances and avoided pushing the new Chinese leadership into a corner so early in its tenure, while allowing more time and opportunity for the perceived 'new thinking' to materialise.

Domestically, Koizumi may well have felt nationalist pressure increasing after his diplomatic rendezvous in North Korea in September 2002 (Pilling 16 Sept. 2002). Although popularly accepted, the trip unwittingly 'opened-up a can of worms', in which Kim Jong-il's apparent goodwill gesture of returning several allegedly abducted Japanese nationals sparked public anger and nationalist rancour in Japan. The highly charged 'abduction issue' and the deadlock in diplomatic negotiations with Pyongyang might have compelled Koizumi to make a 'timely' visit to Yasukuni, to soothe swelling domestic nationalist sentiment. Besides,

Koizumi probably calculated that he could not afford to further compromise his 'nationalist' credentials by skipping his shrine routine and appearing weak on China. This is especially so, in view of the August 2001 advisory group's report of December 2002, recommending the establishment of a 'non-religious' national war memorial in place of Yasukuni, which obviously incensed the nationalists (*YS* 24 Dec. 2002; Yamaori 2003: 44, 47).

Additionally, observers saw the visit as shrewdly timed to bolster faltering support within the LDP during the party's annual convention held days later, following limited progress in Koizumi's domestic economic reform agenda (AP 15 Jan. 2003). Moreover, Koizumi was optimistic that the diplomatic cost of another shrine visit on Japan–China ties would not outweigh the domestic political gains, based on his perception of earlier Chinese reaction. Furthermore, the striking decline in Japanese public images of the Chinese, according to recent public opinion surveys, would have strengthened Tokyo's resolve.[58] Koizumi's pronouncement in December 2002 regarding his intention to continue visiting Yasukuni even in the presence of an alternative memorial, demonstrated his confidence in maintaining a hard-nosed China policy, partly to placate nationalist concerns over Yasukuni's fate, which could be sealed by the advisory group's proposal (*KN* 24 Dec. 2002). That said, Koizumi reportedly did not fully observe the traditional shrine ritual during his third pilgrimage,[59] apparently a symbolic gesture to dilute Chinese and domestic consternations (Yamaori 2003: 44).

Global and regional events prior to the third visit would have had the Koizumi government perceiving a relatively favourable external environment in terms of allied commitment/resolve and bilateral leverage over China to maintain its current Yasukuni policy. Conversely, a seemingly weaker domestic political resolve vis-à-vis nationalist pressure required Tokyo to pursue a tougher foreign policy to boost domestic political support. The international–domestic nexus thus locates Koizumi's position within Quadrant C (Figure 5.2), which stipulated an assertive–nationalist policy option regarding Yasukuni visits, in the context of Japanese–Chinese relations.

The 1 January 2004 visit

Japanese–Chinese tension remained high throughout 2003 following several 'history'-related quarrels, but China's new leadership appeared pragmatic in handling and suppressing them. Although Koizumi decided in October against a visit to China that year, and Wen Jiabao declined an invitation to visit Japan, citing the need for Tokyo to improve the atmosphere to facilitate his trip, this high-level posturing did not impede other levels of governmental exchange. Koizumi was able to meet the Chinese leaders in a 'third country', which reinforced his opinion that a continuing lack of top-level mutual visits would not be detrimental to overall bilateral ties. Moreover, the Japanese government noticed Beijing's new flexibility in managing their bilateral problems, with less mentioning of history and harping on the Yasukuni issue by the Hu-Wen leadership.[60] Despite harbouring reservations about the resumption of normal bilateral summits, Hu

Jintao appeared to encourage exchanges between key officials of both states (Funabashi 2003). Increased bilateral cooperation in various areas, i.e. combating the SARS epidemic, and disposal of bio-chemical weapons left by the Imperial Japanese Army in China, gave further indications of the resumption of amiable ties after the previous Yasukuni falling out. Japan also made a conciliatory gesture by agreeing to Chinese demands for damages inflicted by the Qiqihar poison gas incident, albeit as a form of cooperation and not compensation (*JT* 17 Oct. 2003).

The shrine rows did not appear to compromise their deepening economic ties either, with China poised to overtake the US as Japan's top trading partner in 2004, besides becoming the driver of Japanese economic recovery.[61] Japan was also appreciative of China's efforts in realising the first of several rounds of the Six-Party Talks in August 2003, and understood the significance of Japanese–Chinese cooperation in bringing to fruition the event's objectives. Tokyo's emphasis on maintaining cordial relations with China was evident in the conciliatory measures taken soon after Koizumi's New Year shrine homage, in which the PM reiterated his view of China as Japan's most important partner and valued friend (*AS* 6 Jan. 2004). On 9 January, Koizumi instructed the Japanese delegation to China, comprising the chairs of the respective ruling coalition's PARC, to convey his views to the Chinese side (Wan 2006: 252). This suggests the 2004 pilgrimage was made on the assumption of an ambiguous diplomatic position vis-à-vis China, and that Koizumi had been striking a delicate balance between maintaining satisfactory relations with China for Japan's broader national interests, and satisfying domestic political/nationalist demands for personal political expediency, besides advancing the longer-term goal of 'normal' statehood.

The decision was undoubtedly facilitated by Japan's buoyancy about the continued resolve of the US–Japan alliance under Koizumi's pro-American foreign policy. Japan was prepared to defy growing public disapproval to commit the SDF to assisting in the reconstruction of post-war Iraq, much to the US's delight and China's consternation. Tokyo had earlier pledged US$1.5 billion to support the Iraq reconstruction agenda, prior to President Bush's visit to Japan in October 2003.[62] The premier's allegiance and commitment to Washington's cause endeared him to the Bush administration, which saw a 'special relationship' reminiscent to that of the 'Ron–Yasu'[63] era developing between the two leaders (Daniels 2004: 1), and its positive 'spillover' on US–Japan ties (McCreedy 2004). Indeed, Bush appreciated Koizumi's significance as a crucial ally, for he was probably the only Japanese leader who could successfully augment Japan's security role to support Washington's unpopular Iraq policy and still survive unscathed domestically.[64] Strategically, Koizumi's foreign policy continued to give Japan the perceived favourable external environment and diplomatic leverage over China to affect Tokyo's China policy decision-making, and reinforced Koizumi's determination to stand up to China.

Japanese public approval remained generally strong, and the Yasukuni issue had not undermined Koizumi's political standing. Not only did Koizumi manage to get re-elected as the LDP president on 20 September 2003, he went on to lead the party to electoral victory in the November Lower House election, which secured the political mandate and support necessary to advance his political agenda, including his annual shrine routine. Koizumi's confidence was obviously boosted by his re-election and the degree of public support for his Yasukuni visits, which did not dissipate, despite increased public awareness of the controversy they had courted. However, Koizumi did feel the heat of public opposition towards his plans to dispatch the SDF to Iraq, soon after the November election. A 29–30 November *Mainichi* poll showed that the vast majority of Japanese were either directly opposed or reluctant about sending troops, and were critical of US unilateralism in Iraq (Agawa 2004: 7). A *Yomiuri*-Gallup public opinion poll in mid-December also saw those Japanese who 'do not trust the US' exceeding those who 'trust' it, for the first time (cf. McCreedy 2004: 1), highlighting growing apprehensions about Koizumi's foreign and security policies.

The New Year shrine visit could have been a ploy to divert public attention and mobilise support for the SDF dispatch, at the opening of the new Diet session on 19 January 2004. This is likely, since Chinese hostility over Yasukuni could have easily triggered reactive nationalism and aggravated the 'China threat' perception in Japan,[65] giving weight to the government's argument for broadening its security policy, and the importance of the US–Japan alliance in hedging against an unpredictable China that required the Japanese to continue supporting their ally. On the same note, it provided Tokyo with the justification for advancing a more fundamental nationalist agenda in the revision of Article 9, and for reinstating Japan's normal military role. According to Tamamoto (2004: 15), 'the symbolism of the Yasukuni visits and the bravado associated with the Iraq expedition are not unrelated', suggesting that Koizumi was taking advantage of 'a fabricated air of emergency … to fundamentally transform Japanese national identity from a state of constitutional pacifism to a state than can go to war'. This view is shared by Hughes (2005: 133–4), who asserts that the domestically unpopular SDF deployment to Iraq for post-war reconstruction purposes represents the emergence of an increasingly 'normal' Japan, where 'vital precedents' for future overseas dispatch have been established under the US–Japan pact that can effectively circumvent Article 9, with China arguably part of such calculations.

The timing and indications made before the visit also suggest ingenious statecraft by the Koizumi administration. Koizumi's aide publicly announced in December 2003 that the PM was contemplating a visit to Yasukuni on 15 August of the following year (*JT* 29 Dec. 2003). However, he went on New Year's day, which according to a Chinese observer, appeared to be a calculated move, since a January trip would be less contentious than a visit on the date that had been publicised (cf. Wan 2006: 249, n. 94). If such was the case, then the strategy could have been meant to induce the Chinese into viewing the 'change-of-date' as a minor concession by Koizumi, similar to his compromise in 2001. Furthermore, an early visit would have served to end speculation over the issue and avoid further Chinese pressure (*Nikkei* 3 Jan. 2004; Wan 2006: 251). Likewise, Koizumi might well have anticipated more criticism of his policies that could have compromised approval ratings and put pressure on his Cabinet. Hence, an early visit, especially after the recent election, would be timely, with public approval still relatively propitious.

Koizumi's 2004 visit was, thus, plausibly made based on the ambiguous external conditions, and the relatively favourable domestic environment fostered by recent electoral victory and public support for an assertive China policy. This external–domestic nexus places Koizumi between Quadrant A and B in the NCR model, which indicates a flexible China policy option (visiting Yasukuni), supplemented by moderate policy measures to reduce the diplomatic cost of Chinese reactions.

The 17 October 2005 visit

Alliance commitment/resolve remained positive throughout 2004–5, as Japan enjoyed one of the best periods of relations with the US. During the 'Two-Plus-Two' talks in February 2005, both allies established a 'common strategic objective' in hedging against an increasingly powerful China (Klare 2006). Washington, for its part, remained unusually quiet over Yasukuni and Koizumi's 'aloof' policy towards China (and Korea). Amid mounting international opposition to its highly unpopular Iraq policy, the Bush administration would have treasured the personal ties with Koizumi and Tokyo's unwavering support, and therefore would understandably avoid interfering on issues sensitive to its ally. It has been suggested that the 'special relationship' between Bush and Koizumi had given Japan the kind of leverage never before enjoyed by the junior partner; a leverage which under the NCR hypothesis allowed Koizumi to advance his assertive and somewhat reckless China policy.[66]

As US–Japan relations prospered, Japanese–Chinese ties worsened. This contrasting diplomatic outlook would have Tokyo perceiving an ambivalent external environment that would give domestic politics saliency in China policy-making. Although China maintained a pragmatic approach throughout 2004, it became clear by 2005 that Koizumi's nonchalance over Yasukuni, and Tokyo's assertive posturing and growing international ambition, would be obstacles to improving relations (Zhu 2005: 16–17). Ironically, Beijing's pragmatism in maintaining a functional relationship, despite the shrine rows, allowed Koizumi to continue visiting Yasukuni with the same 'aloof optimism' that such visits would not adversely affect Japanese–Chinese ties.[67]

That said, Koizumi's decision to delay his annual visit until late 2005 could have been due to diplomatic prudence, to prevent Japan from becoming increasingly isolated in the region, and to dodge criticisms during the run-up to the sixtieth anniversary of the end of the Second World War. By early 2005, media speculations were rife that Koizumi would visit at the year's end, since the other prospective dates were considered untimely. *Asahi Shimbun* deduced that a visit in either January (New Year), or April (Spring Festival) would be unwise, after having only recently re-established cordial exchanges with China's leaders, and Tokyo's intention to invite Premier Wen to attend the World Expo in Aichi prefecture in May (*AS* 1 Jan. 2005; Wan 2006: 256). Moreover, with diplomatic rows concurrently brewing between Japan and two other neighbours, South Korea and Russia, over territorial disputes (*Korea Times* 24 Feb. 2005; *Nikkei* 31 Jan. 2005), avoiding another shrine row with Beijing would clearly have been in Tokyo's regional interests (Wan 2006: 258). Likewise, a 15 August visit was ruled out in view of the historical sensitivities concerning the date and the year, while paying homage during the Autumn Festival would have risked opportunities to arrange sidelines meetings with the Chinese leaders at the APEC summit in November (*AS* 1 Jan. 2005).

Koizumi's decision to take the risk demonstrated his resolve and priorities in mollifying domestic sentiments rather than soothing Chinese displeasure. One reason for such foreign policy bravado may have been that Koizumi was neither overly concerned with the decline in Japanese–Chinese diplomacy, nor worried about Japan's growing isolation in Asia, as long as Washington–Tokyo relations continued to prosper and develop into a mature and equal partnership. Some Japanese bureaucrats and observers have suggested that Koizumi's 'skewed' external perspective and his lack of diplomatic finesse can be attributed to his limited foreign policy know-how, and consequential indifference towards the policy area, as well as his lack of affinity with and knowledge about China.[68] Affected by these 'limitations', Koizumi could have thus (mis)perceived a pro-US foreign policy as sufficient in helping realise Japan's external goals. Moreover, Koizumi might have seen the deterioration in relations with China (and Korea) as 'temporary and not fatal while the [Yasukuni] visits promote the long-term strategy of pushing Japan closer to normalcy in international relations' (Huo 2005).

Furthermore, Japanese public images of China were severely dented by the anti-Japanese demonstrations in July–August 2004 and April 2005, and Beijing's endeavour to derail Tokyo's UNSC bid. The annual Cabinet Office polls in 2004–5 saw the level of alienation towards China surging to 58.2 per cent in 2004, from 48 per cent the year before, and then topping 63.4 per cent in 2005.[69] Both the *Asahi* and *Yomiuri*-Gallup polls in November and December 2004 also recorded a similar trend, with a staggering 71.2 and 71 per cent indicating distrust of China respectively (Przystup 2005a: 126; *DY* 16 Dec. 2004). In light of the prevailing public sentiment, it would not have been difficult for Tokyo to rally popular support for an assertive China policy. Whilst public opinion favoured Koizumi standing tall against China, opinions regarding his Yasukuni visit were more ambiguous, as seen in the rather evenly divided *Asahi* poll from November, which indicated 38 per cent support for his Yasukuni routine as opposed to 39 per cent against the visits (cf. Kokubun 2007: 147). However, *Mainichi*'s monthly opinion surveys between April and October 2005 revealed signs of public wariness, with greater numbers opposing his shrine visits (Figure 5.1; cf. Deans 2007: 278). A June 2005 *Nikkei* poll also recorded declining public support, with 42 per cent opposing a visit, and 38 per cent in support. Approximately 69 per cent of those opposing cited concerns over deteriorating ties with neighbouring countries as the main reason (*Nikkei* 20 June 2005), indicating the extent to which Chinese and Korean antagonisms had impacted on Japanese public awareness regarding the wisdom of the Yasukuni visits.

Similarly, domestic political opposition mounted after the fourth visit, with opposition parties periodically attacking Koizumi over his Yasukuni antics (*KN* 22

Nov. 2004). Even the LDP's coalition partner, Shin-Komeito, expressed concerns over the constitutionality of such visits (*KN* 1 Jan. 2004), and implored Koizumi to take the Chinese protest seriously (*JT* 9 Dec. 2004). During a Diet session in January 2004, DPJ's Kan Naoto, criticised Koizumi's antagonistic China policy for undermining Japan's broader national interests, in view of Beijing's importance as a Six-Party Talks partner to promote North Korean denuclearisation (Wan 2006: 253). China's subsequent role in facilitating the 'abduction talks' between Pyongyang and Tokyo, before the February 2004 round of the Six-Party summit, also broadened Japanese awareness of the significance of Chinese cooperation, which increased the diplomatic cost of Japanese–Chinese conflict over future Yasukuni visits (*AS* 16 Feb. 2004; Daniels 2004: 33).[70] Apprehensions were growing within LDP as well, notably among senior party cadres and 'pro-China' factions. In a highly unusual act, Lower House Speaker, Kono Yohei, reportedly met with five former premiers on 1 June 2005 to discuss relations with China, following which a unanimous decision was reached to discourage Koizumi from continuing his shrine visits (AFP 1 June 2005). Even Nakasone weighed in, telling reporters that Koizumi should 'think more about national interests than personal beliefs' and stop his Yasukuni trips (cf. Przystup 2005c: 131).

The *zaikai* also began voicing concerns after the 2004 visit, regarding the negative spillover effect of the Yasukuni problem on bilateral economic relations (*KN* 13 Jan. 2004). Indeed, *Asahi Shimbun* reported Chinese officials' statements indicating that Japan would lose its bids on a lucrative high-speed train project as well as the International Thermonuclear Experimental Reactor Project (ITER), purportedly in retaliation against the January 2004 shrine visit (*AS* 18 Feb. 2004). Fear of Chinese retribution in the economic realm after the April 2005 anti-Japanese riots led Keidanren and Keizai Doyukai to call for the PM to exercise caution on future Yasukuni pilgrimages.[71] In a mid-July *Kyodo* poll, more than half of top Japanese companies surveyed feared that strained ties could adversely affect their business in China (*KN* 02 Aug. 2005). Domestic pressure came from the legal front as well, when the Fukuoka District Court and Osaka High Court ruled against the shrine visits in April 2004 and September 2005 respectively (*JT* 29 June 2006). However, the other court rulings were inconsistent, and would be eventually annulled by subsequent deliberations at the Supreme Court, in favour of Koizumi and his government.[72]

Koizumi appeared unmoved by the domestic apprehension, possibly due to his assessment that Yasukuni visits and China policy would not be detrimental to his overall political position, considering the lack of consensus and fickle-mindedness of the Japanese public on the policy areas concerned. Furthermore, he knew that the public was more concerned with his domestic reform agenda, which remained the 'staple diet' that fed his popularity and power base. Moreover, Koizumi could count on LDP Diet-members and other conservative politicians for support, following the formation of a panel of 116 LDP lawmakers on 28 June 2005 that backed his shrine visit (*JT* 29 June 2005), and subsequent statements by a non-partisan group of 235 conservative lawmakers urging him to visit on 15 August (AFP 2 Aug. 2005). The staunch LDP support had been equally reflected earlier in the adoption of the party's policy platform during its fiftieth-anniversary convention on 18 January 2005, which included the call for a continuation of Yasukuni visits (Reuters 18 Jan. 2005), an agenda that was first introduced in January 2004.

More importantly, it was Koizumi's 'landslide' victory in the 11 September 2005 Lower House election that saw the LDP gaining a significant majority which emboldened and gave him a clear mandate to visit Yasukuni, soon after. The snap election was, in Funabashi's opinion, more of a referendum on Koizumi than his reform agenda. Although difficult to detect since they were 'discreetly under the radar' and 'absent from the pre-election debate', Funabashi (2005) contends that the 'China factor' and Yasukuni were amongst 'the largest (election) issues'. With the context for the pre-election debate set by the 'agitating concern' of a rising China and its challenge to Japan, Koizumi's determination to resist Chinese pressure was in tune with the prevailing Japanese public sentiment, and therefore, a decisive factor in forging the resounding electoral success (Funabashi 2005). Interestingly, Gerald Curtis predicted that the landslide win would give Koizumi the leeway to stop visiting Yasukuni (*KN* 12 Sept. 2005). Koizumi's subsequent homage, nonetheless, indicates that he was not merely doing it for political expedience, but also possibly to fulfil his 'nationalist' convictions following propitious conditions stipulated by NCR.

The 2005 visit, therefore, shared similarities with the previous year's pilgrimage in terms of the conditions that affected and fostered Koizumi's decisions. Both trips were made in an ambiguous external environment, shaped by favourable US–Japan relations but worsening bilateral ties with China. Also similar to 2004, Koizumi visited Yasukuni soon after a successful Lower House election, which precipitated a relatively conducive, domestic political condition that facilitated the visit. Hence, Koizumi's position in 2005 would be in between Quadrant A and B, which stipulates a similar policy option to that of the previous year, in managing the Yasukuni issue vis-à-vis China.

The 15 August 2006 visit

By late 2005, the international environment was no longer favourable for the Koizumi administration to continue exploiting the Yasukuni issue in pursuit of an assertive China policy and other nationalist agendas. As stated, the Bush administration had for the first time 'cautioned' against Koizumi's future shrine pilgrimage, considering its debilitating impact on Japan's ties with two key regional actors, which had undermined Tokyo's position regionally, and the US strategy in Asia (*JT* 12 Aug. 2006). Indeed, based on Bush's insinuation and the veiled disapproval of senior US administration officials, together with Washington's signal for better US–China–Japan ties,[73] the American dissonance became obvious, to the extent that Koizumi was ostensibly denied his coveted address at the joint sitting of the US Congress during his farewell US tour, following strong Congressional opposition towards his 'Yasukuni bravado' (*Nikkei* 1 June 2006; Lim 2007).[74]

From a bilateral perspective, Japan–China political ties could not have got any worse, as tensions escalated amid the ECS quandary, while bilateral negotiations and dialogues at various levels failed to progress, due to dissipating political will caused by the prolonged absence of top-level interactions. Although the Chinese kept the pressure on Koizumi over Yasukuni, Beijing appeared to have allocated greater attention to his prospective successors, to ensure that the shrine routine would not continue under the post-Koizumi administration. This suggests that the Chinese government, having contemplated and accepted the worst-case scenario (namely Koizumi visiting on 15 August), had decided to wait him out (*ST* 16 March 2006; Lam 2006b: 1). Ironically, Koizumi's decision to make his final shrine visit on the controversial date could have stemmed from his anticipation of this shift in Chinese focus and diplomatic pragmatism, which would mean the visit itself having limited impact on Japanese–Chinese diplomacy after his departure.

The domestic conditions were equally disadvantageous, with the strongest opposition yet towards his Yasukuni exploits deriving from across Japan's political spectrum. There was growing unrest within the LDP ranks, with senior members like Kato Koichi, Kono Yohei and Yamasaki Taku urging for a rethinking of the Yasukuni policy, while anti-shrine LDP Diet-members forged a study group in March 2006 to improve Tokyo's regional relations (*IHT* 17 March 2006; Lam 2006b: 8). In fact, a supra-partisan group of 130 Diet-members from the LDP, Shin-Komeito, and the opposition DPJ, was established in October 2005, to advocate for an alternative, non-religious war memorial in place of Yasukuni (*JT* 28 Nov. 2005; cf. Lam 2006b: 8). Differences apparently reappeared between the *Kantei* and MOFA regarding Yasukuni, as reflected by an article written by former Japanese ambassador to the US, Kuriyama Takakazu, in the MOFA-affiliated *Gaiko Forum* that was critical of Koizumi's visits and his China policy direction (Lam 2006b: 10–11). Even the Japanese conservatives spoke against the continuation of Koizumi's actions, due to increasingly strong international and domestic repercussions. In an unprecedented development, Watanabe Tsuneo, head of Japan's largest conservative, centre-right newspaper, *Yomiuri Shimbun*, and one of the most influential public opinion leaders, openly criticised the PM's shrine visits during a *New York Times* interview, and in a leftist journal, *Ronza,* in February 2006 (*NYT* 11 Feb. 2006; *KBS* 13 Feb. 2006). More significantly, Watanabe forged an unlikely alliance with his counterpart from *Yomiuri's* ideological arch-rival, Wakamiya Yoshibumi of the left-leaning *Asahi Shimbun*, to call for a moratorium on future prime ministerial visits (Yoshibumi and Watanabe 2006; Lam 2006b: 10). Both *Yomiuri* and *Asahi* also agreed on a joint project to delve into the question of Japan's war responsibility, which is inextricably related to the Yasukuni ideology (*JT* 29 March 2006). As highlighted earlier, public support for the visit declined considerably, while the *zaikai* officially made clear their opposition (*YS* 10 June 2006). Most ironic of all was Izokukai's appeal to Koizumi to refrain from visiting their sacrosanct site, while proposing a solution amenable to China.

So why did Koizumi proceed with his plan, despite facing unfavourable international and domestic conditions? The answer to this 'anomaly' insofar as the NCR framework is concerned would lie in his judgement that the visit would not matter, or carry any significant political risk, since he was already at

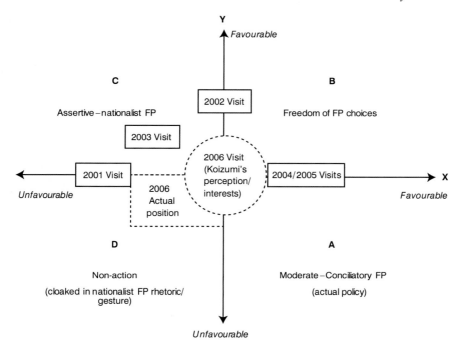

X = Domestic Political Resolve (vis-à-vis domestic nationalist pressure)

Y = Relative Power Position (vis-à-vis disputant state/China)

Figure 5.2 NCR model of nationalism and Japan's China policy preferences on the Yasukuni Shrine issue

the twilight of his premiership. Realistically, the Chinese had 'written him off'[75] and begun concentrating their efforts on the incoming Japanese leadership (*JT* 20 Feb. 2006), while other sources of external and internal pressure would recede if his successor observed the proposed moratorium. Koizumi was also no longer unduly concerned about securing domestic political support for his reform agenda, since he had successfully achieved some of his targeted programmes, and set in motion the forces of change in the Japanese political economy. More so, instead of harming his popularity, a visit on the promised date would have cemented his *kizen* (Funabashi 2005) or 'lionheart' image (Anderson 2004), and reputation as a steadfast leader, in the hearts of millions of Japanese (*JT* 17 Aug. 2006). In this regard, Koizumi could have interpreted the international conditions and domestic processes as indeterminate, rather than determinately unfavourable (Figure 5.2), due to circumstances surrounding the anticipated leadership transition, which gave him the policy flexibility that led to his 'final' visit. His 'nationalistic' action thus conforms to NCR's dictum that state-elites do not necessarily respond effectively to the prevailing decision-making constraints, due to 'intervening' elements, i.e. (mis)perceptions and/or personal interests.

Conclusion

Japan's management of the Yasukuni dispute during the Koizumi administration demonstrates, to an extent, the salience of domestic nationalist pressure (notwithstanding Koizumi's so-called 'normal-nationalist' disposition) in affecting Tokyo's policy decision to sustain the annual shrine routine. That said, the timing and manner in which the visits were executed between 2001 and 2006, and the diplomatic manoeuvring before and after, suggest the prevalence of shrewd and rational rather than purely emotional policy calculation and external–internal balancing, on Tokyo's part, in an effort to simultaneously promote foreign and domestic policy goals. This concurs with NCR's assumptions regarding the extent to which nationalism determines Japan's China policy-making, which can be more or less salient under particular international–domestic conditions, as perceived by Japanese state-elites during specific time periods.

6 Case study II

The East China Sea dispute

The preceding chapter has demonstrated the extent to which resurgent nationalism exacerbates the Japanese–Chinese 'history' problem as manifested in their diplomatic quarrels over Koizumi's visits to Yasukuni-*jinja*. Similarly, bilateral issues concerning maritime territorial integrity and sovereignty are extremely delicate and potentially explosive, as they often arouse nationalistic impulses that galvanise societal and governmental responses 'disproportionate to the material stakes involved' (Roy 2003: 3). Indeed, nationalism is widely perceived to have increased the stakes and retarded possible resolutions of their competing sovereignty and resource claims over the ECS islands and surrounding waters, turning the dispute into a key diplomatic quandary. Utilising the NCR framework, this second case study attempts to assess nationalism's role vis-à-vis other determinants affecting the Koizumi administration's perceptions/calculation and policy options when dealing with China over the ECS maritime territorial dispute. The focus of analysis is on their competing claims over the Senkaku/Diaoyudao archipelago, quarrels regarding natural gas exploration, and alleged Chinese violations of the Japanese maritime boundary within the ECS.

This chapter begins with a background study of the ECS dispute. Particular attention is given to analysing the interactions between domestic nationalist pressure and other external–internal variables within the matrix of Japan's China policy-making, to assess the extent to which nationalism constrains Tokyo's management of this potentially destabilising bilateral conflict.

Background of the ECS dispute

It is essential to elaborate the ECS dispute's origins and multi-dimensional nature, and the contesting legal interpretations involved, as well as its significance to nationalism, to comprehend the intricacies surrounding what is considered to be a perilous set of issues in Japanese–Chinese relations.

Origins and nature of the ECS dispute

The bitter dispute over the ECS comprises several correlated issues, namely their contending territorial claims over Senkaku/Diaoyudao, competition for energy resources and unilateral exploration activities in the adjacent waters, and incursions by Chinese naval and research vessels into the disputed maritime boundaries claimed by Japan. Central to the conundrum is the long-standing territorial dispute over a group of 'islets' and 'barren rocks' called the Senkaku/ Diaoyudao archipelago.[1] These relatively small and uninhabited insular formations are located at the edge of ECS continental shelf, approximately midway between Taiwan and the southernmost island of the Japanese Ryukyu chain, and separated from the latter and Japan's continental shelf by the Okinawa Trough (Su 2005: 46; Dai 2006: 136) (Table 6.1).

Before the 1970s, the Senkaku/Diaoyudao were of limited 'intrinsic value' (Shaw 1999: 12), under-appreciated and regarded as 'worthless' by both Japan and China (Suganuma 2000: 11). Traditionally serving as temporary fishing platforms and shelters, they stirred limited, sustained interests from the eventual claimant-states, and were essentially a dormant issue during the early post-war decades. It was the publication of the UN Economic Commission for Asia and the Far East (UNECAFE) report in 1969, which optimistically predicted the potential existence of abundant hydrocarbon reserves surrounding the archipelago, that triggered the awareness of the concerned parties, and led to the bitter ownership contest between Japan and China (and Taiwan)[2] (Chiu 1999: 4). Since then, it has been identified in both academic and official accounts as one of the most complicated and potentially explosive issues in Japanese–Chinese relations (Whiting 1989: 200; Blanchard 2000: 122–3; Suganuma 2000: 151, 162; Hagstrom 2003: 79; Drifte 2008a: 2).

The dispute was originally between Taiwan (ROC) and Japan over their overlapping concession zones surrounding Senkaku/Diaoyudao, but eventually shifted to a contest between the PRC and Japan, following their diplomatic normalisation in September 1972, and Taiwan's de-recognition as a sovereign state (Su 2005: 47). At first glance, economic considerations, namely the discovery of natural resources, appear to be the catalyst and driver of the islands dispute. Intense competition, especially over the exclusive control of the potentially rich oil and gas deposits in the contested area is to be expected, since both countries are dependent on foreign energy supplies to fuel their gargantuan economies (Drifte 2008b: 33), not to mention the prospects of these islands as future Chinese *Lebensraum* (Jencks 1994: 91). However, the complexity and difficulties in reaching a mutually equitable economic solution thus far, let alone seeking a political resolution to the dispute, point to the significance of political, emotional and strategic sensitivities which have been equally, if not more salient in fuelling the periodic Japanese–Chinese diplomatic confrontations over the archipelago and its surrounding waters throughout the past decades.

The Senkaku/Diaoyudao controversy is inextricably linked to nationalism, and has been predominantly a nationalistic dispute (Shaw 1999: 5; Valencia 2007: 166). To the Chinese, these islands are China's *irredenta*, territories historically belonging to China that have been annexed and continuously occupied by Japan, owing to Japanese imperialism in the past (Taira 2004; Suganuma 2000). Accordingly, they are symbols *sine qua non* to modern Chinese nationalism that

Table 6.1 Senkaku/Diaoyudao archipelago

Japanese Name	Chinese Name	Category	Location Latitude (N)	Longitude (E)	Size (sq.km)	Maximum Elevation (metres)
Uotsuri-shima	Diaoyu Dao	Islet	25° 45'	123° 29'	4.319	383
Kuba-shima	Huangwei Dao	Islet	25° 58'	123° 41'	1.08	117
Minami Kojima	Nan Xiaodao	Islet	25° 44'	123° 34'	0.463	149
Kita Kojima	Bei Xiaodao	Islet	25° 45'	123° 33'	0.302	135
Taisho-Kojima	Chiwei Dao	Islet	25° 55'	124° 33'	0.154	84
Okino Kitaiwa	Dabei Xiaodao	Rock	N.A.	N.A.	0.014	28
Okino Minamiiwa	Danan Xiaodao	Rock	N.A.	N.A.	0.005	13
Tobise	Feilai Dao	Rock	N.A.	N.A.	0.00006	N.A.

Sources: Adapted from Su (2005: 46) and Suganuma (2000: 12)

not only remind the Chinese of Japan's past militaristic transgressions, persistent historical amnesia and skirting of war responsibility, and possible resurgence of militarism (Shaw 1999: 5), but also the need to recover these 'lost territories' as prerequisite for the redemption of China's incomplete sovereignty (Suganuma 2000). Conversely, most ordinary Japanese, especially rightwing nationalists, consider Senkaku/Diaoyudao to be an inalienable part of Japan since their initial discovery by a Japanese national (Chung 2004: 29).

As will be elaborated, symbolic and provocative activities undertaken by nationalists from both sides were responsible for triggering past diplomatic disputes over the islands. Interestingly, the various instances of clashes illustrate the propensity of popular nationalism to pressure and elicit nationalistic responses from the respective governments, suggesting the vulnerability of state-elites to domestic nationalist pressure when managing this highly charged issue. That said, it is worth noting that pragmatism appears to have thus far governed both states' management of past incidents, with concerted efforts being taken to de-escalate bilateral tension. However, with resurgent nationalism raising the stakes of competition for national pride and prestige (Tamamoto 2005b), any resolution or compromise by way of joint development appears bleak, if not almost impossible, as none of the disputant states seem willing to shelve their sovereignty claims. Moreover, compromise by either claimant state would set a precedent that could undermine their bargaining position in other unresolved territorial disputes (Deans 2000: 126).[3] Further complicating the possibility of dispute settlement between Japan and China is the geo-strategic value of the archipelago, straddling key international shipping lanes vital to commerce and energy security, where ownership could carry strategic implications (Suganuma 2000: 13), and affect the evolving regional power dynamics. Suganuma (2000: 11) best captures the complexity of the conflict, noting that 'The cornerstone of the Diaoyu [Senkaku] dispute sprouts from an intricate tapestry of economic interests, geopolitical considerations, symbolic reasons, and historical rights.'

There are three dimensions to the Senkaku/Diaoyudao dispute from the legal perspective (Schoenbaum 2005). The most fundamental concerns sovereignty, which directly affects their respective bargaining position on the subsequent two dimensions, namely their overlapping claims over the ECS continental shelf and maritime boundary, and the right to ownership of the islands' contiguous waters and Exclusive Economic Zones (EEZ), stipulated in the UN Convention on the Law of the Sea (UNCLOS) (Schoenbaum 2005; Dai 2006). Expectedly, the sovereignty issue is the most difficult to resolve (Drifte 2008a/b; Harrison 2005), not only because of the historical-emotional sensitivities involved, but also due to the contrasting interpretations of the sovereignty concept resulting from the vagueness of the UNCLOS.

China claims Senkaku/Diaoyudao based on two interrelated arguments: 'historical discovery' and utilisation documented as early as the Ming Dynasty; and 'territorial cession' along with Taiwan to Japan following Qing China's defeat in the first Sino-Japanese war (Su 2005: 48; Chiu 1999: 9–11). Conversely, Japan establishes its claims via the principles of 'discovery-occupation' and 'effective control' in international law (Hagstrom 2005: 168). The Chinese substantiate their claims by drawing on historical records of early contacts with the islands dating back to 1372 or further (Blanchard 2000: 101; Suganuma 2000: 42–4), citing their functions as shelters for Chinese fishermen, and navigation aids for Chinese 'tributary' envoys to the Ryukyu kingdom, as well as part of the coastal defence system against Japanese *wako* (pirates) (Shaw 1999: 38; Hagstrom 2003: 140–1). The islands' historical ties with and incorporation as part of Taiwan's coastal defence system by the Qing government during the eighteenth century are also alluded to verify the 'territorial cession' argument, where they are considered among the islands 'appertaining or belonging to' Taiwan (Formosa) that were forcefully ceded to Japan in April 1895, under the 'unequal' Treaty of Shimonoseki (Hagstrom 2003: 141–2; Chiu 1999: 10). The Japanese reject the Chinese arguments, asserting that Senkaku/Diaoyudao were *terra nullius* until their subsequent discovery by Koga Tatsuhiro, a Japanese national, in 1884, which eventually led to their formal incorporation into Japan's territory in January 1895, ostensibly after more than a decade of official Japanese survey, and several months before the cession of Taiwan (Su 2005: 49; Hagstrom 2003: 140–1). Further validating Japan's claims have been its 'effective jurisdiction/ control' of the islands since then, apart from the period between 1945 and 1972, when they were grouped together with Okinawa under American occupation (Chung 2004: 28). From the Japanese viewpoint, the islands were indisputably incorporated with the Ryukyus into the 'Nansei Shoto'[4] under the US trusteeship system (Drifte 2008b: 30), before their reversion to Japanese administration under the 1971 Okinawa Reversion Treaty (Taira 2004).

Indeed, the contending interpretations of events leading to and after Japan's Second World War defeat, and the US administration of the islands, further complicate the sovereignty dispute. As understood by the Chinese, the provisions of the 1943 Cairo Declaration and 1945 Potsdam Declaration, and the 1951 San Francisco Peace Treaty (SFPT), effected the return of all territories annexed by Imperial Japan, which included Taiwan and the Pescadores, and supposedly by implication, Senkaku/Diaoyudao, as an appurtenance of the former (Shaw 1999: 39–40). The renunciation of Japanese claims to these territories was apparently reaffirmed in the 1952 Japanese–Chinese Peace Treaty signed between Japan and the ROC as the then-legitimate government of China (Chiu 1999: 18; Su 2005: 48). Accordingly, the Chinese argue that the American occupation of Senkaku/ Diaoyudao was in contravention of these international treaties, and therefore recognise neither Japan's effective control of the islands, nor the US's decision to revert their administrative rights to the latter (Chung 2004: 29). In contrast, the Japanese government maintains that the islands were not part the territories ceded along with Taiwan in 1895, as there was no explicit reference to them under the terms of the Shimonoseki Treaty (Suganuma 2000: 118). Tokyo also asserts that they were neither specifically mentioned in any of the above Declarations/ Treaties, nor did the Chinese government initially raise 'any objections to such omissions' (Hagstrom 2003: 142), let alone challenge the post-war arrangement that placed them under US administration (Su 2005: 48–9; Dai 2006: 147).

To be sure, the ROC did express disagreement with Article 3 of the SFPT, while the PRC denounced it as illegal, since it was signed in the absence of any representative of China, a point used by Beijing to refute Japanese claims of Chinese non-objection to the placement of these islands under American control (Shaw 1999: 41, 121–2; Su 2005: n. 40). However, the Chinese contestations mainly regarded the status of the Ryukyu and Okinawa islands, without specifically referring to Senkaku/Diaoyudao, which according to observers seems to indicate that both Chinese governments were initially unaware of their existence (Hagstrom 2003: n. 282; Shaw 1999: 121).

Meanwhile, Washington's policy was that Senkaku/Diaoyudao were part of its Okinawa administration. Occasionally used by the US military for aerial bombardment exercises (Suganuma 2000: 121–2), the Americans initially grouped them together with Okinawa and Ryukyu as an administrative unit (Blanchard 2000: 121). However, Washington's position concerning the island's sovereignty had become rather ambivalent by the time of Okinawa's reversion to Japan (1971–2), presumably due to the internationalisation of the dispute, and the Nixon administration's budding rapprochement policy towards Communist China that required a more neutral American posture on the issue (Hagstrom 2003: 143; Schoenbaum 2005).[5]

According to Chung (2004: 29), the Japanese–Chinese sovereignty contest over the archipelago became even more 'convoluted' by the 1970s, with both disputant states vigorously incorporating 'the "law of the sea" language of continental shelves and exclusive economic zones' to strengthen their respective claims. The invocation of the UNCLOS provisions invariably leads to quarrels over the other two correlated dimensions. The PRC asserts its claims by concurrently invoking both the Continental Shelf Convention (CSC) and EEZ provision under the UNCLOS. As a coastal state, Chung (2004: 29) states that the basis of China's claims over the islands, and in fact, its 'exclusive jurisdiction over the economic resources in and under the entire ECS', lie partly on the CSC-sanctioned argument that its seabed is a 'natural prolongation of the Chinese continent', demarcated by the Okinawa Trough (Harrison 2005: 6–7). Beijing also validates its claims using the 1982 UNCLOS III provision, which allows a coastal and maritime state to exercise jurisdiction over a 200 nautical miles (nm) EEZ from its shore's baseline (Dai 2006: 136) via its 1992 Territorial Waters Law (TWL) (Hagstrom 2003: 82, n. 177). Conversely, Japan's position as a maritime state only entitles it to invoke the EEZ provision, which supports its claims of a 200nm EEZ spanning across the ECS from the Okinawa/Ryukyu shores that includes Senkaku/Diaoyudao. Japan officially exercised its EEZ claims on 20 July 1996 via legislation from the Japanese Diet (Green and Self 1996: 37). Since the ECS is less than 400nm in width, Japan's maritime territorial claims overlap with those of China, thus complicating a legal solution to the dispute (Su 2005: 46).

By virtue of the UNCLOS, Japan unilaterally limits its claims to a 'median line' equidistant between the Ryukyus and the Chinese mainland (Schoenbaum 2005), one which China does not recognise, for fear of undermining its claims over Senkaku/Diaoyudao. Interestingly, Japan's successful claim to an extended median line in the ECS would depend on the establishment of Japanese sovereignty over the archipelago, a precondition that China is acutely aware of. Since they are located significantly west of Japan, observers construe that possession of Senkaku/Diaoyudao would enhance Tokyo's bargaining position over the location of an agreed median line, insofar as islets (though not rocks) are entitled to their own continental shelf and EEZ (Harrison 2005; Schoenbaum 2005). Harrison (2005: 6) claims that they can be used 'to demarcate the outermost extension of Japanese territory [which] would push part of the median line westward, maximizing the Japanese share of the seabed'. Ferguson (2004a) confirms that ownership would entitle Japan to approximately 'an additional 40,000 square kilometers of EEZ', bringing extra resources to the Japanese nation's coffers. Such legal provisions not only make the possession of these uninhabited islands all the more significant to both parties, but the legal ambiguity, in Drifte's (2008b: 31) opinion, promotes contending interpretations that complicate resolution to their sovereignty claims over the archipelago, and correspondingly hinders the delimitation of the related maritime borders.

As would be expected, both Japan and China hold a rigid position in the Senkaku/Diaoyudao dispute. The Japanese government appears most reluctant to negotiate on the issue, asserting the islands as an 'integral part' of Japanese territory, and even denies the existence of any sovereignty dispute over them (Drifte 2008a: 5).[6] Apart from their economic value, these islands are important to Japanese geopolitical and strategic interests in that they straddle sea-lanes vital to Japan's economic, energy and military security (Suganuma 2000: 13). Furthermore, Japan has unresolved disputes with Russia and South Korea over the Northern Territories/Kuril and Takeshima/Tokdo Islands, respectively, and is understandably reluctant to defer Japanese claims to Senkaku/Diaoyudao in favour of joint exploration and development with China, 'lest this set a precedent that would jeopardize Japan's position' (Harrison 2005: 6) in those disputes. Although both governments have taken a pragmatic stance and avoided military conflicts over the ECS, the intertwined notions of nationalism and maritime territorial sovereignty are increasingly constraining their policy options, especially in the wake of resurgent nationalism in both countries. In Japan's case, domestic nationalist activities have not only been responsible for several bouts of diplomatic disputes with China over the islands since the 1970s, but rising Japanese nationalism has also ensured that they remain a highly visible foreign policy issue, which limits Tokyo's options when dealing with Beijing.

Domestic nationalist pressure and 'internationalisation' of the ECS dispute

As mentioned, the ECS was essentially a non-issue until the UNECAFE's revelation of potentially rich petroleum deposits in the waters off Senkaku/Diaoyudao. It reportedly estimated the potential existence of an excess of 'between 10 to 100 billion barrels' of oil in and under the continental shelf between Japan and Taiwan, notably where the islands are located (cf. Chung 2004: 32). A subsequent Japanese government survey strengthened the speculation, estimating 'well over

94.5 billion barrels of quality oil' trapped in the seabed to the north-west and south of the archipelago (Harrison 2005: 6). As major oil importers, the news predictably triggered competing sovereignty claims by Taiwan and Japan.

The territorial dispute first manifested in September 1970, when Japanese police evicted a group of Taiwanese reporters from one of the islets after their symbolic effort to plant a Taiwanese flag, which elicited anti-Japanese protests and inspired the establishment of overseas movements to defend Chinese interests in Senkaku/Diaoyudao (Downs and Saunders 1998–9: 126). The incident prompted Japan to officially reassert its sovereignty over the islands, but Tokyo publicly favoured the idea of deferring the ownership claims for joint exploration and development of the disputed areas with Taipei, and even Seoul (Chiu 1999: 7). This led to negotiations between representatives from the three governments in November–December 1970, which saw the formation of a 'Liaison Committee' (Suganuma 2000: 132) to facilitate discussions of a tripartite 'development cooperation' for the ECS (Chung 2004: 32).

Despite its silence during the early stages of the sovereignty dispute, the PRC's exclusion from the joint development negotiations saw Beijing wasting no time in denouncing the plans and thereafter officially staking Communist China's claims over the islands (Blanchard 2006: 214; Chiu 1999: 9).[7] China's intervention virtually halted all plans for development cooperation in the disputed waters (Chung 2004: 35), and brought the 'sovereignty question' back into the limelight; this erupted again in 1971–2, following the US decision to revert the islands' administrative rights to Japan. Washington's neutrality on the sovereignty issue notwithstanding, the Okinawa Reversion Treaty's provision prompted fierce public demonstrations across North America, Hong Kong and Taiwan, as well as diplomatic protests from Beijing and Taipei (Shaw 1999: 14–15). The controversy subsided after Japan and China, in their capacity as the official claimant states, agreed to shelve the issue to facilitate diplomatic normalisation (Drifte 2008a: 4–5).

The next round of diplomatic contention occurred in April 1978, when the ultra-nationalist group, Nihon Seinensha, erected a lighthouse on Uotsuri-shima, the largest of the Senkaku/Diaoyudao islets, in an attempt to stake Japan's claims over the disputed archipelago. The provocative action took place following sustained, albeit unsuccessful efforts by rightwing 'anti-China' politicians to link the sovereignty issue to the bilateral negotiations for the Japanese–Chinese PFT (Bedeski 1983: 35–7). Since the resumption of the talks in February 1978, pro-Taiwan and anti-PFT Diet-members led by the LDP's rightwing Seirankai had been pressuring the government to extract a favourable resolution to the Senkaku/Diaoyudao dispute from China as a precondition for the inclusion of the so-called 'anti-hegemony' clause in the PFT (Chung 2004: 36; Shaw 1999: 16). Seeking a 'win–win' solution, the anti-PFT forces thought they could either derail the PFT negotiations by assuming an uncompromising position over Senkaku/Diaoyudao, or at least draw the islands as a 'bargaining chip' from the Chinese for Japan's agreement to include the controversial clause (Chung 2004: 36). China forcefully remonstrated against the political affront by dispatching a fleet of more than 100 allegedly armed fishing vessels to the disputed waters to encircle the islands

(Blanchard 2006: 215).[8] Instead of eliciting a conciliatory posture from Japan, the Chinese action galvanised Japanese nationalist convictions that saw Seirankai members erecting a makeshift beacon before collaborating with Nihon Seinensha to construct the lighthouse (Chung 2004: 41). A series of assertive diplomatic exchanges ensued before eventually abating, with both governments agreeing 'to shelve the sovereignty issue for future negotiations' to facilitate the 'more important' goal of realising the PFT (Takamine 2005: 453–4).[9]

Following a twelve-year hiatus, the sovereignty dispute reignited in September 1990, when the Japan Maritime Safety Agency (J-MSA) reportedly decided to recognise the Seinensha-built lighthouse as an 'official navigation mark' (Su 2005: 47), and permitted its renovation (Chung 2004: 42). The decision triggered instantaneous reaction from Taiwanese authorities, who lodged an official complaint to the Japanese government before dispatching two fishing boats filled with athletes carrying an Olympic torch to the islands to symbolise Taiwan's claims (Deans 2000). Despite intense media scrutiny, the J-MSA 'forcefully' prevented their landing, drawing more media criticism and public demonstrations in Taiwan and Hong Kong (Whiting 1992: 48). Although this was largely a dispute between Taiwan and Japan, the PRC did respond, albeit belatedly and reluctantly, by joining the chorus of denunciation of Japan's claims and demanded the Japanese authorities curtail the activities of ultra-nationalist organisations (Downs and Saunders 1998–9: 128–9). China's low-profile response probably reflected its gratitude and recognition towards Japanese support in the aftermath of the 1989 Tiananmen Incident, which saw Beijing employing mild rhetoric rather than concrete actions to challenge Tokyo's intransigence (Whiting 1992: 48). Following both sides' reiterations of claims to the islands, the sovereignty issue was indecisively shelved again to prevent it from undermining the amicable atmosphere of the bilateral ties.

Controversy soon re-emerged in 1992 following the promulgation of China's TWL, which explicitly located Senkaku/Diaoyudao within Chinese territorial waters, much to Japan's consternation (Hagstrom 2003: 82). Subsequent ratification of the UNCLOS, and the updating of continental shelf and EEZ claims by both governments in 1996, ratcheted up bilateral tension (Su 2005: 47). Fuelled by provocative nationalist actions and counteractions from both sides, the already simmering dispute culminated in a protracted diplomatic crisis that saw both governments initially playing to the nationalist tune and taking assertive stances, before scrambling to defuse the potentially explosive situation that threatened to spiral out of rational control after the dispute suffered its first casualty.

The 1996 incident started when Nihon Seinensha made yet another attempt to assert Japan's claim by constructing a lighthouse on Kita-Kojima, one of the smaller Senkaku/Diaoyudao islets, days before the Japanese Diet ratified its EEZ claims, which encompass the contested archipelago. Apparently timed to put pressure on and influence the Diet resolution (Chung 2004: 43–4), Seinensha's action and Tokyo's assertiveness over the issue, including PM Hashimoto's 'timely' visit to Yasukuni, emboldened the Japanese nationalists (Downs and Saunders 1998–9: 133; Green 2001: 86). Thereafter, another *uyoku* organisation known as the Senkaku Islands Defence Association erected the *Hinomaru* on

Uotsuri-shima, while Seinensha continued testing Chinese patience with further provocative activities on the islands (Chung 2004: 44). Public demonstrations reverberated from Hong Kong and Taiwan in response to the provocations. The Chinese government reacted more firmly this time around, lodging diplomatic protests against Tokyo's assertion of claims, and criticising the Japanese authorities for their alleged indifference in curtailing the nationalist activities.

Under pressure from domestic nationalist forces during the period of high nationalism, both governments had to demonstrate their nationalist credentials by appearing assertive and uncompromising, although 'behind-the-scenes' negotiations were conducted to prevent further escalation of the dispute (Bong 2002; Chung 2004). Nonetheless, subsequent clashes between Chinese protesters attempting to land on the islands and the J-MSA which tried to prevent their landing, resulted in the death of a Hong Kong activist, which led to more virulent, popular anti-Japanese demonstrations across Greater China (Bong 2002: 81).[10] The controversy receded after Beijing took measures to rein in nationalist sentiments and settled for a diplomatic compromise, in which Tokyo, though refusing to demolish the Kita-Kojima lighthouse, agreed not to recognise it.

These past disputes demonstrate the propensity of nationalist groups in Japan to manipulate the Senkaku/Diaoyudao issue to advance their parochial agenda, and in so doing, trigger reactive popular Chinese nationalism that leads to diplomatic rows between the two governments. They also suggest the salience of domestic nationalist pressure in constraining Japan's behaviour vis-à-vis China, where the Japanese state is inclined, to an extent, to assuage nationalist demands by standing firm on the sovereignty dispute.

Nonetheless, the fact that none of these diplomatic crises led to military engagements, and Tokyo's willingness to settle for compromises to de-escalate bilateral tension, suggest the prevalence of other determinants and limits of nationalism in shaping Japanese policy options over the ECS dispute, and its overall China policy, for that matter. For example, the prompt containment of the crises in the early 1970s can be attributed to the prevailing Cold War international environment and US policy shift towards the PRC that drove Japan to prioritise Japanese–Chinese reconciliation. Similarly, the willingness of Japanese state-elites to 'dismiss' sustained domestic nationalist pressure during the 1978 crisis highlights the importance of securing the PFT to substantiate the *de facto* 'strategic alliance' with China against a common security threat in the Soviet Union (Zhao 1996: 193–5). These instances reflect NCR assumptions regarding the salience of external variables vis-à-vis domestic considerations, i.e. nationalist pressure affecting state behaviour/preferences, under structurally determinate or high-pressure international conditions. Conversely, the protracted diplomatic row and Japanese assertiveness in managing the 1996 incident suggest increased domestic nationalist leverage in China policy-making, under a relatively low-pressure post-Cold War international environment. Furthermore, a perceived favourable relative power position vis-à-vis China, in terms of 'alliance commitment/resolve' and bilateral exchanges, allowed Tokyo to exercise rather more nationalistic posturing during the dispute, which mirrors the NCR dictum.

This leads to the question regarding the extent to which domestic nationalist pressure affects Japan's policy options when managing the ECS problem between 2001 and 2006, and whether they are directly induced by the emotional properties of nationalism and identity politics, and/or calculated responses by the Koizumi administration for domestic and diplomatic expediency. Indeed, the Japanese government has displayed a more assertive attitude vis-à-vis China over the ECS issues since 2001, following revitalised domestic nationalist impulses, and the advent of a nationalist-oriented leadership in Japan. The islands' sovereignty dispute has also become more complicated. Besides the occasional provocation by nationalists from both countries, China's growing physical presence in the contested waters via repeated ship incursions into the area, and its unilateral decision to develop gas fields at the fringe, albeit on the Chinese side of the median line, have broadened the scope of the conflict and increased the frequency of diplomatic quarrels. Against the backdrop of a fluid external environment and regional power shifts that perpetuated Japanese insecurity towards the Chinese, an NCR analysis of the interactions between nationalism and these changing external dynamics can help explicate nationalism's salience in shaping Japan's China policy over the ECS dispute.

Nationalism and the international–domestic nexus in Japan's China policy-making over the ECS dispute

In view of its multi-dimensional nature and constant recurrence throughout the period of investigation, an overview of the ECS conflict is elaborated, before applying the NCR model to assess nationalism's salience against other variables in affecting Japan's management of: (1) the Senkaku/Diaoyudao sovereignty contest; (2) Chinese incursions into the disputed waters; and (3) the natural gas dispute.

An overview of the ECS conflict (2001–2006)

The ECS remained a 'sea of simmering conflict' (Curtin 2005b) even after Japan and China managed to rein in their strident diplomatic row in 1996, with occasional incidents involving provocation by nationalists from both sides eliciting rhetorical exchanges between the two governments throughout the twilight of the twentieth century.[11] The Chinese have also increased their physical presence in the disputed waters off Senkaku/Diaoyudao since 1999 via the dispatch of scientific research vessels, under the pretext of conducting maritime research (Su 2005: 47). The frequency of Chinese vessel sightings in the area has risen spectacularly since 1998, including suspected PLA-Navy intelligence-gathering activities to map the sea floor for future Chinese submarine operations (Drifte 2003: 56–7; Goldstein and Murray 2004).[12]

Viewed by Japan as a violation of the UNCLOS, these repeated Chinese forays into the Japanese-claimed EEZ has become a key diplomatic irritant, which led to bilateral negotiations in September 2000 for the establishment of a

mutual advanced notification mechanism regarding maritime research activities
(Przystup 2001a: 93). Although both sides reached an agreement in February
2001, the 'prior notification' mechanism appeared vague on the definition of
research activities and geographical area involved (*JT* 14 Feb. 2001; Drifte 2008a:
18–20).[13] This eventually saw China rescinding its obligation several months
later, with the 'illegal' return of Chinese ships to the contested waters (*KN* 18
July 2001).[14] China's failure to observe the agreement drew strong criticism from
Japan, and growing security concerns regarding Chinese intentions in the ECS,
let alone capabilities, given the PLA-Navy's rapid expansion (NIDS 2002: 214).
Tokyo released an incriminating five-year review of China's maritime activities
within Japanese EEZ on 26 July 2001, soon after the Chinese violation, which
highlighted possible military intelligence operations in the areas concerned (*YS*
26 July 2001). Meanwhile, FM Tanaka took the matter up with her Chinese
counterpart during the ARF meeting in Hanoi, where the Yasukuni issue was also
raised (Przystup 2001c: 112).

The incursions halted temporarily after August 2001, with no violations
reported until year's end, when a *fushinsen* appeared in the disputed waters.
Subsequently identified to be North Korean, it was intercepted by and exchanged
fire with the JCG before sinking off the Chinese EEZ (Samuels 2007–8: 96). The
incident triggered protracted diplomatic exchanges between Japan and China that
lasted well into 2002 concerning alleged Japanese aggression, the prospect of
raising the sunken ship, and speculations of Chinese involvement in supplying the
vessel, prior to its meeting its fate (Przystup 2002b: 99–101).

Although relatively quiet throughout 2001–2, the Senkaku/Diaoyudao
dispute resurfaced early in January 2003, when Japanese media reported that the
government had controversially leased three of the islets, Uotsuri-shima, Kita-
Kojima and Minami-Kojima, from their Japanese owner (*YS* 31 Dec. 2002). The
revelation prompted diplomatic protests from the Chinese MFA on 3 January,
and Vice-FM, Wang Yi, two days later (Reuters 3 Jan. 2003; *KN* 5 Jan. 2003).[15]
Japanese Vice-FM, Takeuchi Yukio, responded with the usual reiteration of Japan's
rightful claims to the archipelago, but called for a 'cool-headed approach' to avoid
damaging overall ties (Przystup 2003b: 101). Despite mutual governmental effort
to contain the issue, Chinese nationalists were not prepared to go silent without
responding to what was perceived as a move by Japan to strengthen its sovereignty
claims. On 22 June 2003, a group of mainland Chinese and Hong Kong activists
attempted to land on the islands, but was 'appropriately' repelled by the JCG
(AFP 23 June 2003). Japanese rightwing-nationalists retaliated with a landing
in August, prompting protests from Beijing (*KN* 26 Aug. 2003). The Chinese
activists remained undeterred as they regrouped and made further landing attempts
in October (*SCMP* 10 Oct. 2003). Meanwhile, Chinese maritime incursions were
limited in 2003, with the JDA detecting only eight such 'intrusions' (Przystup
2004a: 109). Nonetheless, the spotting of a Chinese Ming-class submarine in
international waters close to Senkaku/Diaoyudao on 12 November did raise
Japanese concerns regarding China's stealthy strategy in establishing a forceful
presence in the ECS (*JT* 13 Nov. 2003).

On 14 January 2004, two fishing vessels carrying twenty Chinese activists sailed to Senkaku/Diaoyudao in what was their third attempt since the previous June to land on the islands (AFP 15 Jan. 2004). The vessels subsequently turned back after being intercepted and denied by JCG ships on 15 January (*JT* 16 Jan. 2004). The media reported that the Chinese boats were attacked with water cannon by ten Japanese ships, causing injury to a Chinese crew (BBC 15 Jan. 2004). Interestingly though, the incident was not reported in the Japanese media (Ferguson 2004a). The relatively inconspicuous incident served as the precursor to the next diplomatic clash over the islands in March 2004, which saw the dramatic arrest of Chinese activists by Japanese authorities following their successful fourth landing attempt. Preceding the incident was the resumption of illegal Chinese activities in the disputed waters, which prompted a MOFA protest.[16]

On 24 March, seven mainland Chinese activists from the China Federation for Defending the Diaoyu Islands landed on Uotsuri-shima/Diaoyu Dao, after successfully evading the JCG patrol ships (*JT* 25 March 2004). According to Curtin (2004b), after spending hours planting the Chinese flag, giving mobile phone interviews to the Chinese media and avoiding capture, they were finally taken into custody by the Okinawa Prefectural Police for violating the Immigration Control and Refugee Recognition Law (*KN* 24 March 2004). The incident was significant in that it marked the first time mainland Chinese nationals were directly involved and detained for landing on Senkaku/Diaoyudao (Su 2005: 47). The Japanese government lodged an immediate protest, and the Chinese authority responded by denouncing the provocative action, and demanded the release of the detainees amid popular Chinese protests outside the Japanese embassy in Beijing, where Japanese flags were purportedly burnt (*MDN* 25 March 2004). In Tokyo, indignation flared up as rightwing politicians and the media engaged in nationalistic rhetoric to assert Japan's claims, while Nihon Seinensha announced its intention to send another expedition to the island in a 'tit-for-tat' response to Chinese provocation (Curtin 2004a; AFP 25 March 2004). The Japanese government decided against pressing criminal charges, and instead deported the activists on 26 March, in an effort to defuse the situation (BBC 26 March 2004). The following day, FM Kawaguchi called on her Chinese counterpart, Li Zhaoxing, to prevent a recurrence of the incident, and protested at the flag burning (*KN* 27 March 2004). This episode of the ECS dispute not only resulted in the cancellation of scheduled bilateral talks on the UNCLOS (*JT* 1 April 2004), but also saw the Diet promptly passing an unprecedented resolution addressing Senkaku/Diaoyudao as an issue of Japanese territorial integrity (*DY* 1 April 2004).[17] Despite being 'diluted',[18] the motion drew instant denunciation from the Chinese MFA (XNA 1 April 2004).

By late May 2004, the territorial row had developed into a maritime boundary and energy dispute involving Japanese contestations over Chinese repeated incursions into Japan's EEZ, and more contentiously, exploration activities in the ECS natural gas fields close to, albeit on the Chinese side of, the so-called 'median line'.[19] Bilateral tension began to brew after both sides disagreed over the delimitation issue in the rescheduled UNCLOS meeting on 22 April 2004. The Chinese continued their 'illegal' research forays, leading to MOFA's official protest on 13 May, several days after the JCG discovered a Chinese vessel operating near Uotsuri-shima (BBC 13 May 2004). Despite Beijing's refutation, the ship left the disputed waters a day after MOFA's protest (BBC 14 May 2004).

However, Japanese media reports emerged in late May concerning China's construction of exploration facilities in close proximity to the ECS median line (Liao 2007: 40). Confirmation by the Japanese government on 7 June prompted media and LDP pressure for a strong response to the Chinese actions (*KN* 8 June 2004; Przystup 2004b: 125). Concerned that the Chinese exploration activities would siphon off gas from the Japanese side of the demarcation line, Tokyo requested Chinese exploration data during the Foreign Ministers meeting at the sidelines of the Asia Cooperation Dialogue on 21 June (Takahashi 2004). Beijing declined, and instead proposed joint development, which drew Japanese scepticism, due to concerns over the Senkaku/Diaoyudao sovereignty status (Drifte 2008a/b).[20] The deadlock led to METI chief, Nakagawa Shoichi, declaring on 29 June Japan's intention to start its own exploration of the area (AFP 29 June 2004), which the Japanese promptly initiated on 7 July, despite Chinese apprehension and mutual calls to resolve the issue through 'peaceful consultation' (AFP 7 July 2004; Przystup 2004c: 117). Bilateral tension continued to simmer, with China reportedly granting exploration rights to Chinese companies in areas allegedly within Japan's EEZ (BBC 17 Oct. 2004). Mutual consultation did not materialise until late October 2004, when working-level talks finally began in Beijing.[21] Although the talks failed to yield any solution, both sides agreed to maintain the dialogue (BBC 25 Oct. 2004).

Meanwhile, Chinese incursions into the Japanese EEZ intensified throughout July–August 2004, with various sightings of research and naval ships conducting oceanographic surveys reported around the vicinity of Senkaku/Diaoyudao and Okinotorishima,[22] fuelling speculations over China's intention to expand its naval/submarine operations, and to undermine Japan's maritime resource survey in the ECS (Tkacik 2004; Przystup 2004c: 119). Already reflected in the *Defense of Japan*, approved in July, which called for vigilance over Chinese military development, Japan's security concerns were further heightened on 10 November 2004 by the discovery of an unidentified submarine travelling submerged through Japanese waters off Okinawa (*JT* 11 Nov. 2004).[23] Subsequently identified as a Chinese Han-class nuclear submarine, the incursion led to 'the highest alert levels' in post-war Japan (Fanell 2006), as MSDF destroyers and planes tracked the vessel for two hours, while it manoeuvred towards Chinese waters (Takamine 2005: 440; Ferguson 2004b).[24] On 12 November, MOFA protested at the incursion and demanded an apology (AFP 12 Nov. 2004), but the Chinese MFA refused to respond, pending on its ongoing investigation over the incident (Reuters 13 Nov. 2004). Meanwhile, reactive anti-Chinese nationalism unfolded in Japan, fuelled by a barrage of speculation, rhetorical attacks and critical statements by the Japanese media and political parties (Chan 2004). The controversy finally ended on 16 November, when China accepted responsibility, attributing the incident to 'technical errors' during training routines (Przystup 2005a: 122), and extended what Japan quickly interpreted to be an 'apology' (Chan 2004).[25]

The submarine incident nonetheless exacerbated Japan's perception of China as a security concern, which already saw the JDA developing contingency plans envisaging the possibility of a Japanese–Chinese military confrontation over the ECS resources and territorial claims, in conjunction with the drafting of the new National Defence Programme Guidelines (NDPG) (Dai 2006: 140). Besides strengthening the US–Japan alliance via the 'Two-Plus-Two' talks in February 2005,[26] Japanese press also reported in March 2005 on Tokyo considering the establishment of a stronger military presence in Okinawa's southernmost islands near Senkaku/Diaoyudao, ostensibly to counter growing Chinese presence in the area (Przystup 2005b: 114).

The disputes over EEZ encroachment and natural gas exploration continued to fester during early 2005. In February, Japan accused China of extending its exploration activities beyond the median line into Japanese EEZ,[27] and demanded a cessation of activities and made a renewed request for the provision of exploration data, which Beijing promptly rejected (Harrison 2005: 4; Przystup 2005b: 115; Brooke 2005). Bilateral tension was also aggravated by Tokyo's controversial decision to place the Seinensha-built lighthouse on Uotsuri-shima under state control, eliciting instantaneous Chinese diplomatic and popular protest (*KN* 9 Feb. 2005). This was followed by other reported decisions between early March and June to develop, erect a lighthouse and provide an address for Okinotorishima, to substantiate Japan's claims to an extended EEZ (AFP 20 June 2005; Yoshikawa 2007).[28] Japan's decision to consider the application and granting of exploration rights in the ECS to Japanese oil companies in April 2005 produced further Chinese consternation (Harrison 2005: 4–5). Compounded by other issues mentioned in previous chapters, bilateral ties spiralled dangerously downward in April 2005, as anti-Japanese demonstrations spread across Chinese cities. Mutual efforts to de-escalate tensions in the aftermath saw both sides resuming bilateral consultations on the ECS issues on 30–31 May. The second-round talks again ended fruitless as disagreement over each other's requests and proposals for joint development stalled the progress of seeking a resolution to the dispute (*JT* 1 June 2005), prompting METI to grant exploration rights to Teikoku Oil on 14 July (Jiji 14 July 2005).

The ECS gas dispute continued to escalate, with both sides pushing ahead with their unilateral development plans. The third round of consultation on 30 September–1 October ended in deadlock, while the fourth, planned for 19 October, was effectively stymied by Koizumi's Yasukuni visit two days earlier, and so the prospect of a resolution appeared dim. Meanwhile, the ECS became increasingly volatile as the presence of Chinese navy warships near the Shirakaba/Chunxiao gas fields in September 2005 compelled the LDP to legislate for the protection of Japanese exploration activities, which was subsequently approved on 10 March 2006 (*SCMP* 14 Sept. 2005; Przystup 2006a: 116).[29]

Semi-formal talks resumed in January 2006, leading to the recommencement of official consultations in March, but yielded no progress. China advanced a joint development proposal in the Beijing dialogue, which Japanese diplomats agreed to bring back for further study (AFP 7 March 2006). However, the 'provocative' proposal, which called for joint development of two areas, one near the median line but in the waters disputed by Japan and South Korea, and the other in the vicinity of Senkaku/Diaoyudao, was immediately rejected by key members of the cabinet like Abe Shinzo and Aso Taro (AP 8 March 2006). It also elicited calls for countermeasures against continuing Chinese exploration activities (*KN* 15 March 2006), including a military response in the event of unprovoked Chinese attack on Japanese vessels operating in the disputed waters.[30] Indeed, the SDF planned to conduct joint exercises with the US Marines between 9 and 27 January 2006, focusing on the ECS, including the defence of Senkaku/Diaoyudao (*Nikkei* 31 Dec. 2005). Despite further working-level dialogues in May and July 2006, a resolution over the natural gas dispute remained elusive (*JT* 19 May and 11 July 2006),[31] as Koizumi's premiership drew to a close in September. Incidents concerning the ECS dispute continued to occur during the early months of the Abe administration, against the backdrop of improved bilateral ties, as the new PM sought to mend fences with China.

A neoclassical realist interpretation of nationalism and Japan's China policy towards the ECS dispute

The following section maps the Koizumi administration's perceived position during the related ECS incidents within the NCR model, via the assessment of and inferences on the prevailing international–domestic conditions and actors/factors, and their interactions that influenced Japan's China policy-making. Although the analysis draws attention to all three dimensions of the ECS dispute, empirical attention is devoted to specific incidents, namely the 2004 Senkaku/Diaoyudao debacle involving the detention of Chinese activists, the Chinese submarine intrusion in November of the same year, and the natural gas exploration issue, which is addressed as a protracted dispute between 2004 and 2006.

The Senkaku/Diaoyudao incidents (2003–2004)

Japan's management of the events leading to the March 2004 diplomatic row over Senkaku/Diaoyudao highlights the interaction between domestic nationalist pressure and Japanese state-elites' perceptions/calculation regarding the prevailing external environment and their domestic political resolve, which constrained their policy options towards China. Internationally, the post-Cold War conditions stipulated in the previous case study, namely a fluid external environment and strengthening allied commitment/resolve (via the US–Japan alliance) provided the Koizumi administration with an opportunity to redress Japan's traditionally deferential diplomacy towards China. The presence of such an environment, against the backdrop of domestic nationalist undercurrents, had Tokyo demonstrating greater resolve in asserting its sovereignty claims over Senkaku/Diaoyudao from the 1990s onwards. This is reflected in its assertive posturing during the 1996 incident, and subsequently, what observers noticed as an incremental strategy to strengthen its 'effective control' over the islands (Su

2005; Chung 2004).[32] Indeed, this Japanese strategy was responsible for the 2004 dispute, beginning with the media revelation on Tokyo's controversial leasing of the three islets in January 2003 that instigated a series of landing attempts by Chinese nationalists between June 2003 and March 2004 to challenge the Japanese state's action.

In many ways, Tokyo's decision to lease the islands was ushered by similar external–domestic conditions perceived by the Koizumi administration to those that encouraged the premier's third Yasukuni visit in January 2003. What were the conditions leading to the March 2004 Senkaku/Diaoyudao dispute, and to what extent was Tokyo's assertive handling of the incident attributable to domestic nationalist pressure? For a start, the prevailing international environment that facilitated Koizumi's New Year's Day 2004 shrine visit remained relatively unchanged, especially in terms of Japan's growing confidence towards a vastly improved US–Japanese relationship serving as the fulcrum for its more assertive and nationalistic China policy. Besides providing logistical support in the Indian Ocean and pledging financial assistance for US policy in Iraq, Koizumi's effort to strengthen the US–Japan alliance reached a new threshold in February 2004 with the successful deployment of the Ground-SDF (GSDF) to Iraq, despite domestic scepticism (*JT* 4 Feb. 2004). At about the same time, the debate on constitutional amendment of Article 9 to facilitate Japan's right for collective self-defence under the alliance framework was also gathering momentum (Przystup 2004a: 107), not to mention Tokyo's earlier decision in December 2003 to proceed with the acquisition and deployment of TMD (C. W. Hughes 2006: 2). As stated, this conspicuous pro-American stance endeared Koizumi to the Bush administration, where the budding 'special relationship' between the two leaders, and Washington's appreciation of its Japanese ally, led to an unusual absence of American *gaiatsu* on Japan's China policy. This plausibly contributed to Tokyo's boldness in advancing some of its nationalist goals at the expense of Japanese–Chinese ties. On a more specific note, Japanese policy-makers would have taken comfort in the 1997 US–Japan Defence Guidelines' implicit acknowledgement,[33] and later on, the Armitage Doctrine's more explicit statement, regarding the geographical coverage of the US–Japan Security Treaty that allegedly included the Senkaku/Diaoyudao archipelago, despite Washington's enduring neutrality on its sovereignty status (Tkacik 2004).[34] The perception of a favourable 'alliance commitment/resolve' would have emboldened Tokyo to adopt a strategy of 'calculated assertiveness' over the ECS dispute.

The same cannot be said about the bilateral conditions vis-à-vis China. Their robust economic relationship notwithstanding, diplomatic ties noticeably deteriorated in 2003 following the previously mentioned 'history'-related incidents, which culminated in Koizumi's January 2004 visit to Yasukuni. China's Hu-Wen leadership had initially appeared pragmatic and prepared to promote better ties with Japan, which included less harping on about 'history', and its somewhat restrained, if not muted, response towards the June 2003 Senkaku/Diaoyudao incident.[35] However, Koizumi's obstinate Yasukuni policy instantaneously undermined the prospects for improving political relations as the New Year dawned.

That said, the presence of extensive high-level exchanges during the first quarter of 2004 (i.e. China visits by senior members of Japan's ruling coalition, vice ministerial-level coordination for the February 2004 Six-Party Talks, resumption of bilateral defence dialogue after a three-year hiatus) (Przystup 2004a: 107–8) gave the impression that Beijing was willing to maintain a functional relationship, despite the protracted 'political chill'. Also, China's continued low-key response towards alleged Japanese heavy-handedness during the Senkaku/Diaoyudao incident on 14–15 January, despite ongoing Chinese discontent about the Yasukuni visit, equally boosted Tokyo's 'quiet confidence' in the Hu-Wen leadership's 'new thinking' on Japanese–Chinese diplomacy. Indeed, Beijing's response to the 'controlled aggression' of the JCG during the episode was unusually mellow, in that no diplomatic protests were lodged other than the mild rhetoric issued by the Chinese media (Urabe 2004a).[36] Such ambiguous signals from Beijing plausibly encouraged Japanese policy-makers to maintain 'cautious optimism' in re-establishing a more realistic relationship with China, which included advancing Japan's interests more forcefully in the ECS. Japanese confidence of Chinese pragmatism was likewise boosted by their flourishing trade ties and economic interdependence, along with Tokyo's calculation that its 'friendly' gestures over the Qiqihar poison gas incident and Koizumi's reassurance to the Chinese following his Yasukuni visit, would have bought Japan some goodwill in Beijing.

In fact, Japan's 'low-risk' estimation of an assertive policy option in the March 2004 incident was vindicated by another relatively mild official Chinese response, reflected by 'calm and subdued' reporting from the *People's Daily* (cf. Urabe 2004b) and the usual official reiteration of Chinese claims,[37] against the outbreak of 'relatively low-key' popular protests (Blanchard 2006: 220).[38] Beijing even prevented the departure of another planned Chinese 'tour' to the islands in the aftermath, possibly to quell growing anti-Japanese sentiments in China (*DY* 29 March 2004). Considering the above atmosphere, the Koizumi administration would have anticipated ambiguous diplomatic leverage over China.

Domestically, the Koizumi administration was reaping the fruit of the November 2003 Lower House electoral success, which provided a relatively favourable political environment vis-à-vis its detractors (i.e. left-wingers/pacifists and China sympathisers) and more importantly, the mandate to advance an assertive China policy. Meanwhile, the timing of the March 2004 Senkaku/Diaoyudao incident was, according to Curtin (2004b), 'particularly unpropitious', insofar as the general public mood towards China was severely affected by anti-Chinese sentiment triggered by sensational media reporting on the 'macabre' murder trial of Chinese students accused of brutally killing a Japanese family in Fukuoka (*JT* 24 March 2004). With the Japanese public appalled by the crime, nationalist politicians exploited the popular mood, their rhetoric inciting anti-Chinese nationalism and their stereotyped 'China threat' perception (Curtin 2004a). Compounded by recent commotions over the resumption and intensification of Chinese vessel intrusions into Japanese waters, the prevailing domestic milieu undeniably amplified the event that unfolded in Senkaku/Diaoyudao, which received extensive coverage from the Japanese media. Besides the nationalistic actions of politicians and pressure groups, media pressure also constrained Tokyo's policy options, with the likes of *Yomiuri Shimbun* blaming as much the Japanese government's past inaction as the Chinese state's intransigence over the ECS for the debacle (Katsumata 2004; Curtin 2004a). The 'highly visible' Chinese provocation thus necessitated a strong, discernible response from a Japanese government under intense media and public scrutiny, which plausibly explained the punitive action taken against the Chinese activists, backed up by official protests via diplomatic channels.

That said, domestic political apprehension about Koizumi's hard-line China policy was also evident, especially after his January 2004 shrine pilgrimage. Considering the domestic concerns over potential economic repercussions, and the diplomatic cost of Japanese–Chinese falling out on the North Korean problem (Daniels 2004: 33), the Koizumi government would presumably need to prudently manage the territorial row that followed. Hence, besides defusing the situation, Tokyo's relatively swift decision to deport rather than prosecute the activists could be interpreted as a conciliatory gesture to undercut the diplomatic damage incurred by the assertive action taken initially (*JT* 27 March 2004).[39] Indeed, some government officials contended that the wishes of the 'China-friendly' CCS Fukuda may have influenced the decision (*JT* 28 March 2004), while senior MOFA officials interviewed defined it as a move out of politico-diplomatic rather than legal considerations.[40] Koizumi's 'conciliatory tone' and 'use of measured words' (Curtin 2004a) in his effort to reduce bilateral tension immediately after the arrest also confirms this observation.[41]

Japan's policy options during the March 2004 incident were, therefore, plausibly conditioned by the anticipation of ambiguous external conditions, with enhanced alliance commitment/resolve via the US–Japan ties, but ambivalent diplomatic leverage over China, as the mixed signals from Beijing, despite recent history-related enmity, provided an indeterminate environment for policy flexibility. Meanwhile, an initially encouraging domestic environment fostered by electoral victory and public support for an assertive China policy, then adding in 'reactive' anti-Chinese nationalist pressure fuelled by recent events, generated an external–domestic nexus that saw the Koizumi government moving into a position between Quadrant C and D in the NCR framework. The preferences of action taken by Tokyo reflected NCR's dictum, which required a mix of assertive–nationalistic (highly visible) policy options to appease nationalist demands, complemented with conciliatory gestures to reduce the diplomatic cost of potential Chinese blowback.

Chinese submarine intrusion (November 2004)

According to the NCR schematics, Japan's management of the submarine incident suggests that Japanese policy-makers may have perceived the external environment leading to the episode to be relatively indeterminate. Japan continued to enjoy exceptionally good ties with the US via the Bush–Koizumi 'special relationship', and Tokyo had shown unprecedented resolve in passing legislation circumventing Article 9 to meet the expectations of the alliance. Understandably, a sense of 'quiet confidence' did reverberate in Kasumigaseki's 'corridors of power' regarding the maturity and value of the alliance as a deterrence against potential Chinese belligerence in the ECS.[42] Indeed, it is not far-fetched to suggest that Japan's assertiveness in advancing its interests in the disputed waters after Koizumi took office was partly derived from such perceptions/calculation.

However, such optimism could have been somewhat dampened after the March 2004 Senkaku/Diaoyudao dispute, especially regarding American obligations to meet Japanese expectations to defend Japan's maritime territorial interests in the ECS. Washington's neutrality and strategic ambiguity, demonstrated by the US State Department's 'impartial' response to the March incident (AFP 24 March 2004) could have awakened Tokyo to the stark reality of possible US non-commitment/ intervention in the event of a Japanese–Chinese confrontation in the contested waters.[43] Japanese policy-makers were also becoming aware of Washington's qualitatively different attitude towards Tokyo's handling of Japanese–Chinese schisms, which appeared more tolerant of Koizumi's obstinacy on 'symbolic' disputes like Yasukuni and history, compared to the 'real' and potentially explosive nature of the ECS conflict. With the American military juggernaut overstretched by commitments in Iraq and Afghanistan, and the significance of Chinese partnership in the 'war on terror' and North Korean nuclear brinksmanship, it was in the US interest to see the ECS status quo maintained. In this sense, Tokyo's policy options during the following submarine row would have been partly affected by perceptions of ambiguous allied commitment/resolve towards the dispute.

Conversely, bilateral relations with China had been in decline since the Senkaku/Diaoyudao incident in March 2004, despite burgeoning trade ties[44] and mutual efforts to advance cooperation via multilateral platforms like the ASEAN-Plus-Three and Six-Party Talks. The Chinese leadership tried to maintain a degree of pragmatism towards Japan, but the Yasukuni issue rapidly developed into a 'diplomatic *faux pas*' that constrained its policy options on other areas of bilateral exchange. Indeed, Chinese activities and the incremental encroachment in the ECS demonstrated, to some extent, the Hu-Wen leadership's depleting goodwill towards the Koizumi administration, apart from susceptibility to domestic nationalist pressure to rethink their 'new thinking on Japan'. Premier Wen's belated altercation with FM Kawaguchi over the Senkaku/Diaoyudao incident during a 'fence-mending' meeting in Beijing early April (*JT* 4 April 2004) signifies the Chinese leaders' hardening attitude in the face of growing nationalist pressure at home. China's decision to start exploration in Shirakaba/Chunxiao in May, and its impertinence towards repeated Japanese requests for suspension of exploration and data sharing on the contested gas fields, also ratcheted up bilateral tension. The spectre of heightened competition for energy resources in the ECS loomed throughout the remainder of 2004, with bilateral consultations yielding more frustration than resolution (van Kemenade 2006: 71–2). The prickly atmosphere was likewise aggravated by the resumption and intensification of 'illegal' research activities by Chinese vessels, notably between July and August, as well as anti-Japanese fervour during the Asia Cup football tournament that culminated in mob-like demonstrations directed against the Japanese entourage following China's defeat to Japan in the final. The Chinese also reportedly took exception to Tokyo's linking of Chinese military development with its decision to reduce ODA loans (*JT* 11 Nov. 2004),[45] and were offended by JDA's call for vigilance and contingencies to counter China's military intentions (*KN* 7 Nov. 2004; *CD* 10 Nov. 2004). Altogether these issues set the stage for the diplomatic showdown over the submarine incident in November 2004.

In the domestic context, the Koizumi government faced increased nationalist pressure to act more decisively in asserting Japan's sovereignty over Senkaku/Diaoyudao, especially after its perceived 'docile' handling of the March 2004 incident had left Japanese nationalists fuming. Indeed, pressure began to mount almost immediately, beginning with the first-time adoption of a resolution aimed at 'preserving [Japan's] territorial integrity' by the Diet's House of Representatives Security Committee on 30 March 2004 that requested the government to 'forcefully promote all sorts of measures, including diplomatic efforts' to defend Japanese territorial sovereignty (cf. Przystup 2004b: 124). According to Przystup (2004b: 124), although 'initially cool to the resolution', the Japanese government, presumably under duress, eventually agreed to the committee's adoption of the revised version.[46]

Nationalist assertions of Japanese sovereignty over the islands continued with Land Minister, Ishihara Nobuteru,[47] calling on the government to construct a lighthouse or heliport on Senkaku/Diaoyudao during a public speech on 3 April (BBC 3 April 2004), followed by the formation of the LDP–DPJ-led, non-partisan, Diet-members Association to Defend Japan's Territorial Integrity, several days later (Przystup 2004b: 131). The LDP, through its working group on maritime interests, also pressured the government to adopt a comprehensive national strategy on maritime-related issues, and initiate unilateral exploration on Japan's side of the median line, in June, followed by a proposal to bolster the JCG in terms of personnel and equipment, a month later (*KN* 11 June 2004; Przystup 2004b: 133; 2004c: 119).[48]

Meanwhile, on the popular front, a Japanese *uyoku* rammed a bus into the Chinese consulate in Osaka on 23 April 2004, apparently to protest at China's claims over Senkaku/Diaoyudao (*MDN* 23 April 2004). The media also reported earlier in the month that Seinensha members would go ahead with initial plans to land on the islands (Reuters 7 April 2004). Popular anti-Chinese sentiment was likewise heightened by agitated reporting in the Japanese media of Chinese activities in the ECS, and widespread anti-Japanese hostility during the mentioned football tournament. Sustained media pressure in reaction to continuous Chinese maritime probing began to constrain the Japanese government's capacity to opt for a moderate approach in managing the debacle.[49] For instance, the conservative and usually pro-establishment *Yomiuri Shimbun* published several scathing editorials in June 2004, attributing the government's failure to decisively address the ECS issues to its fixation on mollifying China. The editorials specifically blamed it on the work of pro-China forces and MOFA's indifferent attitude, and called for the *Kantei* 'to exert strong leadership on the issue' (cf. Przystup 2004b: 125).

In fact, Japan's 'nationalist-rightwing' press apparently played a key role in forcing Tokyo to abandon its cautious diplomatic response towards the submarine incident. According to observers, the Koizumi administration initially played down the issue when it first occurred on 10 November, with the JDA hesitating to speculate about the vessel's identity, while MOFA remained tight-lipped about the incident (*IHT* 12 Nov. 2004; Chan 2004). The Japanese media, led by *Yomiuri* and *Sankei*, were less courteous, strongly speculating the 'intruder' to be a Chinese submarine, and taking the Koizumi government to task for what was perceived to be its 'slow and ineffective' response in defending Japanese oceanic security, with the former demanding 'a no-compromise policy' (cf. Curtin 2004b; *DY* 11 Nov. 2004). Meanwhile, a 'united front' of political leaders 'upped the ante' with statements criticising the latest Chinese provocation (Chan 2004).[50] Intensified media pressure and concerns over domestic repercussions forced Tokyo to take a more strident approach, as reflected in the subsequent decision to declare the vessel's identity, and the MOFA's protest and demand for a Chinese apology (Curtin 2004b). Further nationalist outcry dominated both papers' editorials, in an attempt to incite anti-Chinese nationalism, specifically (*DY* 13 Nov. 2004),[51] and raise the general level of popular nationalistic sentiment, in anticipation of the ongoing negotiations in Pyongyang over the abduction issue (*JT* 10 Nov. 2004; Curtin 2004b).

Although the Japanese government took a hard-line posture by adamantly maintaining the vessel's identity as Chinese, despite Beijing's initial refusal to acknowledge this and insufficient 'hard' evidence to validate its origin, it also carefully avoided excessively acerbic rhetoric throughout the controversy that could escalate tension (Przystup 2005a: 122). Tokyo was quick to accept Beijing's subsequent admission, even interpreting its 'halfhearted' expression of regret as an 'apology' to close the episode (Chan 2004). This plausibly indicates the Koizumi government's diplomatic manoeuvres to strike a balance between appeasing nationalist demands and not adversely affecting bilateral ties, based on its perceptions/calculation of the prevailing external–domestic situation. Indeed, it could be that Koizumi wanted a swift and amicable settlement to ensure the long-awaited bilateral summit with Hu Jintao would materialise at the APEC's sidelines in Chile, days later, after a difficult year of relationship (*IHT* 18 Nov. 2004). Likewise, Curtin (2004b) observes that the earlier decision to escalate the submarine issue could be based on a 'calculated-risk' that this round of Japanese–Chinese altercation would be quickly overshadowed by a fresh eruption of the North Korean abduction issue, soon after.[52]

Japan's policy options during the submarine episode again reflect the NCR model's hypotheses, insofar as the perceptions/calculation of an increased vulnerability to domestic nationalist pressure, compounded by a relatively indeterminate external environment (i.e. unfavourable diplomatic leverage vis-à-vis China and ambiguous allied commitment), locate the Koizumi administration's position more within Quadrant D (see Figure 6.1). This explains the measured response cloaked in nationalistic rhetoric to simultaneously satisfy external and domestic imperatives.

Natural gas exploration dispute (May 2004–September 2006)

Unlike the other two ECS contentions, the natural gas dispute has not triggered specific diplomatic clashes, despite gradually festering into a potentially volatile conflict during the period of investigation, due to unilateral actions and counteractions from both sides. One can observe that the Japanese government has maintained its assertiveness, taking tangible, calculated measures periodically to assert Japan's claims in response to Chinese effrontery. Yet such assertions have also been arbitrated by moderate policy behaviour that saw Tokyo agreeing to participate in protracted and unproductive dialogues, even as Beijing continued to defy its requests and proceed with its own plan. The NCR dictum suggests these 'ambiguous' policy options as reflecting state-elites' perceptions/calculation of the prevailing external–domestic conditions and processes during a particular time and context, which affected their decisions.

As highlighted, the natural gas issue erupted in May 2004, following Chinese exploration in Shirakaba/Chunxiao that prompted repeated Japanese protests, and requests for suspension of survey and data provision. China's lackadaisical attitude elicited a tougher Japanese response, with METI deciding to conduct surveys on Japan's side of the median line in July 2004 (*KN* 9 July 2004),[53] leading to Chinese calls for working-level dialogues on the issue that brought several rounds of fruitless consultations between 2004 and 2006, beginning in October 2004 (Drifte 2008a; Valencia 2007). It is arguable that Tokyo's measured responses during the nascent stages of the natural gas dispute mirrored the perceived external environment and domestic conditions elaborated in the 'submarine incursion' analysis, as both issues occurred at almost the same time and context. This means discernible policy actions (declaration of intent followed by concrete, albeit low-risk launching of surveys), mediated by persistent requests for Chinese cooperation and agreement to bilateral exchanges (the dialogues) that were required to keep diplomatic channels open for peaceful resolution, while avoiding serious escalation of the situation.

Nonetheless, the dispute became volatile in 2005, with Japan visibly advancing its interests amid serious deterioration in politico-diplomatic relations caused by a tempestuous mix of issues. Specifically, bilateral conditions vis-à-vis China became unfavourable, despite the promising late 2004 'sideline summitries' in Chile and Vientiane, and various levels of bilateral engagement during the first quarter of 2005 (Przystup 2005b: 110–12), including the establishment of the Vice-Foreign Ministerial Comprehensive Dialogue (Reuters 24 June 2005). On the security front, China was concerned about the strategic implications of the February 2005 'Two-Plus-Two' talks, and upset by Japanese attempts to subvert the lifting of the European Union (EU) arms embargo on the Chinese, especially with METI chief Nakagawa and PM Koizumi lobbying to dissuade their French counterparts from doing this.[54] The adoption of the Anti-Secession Law in March was clearly a strong Chinese response to the development in US–Japanese security cooperation, not to mention Beijing's strengthened resolve to oppose Tokyo's bid for a permanent UNSC seat that started gaining momentum from late 2004 (Marquand 2005).

The maritime territorial dispute, likewise, escalated in February 2005, fuelled by the Japanese government's controversial decision to take administrative control of Senkaku/Diaoyudao, and other endeavours to strengthen claims to sovereignty, i.e. Okinotorishima,[55] against the backdrop of persistent Chinese encroachment on the Japanese-claimed EEZ and exploration activities at the fringes of the median line. The large-scale anti-Japanese demonstrations in April, in reaction to the plethora of Chinese grievances, including a fresh eruption of the Tsukurukai textbook controversy, further aggravated Japanese–Chinese tension. Although there were mutual efforts to resuscitate the flagging ties, Koizumi's Yasukuni exploits, as elaborated in the previous chapter, ensured that the political chill remained throughout 2005, which effectively subverted the progress of resolving the ECS dispute via consultation. Indeed, Japan's intention to use the scheduled 19 October dialogue to force a definitive solution to the issue was squandered by Koizumi's Yasukuni visit, two days earlier, which saw China temporarily cancelling all diplomatic exchanges with Japan (van Kemenade 2006: 73). Whether Beijing was deliberately 'buying time' (Curtin 2005b) by keeping the ECS negotiations deadlocked has remained unproven, but China's aforementioned military presence and provocative actions in the contested waters unquestionably made the situation more perilous.[56] The unfavourable bilateral conditions with China suggest the need for Japan to maintain a cautious approach in managing the natural gas issue.

In terms of alliance commitment, Japanese policy-makers may have remained doubtful of Washington's resolve when it came to defending Japan's ECS claims, the new impetus from the 'Two-Plus-Two' talks notwithstanding. To be sure, one can argue that Tokyo could have taken heart from the talks, plausibly in the shape of discreet reassurance from its American ally, to counter potential Chinese belligerence in the ECS. This was especially so after the submarine incident and the repeated ECS forays, which were widely perceived by observers as China's attempt 'to probe where the bedrock of the US-Japan alliance begins' (Tkacik 2004). Also, one can construe the Joint Statement to be as much a value-added deterrence as a veiled American caution against potential Chinese 'adventurism' in the Taiwan Strait and ECS, besides serving as a 'safety valve' to keep domestic nationalist pressure for a more independent Japanese military solution in check.[57] That said, the continuous absence of explicit and firm articulation of the US position, despite Washington's reassurances over the years, and given the other perceived external constraints vis-à-vis China, would have meant that a policy of calculated assertiveness mixed with diplomatic prudence serves Japanese interests best in the ECS. Specifically, while Tokyo needs to demonstrate a degree of assertiveness, it also has to pursue joint development as 'the best means for unlocking the impasse' (Curtin 2005b; Takahashi 2004), and to avoid adversely affecting the ECS status quo.

The Koizumi government would be required to demonstrate assertiveness in the natural gas dispute, not only to protect Japan's oceanic resources and security in the name of the national interest, but also to soothe nationalist demands for domestic political expediency. Unquestionably, nationalist pressure continued to mount in reaction to Chinese defiance towards repeated Japanese requests and proposals to facilitate a resolution of the dispute. The reputedly 'hawkish' METI chief Nakagawa[58] consistently pursued an assertive stance on the issue from mid-2004, and his televised address in February 2005 regarding the likelihood of Chinese siphoning off Japanese resources via their exploits in Shirakaba/Chunxiao fuelled both nationalist and public hostility towards China (AFP 20 Feb. 2005). On the political front, the DPJ advocated a Diet legislation draft in March to protect Japanese ships engaged in exploration activities in the disputed area (Przystup 2005b: 116), while members from the LDP, Shin-Komeito and DPJ increased pressure on the Japanese government to proceed with the granting of exploration rights after aerial observation of Chinese activities in the ECS during early April (Fanell 2006). Nationalist pressure also emerged in the form of reactive, popular anti-Chinese nationalism that reached a high, following the anti-Japanese demonstrations in China, with a string of 'vandalism and harassment against Chinese businesses, schools, and diplomatic establishments reported across Japan between April 11–19' (Chan and Bridges 2006: 129). Although chiefly triggered by the Chinese demonstrations, these xenophobic activities reflected pent-up frustration amongst Japanese nationalists towards perceived Chinese bullying and obstinacy over a range of issues, including the ECS natural gas dispute (Tsunekawa 2006: 7, 19–20). Indeed, Tokyo's decision to proceed with unilateral exploration plans soon after, and Koizumi's dismissal of concerns that it could further strain Japan–China ties (Przystup 2005c: 126), suggest the salience of domestic pressure, nationalist or otherwise, in determining the assertive policy response.[59]

Japan's posture on the gas exploration issue remained unchanged throughout 2005, as sustained nationalist pressure required the Koizumi administration to stand tall against China. The METI, personified by Nakagawa, continued to pursue a hardnosed approach, accusing China of deliberately prolonging the consultations, while pushing ahead with its exploration activities in Shirakaba/Chunxiao, and then extending to Kashi/Tianwaitian, despite Japanese protests (Curtin 2005b). Media pressure also derived from *Yomiuri Shimbun*'s October editorial that reiterated the conventional wisdom of Chinese 'time buying' and raised the possibility of such manoeuvres as a Chinese strategy to turn their development of the gas fields into 'a *fait accompli*', especially in the absence of Japanese counteractions (cf. Curtin 2005b). Unsurprisingly, such agitated reporting galvanised Japanese public opinion, which saw 70 per cent of respondents agreeing that China should cease its operations in the ECS during a mid-October *Yomiuri* poll, with 65 per cent favouring unilateral Japanese development of the disputed area, if Beijing refused to comply (Przystup 2006a: 116). Interestingly, the same poll recorded an 'almost evenly divided' opinion on Koizumi's Yasukuni visit (cf. Curtin 2005b), suggesting that public support for a forceful China policy was more cohesive on the ECS dispute compared to symbolic issues. This inadvertently meant greater pressure on the Koizumi government to maintain, if not increase, its assertiveness on the former issue, amid mounting public impatience. As mentioned in Chapter 5, the LDP's landslide victory in the September 2005 Lower House election was driven as much by Koizumi's domestic reform agenda as his uncompromising

China policy. It is plausible to suggest that Tokyo's posturing before the snap election, which included its assertive stance on the ECS natural gas dispute, reflected Koizumi's sensitivity towards the prevailing public mood, which he masterfully rallied to his political advantage.

Also, unlike Yasukuni, there was a unified opinion between the LDP and DPJ on a forceful ECS policy, with both parties advocating legislation in late 2005 to protect Japan's EEZ against foreign encroachment.[60] Political elites, namely DPJ's president Maehara and FM Aso, even amplified the 'China threat' theory with their provocative remarks, purportedly in response to China's military development and its related activities in the ECS (*CD* 3 April 2006).[61] Whereas the LDP-coalition government later backtracked on Aso's remark, the DPJ adopted the 'China threat' perception as its official view on 23 January 2006 (Przystup 2006b: 126). Meanwhile, the prospective LDP candidates to succeed Koizumi in September 2006 also began playing to the nationalist tune, with Abe and Aso leading the chorus of criticisms on China over Yasukuni and the ECS, ostensibly to boost their nationalist credentials. As revealed, both firmly rejected China's proposal for joint development that was forwarded to the Japanese delegation when dialogue resumed early March 2006 (*AS* 9 March 2006). Abe also reportedly chided Sasae Kenichiro, MOFA's AOAB director-general, for not rejecting it outright during the talks (Przystup 2006b: 123), while Aso advocated 'countermeasures' if China proceeded with gas production in Shirakaba/Chunxiao (*KN* 15 March 2006). To be sure, these confrontational/nationalistic expressions were often moderated by conciliatory posturing of other policy-makers, like the new 'pro-China' METI chief, Nikai Toshihiro, who called for level-headedness in dealing with the ECS issue.[62] In fact, Nikai reportedly rebuked Aso for his provocative, yet unproductive recommendation, highlighting the emerging schism between METI and MOFA over the dispute (*AS* 20 March 2006). Ironically, METI was perceptively more confrontational during the earlier stages, notably under Nakagawa, while MOFA, before Aso, was more tactful. This suggests that the leadership's 'nationalistic' disposition tends to personify the policy orientation of Japanese bureaucracies.

Overall, it is viable to suggest that the Koizumi government had been under consistent pressure from domestic forces to adopt and maintain an assertive–nationalistic policy towards China over the ECS natural gas dispute since its outbreak in mid-2004. Japan's pressure on China to suspend exploration activities and share geological data on the disputed gas fields as preconditions for joint development negotiations, as well as visible moves to protect Japanese interests in response to the Chinese refusal to cooperate, imply, to an extent, the influence of domestic nationalist impetus on such policy behaviour. An ex-METI senior vice-minister even conceded that the ECS became problematic following Nakagawa's 'nationalistic' overtures and posturing,[63] while a former Japanese ambassador to China conceded that Diet and LDP pressure made any Japanese concession or 'peaceful solution' to the issue difficult.[64] Indeed, Tokyo's tough stance, despite informed opinions that full-scale gas production in the ECS is neither economically viable, nor cost-effective for Japan, compared to importing from cheaper neighbouring sources, i.e. Russia and South-East Asia, goes on to support such a view.[65]

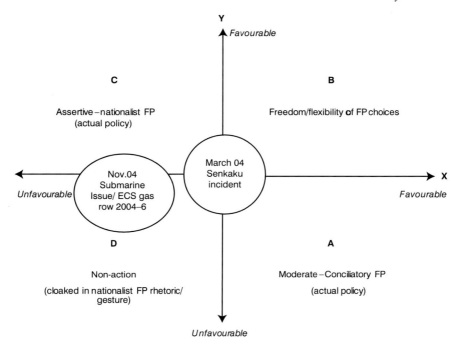

Y

Favourable

C

Assertive–nationalist FP
(actual policy)

B

Freedom/flexibility of FP choices

Unfavourable

Nov.04
Submarine
Issue/ ECS gas
row 2004–6

March 04
Senkaku
incident

X

Favourable

D

Non-action

(cloaked in nationalist FP rhetoric/
gesture)

A

Moderate–Conciliatory FP

(actual policy)

Unfavourable

X = Domestic Political Resolve (vis-à-vis domestic nationalist pressure)

Y = Relative Power Position (vis-à-vis disputant state/China)

Figure 6.1 NCR model of nationalism and Japan's China policy preferences on the ECS dispute

Conversely, Japanese policy-makers (Chinese, as well) would have estimated the risk of a Japanese–Chinese military conflict to be low, since the dispute over natural gas *per se* is arguably 'non-zero-sum', insofar as both countries are able to source it from regional suppliers, and that the calculated costs and benefits favour joint development.[66] Thus, a degree of nationalistic 'brinksmanship' and 'grandstanding' in dealing with the Chinese would not be overly damaging to Japan's overall interests. However, the fact that Tokyo has (1) tolerated Beijing's continuous defiance, despite its repeated request for cooperation, (2) demonstrated willingness to participate in protracted, yet unprogressive consultations, and (3) hesitated to adopt countermeasures, as reflected by the relatively sluggish proceedings in granting exploration rights to Teikoku Oil, let alone permitting actual drilling, also suggest the limits of nationalism in Japan's China policy-making.[67]

A neoclassical realist interpretation would emphasise the prevailing external conditions elaborated earlier, and their interactions with domestic imperatives that plausibly contributed to Tokyo's 'measured' approach of discernible, albeit calculated assertiveness, mediated by diplomatic prudence, when dealing with

Beijing over the issue. Indeed, whilst Japan took incremental counteractions, Koizumi continued to call for both sides to transform the ECS from a 'sea of confrontation to a sea of cooperation' (Przystup 2005c: 126; Drifte 2008a/b). He also replaced the so-called 'China-bashing' Nakagawa with the 'pro-Beijing' Nikai as one of Japan's key bureaucratic actors in the dispute during the October 2005 Cabinet reshuffle. Such conciliatory gestures plausibly reflect perceptions/ calculation of a less-sanguine external environment, characterised by ambiguous alliance support and adverse bilateral conditions vis-à-vis China, which require Japanese state-elites to adopt restrained policy preferences. Arbitrated by relatively intense domestic nationalist pressure, the external–domestic nexus would have informed their perceived location within the NCR diagram, and therein the stipulated policy option. This generalised policy trend is essentially based on the assessment of the natural gas issue being a protracted conflict, and therefore, does not account for variations in state-elites' perceptions that led to specific manifestations of Japanese policy behaviour at particular points during the period of investigation.

Conclusion

Japan's management of the ECS maritime territorial issues during the Koizumi administration implies the plausible salience of domestic nationalist pressure affecting its policy choices. However, unlike the predominantly symbolic nature of the Yasukuni problem, the ECS dispute is real/tangible, and has the potential to escalate into armed confrontation amid a volatile concoction of chauvinistic nationalist passion and military brinksmanship. Accordingly, NCR's dictum expects Japanese state-elites to be more constrained by the relative determinacy of the ECS issues. The measured responses and diplomatic manoeuvres undertaken clearly suggest the prevalence of reason over passion (Gries 2004), and balancing, on Tokyo's part, to simultaneously advance its foreign and domestic policy goals. This demonstrates the extent to which nationalism determines Japan's China policy-making, which, under particular external–domestic conditions and time context, as perceived by Japanese state-elites, can be more or less salient vis-à-vis other variables in shaping their policy options. Indeed, the breakthrough in June 2008, where both sides reached an agreement to jointly develop the disputed ECS gas fields, further underscores nationalism's limitations in Japanese policy-making (Yoshida and Terada 2008).

Conclusion

This book has striven to assess nationalism's role and salience in shaping Japan's relations with China during the Koizumi administration. It has earmarked important questions which required investigation pertaining to the conventional wisdom regarding the effect of nationalism in weakening their bilateral ties. By incorporating an NCR analytical model, this volume has sought to explicate why, how, when and the extent to which resurgent nationalism has affected the perceptions and calculation that determine Japanese policy options towards China. This is especially the case when managing nationalist issues in the presence of other factors that simultaneously influence their bilateral interaction.

This chapter attempts, first, to summarise the empirical findings from the case studies of the Yasukuni Shrine and ECS disputes, by re-engaging the research questions and identifying the commonalities and differences between the two issue areas, to establish nationalism's causality vis-à-vis other determinants in Japan's China policy and the bilateral ties. This is followed by an evaluation of the feasibility and relevancy of the NCR analytical construct in addressing the 'national' question, as compared to conventional IR and constructivist/area studies frameworks that dominate the literature on Japanese–Chinese relations. The concluding section delineates this study's implications for future IR-oriented investigations of Japanese–Chinese diplomacy, and generally, interstate relations that are obfuscated by domestic-ideational problems, i.e. nationalism and identity politics. Perhaps most emphatically, it highlights the progressiveness of IR realism via NCR in addressing its 'Achilles' heel' of domestic-ideational theorising, to advance a more wholesome explanation of state behaviour in international relations.

Empirical findings

The analyses of the Yasukuni and ECS disputes reveal a number of cross-case empirical commonalities and differences, with regard to nationalism's impact on Japan's China policy prescriptions for the respective issue areas. The findings of this section are guided by the central research question, which investigated the manner, conditions and the extent to which nationalism affects Japanese state-elites' perceptions/calculation and policy options towards the Chinese, when managing these nationalistic-flavoured bilateral issues. They are also formulated around correlated questions regarding its salience vis-à-vis other determinants in constraining Japan's preference of action, and whether these other imperatives exacerbate or mitigate nationalism in the policy-making process.

The salience and limits of nationalism

For a start, this investigation found that in both case studies, nationalism, defined in terms of domestic nationalist pressure and/or nationalistic-rightwing conviction of key state-elites, was, to some extent, responsible for the Japanese government's policy options that aggravated diplomatic conundrums and periods of sustained political tension with China. For reasons of identity and/or politico-strategic expediency, nationalism was unequivocal in fuelling the Japanese–Chinese disputes over Yasukuni and the ECS. Nationalist passion and emotions were indubitably involved in arousing Japanese pride and prejudices vis-à-vis the Chinese. So was their strategic instrumentalisation by Japanese state-elites in foreign policy-making, to advance both personal political goals and the nationalist agenda of historical revisionism and maritime territorial sovereignty.

However, nationalism, though salient, did not appear to be the primary determinant of Tokyo's external behaviour. Indeed, neither case study depicted instances of Japanese–Chinese altercations festering beyond strident rhetorical exchanges and measured diplomatic responses that stopped short of hostile actions, despite the nationalistic sensitivities surrounding both issues. The fact that none of the disputes escalated into violent confrontations suggests that nationalist passion and emotions do not automatically render the 'rationality' of state-elites obsolete, and that domestic nationalist pressure does not necessarily translate into assertive–nationalist policy options. A clear example of such behaviour can be drawn from Japan's management of the ECS natural gas dispute. As described, the Japanese government encountered significant domestic nationalist pressure for more decisive action in dealing with China, following its perceived 'soft handling' of the Senkaku/Diaoyudao and submarine incidents, and especially after reports of Chinese encroachment and alleged exploration activities at the fringes of the ECS median line. Yet, despite nationalist pressure and Chinese provocations, the Koizumi administration did not opt for an outright assertive-nationalist policy, in a 'tit-for-tat' action to stake Japan's claim that would have risked a high-seas confrontation with the PLA-Navy. Instead, a policy of discernible, albeit calculated assertiveness modulated by diplomatic prudence was preferred, to advance a more pragmatic solution to the dispute.

Similarly in the Yasukuni Shrine row, Koizumi's annual pilgrimages at the expense of Japanese–Chinese political relations demonstrated nationalism's salience in shaping his nonchalant policy towards China. However, notwithstanding fervent nationalist calls for a more forthright treatment of his 'original' Yasukuni pledge (annual homage on 15 August), the timing, policy options and diplomatic manoeuvres undertaken by Koizumi and his government during each of the six shrine visits indicate state-elites' astute perceptions/calculation and shrewd statecraft, rather than purely nationalistic passion and emotionally laden decision-making. Koizumi's decision to avoid the contentious date in all but his last Yasukuni visit (most vividly depicted by his 'eleventh hour' 'change-of-date' strategy in August 2001) further confirms this observation.

The extent to which nationalism affected foreign policy-making was demonstrated by the differences in Japanese state-elites' treatment of and attitude towards the two issue areas of history and security (symbolic/intangible versus real/tangible), especially when it came to suppressing or allowing the neo-nationalist agenda to manifest in China policy-making. It is obvious that the Koizumi administration was generally more prepared to pander to nationalist demands to advance an assertive–nationalist policy over the history-oriented Yasukuni dispute, due to the symbolic and less risk-adverse nature of the issue. Conversely, its inclination to modulate between assertive and moderate policy options, when managing the security-oriented ECS dispute, connotes its readiness to rein in or divert excessive nationalist pressure to other less tangible issues, considering the real and potentially explosive nature of maritime territorial disputes. The qualitatively different treatment of and policy approach towards these two issue areas, as reflected by Koizumi's cavalier attitude in advancing the neo-nationalist revisionist history agenda via the Yasukuni issue, while embracing a cautious and measured response towards the ECS conflict, evidently highlight the limits of nationalism in affecting Japan's China policy.

Overall, the evidence from both case studies shows that Japan's China policy is determined by much more than the nationalistic and emotive goals of reinstating Japanese pride and identity via the reinterpretation of history, and the defence of Japanese maritime territorial sovereignty. Rather, foreign policy reflects the broader national interests of the Japanese state/state-elites, defined in terms of realising a combination of pragmatic external goals and domestic agendas. In both cases, 'sensibility and reason' appear to have overridden 'sense and passion' in Japanese policy-making, despite the latter combination being popularly, albeit mistakenly perceived as the driving force behind Koizumi's hardnosed Yasukuni policy towards the Chinese. It is undeniable that Koizumi's obstinacy in the Yasukuni debacle was, to an extent, the result of intense domestic nationalist pressure and plausibly his personal nationalist convictions. However, it was also evident that such behaviour only manifested itself because of the symbolic rather than tangible nature of the dispute. More significant was Koizumi's over-emphasis and dependence on a pro-US foreign policy, where the anticipation of favourable US–Japan relations vis-à-vis China facilitated his shrine bravado. It is likewise true that Koizumi and several key Cabinet members have been commonly regarded as 'neo-conservatives' and/or 'normal-nationalists' (Samuels 2007a/b), who long for the revival of Japanese pride and prestige in the international arena. Yet, in most of the diplomatic incidents discussed, their nationalistic demeanour did not appear to cloud their judgement and policy deliberation, nor did these so-called 'normal-nationalists' indiscriminately pursue nationalistic policy options vis-à-vis China, to advance the more parochial dimensions of Japanese national interests. These empirical observations, though not denying nationalism's salience in Japanese policy-making, suggest the need to redress the common misinterpretation regarding its primacy in shaping Japan's contemporary relations with China.

Abe Shinzo's initiatives to resuscitate political relations with Beijing upon assuming office in September 2006 further demonstrated the limits of nationalism in China policy-making. Despite his renowned hawkish, anti-China stance and nationalist candour, Abe exhibited his pragmatic side by making the PRC his maiden official overseas destination,[1] in an attempt to seize the opportunity to restore leadership summits and mutual state visits that had been frozen since 2001, owing largely to Koizumi's Yasukuni intransigence. During their summit, both Abe and the Chinese leadership agreed to build 'a mutually beneficial relationship based on common strategic interests', which was a qualitative improvement on the 1998 pledge of 'a partnership of friendship and cooperation' (Nabeshima 2006). They also agreed to strengthen bilateral relations by 'turning the wheels' of politics and economics simultaneously, instead of maintaining the *seikei bunri* principle, and establishing bilateral panels to study the 'history' and ECS issues (Nabeshima 2006). Perhaps nationalism's centrality was most evidently dismissed by Abe's observation of the Yasukuni moratorium during his inaugural stint as premier. Taken together with this hindsight, the empirical evidence does not appear to support the conventional wisdom regarding rising nationalism being the dominant feature of the bilateral relationship, or the primary driver of Japan's China policy.

Nationalism's efficacy vis-à-vis other variables

This brings us to a second, correlated conclusion that views nationalism's saliency as being dependent on its interaction with other variables, which can either mitigate or exacerbate its efficacy, and which, under particular conditions and contexts, can be more prevalent in determining Japanese policy options. Both case studies have shown that domestic nationalist pressure does not act in isolation to determine Japan's China policy-making, even though both issue areas are genuinely rooted in the nationalist ideology and fuelled by nationalist passion. Rather, nationalism's salience depends on Japanese state-elites' perception of the prevailing external environment, and the domestic political conditions that affected their policy calculations. In particular, the Koizumi administration's pursuance of a nationalistic–assertive China policy reflects its perceptions of a sanguine external environment, defined in terms of an advantageous relative power position vis-à-vis China. Such perceptions were forged mainly by a combination of favourable alliance commitment/resolve via the US–Japanese alliance, and bilateral leverage over Beijing, as well as limited economic cost to their deepening interdependence. Conversely, a perceived disadvantageous or ambivalent power position has almost always induced less palpable nationalistic policy options that come either in the form of non-action masqueraded in nationalist rhetoric, a tangibly moderate-conciliatory policy, or a discernibly assertive policy modulated by appeasing measures. Mediating Tokyo's decision-making were the developments in the domestic political context, namely the magnitude of official and popular nationalist-rightwing vis-à-vis pacifist-leftist/opposition political pressure for a more assertive or moderate China policy, the personal politico-ideological convictions of state-elites notwithstanding.

Both cases have shown limited instances where the Japanese government chose an outright nationalistic policy option, following its perception of a favourable power position vis-à-vis China. Instead, the most favoured option appeared to be a combination of assertive-cum-moderate behaviour that reflected Tokyo's predominant perception of ambiguous external conditions leading to the various diplomatic clashes. However, a more important observation lies with the fact that Japan's behaviour towards China was primarily constrained by external impetus, an observation that is theoretically consistent with the NCR dictum espoused by this study. Indeed, in both cases, the choice between nationalistic and moderate policy options essentially hinged on state-elites' perceptions of the external environment, which delineated the parameters of Japan's policies in the context of Japanese–Chinese relations. Empirically, the Koizumi administration appeared more willing to support the neo-nationalist agenda, or allow domestic nationalist pressure to affect its China policy, to varying degrees, under a perceived favourable or ambivalent external environment. Conversely, it exercised diplomatic prudence, suppressing domestic nationalist sentiments, when the external environment was perceived as unfavourable. Such policy behaviour clearly reflects NCR's presuppositions regarding domestic variables gaining salience and assuming a relatively independent function affecting foreign policy, under low-pressure or ambiguous external conditions, and vice versa during periods of high external pressure.

Yet both case studies demonstrate that the prevailing external environment did not directly translate into specific preference of action, but had to be mediated by domestic variables in the guise of nationalist pressure and other political processes, and more fundamentally by the 'fuzzy' perceptual lenses of Japanese state-elites who served as the final arbiter of the specific policy options (G. Rose 1998; Sterling-Folker 1997: 19). In other words, it was unit-level causality in the shape of key decision-makers within the Koizumi administration that intersubjectively defined the external conditions which, calculated together with the other domestic impetus, shaped the respective policy options and diplomatic manoeuvres vis-à-vis China. Again, this conclusion not only conforms to NCR's theoretical underpinnings that posit a causal role for domestic variables like nationalism in foreign policy analysis, but also evidently justify its advocacy for explicit domestic-level theorising, which under particular conditions can be effective in constraining state behaviour.

As noted, the Koizumi administration mostly perceived the external condition and relative power position vis-à-vis China to be ambiguous. Meanwhile, its domestic political resolve over nationalist pressure leading to the incidents in both cases was largely unfavourable. Straddling the external–domestic nexus, the anticipated position predisposed Tokyo's preference towards visible, assertive–nationalist responses moderated by conciliatory measures when dealing with Beijing. This apparent 'balancing' act of satisfying nationalist demands domestically while appeasing the Chinese externally also validates the NCR-centred argument regarding state-elites' inclination to strike a balanced foreign policy of simultaneously pursuing nationalistic goals and the broader national interests. In the Japanese case, these potentially divergent goals were defined in terms of the quest for national pride and prestige, and 'normal statehood', on one hand, and a stable Japanese–Chinese relationship for mutual economic and strategic benefits, on the other. Time and again, 'trade-offs' occurred in the form of pursuing 'damage-control' measures to compensate for the initial provocative actions (i.e. visiting Yasukuni, detaining Chinese activists in Senkaku/Diaoyudao and pursuing unilateral exploration plans in the ECS), where pragmatic considerations like preventing further escalations of diplomatic tension and sustaining flourishing economic ties to fuel Japan's economic vitality were prioritised over narrower nationalist objectives.

Another interesting empirical point to note is that, in most of the contentious episodes, the Koizumi administration chose the expected policy options that reflected its anticipated position resulting from the interplay between external and domestic dynamics. However, Koizumi's controversial decision to visit Yasukuni on 15 August 2006 seemed anomalous, since the unfavourable external environment and domestic political resolve would have required him to adopt non-action, or a conciliatory policy option. Yet, when interpreted from NCR's perspective, his 'nationalistic' action conforms to the assumption that state-elites do not necessarily respond effectively to the stipulated decision-making constraints, due to domestic 'intervening' elements. In this respect, the decision arguably reflected Koizumi's anticipation that a shrine visit during his last weeks in office would not trigger debilitating international and domestic political repercussions, but would support his intention to 'immortalise' his personal political image as the leader who stood tall against China, and even, plausibly, fulfil his nationalist convictions.

As concluded earlier, the perception of an advantageous relative power position vis-à-vis China, forged by a combination of favourable US–Japan alliance commitment/resolve, diplomatic leverage over China and sustainable economic interdependence, tended to allow domestic nationalist impetus greater room to shape Japan's China policy. Individually, and collectively, these external dynamics also exhibited mitigating and exacerbating effects on nationalism's efficacy. In both case studies, it was apparent that favourable allied commitment/resolve in the shape of a strengthened US–Japanese alliance was a decisive external factor influencing Koizumi's China policy orientation. Both cases demonstrate that the perception of the prevailing relative power position vis-à-vis China significantly depended on the Japanese government's anticipation of the atmosphere of US–Japan ties, the proximity between Tokyo and Washington vis-à-vis Beijing in the US–Japan–China 'triangular ties', and American *gaiatsu*, pertaining to the two issues. Undoubtedly, such estimations were engendered by Koizumi's 'grand strategy' of hitching Japanese foreign policy to that of their American ally to facilitate the quest for 'normal' statehood, and a greater international role and recognition. Since Japanese–Chinese relations have traditionally been and continue to be greatly affected by their relationships with the US, Washington's encouragement and appreciation of Japan's overtly pro-American foreign policy, obviously, gave Tokyo the impression of greater leverage over Beijing in their 'strategic triangularity' (Soerensen 2006). This expectedly boosted Koizumi's confidence in advancing an assertive and occasionally 'aloof' China policy.

In particular, this book has determined that Koizumi's Yasukuni policy was largely facilitated by the post-'9/11' expansion of US–Japanese security relations under the aegis of their alliance. Japan's unwavering support for US external/security agenda endeared Koizumi to the Bush administration, and the 'Bush–Koizumi special relationship' led to minimal American *gaiatsu* on Japanese diplomacy towards China, at least on 'history'-related quarrels. Indeed, Washington, for most part, maintained its silence and tolerated the Japanese PM's Yasukuni antics, despite their debilitating impact on Japan's Asia policy, and the corresponding repercussions to US regional strategy. However, when it came to the security-oriented ECS conflict, Washington was more prepared to vocalise its 'impartiality' (e.g. during the 2004 Senkaku/Diaoyudao dispute), apparently to send a clearer signal to Tokyo regarding possible US 'non-commitment' in the event of an ECS contingency, and its preference for the status quo, to dissuade further provocative actions from its Japanese ally. Both instances not only demonstrated the prevalence of 'alliance commitment/resolve' impinging on the Koizumi administration's perceptions/calculation of its relative power position vis-à-vis China, but also in exacerbating as well as mitigating nationalism's role in Japan's China policy-making. In fact, the general assertiveness of Koizumi's China policy gave the impression that he was willing, to some extent, to discount other policy determinants, to advance the neo-nationalist agenda and upset the Chinese in the process, for as long as propitious US–Japanese ties were in place. It is, therefore, viable to deduce that the correlation between Washington's alliance commitment and the 'strategic empowerment of nationalism' (Bong 2002: 266) by Japanese state-elites denote what observers acknowledge as Japan's 'dependent nationalism', one which is only feasible via American encouragement (McCormack 2007; Tsunekawa 2006).

The prevalence of the alliance factor in Japan's external calculus invariably connotes the limits of economic interdependence and other external–domestic determinants in moulding its China policy. As previously described, Koizumi's aloofness in continuing with the shrine visits, despite the threats of Chinese economic retributions and, more ominously, following the massive anti-Japanese demonstrations in 2005, indicates Koizumi's willingness to risk damaging Japanese–Chinese economic ties. Likewise, Tokyo's forceful detention of Chinese activists during the March 2004 Senkaku/Diaoyudao incident, regardless of the earlier Chinese veiled threat to undermine Japanese bid for a lucrative Shinkansen project, in the wake of Koizumi's New Year shrine visit, further allude to the limits of economic interdependence in mitigating nationalistic tendencies in Japan's China policy. However, it has to be clarified that these specific instances do not adequately represent the full impact of economic considerations on Japanese policy-making, especially when viewing their bilateral ties from the broader and longer-term perspective. On the contrary, the 'damage-control' measures and swift diplomatic 'fence-mending' by Japan (and China) following several of the bilateral altercations suggest economic interdependence as having a much more constraining effect on Japanese state-elites' decision-making. Thus, despite limited contextual evidence indicating the impact of specific economic considerations on Tokyo's policy calculations during the various diplomatic contentions, it is still credible to deduce that their flourishing bilateral trade and investment relations did factor in Japan's pragmatic posturing, especially when her long-overdue economic recovery had much to do with China's robust economic growth and burgeoning domestic consumption. Moreover, with China becoming Japan's top trading partner from 2004, and Japanese investment pouring into the Chinese mainland against the backdrop of popular anti-Japanese fervour, rational and calculated policy judgements, rather than purely emotional responses that could undermine Japanese business interests, appeared to be Tokyo's *modus vivendi* towards Beijing.

Furthermore, China's 'comfortable' acquiescence of the *seikei bunri*-styled relationship, epitomised by the 'cold politics, hot economics' arrangement, gave the impression of both governments operating a 'double-track' approach when managing the political and economic dimensions of their diplomacy (Drifte 2003: 19). If true, this hypothesis would have offered Tokyo more flexibility in terms of policy choices towards Beijing without being overly concerned about Chinese economic retribution. It would have equally explained the Koizumi administration's relatively indifferent perceptions/calculation of its diplomatic leverage vis-à-vis China, especially in the majority of the Yasukuni incidents discussed, which partly encouraged his obstinate shrine policy. Similarly, Tokyo's 'calculated assertiveness' in the submarine and gas disputes, despite the unfavourable diplomatic conditions with China, partly reflects its confidence towards Beijing's economic pragmatism in mitigating excessive Chinese responses to escalate the disputes. This evidence highlights the correlation between economic interdependence and Japan's perception of its bilateral leverage over China, where the latter was, to an extent, dependent on Japanese state-elites' consideration of the former. More significantly, they illustrate not only the moderating, but also exacerbating attributes of economic interdependence on nationalistic tendencies in Japan's China policy-making, where increased confidence in the positive effects of greater interdependence actually encouraged Japanese state-elites to be less restrained in pursuing nationalistic policies.

As for domestic politics, both case studies demonstrate, to varying degrees, the causality of inter/intra-party political competition and the affective role of domestic, non-state actors in Japan's China policy-making. They also highlight the intertwined relations between domestic politics and nationalism, where Japanese state-elites demonstrated the inclination to indulge in nationalist politics, and propensity to stoke nationalist sentiment for domestic political expediency, all of which contributed to Japan's assertive–nationalist policy options (actual and rhetorical), when managing the two issue areas. Indeed, both cases testify to the changing dynamics of intra-LDP politics, whereby the ascendancy of nationalistic-rightwing and 'anti-China' forces via the Seiwa-kai faction, diplomatic *zoku*, the PARC, and various Diet-member groupings, engendered a more assertive and *realpolitik*-oriented China policy. This policy shift was encouraged by waning leftwing opposition and the resulting drift of Japanese mainstream politics to the right. Furthermore, despite its political opposition on symbolic issues like the Yasukuni visits, the then-largest opposition party, DPJ, revealed that it can be as nationalistic as the LDP, if not more so, when it comes to defending Japanese interests in the ECS, or fuelling the 'China threat' notion. Meanwhile, PM Koizumi's promotion of 'neo-conservative' elites to key Cabinet positions also saw China policy-making becoming relatively dependent on these central decision-makers' political resolve vis-à-vis domestic nationalist pressure, their own nationalistic convictions aside. Additionally, the enhanced foreign policy-making leverage of the Cabinet and the *Kantei* saw MOFA's traditionally moderating influence on China policy diminished. Meanwhile, Koizumi's pro-US external orientation facilitated the ascendancy of so-called 'American school' bureaucrats at the expense of 'China school' officials within the MOFA setup. These domestic political transformations, among others, allowed the mainstream neo-nationalist/neo-conservative version of 'American-dependent' nationalism to take root at the apex, legislative and the bureaucratic levels of Japanese policy-making during Koizumi's premiership.

Moreover, in both cases, nationalist pressure groups, the Japanese media and public opinion became important sources of nationalistic-oriented political pressure affecting Tokyo's policy deliberations. Likewise, members of state-elites like Koizumi, Abe, Aso and Nakagawa all demonstrated the inclination to instrumentalise 'anti-China' nationalism to appease these non-state actors, in their efforts to advance both neo-nationalist and personal political agendas. Conversely, the traditionally salient, non-official mitigating forces of pacifist pressure groups and *zaikai* appeared less effective in suppressing nationalist tendencies. This was vividly demonstrated by the Koizumi administration's rebuffing of their calls for a moratorium of prime ministerial Yasukuni visits.

Overall, one can conclude that domestic politics remains a salient determinant, exhibiting both exacerbating and mitigating influence on nationalistic tendencies in Japan's China policy-making. However, like nationalism, it has appeared more effective under sanguine or ambiguous relative power positions vis-à-vis China, as perceived by Japanese state-elites, who were more prepared to accommodate domestic political imperatives in their policy decision-making under such external conditions. This again corresponds with NCR's assumptions regarding the primacy of external constraints in delineating the parameters of state behaviour, and the causality of domestic political processes in determining the specific preference of action.

Theoretical findings and reflections on neoclassical realism

On the whole, the NCR framework fared relatively well in answering and meeting the research questions and objectives of this book. First and foremost, it was accommodative towards the 'national question', in that nationalism and identity politics were aptly and deductively operationalised as a 'domestic' variable within its construct, as well as systematically assessed in terms of their interaction with and salience over structural-material determinants that conventionally governed mainstream theories. Indeed, unlike the mainstream realist and liberal constructs' inclination to either discount or introduce it as an addendum in their analysis, the NCR model gave nationalism adequate emphasis by juxtaposing it within its external–domestic nexus to demonstrate its interplay with the external constraints and domestic political process involved in Japan's China policy-making. Although foregrounding on basic realist assumptions, NCR's hospitability towards non-material, unit-level variables helped theoretically bridge the supposedly incompatible assumptions of structuralist and cultural–ideational theories; and enabled this study to generate relatively novel, realist-based conclusions about nationalism in Japan's relations with China.

As anticipated, NCR's unequivocal acceptance of nationalism's function in foreign policy-making helped realise two fundamental objectives of this book. These were (i) to determine the meanings and manifestations of nationalism in contemporary Japan, and reveal its correlations with Japanese domestic politics and foreign policy; and (ii) to systematically assess its impact vis-à-vis other variables on Japan's China policy that defined the atmosphere of their bilateral relations. Specifically, the 'bridging qualities' of NCR's assumptions facilitated this book's responses to the related central research question of why, how, when and to what extent nationalism affected Japanese external behaviour, interests and goals in relation to China. On why nationalism and nationalist politics mattered in Japan's China policy-making, the NCR analysis employed the constructivist-style methodology of scrutinising the ideational (history, culture, ideology), psychological (perception, images, attitudes) and material (power, capabilities, prestige) dimensions of Japanese nationalism, to cultivate a deeper appreciation of its contemporary meanings, agendas, driving forces and typically anti-Chinese manifestation in post-Cold War Japan. This exercise was deliberately meant to bring to light the underlying passion and emotions that drove the nationalist logic, which made Japanese nationalists, and to an extent the general public, so resolute in defending what they perceive to be their national identity and territorial sovereignty, and their eagerness to defy the Chinese. In so doing, it also alludes to nationalism's growing influence within Japanese domestic politics, and its anticipated impact on Japan's behaviour towards China.

The analysis also dealt with the 'unit-level' intricacies of identifying the actors and processes involved, to infer the linkage between nationalism and foreign policy; namely how nationalism intersected with actor interests and wielded its influence in policy-making. To be fair, the empirical findings were not affirmatively conclusive, both in ascertaining the nationalistic convictions of key actors and establishing a direct linkage between nationalist pressure and policy decisions. It was also difficult to objectively verify that nationalist passion drove Japanese state-elites to behave the way they did during the instances of diplomatic contention. Yet both case studies demonstrate that nationalism's saliency did not solely derive from unadulterated passion and emotions. Japanese state-elites also invoked nationalism's instrumentality for politico-strategic purposes, underscoring its efficacy in foreign policy-making, when strategically empowered by the power-wielders as a political tool (Bong 2002: 266). Moreover, the widely reported personalities, ideological dispositions and affiliations, and actions/reactions as well as opinions and statements by key actors, before and during the periods of disputes, provided ample evidence that enabled the credible assertion of nationalism's effective role in Japan's China policy-making.

In responding to the questions of when, and the extent to which nationalism affected Japanese state-elites' China policy decisions, both case studies largely conformed to NCR's assumptions regarding nationalism's causality under particular external conditions and the domestic political process. The NCR schema also shed light on the inquiries concerning the saliency of other variables, and their exacerbating and/or mitigating impact on nationalism in Japanese policy-making. True to its realist pedigree, the NCR analysis, although recognising the causality of nationalism and/or other domestic sources on Japanese behaviour towards China, also affirms the centrality of 'power' in international politics. To reiterate, NCR 'holds that the international environment in which states interact is the primary determinant of their interests and behaviour' (Taliaferro 2006: 479–80), and that relative power position establishes 'the basic parameter of a country's foreign policy' (G. Rose 1998: 146). The Koizumi administration's external behaviour, when dealing with China over the Yasukuni and ECS disputes, echoed these assumptions, in that its policies largely hinged on its perceptions/calculation of the external environment, defined in terms of its relative power position vis-à-vis the disputant state, China. Domestic politics and nationalist pressure obviously factored in Tokyo's calculations, and key members of the administration did exhibit willingness to satisfy nationalist demands and/or their personal nationalist passion, or gain political mileage by advancing nationalistic policies to varying degrees. However, the extent of nationalism's manifestation and the level of policy assertiveness were constrained by the external conditions noted earlier, indicating consistency between the empirical findings and NCR's realist-centred premise. That said, NCR's auxiliary assumptions also indicate that external constraints limit but do not determine specific foreign policy choices, and that states do not always respond effectively to the exigencies of the impending environment. One can thus explain the supposed anomaly to the realist dictum in the case of the 2006 Yasukuni visit via this NCR notion regarding the likelihood of states/state-elites responding inappropriately to external imperatives, due to unit-level 'intervening' factors. This instance can be arguably attributed to Koizumi's perceptions, nationalist conviction and personal expedience.

From a comparative perspective, NCR's 'integrative framework' certainly has its advantages over the rigid constructs of 'Waltzian' realism and neo-liberalism in understanding nationalism and other domestic–ideational sources, which, together with the preferred variables of these orthodoxies, concurrently influenced Japan's relations with China. As mentioned, its foregrounding on realism's fundamental tenets and deductive incorporation of unit-level variables endowed the NCR analysis with 'operational flexibility' and greater explanatory power. That made it robust, yet meticulous and better equipped to analyse variations in state behaviour and international relations.

Specifically in the case of this book, NCR offered far better insights into the workings and internal attributes of Japanese (nationalist) politics and China policy-making that both neo-realist and neo-liberal studies commonly missed, or marginalised, due to their presupposition of such sources as a given. NCR facilitated the systematic assessment of nationalism as both a power and ideational variable without negating the significance of the constraints imposed by the external environment on Japanese policies towards China. This allowed a more inclusive explanation of the parameters and variations in Japanese policy, especially with regard to nationalism's impact in particular conditions and contexts, compared to neo-realism's preoccupation with systemic–structural constraints, which in Waltz's own admission 'does not dictate exactly how each state will respond within those parameters' (cf. Taliaferro 2006: 482). Similarly, the neo-liberals' central variables also proved deficient on their own in explaining the anomaly of worsening Japanese–Chinese relations against the backdrop of deepening economic interdependence ('cold politics, hot economics'), without the necessary domestic inputs espoused by NCR. Hence, rather than attributing Japan's deteriorating relationship with China solely to the intricacies of balance-of-power politics and changing power dynamics, or the downside of interdependence and under-institutionalisation of their bilateral framework, NCR evinced that domestic nationalist wherewithal and political exigencies were as much causal in Tokyo's China policy deliberations as the exacerbating consequence of their interaction with the neo-realist/neo-liberalist interpretations that led to the contemporary outcomes in Japanese–Chinese ties.

Although its advocacy for unit-level explanation has brought accusations of 'reductionism', the NCR analysis proved critics wrong by demonstrating that the bilateral outcomes and Japan's behaviour towards China did not rest solely on the causal properties of unit-level variables. Also, unlike 'reductionist' theories, it did not rely on domestic attributes to do most of the explaining (Taliaferro 2006: 481–2). Meanwhile, the charges of NCR's so-called violation of realism's structural logic are, in Taliaferro's (2006: 480, 482) contention, due to their widely misinterpreted notion that IR realism is a rigid research schema 'whose "hard core" is synonymous' with neo-realism. In actuality, both NCR and neo-realism are part of its broader research programme.

NCR also fared better than constructivism in explaining why nationalism/ identity politics, though efficacious, was not the primary driver of Japan's China policy. Although embracing the constructivist approach of scrutinising domestic–ideational sources, it did not forsake the international forces that equally constrained Japan's policy-making, nor over-emphasise sense over sensibility, or passion over reason (Gries 2004), on the part of Japanese state-elites, which explained their reluctance to pursue determinative policies to defend Senkaku/ ECS, or be forthright in visiting Yasukuni. Moreover, unlike constructivist studies, NCR does not deny the services of a working analytical model, which in this book allowed the systematic theorisation of the relevant variables that helped generate comparatively more intelligible explanations of how, when, and to what extent nationalism affected Japan's China policy-making.

It is, henceforth, reasonable to conclude that NCR has generated robust interpretations, and relatively insightful explanations of nationalism's functions and impact on Japan's relations with China. Its merits include: (1) the provision of a clear, operational framework, through which the interplay between nationalism and power politics becomes intelligible and assessable in Japanese China policy-making; and (2) its fostering of both intra- and inter-paradigm exchanges, which helped reduce the 'analytical myopia' within mainstream and alternative IR constructs when theorising their nationalism-tainted bilateral relationship. Together, they facilitated the formulation of reasonably novel IR-based conclusions about the stipulated research problems.

Implications for future research

This book has demonstrated via NCR the continued relevance and progressiveness of IR realism in the analysis of Japan's contemporary relations with China. By deductively introducing non-traditional reasoning, it has taken steps to address the 'Achilles' heel' of mainstream realism, and enhance the explanatory power of the realist paradigm on the international relations of regions like East Asia, which are facing emerging power competitions, and which are baffled by clashing nationalisms, memories and identities (Berger 2003).

There are, however, noticeable caveats to this modestly defined study. Theoretically, critics may argue that, although the domestic 'black box' was exposed, some areas of unit-level theorising remained inconspicuous in this investigation. Specifically, the linkage between nationalism and the intersubjectivity of state-elites' perceptions and socio-psychological dimensions of decision-making were not thoroughly developed and exhaustively elaborated. And there were the aforementioned difficulties in affirmatively linking nationalism and intention to specific policy decisions, following the limitations of empirical materials. Indeed, it is difficult to make objective inferences on such intersubjective dimensions of policy-making and validate them, without substantial written, and/or verbal evidence from the protagonists themselves, or those closest to them (i.e. personal memoirs, interviews), an 'empirical luxury' that remains unavailable due to the recentness of events and the sensitivities that still surround the issue areas. Moreover, as professed in the Introduction, this was never intended to be a socio-psychological/ideational study of Japanese nationalism and/or policy-making *per se*, but merely an attempt to introduce an IR-oriented analysis that operationalised nationalism as both a power and ideational determinant, to assess its causality in Japan's China policy-making. This explains the modest theorisation of the intersubjective linkages mentioned, as the study's limitation called for greater emphasis to be given to theorising the external–domestic interplay, and lesser on those domestic linkages. Undoubtedly, these caveats and limitations require further treatment via a more advanced NCR construct, and this should be the avenue for future research, once 'first-hand/primary-level' empirical information becomes more readily available. In addition, the NCR model can be utilised to investigate similar research problems, from either the Chinese or a comparative perspective, an area beyond the scope of this book.

Lastly, bearing in mind NCR's relative capacity to generate predictions of state behaviour, students of Japanese–Chinese relations and NCR should look at developing more elaborative models to guesstimate the future direction of bilateral ties. Based on this volume's findings, it is credible to envisage nationalism becoming increasingly salient in Japanese politics and foreign policy for the foreseeable future, as Japan drives towards 'normal statehood'. For this reason, relations with China are likely to continue to struggle, as domestic nationalist pressure increasingly constrains Japanese (and Chinese) state-elites' management of issues endemic to the bilateral ties. However, nationalism's dynamism would largely depend on American encouragement, considering its contemporary attributes and Japan's trademark dependency on its ally, and for as long as the 'neo-conservative/normal-nationalist' discourse (Samuels 2007a/b) remains dominant.

With the future of Japanese–Chinese ties and East Asia's well-being partly resting on Tokyo and Beijing's ability and political will to suppress their confrontational nationalisms, the onus is on Washington to prudently manage the US–Japan alliance and promote more equidistant relations with both governments within their emerging 'triangular' framework. This would help constrain overly nationalistic tendencies in policies towards each other. On Japan's China policy, *gaiatsu* from the US, together with other strategic and economic considerations, and domestic actors that act to preserve their interests in maintaining good relations with China, would remain as credible mitigating factors against excessive nationalistic preoccupations in Tokyo's policy-making process. One would, therefore, expect a kind of 'pragmatic nationalism tempered by diplomatic prudence' (Zhao 2005: 132) to prevail in Japan, where parochialism is mediated by sensible considerations that befit the behaviour of an interdependent and status quo power. On that note, Japanese–Chinese diplomacy would remain volatile, as Japanese policy-makers strive to delicately balance their pursuit of both nationalist and pragmatic goals. However, in a 'trade-off' situation, the former is unlikely to supersede the latter, or become the primary driver of China policy-making in Japan.

Appendix

Map of the East China Sea: area of dispute

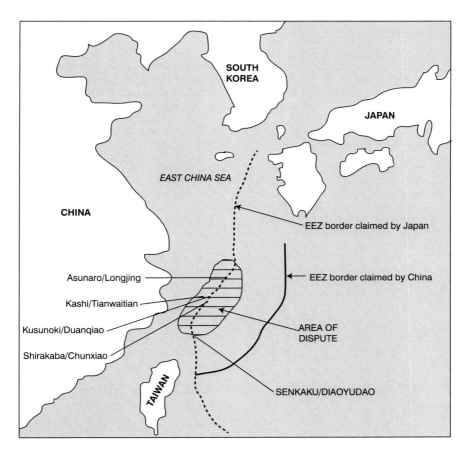

Source: Adapted from *The New York Times*, 28 March 2005.
[http://www.nytimes.com/imagepages/2005/03/28/business/20050329_JOUS_GRAPHIC.html]

Notes

Introduction

1 The Japanese equivalent term is *seirei keinetsu*.
2 Although Bong (2002) introduces a realist-oriented sub-hypothesis, which he claims to be in the mould of NCR, the overall conceptualisation and operationalisation of his 'legitimisation strategy model', as well as both theoretical and empirical arguments, ontologically reflect the Putnamesque 'two-level game' rather than NCR's logic and assumptions.
3 Among the notable terms introduced to define the various manifestations of nationalism include 'banal' (Billig 1995), 'assertive' (Whiting 1983), 'reactive' (Zheng 1999), 'pragmatic' (Zhao 2000, 2005), 'confident' (Rose 2000), 'cultural' (Yoshino 1992), 'wounded' (Gries 2004) and 'dependent' (McCormack 2000; Tsunekawa 2006). See Chan and Bridges (2006: 129–30 nn. 5–11).
4 See Ch. 3 for a discussion of nationalism, generally, and Japanese (neo-)nationalism in particular, especially the mentioned manifestations, and contributors of the terminologies, i.e. McCormack (2000), Kingston (2004), Samuels (2007a/b), among others.
5 Officially upgraded to 'ministry' status on 9 Jan. 2007, the JDA is now referred to as the Ministry of Defence (MOD), Japan. This book uses the former name in view of the stipulated period of investigation.
6 This term is referred to as 'patron commitment' in Cha's (2000) NCR-oriented study.
7 The given time period is mainly, though not exclusively, based on the specific period leading to the respective diplomatic rows between Japan and China over the selected case studies, and the immediate aftermath.
8 For works with similar assumptions from which this book draws its ideas, see Downs and Saunders (1998–9), Bong (2002), Brooks (1997) and Fearon (1994).

1 Interpreting nationalism in Japanese–Chinese relations

1 The inter/intra-disciplinary debate (notably on IR versus area studies) in this section draws ideas/arguments from Caroline Rose (1998: ch. 2) and theory-based works focusing on the contending debates within IR studies like Desch (1998), Gideon Rose (1998) and Zakaria (1992).
2 Rather than pitting one theoretical paradigm against the other (i.e. realism versus liberalism, or constructivism) Desch (1998: 155–6) contends that the theoretical divisions are best explained 'across two dimensions: domestic versus international, and material versus ideational'.
3 Whilst structural-realists in the Waltzian tradition assume that the structural attributes of international anarchy govern state behaviour/preferences, systemic-level constructivists

like Wendt (1992) argues that 'Anarchy is What States Make of It', where the international system is a social and cultural construct, defined by states (units) within it.

4 According to Gideon Rose (1998: 157–61), perception, notably that of political and foreign policy elites is regarded by most neoclassical realists as an important domestic variable, with some making perceptual factors central to their analytical framework.

5 Without sacrificing the fundamental realist premises, namely the primacy of relative power and structural constraints, NCR holds the 'middle ground' between neo-realism and constructivism (G. Rose 1998: 152), a position that offers greater explanatory power compared to the two extremes, insofar as the synthesis of systemic–material and domestic–ideational factors makes NCR analysis more detailed, and non-exclusive.

6 This variable draws ideas from and is partially based on the concepts of 'patron commitment' introduced in Cha's (2001) NCR-oriented analysis. It adopts the generally shared assumption that perceptions of favourable alliance commitment/ resolve would encourage states to seek more self-serving external policy goals (i.e. nationalist goals), and vice versa.

7 This paragraph's line of argument is partly developed based on the NCR-oriented works of Desch (1998) Taliaferro (2006) and Sterling-Folker (1997).

8 According to Sterling-Folker (1997: 19–20), the domestic process, serving as an 'opaque filter' through which assessments, choices and judgements are made regarding the international realm, would not only 'inhibit actors from objectively judging choices, behaviours and outcomes', but could even act as 'a barrier to their survival during time of major external crisis'.

9 According to Sterling-Folker (1997: 4–5), since realism is essentially an environment-based theory, while liberalism claims to be a process-based theory, the incorporation of domestic factors as process-based variables by the former is deductively consistent compared to the latter. The ontological nuance makes this book's framework theoretically different from previous works like those of Bong (2002) and Chung (2004) that employ the liberal-oriented 'two-level-game' or other mid-range constructs.

10 The hypotheses H1–H6 are adapted and modified from Bong (2002: 18, 20–3) and Downs and Saunders (1998–9). Comparable hypotheses and models are found in other 'mid-range' theoretical conceptualisations. See Mastanduno *et al.* (1989), and Cha (2000), among others. What differentiate this book's NCR-based hypotheses from the 'two-level-game', or other mid-range hypotheses adopted by the likes of Bong (2002) and Downs and Saunders (1998–9), are theoretical nuances like: (i) its espousal of the primacy of external factors; (ii) nationalism's 'intervening' role on state-elites' intersubjective perception of the external–domestic conditions; (iii) auxiliary assumptions regarding the potential irrationality of state behaviour; (iv) ontological positioning of the 'external' as environment rather than process-based variables; and (v) conceptualisation of analytical framework.

11 In fact, the 'theoretical degeneration' critique of realism and especially NCR by Legro and Moravscik (1999) was, according to neoclassical realists, due to their misinterpretation of the realist canon and overly rigid labelling of IR realism, and preoccupation with 'paradigmatism' (Feaver *et al.* 2000).

2 The trends, developments and dynamics in Japanese–Chinese relations

1 The conclusion of the Sino-Soviet Treaty of Friendship, Alliance and Mutual Assistance on 14 Feb. 1950 incorporated the People's Republic of China (PRC) into the Soviet's Cold War alliance framework.

2 In 1950, unofficial bilateral trade amounted to less than US$60 million, comprising mostly Chinese soybeans, salt, coal and iron exports to Japan, and Japanese exports of textile machinery, steel, engines and pumps to China (Taylor 1996: 3).

3 The 'L-T trade agreement' represented Liao Chengzhi and Takasaki Tatsunosuke, the names of the two 'semi-formal' representatives used to facilitate bilateral trade (Iriye 1996: 54). According to Caroline Rose (1998: 47), this 'friendly trade' system was limited to Japanese companies designated as 'China-friendly', specifically those permitted to trade with China via their acceptance of the preconditions set by the Chinese government.

4 The incident took place in May 1958, when a Japanese youth tore down a Chinese flag at a Chinese stamp exhibition held in a shop in Nagasaki (C. Rose 1998: 44–5).

5 Beijing's displeasure towards Tokyo began to mount by mid-1950s, when the Hatoyama administration, under pressure from Washington, failed to respond to persistent calls for the establishment of a Chinese resident trade mission in Tokyo, as stipulated in their first two unofficial trade agreements (Burns 2000: 38). The arrival of the 'pro-Taipei' Japanese premier and ex-member of the Tojo war cabinet, Kishi Nobusuke, caused further deterioration with his Taiwan visit, and efforts to remilitarise Japan under the proposed revision of the US–Japan security treaty.

6 According to Burns (2000: 40), while agreeing to the 'One-China' policy, Tanaka was able to secure Chinese acquiescence over Japan's intention to maintain non-diplomatic relations with Taiwan via trade offices that doubled-up as *de facto* political representatives, in an arrangement similar to that of the Japanese–Chinese 'pre-normalisation' framework. Both sides also agreed to shelve their territorial dispute over Senkaku/Diaoyudao, and China, on its part, agreed to renounce war reparations claims worth around US$50 billion (Lee 1976: 10, cf. Yahuda 1996: 84).

7 Bilateral trade leapt up within the first few years of diplomatic normalisation, with Japan emerging as China's largest trading partner (Iriye 1992: 127).

8 Japan's initial reluctance to conclude the PFT was due to concerns over the controversial 'anti-hegemony clause' that could antagonise the USSR, and its desire to maintain an 'equidistant' policy with all neighbours, including the communist superpower. Also, the indecision in resolving the Senkaku/Diaoyudao dispute during the 1972 joint communiqué saw its untimely resurfacing as a problem that delayed the PFT negotiations. However, besides shelving the territorial dispute, Japan's acceptance of and China's reciprocal decision to include a 'disclaimer' to neutralise the implication of the contentious clause exemplified both sides' pragmatism in realising a progressive relationship (Bedeski 1983: 31–2).

9 Japan's ODA to China comprises yen loans, technical cooperation, and grant aid/ assistance. For a record between 1980 and 2004, see MOFA (2006: 41).

10 Between 1979 and 1999, Japan provided 41.91% of the total major foreign government loans to China, making it by far the largest contributor, followed by Germany with a mere 9.86% (Mori 2007: 32).

11 In the 'June 4', 1989 incident, the Chinese government took drastic measures to quell student-led pro-democracy and anti-government demonstrations at the heart of the Chinese capital that saw the PLA launching what Western media described as a forceful and 'bloody' crackdown/'massacre' (Drifte 2003: 29–32).

12 During PM Kaifu's 1992 visit to China, a new ODA guideline was announced, stipulating that disbursement to recipient countries would be based on, among others: (i) trends in defence expenditure, (ii) development and production of WMD, (iii) efforts to promote democratisation, and (iv) respect for basic human rights and freedom (cf. Shambaugh 1996: 87).

13 Drifte (2003: 44, 88) highlights Japanese elite concerns over China's military modernisation, which, among others, included the so-called 'Higuchi Report' that made veiled references to the 'Chinese military challenge'.

14 Although Japan's annual defence budget rarely exceeded 1% of its annual GDP (except during the Nakasone administration), it was still comparatively large, due to its gargantuan national economy.

15 The Olympics Committee of Asia controversially extended an invitation to Taiwan's President Li Denghui to attend the 1994 Asian Games in Hiroshima, triggering strong Chinese protests and threats of boycott (Takagi 1999: 28). Although Tokyo caved in to the protest by thwarting Li's visit, it did not budge in inviting Vice-Premier, Xu Lide, to attend the Games in his place, marking the first high-ranking visit by Taiwan's elite since 1972 (Takagi 2006: 118). Tokyo also invited Taiwanese officials to the Osaka APEC conference months later, where a meeting held between the two trade ministers broke a 22-year moratorium on ministerial-level summits between the two sides (Shambaugh 1996: 92).

16 According to Takahara (2004: 166), Obuchi was also under pressure from the LDP to rebuke the Chinese demand for an apology. The Japanese premier presented a 'diluted' declaration stating Japanese 'war responsibility' and 'deep remorse' (cf. Rose 2005: 106), which fell short of an apology similar to the one given to Korea.

17 The so-called 'Armitage Report on US–Japan Relations' (October 2000), published by a foreign policy expert group headed by Richard Armitage, which advocated a strengthened US–Japan security partnership, was widely perceived to reflect the Bush administration's policy towards Japan (and China). For details, see Armitage *et al.* 2000.

18 The 'new thinking on Japan' refers to the intellectual voices in Beijing's academic circle, i.e. Ma Licheng and Shi Yinhong, calling for the abandonment of the 'history' card in favour of pragmatic engagement with Japan, which apparently reflected the Japan policy direction of the new leadership of Hu Jintao and Wen Jiabao (see Ma 2003; Gries 2005b).

19 Among the 'bloc-imposed' trade barriers were the China Committee (CHINCOM) and Coordinating Committee (COCOM) restrictions, enacted following the outbreak of the Korean War (Iriye 1996: 52–3).

20 According to Wang (2000: 364), Tokyo voiced its disapproval of Chinese belligerent actions during the 1996 Taiwan Strait crisis, but refrained from officially endorsing the US aircraft-carrier battle groups' deployment from its bases in Japan, to avoid aggravating Chinese suspicion of US–Japan collusion to intervene in the Taiwan issue. Likewise, fierce debate took place in the Japanese Diet regarding the definition of the revised scope of the US–Japan Security Guidelines. According to Wang (2000: 369–72), Japanese policy-makers were concerned that it could violate Article 9 and draw Japan into an unwanted military confrontation with China. The enactment of the three security bills in 1999 was therefore meant to give Japan 'strategic ambiguity' with regard to the provision of logistical support to US military operation in Taiwan (Wang 2000: 371). This diplomatic manoeuvre was apparently aimed at alleviating the alliance dilemma of 'entrapment and abandonment', and maintaining the Taiwan status quo (Green 2001: 90–2, 106).

21 Drifte (2003: 18) calls such Japanese behaviour 'deferential' policy or 'deference to China'. Both terms are used intermittently in this book to describe this particular Japanese behaviour towards the Chinese.

22 The history textbook, Yasukuni-*jinja* and Kyoto dormitory controversies coincided with major events and developments in Chinese domestic politics in the 1980s, i.e. the 12th and 13th CCP Congresses in 1982 and 1987, respectively, and the reshuffling of top leadership in 1985 (Kojima 2000: 41).

23 A former Senior Vice-Minister at the Cabinet Office claims that Japan's basic policy stance towards China remained unchanged, but opines that the 'Koizumi factor' made the difference. Interview (Tokyo, 19 March 2007).

24 According to senior 'pro-China' LDP politician, Kato Koichi, the Seiwa-kai, to which both Koizumi and Abe belong, is predominantly 'anti-China' and 'pro-US'. This faction contends that good ties with the latter do not coexist well with the former, which necessitates a trade-off. Interview (Tokyo, 19 March 2007).

3   Theories of nationalism and its manifestations in Japan

1   Guibernau (1996: 47) defines 'nation' as 'a human group conscious of forming a community, sharing a common culture, attached to a clearly demarcated territory, having a common past and common project for the future, and claiming the right to rule itself'. Conversely, a 'state' in Max Weber's (1948: 78) definition refers to 'a human community that claims the monopoly of the legitimate use of physical force within a given territory'. These definitions highlight the nation as multi-dimensional: it is psychological, cultural, territorial, political and historical; the state, with its primarily political and territorial features, appears much more limited in substance.

2   Scholars generally agree that nationalism and national consciousness are intimately linked to the idea and experiences of war, and share a mutually reinforcing relationship (Fujiwara 2001: 37; Posen 1993; Van Evera 1994).

3   This book concurs with Gries's (2004: 9) interpretation of 'national identity', which he loosely defined as 'that aspect of individual's self-image that is tied to their nation, together with the value and emotional significance they attach to membership in the national community'. And, 'nationalism', Gries (2004: 9) contends, refers to 'any behaviour designed to restore, maintain, or advance public images of that national community'.

4   Conroy (1955: 821) concedes 'there was at most "national consciousness" in Japan before 1868'. Meanwhile, McVeigh (2004: 42) and Yoshino (1992: 46–9) suggest the existence of an 'elitist proto-nationalism' promoted by 'Nativist Studies (*Kokugaku*)' and 'Mito School' intellectuals that sought to divorce Japan's past from Chinese influences by emphasising 'the uniqueness of the Japanese imperial lineage', and which also initiated the nascent discourse on reform and defence against Western encroachment. These 'proto-nationalist' elites were responsible for inspiring the domestic-oriented *sonno* (revere the emperor) movement, which later on incorporated the externally directed and xenophobic *joii* (expel the barbarian) slogan that eventually led to the successful *coup d'état* of the Tokugawa *bakufu* and the restoration of the imperial political system in 1868 (Brown 1955: 58–61, 76–90; Stronach 1995: 36).

5   The Emperor became the divine embodiment of the Japanese nation and state, and was placed at the centre of Japanese life, serving as both spiritual and political leader who required ultimate devotion from and the undying loyalty of its subjects (Stronach 1995: 40). Indeed, the 'invented' mysticism surrounding the Emperor's status and its preponderance in the Japanese consciousness was a vital element of modern Japanese identity, and 'a key renovationist symbol' (McVeigh 2004: 42–3) of the Meiji state, serving as the rallying point for Japan's emergence as a modern, powerful and distinctive nation-state.

6   According to McVeigh (2004: 34), to mobilise the masses for political loyalty and national regeneration via a state-oriented nationalism (*kokka shugi*), the *Sat-Cho* oligarchs also introduced the mythical yet practical idea of *kokutai* (a continuous national historical essence) (cf. Najita 1980: 47) to indicate Japan's 'immutable' and 'national character'. It served along with other concepts and ideals like *minzoku* (nation), *tanitsu minzoku* (homogeneous nation), *seikyo itchi* (unity of politics and religion) and *kokumin dotoku* (national morals) as 'key conceptual building blocks' of pre-war nationalism (McVeigh 2004: 28, 43).

7   The 'dependent' nature of Japan's post-war nationalism has been noted in several works, i.e. McCormack (2000, 2007), Kingston (2004) and Tsunekawa 2006). This term is utilised throughout the book.

8   During this period, McCormack (2000: 247) saw the Japanese society as riddled with the problems of homelessness, violence in schools, high rates of suicide and truancy, and social and spiritual unease.

9 By 1997, Japan had seen three changes of government, five premiers, and the sharing of power by eleven political parties, all since the LDP temporarily lost its power in 1993 (Jameson 1997: 1)

10 *Nikkyoso*, or Japan Teachers' Union, once the staunchest opponent of nationalist indoctrination in the post-war education system and curriculum, has seen its influence gradually weakened, especially in the battle for control over textbook content and the national flag and anthem issue (Itoh 2001).

11 Cyberspace has become a major disseminator of neo-nationalist ideas, especially among Japanese youth, whereby 'revisionist' websites like *Channel-2* (*ni-channeru*) (see http://www.2ch.net/) score an average 7 million monthly hits (Tanamichi 2005: 35), and *Channel Sakura* is another popular site for nationalistic bloggers (Johnston 2007: 114). *Manga* or Japanese comics are also hugely popular and influential. Among the revisionist *manga* included *Sensoron* (On War) by Kobayashi Yoshinori, which sold more than 700,000 copies, George Akiyama and Huang Wen-Hsiung's *Chugoku Nyumon* (Introduction to China) that sold 180,000 copies, and Yamano Sharin's *Kenkanryu* (Hating the 'Korean Boom') 450,000 copies (Sasada 2006: 118).

12 Interviews with Sasajima Masahiko, Senior Staff, *Yomiuri Shimbun* (Tokyo, 1 Feb. 2007); Soeya Yoshihide, Professor, Faculty of Law, Keio University (Tokyo, 20 Feb. 2007); ex-Senior Vice-Minister, METI (Tokyo, 5 June 2008).

13 Interview with Gilbert Rozman, Musgrave Professor of Sociology, Princeton University, USA (Tokyo, 31 Jan. 2007).

14 Samuels's (2007a/b) categorisation of Japanese nationalists, e.g. 'neo-autonomists', 'normal-nationalist', 'neo-conservatives' and 'realist', will be used intermittently throughout this book.

15 This is exemplified by the 'neo-nationalistic' writings of prominent liberal/progressive scholars like Kato Norihiro which were published by liberal-oriented publishers, i.e. *Iwanami*, *Kodansha* and *Heibonsha* (McCormack 2000: 253).

16 These features of state/official nationalism are noted in Zhao's (2000) description of Chinese nationalism. They are equally applicable to explaining state/official nationalism in Japan.

4 Nationalism, Japan's China policy-making and Japanese–Chinese relations

1 Interview (Tokyo, 9 June 2008).

2 Ishihara Shintaro, renowned for his 'anti-China' stance, has blamed Chinese citizens for Tokyo's rising crime rates, and used the derogatory terms *Shina* and *sangokujin* to refer to China and Chinese residents in Japan. His explicit 'pro-Taiwan' position, denouncement of the Nanjing massacre as a Chinese historical fabrication, and claims of a 'China threat' also underline his anti-Chinese sentiment (Hood 1999: 4).

3 This section's elaboration draws inspiration from Hagstrom (2003), Hook *et al.* (2005), and Tanaka (2000).

4 The Diet passed the Basic Law for the Reform of Central Government Ministries and Agencies in March 1998, which carried out the restructuring of ministries and agencies, and strengthening of executive powers of the prime minister and cabinet secretariat (Tanaka 2000: 7). The law officially came into effect on 1 Jan. 2001.

5 PM Tanaka's leadership was instrumental in the rapid normalisation of Japanese–Chinese relations in Sept. 1972, while both Nakasone and Takeshita have devoted years to building up 'pro-China' support within the LDP, and establishing formal and informal networks with Chinese state-elites (Hook *et al.* 2005:59; Zhao 1993). Conversely, Koizumi was arguably a key factor in the deterioration of contemporary Japanese–Chinese diplomacy (Lam 2005).

6   Tanaka (2000: 5) sees the CCS as the most important figure in the PM's support staff, usually appointed from the same LDP faction as the presiding PM. Although assigned to primarily domestic-oriented tasks, the likes of Gotoda Masaharu, Fukuda Yasuo and Abe Shinzo have been influential in foreign policy (Lam 2005).

7   This is an opinion shared by most interviewees. Also, for instance, former MOFA Director of NAAB, Okamoto Yukio, was promoted to be Koizumi's top diplomatic aide in April 2003 (Shinoda 2007).

8   The JCG, formerly Japan Maritime Safety Agency (J-MSA), got directly involved in the Senkaku/Diaoyudao dispute with China (Samuels 2007–8). Meanwhile, the MOE/MEXT has been implicated in the textbook rows since 1982, notably for its alleged acquiescence in historical revisionism (Hook *et al.* 2005: 52).

9   Indeed, even the China Division in 2007 was no longer headed by 'China school' bureaucrats, i.e. Akiba Takeo was American-trained, and served previously in the MOFA's NAAB.

10 The president normally assumes the PM position when the LDP serves as the dominant ruling party.

11 Among the LDP factions between 2001 and 2006 were Seiwa Seisaku Kenkyukai (Seiwa-kai), Keisei Kenkyukai (Keisei-kai), Shisuikai, Kochi-kai, Kinmirai Seiji Kenkyukai and Taiyukai. The Seiwa-kai (ex-Fukuda/Mori/Machimura faction) is known to be more hawkish, rightwing, pro-US/Taiwan and anti-China. It replaced the moderate and 'pro-China' Keisei-kai (ex-Tanaka/Takeshita/Hashimoto/Tsushima faction) as the most powerful LDP faction during Koizumi's premiership. See Park (2001).

12 Interview with Kato Koichi, senior LDP Diet-member (Tokyo, 19 March 2007).

13 According to Takamine, LDP foreign policy expertise has been enhanced by Diet-members who previously served as foreign minister/vice-ministers. Specifically, ex-Upper House and *gaiko-zoku* member, Takemi Keizo, was arguably amongst the most influential LDP politician during the Koizumi era in China policy-making, due to his vast knowledge of China and Taiwan, and personal connections with MOFA bureaucrats. Other influential *gaiko-zoku* members include Kono Taro, Shiozaki Yasuhisa, Aso Taro and Abe Shinzo (Takamine 2006: 84–5).

14 Press members normally obtain heavily regulated news information via attachment to a particular government agency/political party, thus, potentially undermining the impartiality of the news (Hook *et al.* 2005: 68).

15 Interview with Kokubun Ryosei, Professor/Director, Keio Institute of East Asian Studies (Tokyo, 27 Feb. 2007)

16 Apparently, under Ishihara, the Tokyo Metropolitan government had substantially scaled down activities of its sister-city relations with Beijing (Jain 2006: 129).

17 Observers deemed the Koizumi administration to be amongst the most hawkish and nationalistic in post-war Japan, with many cabinet members, such as CCS Abe Shinzo, FM Aso Taro, Defence chief Nukaga Fukuhiro, and METI ministers, Hiranuma Takeo and Nakagawa Shoichi, among others, identified as nationalist-inclined, or sympathetic towards domestic nationalist movements, due to their common political stance and/or familial background.

18 With these forces at work and, even more significantly, the current public sentiment, a Cabinet Office senior vice-minister went as far to assert that efforts by Japanese politicians that ran counter to prevailing public opinion, i.e. defending China's position, would be 'some sort of a political suicide'. Interview (Tokyo, 19 March 2007).

19 It was also known by Japanese as the Fifteen Year War, Greater East Asia War, and recently the Showa War as renamed by the *Yomiuri Shimbun* (Samuels 2007a: 130).

20 Examples include the Molotov cocktail attack on the residence of Doyukai's head, Kobayashi Yotaro, and the arson attack on the house of 'pro-China' LDP politician

Kato Koichi by *uyokus*, following their respective criticisms of Koizumi's Yasukuni visits (McCormack 2007: 24; *AS* 19 Aug. 2006).

21 PM Muruyama's intention to obtain a Diet resolution of a 'clearly-worded' formal war apology was staunchly opposed by half of his coalition cabinet (Austin and Harris 2001: 51). Also, 5 million Japanese and a quarter of Diet-members petitioned against it (Yang 2002: 18). Although he made the apology personally on 15 Aug. 1995, Muruyama only managed to muster limited Diet support for the adoption of a 'watered down' resolution (Miller 2002: 3).

22 Its passing of the screening process together with other 'revisionist' books plausibly indicated MOE/MEXT's tacit acquiescence, and political support from the Diet, notably the Diet-members League for the Passing on of a Correct History, led by the likes of Nakagawa Shoichi and Abe Shinzo (McCormack 2000: 250, Mori 2007: 57–8).

23 Japan's defence budget of over US$41 billion in 2006 was 'one of the five largest in the world' (Samuels 2007b: 63). The SDF also possesses power-projection capabilities that include what essentially is a blue-water navy comprising submarines and Aegis-class destroyers at Yokosuka, Sasebo and Kobe, and an air-force of medium/long-range air-superiority fighter-aircrafts and airborne refuelling capabilities (Roy 2003: 2; Drifte 2003). Observers see such offensive-based weaponry as contradicting the SDF's definition as a 'self-defence force' and Article 9 (Wu 2000; Roy 2003). For analyses of Japan's gradual 'remilitarisation', see Hughes (2005).

24 Japan's security role has expanded unprecedentedly since the '9/11' incident. This includes the introduction of so-called 'emergency legislations' like the 'Anti-Terrorism Special Measures Law' and the 'Bill to Respond to Armed Attacks', which give Japan the flexibility to participate in military activities in conjunction with the US, and to initiate the use of force in respond to armed attacks (NIDS 2003). The subsequent dispatch of MSDF refuelling vessels to the Indian Ocean under Operation Enduring Freedom represented Japan's active participation in overseas military operations, for the first time since the Second World War. Tokyo also dispatched Ground-SDF (GSDF) personnel to support the US 'coalition of the willing' in the post-war reconstruction of Iraq.

25 North Korea's security 'threats' to Japan include its nuclear weapons programme, missile tests that expose Japan's lacklustre and inadequate security measures, incursions of *fushinsen*, and the emotionally charged abduction issue, in addition to Pyongyang's reputed anti-Japanese stance, belligerence and lack of conformity to international norms and practices.

26 Japanese observers are generally concerned at the prospect of China's unsustainable economic growth under an authoritarian political system (Shirk 2007: 18) triggering serious internal socio-political and economic upheavals that may undermine the CCP regime's survival. The collapse of the PRC could spawn regional instability reminiscent of the Soviet disintegration, i.e. emergence of more unstable, anti-Japanese states, and exodus of refugees, etc. (Shambaugh 1996: 86). Similarly, a weak Chinese state may manipulate anti-Japanese nationalism, and adopt an aggressive posture on the Senkaku/Diaoyudao dispute and Taiwan, to bolster national unity and political legitimacy (Roy 2005: 206).

27 In 2002, China reported an annual increase in military expenditure of approximately 19.4% compared to the year before, marking the highest jump in recent years (NIDS 2003: 185). In 2006, the annual budget was set to increase by another 14.7% (*PD* 5 March 2006; Shirk 2007: 73)

28 According to the US Dept of Defense estimates, China's annual military spending totals around US$65 billion, over three times more than the Chinese government announcement (Bitzinger 2003: 3).

29 China has published defence white papers, biennially, since 1998. E.g. see State Council Information Office (SCIO) 2004.

5   Case study I: the Yasukuni Shrine dispute

1 *Tokyo Shokonsha*, meaning 'shrine for inviting the spirits' (Tokita 2003:48), was originally established to console the souls of those who perished during the crucial Boshin civil war, which paved the way for the birth of modern Japan under the Meiji Restoration. It eventually included the enshrinement of those who had died for the nation since 1853, notably during engagements with external forces to prevent foreign encroachment, and domestic revolts in the immediate post-Tokugawa period, i.e. Saga incident, Seinan War and Satsuma rebellion (Gardner 2002: 666–9: Breen 2007: 13).

2 Yasukuni was also classified as a *gokoku-jinja*, meaning 'protector of the nation shrine' (Harootunian 1999: 148).

3 They included non-military personnel, i.e. those who died in the line of duty, such as nurses, volunteers and those drafted through the National General Mobilisation Law to serve directly and indirectly in Japan's war machinery, as well as children who died in the line of fire (Breen 2004: 82; Gardner 2002: 669–70).

4 In my interview, Noda Takeshi, the senior LDP Diet-member, comments that Yasukuni is important for Japan, because of its relations to the acceptance and denial debate regarding Japan's war responsibility, and the results of the Tokyo War Crimes Tribunal. According to Noda, despite Japan's official acceptance of the tribunal's judgment, many ordinary Japanese cannot fully accept this, because, to them, the US was also, in some ways, responsible for the war. Such popular perceptions are closely related to the sentiment over Yasukuni, where the executed war criminals are 'criminals' because of the tribunal's 'lopsided' judgment. Since the judgment is perceived to be unfair, the so-called 'war criminals', in the eyes of this cohort of Japanese, are not criminals after all, and therefore, it is not a problem they are enshrined at Yasukuni. Indeed, those executed were eventually enshrined because of such opinions in Japan. In this sense, their enshrinement is symbolic of the challenge to conventional logic of the war. Noda is the former secretary-general of Hoshuto (New Conservative Party), who together with his LDP and Shin-Komeito counterparts, Yamasaki Taku and Fuyushiba Tetsuzo, visited China in July 2001, where they were believed to be heavily involved in the diplomatic negotiations, prior to Koizumi's first trip to Yasukuni. Interview (Tokyo, 26 May 2008).

5 According to documents on the Yasukuni problem released by the National Diet Library on 28 March 2007, the Japanese government did conduct discussions on the enshrinement of Class-A war criminals with Yasukuni officials in 1969, some nine years before the 'secret' enshrinement. Among the documents released are lists dating from 31 Jan. 1969, presented during a meeting between then-Health and Welfare Ministry and Shrine officials, containing names of Class-A war dead eligible for enshrinement, highlighting the common view between the government and Yasukuni on this matter. Both the Ministry and Yasukuni also agreed not to publicly reveal the idea, a decision apparently linked to the constitutional issue regarding the separation of religion and state (*JT* 29 March 2007).

6 Although it is a Japanese custom to mourn the dead, the Yasukuni rituals, concepts and doctrines are, apparently, qualitatively different from those observed in traditional Shinto shrines (Breen 2004: 82).

7 Eirei ni kotaeru kai claims a 1.2 million-strong membership across Japan (Breen 2004: 87).

8 According to Breen, the Yasukuni Worship and Tribute Society was established in 1999 to mark the 130th anniversary of Yasukuni Shrine. Membership derives mostly from other rightwing organisations. The society is responsible for several shrine development projects, deemed crucial to its long-term strategy of 'laying the foundation of new believers, and ensuring the transmission to successive generations of the lessons of the war dead' (Breen 2004: 87). Among the key development

projects included the refurbishment and expansion of the Yushukan museum that was completed in 2002 (Breen 2004: 87).

9 Japan's post-war premiers who paid homage at Yasukuni were Shidehara, Yoshida, Kishi, Ikeda, Sato, Tanaka, Miki, Fukuda, Ohira, Suzuki, Nakasone, Hashimoto and Koizumi (see Deans 2007: 273, table 1). All LDP PMs before 1985, from Kishi to Nakasone, visited the shrine (Shibuichi 2005: 205). Following strong international protests, Nakasone's successors from the LDP, i.e. Takeshita, Uno and Kaifu kept away from Yasukuni. The post-Cold War era has seen three LDP premiers (Miyazawa, Hashimoto and Koizumi) visiting the shrine. Those who did not visit were non-LDP premiers, i.e. Hosokawa, Hata and Muruyama (Shibuichi 2005: 205).

10 Noda Takeshi sees Yasukuni as a big issue for the Chinese leadership, because of its link to Chinese nationalism and the legitimacy of the CCP. According to Noda, China's understanding of the war is very much focused on the view of Japan being the aggressor and China its victim. The Chinese view the war criminals enshrined at Yasukuni as the major problem. Therefore, any Japanese PM visit to Yasukuni would trigger Chinese perceptions that Japan is trying to justify its role in the war. Interview (Tokyo, 26 May 2008).

11 It was originally called the Japan Welfare Federation of War-Bereaved Families in English, but was later renamed as the JABF. According to Tamamoto Masaru, Senior Fellow at the Japan Institute of International Affairs (JIIA), the real motivation and original objective behind Izokukai's formation was economic, namely to seek war pensions rather than venerating the war dead. This suggests pressure groups utilising nationalism as a political tool to pressure the Japanese government for their own political-economic agenda. Interview (Tokyo, 31 Jan. 2007).

12 The late Emperor Hirohito, posthumously known as Emperor Showa, visited Yasukuni eight times in the post-war period (Deans 2007: 273), but stopped after the enshrinement of the Class-A war criminals in 1978.

13 For instance, Beijing did not reprimand Suzuki for his 15 Aug. 1982 visit, despite coinciding with the history textbook row (Wan 2006: 237). It did express 'mild' displeasure during Nakasone's 1982 visit via the official mouthpiece, *Renmin Ribao*, followed by similar 'soft' protests in 1983 and 1984 (Shibuichi 2005: 207).

14 Nakasone explained in his memoirs that he stopped his shrine visits in response to a personal request from Hu Yaobang, the Japan-friendly CCP General Secretary, with whom he developed personal ties. Apparently, Nakasone's visit in 1985 had forced Hu into a tight corner (cf. Kokubun 2007: 153).

15 Hashimoto, however, insisted that his Yasukuni visit in 1996 was 'official', not 'private' as many had believed, when queried by the press, prior to the April 2001 LDP presidential election (*KN* 17 April 2001).

16 Kato Koichi, Koizumi's ex-political ally, described him as 'a politician who depends much on emotions and intuition, instead of logic and reason when making decisions … and also not one to listen to the advice of others' (Yoshida 2005, cf. van Kemenade 2006: 49). This was reiterated by Kato during my interview with him, an opinion that was equally shared by Japanese 'China' experts, like Takagi Seiichiro, Kokubun Ryosei, Soeya Yoshihide and Mori Kazuko, interviewed in Jan.–March 2007 and May–June 2008.

17 Interview with a senior official at the China and Mongolia Division, MOFA, Japan (Tokyo, 21 Feb. 2007).

18 According to my interviewees, Hashimoto's decision was probably due to: (i) the negative experience and repercussions following his previous Yasukuni visit as PM; (ii) his knowledge and experience on the intricacies of foreign affairs and diplomacy, which may have prompted his statesman-like considerations to maintain the thawing relationship with China; and perhaps, (iii) a 'miscalculation' of his domestic power base and influence. Hashimoto may have thought that his declaration would not have any damaging impact, since he had already visited Yasukuni during his premiership, and

that he could count on his personal affiliation with Izokukai and support from military veterans/pensioners organisations, considering his influential position as then-Welfare Minister. This 'miscalculation' was strategically exploited by Koizumi. Interviews with Nakai Yoshifumi, Professor of Political Studies, Gakushuin University, Tokyo (1 March 2007); and Tomoda Seki, Director-General, JIIA (Tokyo, 7 Feb. 2007).

19 Despite strong pressure from Beijing, Tokyo allowed the former Taiwanese president to visit Japan on 22–26 April 2001, under the pretext of seeking medical treatment. China retaliated by cancelling the planned visit to Japan in May 2001 by Li Peng, the NPC Chairman and former Chinese premier (*JT* 26 April 2001).

20 A bilateral trade dispute broke out when Japan imposed temporary safeguard measures on shitake mushrooms, leeks and *tatami* straws imported from China, on 23 April 2001, provoking Beijing to retaliate by raising tariffs on imports of Japanese automobiles, air-conditioners and mobile phones on 19 June 2001 (Przystup 2001b: 93–4).

21 The secretaries-general were Yamasaki Taku of LDP, Fuyushiba Tetsuzo of Shin-Komeito, and Noda Takeshi of Hoshuto. The trio reportedly carried with them Koizumi's personal letters to the Chinese and Korean leaders expressing his commitment to maintaining friendly ties with the two countries (Jiji 2 and 6 July 2001).

22 In his keynote speech at the Boao Forum, Koizumi stressed that China is not an economic threat to Japan but an opportunity (*JT* 13 April 2002).

23 *Asahi Shimbun* reported on 9 Aug. 2002 the postponement of Koizumi's scheduled China trip to mark the thirtieth anniversary celebration of diplomatic normalisation, apparently following Beijing's recommendation to avoid a visit during the Sixteenth CCP Congress, and Tokyo's intention to arrange one after the event to enable him to meet China's new leadership. However, observers see Koizumi's unwillingness to satisfy Chinese demand to stop his Yasukuni visits as central to the suspension of this symbolically important trip (*AS* 9 Aug. 2002; Wan 2006: 247).

24 According to Zhu (2005: 16), the Chinese authorities did tacitly accept responsibility for the damage to Japanese-related facilities, when Vice-FM Qiao Zonghuai expressed regrets to Japanese ambassador Anami Koreshige, and promised compensation. However, Chinese FM Li Zhaoxing refused to apologise to his Japanese counterpart, Machimura Nobutaka, in a subsequent meeting on 17 April.

25 Koizumi strongly hinted that he would continue visiting Yasukuni during a Lower House budget session on 16 May 2005, a day before Wu Yi's arrival (XNA 16 May 2005). The Chinese leadership initially remained cool, hoping the trip would result in more conciliatory tone from Koizumi, but was subsequently offended when Koizumi made his intention clear a day before the scheduled meeting (Curtin 2005a).

26 See Michael Green's remark on Yasukuni visits in 'Simply stopping Yasukuni visits won't solve problem: ex-Bush aide', *Kyodo News*, 4 Feb. 2006. For other expert opinion, see 'US walks fine line on Japan shrine: response cautious to dispute among allies and trade partners', *International Herald Tribune*, 21 Oct. 2005.

27 Nonetheless, Koizumi reportedly told President Bush in Nov. 2005 that he would not stop his Yasukuni routine even if the US requested him to do so (*KN* 21 Jan. 2006).

28 For a similar interpretation regarding the plausible correlation between the Cold War/ Soviet threat factor and the respective Japanese premiers' attitude towards Yasukuni visits, see Shibuichi (2005: 207–9, 212–13).

29 The Bush administration's hard-line China policy was evidently spelt out in Condoleeza Rice's article in *Foreign Affairs* (Rice 2000).

30 A US administration official, speaking under the condition of anonymity, voiced concerns regarding the negative repercussions of Koizumi's planned Yasukuni visit on Japan–ROK relations in early Aug. 2001 (*KN* 3 Aug. 2001).

31 Fukuda reportedly received guidance from Koga Makoto, Izokukai's deputy chief, regarding the possible option for Koizumi to visit between 13 and 16 Aug.

in conjunction with Obon, which apparently, crucially helped resolve Koizumi's dilemma (*YS* 17 Aug. 2001).

32 Kato Koichi revealed that he acted as the intermediary between the Chinese authorities and Koizumi on 'negotiations' over the Yasukuni issue. Prior to his dinner-cum-discussion with Koizumi at the PM residence, together with Yamasaki Taku on 11 Aug., Kato spoke to the Chinese side several times. Finally, via a cell-phone conversation with the Chinese intermediary, who was at Beidaihe (the resort for China's leaders/VIPs), Kato was told that the Chinese would tolerate it if Koizumi made just one visit, and avoided 15 Aug. Interview (Tokyo, 27 May 2008).

33 However, opinions do differ, with some observers such as Okazaki Shigenori (2005: 23) branding Koizumi as 'the most hawkish, rightwing prime minister since the end of World War II'.

34 Koizumi's approval ratings during the early days of his premiership recorded unprecedented highs of above 80%, with *Mainichi* polls recording 85%, *Nikkei* 80%, and *Kyodo* 86.3% (*KN* 30 and 28 April 2001).

35 A significant majority of my Japanese interviewees contend that Koizumi's resoluteness on visiting Yasukuni was due to his personal convictions and personality, both of which are not necessarily driven by nationalism.

36 Shibuichi (2005: 210) opines that Koizumi's pledge to reform the domestic economy antagonised many influential pressure groups from sectors like construction, postal services, agriculture and small-and-medium-size enterprises that traditionally supported the LDP.

37 Interview with ex-senior vice-minister, METI, Japan (Tokyo, 5 June 2008).

38 It is also plausible that Koizumi foresaw the need to rally nationalist-rightwing support in his desperation to make his third attempt at the LDP presidential post successful.

39 Interview (Tokyo, 9 June 2008).

40 The three Cabinet members were Finance Minister, Shiokawa Maajuro, METI chief, Hiranuma Takeo, and Public Safety Commission chairman, Murai Jin. Five of the remaining 14 ministers declined to publicly state their intentions (*JT* 8 Aug. 2001).

41 For instance, according to a *Mainichi* poll on 28 May, 44% of respondents saw nothing wrong with Koizumi's visit, while 46% thought that worshipping in a private capacity was acceptable, with only 7% disagreeing with his planned visit (cf. Takashina 2001: 50).

42 Observers like Prof. Kubo Fumiaki reportedly suggested that the rift between Koizumi and Tanaka would lead the PM to depend on CCS Fukuda and his aides to manage Japan's foreign policy, as Tanaka could no longer be trusted over policy matters (*JT* 4 Aug. 2001). Tanaka would eventually be forced to resign in Jan. 2002.

43 According to observers, Nonaka was one of the LDP 'Old Guard', i.e. defender of the old political-economic system that Koizumi was hoping to destroy (*JT* 24 Feb. 2001; Anderson 2004; Hiwatari 2005). Nonaka's intervention in the Yasukuni issue, therefore, bore limited results, as Koizumi apparently did not pay attention to him (Wan 2006: 239).

44 The close relationship between Koizumi, Yamasaki and Kato was popularly known as the 'YKK' clique. Indeed, Kato confirmed that Koizumi requested a 'dinner-cum-discussion' meeting with Yamasaki and himself at the PM's official residence on 11 Aug. 2001, where the 'change-of-date' strategy was deliberated. Interview (Tokyo, 27 May 2008).

45 Koizumi expressed his 'profound remorse and sincere mourning to all the victims of war' in a press statement issued just before the visit, apparently in a final effort to soothe Chinese and other Asian neighbours' resentment, and cushion the negative external repercussions. The PM also provided reasons for his decision to change the date of his visit to appease the nationalists (BBC 13 Aug. 2001). See MOFA (13 Aug. 2001) 'Statement of Prime Minister Junichiro Koizumi' (provisional translation): <http://www.mofa.go.jp/announce/pm/koizumi/state0108.html> (accessed June 2007).

46 According to UCLA's Ronald Morse, Koizumi's visit might relate ultimately to his impulse for political survival, as failure to go might have angered the nationalist cohorts and damaged his political position (AP 3 Aug. 2001). Koizumi's expression of 'deep shame' for not fulfilling his promise to visit on 15 Aug. was an attempt to appease domestic nationalist displeasure (AFP 13 Aug. 2001).

47 According to Wang (2002: 118), Koizumi's visit to the Memorial Museum of the Chinese People's War of Resistance against Japanese Aggression, was the first by a Japanese premier. He also laid a wreath at the symbolic 'Great Wall' that symbolises Chinese heroic resistance against the Japanese.

48 Interview (Tokyo, 9 June 2008).

49 Moreover, it was the Chinese who extended the invitation to Koizumi to attend the biennial Boao Forum in 2002, which suggested that Beijing was warming to the Japanese premier after an inopportune start (Drifte 2003: 129).

50 Tanaka Makiko was very popular, especially among women voters, besides being the daughter of former premier, Tanaka Kakuei, whose faction once wielded the most power in LDP politics (Murata 2006: 43–4).

51 Indeed, both *Yomiuri* and *Mainichi* public surveys conducted between 20 and 21 April 2002 showed Koizumi's support rate slipping to new lows of 47.9 and 42%, respectively, leading observers to view the visit as being aimed at winning votes (especially from Izokukai) in two by-elections and a prefectural governor election on 28 April (Reuters 23 April 2002).

52 Tanaka contends that Koizumi would have visited Yasukuni 'quietly, without notifying the media' if it was intended to be a private affair. According to Tanaka, Koizumi arrived at Yasukuni at 8:30am, but only proceeded with the ceremony after 'wasting one hour waiting' for the media to arrive, suggesting that he intended to publicly convey that it was a 'prime ministerial visit'. Moreover, Koizumi apparently published 'Thoughts on a visit to Yasukuni Shrine' after the visit, making clear that there had been 'careful preparations' (Tanaka 2003).

53 Indeed, the only reported gesture by Koizumi soon after the visit was his decision to write a letter that would be delivered by Shin-Komeito's head Kanzaki Takenori to President Jiang Zemin, to reaffirm Japan's intention to strengthen ties with China (Jiji 23 April 2002).

54 According to Wan (2006: 248), Koizumi's perception suggests that 'he believed Chinese reactions to date had been in an acceptable range of severity – strong discontent expressed in a symbolic manner without having an impact on vital China–Japan bilateral interests'.

55 Koizumi cordially met Zhu Rongji at the Asia–Europe Meeting (ASEM) in Copenhagen on 22 Sept. 2002 (BBC 23 Sept. 2002), and then Jiang at Mexico's APEC summit on 27 Oct. 2002 (XNA 28 Oct. 2002).

56 *Yomiuri* subsequently reported from a source close to the *Kantei* that the timing of the 'surprise' visit had been 'elaborately orchestrated' since late 2002, to take into account key domestic and external political agendas (*DY* 16 Jan. 2003).

57 The rightwing *Sankei Shimbun* ran a full-page coverage of the 'New Thinking' debate in China, and made several proposals for the improvement of Japanese–Chinese ties (*SS* 10 Jan. 2004, cf. Lam 2004: 10).

58 See Figure 2.1 for the declining trend in the annual Cabinet Office public opinion survey on perceptions/images of China (especially Oct. 2002).

59 Koizumi reportedly took a deep bow, instead of performing the usual two bows, two hand claps, and one final bow of traditional Shinto worship, ostensibly hoping that it would be perceived by his domestic and external detractors as a 'non-religious' form of respect (Yamaori 2003: 44).

60 For instance, during the St Petersburg summit, Hu did not raise the Yasukuni issue in his talks with Koizumi, although he did comment generally on the history issue (*YS* 31 May 2003).

61 China accounts for 80% of Japan's export growth in 2003, with the total value of Japanese exports to China increasing 33.2% from the previous year, hitting a record high for the fifth consecutive year (*DY* 2 March 2004; Glosserman 2004).

62 The timing of the pledge, which came ahead of Bush's visit, was apparently a move to demonstrate that it was not made under US pressure (*JT* 16 Oct. 2003).

63 This refers to the close relationship forged by Ronald Reagan and Nakasone Yasuhiro that saw a significant warming of US–Japan relations during their tenures as heads of state.

64 Interview with Kokubun Ryosei (Tokyo, 27 May 2008).

65 Japanese public scepticism regarding China's 'peaceful rise' was equally fuelled by the success of Chinese manned space mission in Oct. 2003, which triggered concerns over China's advanced military development.

66 Indeed, Kato Koichi recalled Bush saying that he did not want to put Koizumi in an awkward position over Yasukuni, underscoring the constraints on Washington's handling of the issue. Interview (Tokyo, 27 May 2008).

67 High-level bilateral exchanges/consultations continued on, despite Beijing's displeasure over Yasukuni, as seen in the sideline meeting between the two foreign ministers in Hanoi's ASEM summit in Oct. 2004 (SCMP 10 Oct. 2004). Similarly, the Hu–Koizumi and Wen–Koizumi summits at the Nov. APEC and ASEAN-Plus-Three gatherings in Chile and Laos, respectively, proceeded, even though relations were strained by the Chinese submarine incident in Nov. 2004 (AFP 22 Nov. 2004; BBC 30 Nov. 2004).

68 According to several of my interviewees, Koizumi was not particularly interested in foreign policy, and had limited experience and knowledge in the field before assuming the premiership. This partly explains why Koizumi devoted his efforts predominantly to realising domestic policy objectives, while hinging Japan's external strategy on the US–Japan ties. His assertive China policy was also possibly influenced by his political and personal background, notably his affiliation with the pro-Taiwan Seiwa-kai faction, and supposedly limited knowledge and interests about China. Apparently, Koizumi's 2001 trip was only his second visit to China. Interview with former Assistant Director, China and Mongolia Division, MOFA Japan (Tokyo, 13 March 2007). Opinion also shared by Kokubun Ryosei, Tomoda Seki and Zhao Quansheng in their respective interviews.

69 See Figure 2.1 in Ch.2.

70 China's Vice-FM, Wang Yi, reportedly told LDP policy chief, Nukaga Fukushiro that China had approached North Korea to open the avenue for resolving the abduction issue with Japan, before the Feb. 2004 Six-Party Talks (*AS* 16 Feb. 2004).

71 The main critics of Koizumi's actions came from Okuda Hiroshi, Chairman of Keidanren and Chief Executive Officer (CEO) of Toyota, Kobayashi Yotaro, Chairman of Fuji Xerox, and Kitashiro Kakutaro, Chairman of both Keizai Doyukai and IBM Japan (Lam 2006b: 10).

72 There were, indeed, mixed lower court rulings on the issue, with Osaka and Matsuyama district courts dismissing the Yasukuni lawsuits on 27 Feb. and 16 March 2004, respectively (*MDN* 27 Feb. and 16 March 2004). On 13 May 2004, the Osaka District Court also ruled Koizumi's Yasukuni visit as private in nature (*MDN* 13 May 2004), while the Chiba District Court ruled against plaintiffs seeking compensation for his 2001 shrine visit (Przystup 2004a: 114–15; 2004b: 127–8; 2005a: 132). However, on 23 June 2006, Japan's Supreme Court rejected the lawsuit filed against Koizumi's 2001 Yasukuni visit, without giving any judgment on the constitutionality of the visit (XNA 23 June 2006).

73 For veiled comments from senior US officials, i.e. US Deputy Secretary of State, Robert Zoellick, and Deputy National Security Adviser, Jack Crouch, see 'U.S. official seeks March realignment plan, better Japan–China ties', *Kyodo News*, 24 Jan. 2006. See also 'US says frustrated over Japan's strained Asian ties', Reuters, 19

Nov. 2005, for Assistant US Secretary of State, William Hill's 'frustration'. Indeed, observers perceive Zoellick's influential speech to the National Committee on US–China relations on 21 Sept. 2005 calling for the engagement of China as a 'signal' to Koizumi, and Tokyo, to 'reassess' Japan's China policy direction (Zoellick 2005).

74 The strongest opposition came from the Chairman of the House's International Relations Committee, Congressman Henry Hyde. In a leaked letter to House Speaker, Dennis Hastert, Hyde stated that if the PM visited Yasukuni as expected, after he addressed the Congress, 'Mr. Koizumi would dishonor the place where President Franklin Roosevelt made his "Day of Infamy" speech after the Japanese attack on Pearl Harbor' (quoted in *IHT* 24 June 2006). Congressman Hyde had voiced concern back in Oct. 2005 regarding regional Yasukuni fallout following Koizumi's 2005 visit (*IHT* 28 Oct. 2005).

75 On 8 Feb. 2006, China's State Councillor, Tang Jiaxuan, told the visiting Japan–China Association head, Noda Takeshi, that the Chinese has 'written off' Koizumi and expected nothing from him during the remainder of his office (Przystup 2006b: 124).

6 Case study II: the East China Sea dispute

1 The geological terms 'islets' and 'barren rocks' are commonly noted (Drifte 2008a/b; Hagstrom 2003: 80). According to observers, the islands are called 'Senkaku', 'Senkaku Shoto', 'Senkaku Retto', 'Senkaku Gunto', meaning 'Pinnacle rocks' in Japanese. 'Tiaoyu' or 'Tiaoyu tai', meaning 'Fishing platform', is their Chinese name (spelled in the Wade-Giles Pinyin system widely used in Taiwan and Hong Kong). In the PRC, they are known as and spelled 'Diaoyu Dao' or 'Diaoyu Tai' in the Hanyu Pinyin system (Su 2005: n. 1; Suganuma 2000: 93). These islands are also called 'Pinnacle Islands' for convenience and neutrality sake by Western scholars (Hagstrom 2005). This study calls them 'Senkaku/Diaoyudao' or 'Senkaku/Diaoyu Islands', to avoid a biased slant towards either disputant state.

2 This study considers Taiwan's claims over Senkaku/Diaoyudao as similar and in tandem with those of the PRC, and thus treats them as a single claim under the name of China.

3 Apart from the history-induced Chinese ultra-sensitivity towards issues concerning extraterritoriality, the PRC is still engaged in a multitude of sovereignty disputes with neighbouring states, such as the South China Sea archipelagos of Paracel and Spratly, and secessionist movements in Tibet, Xinjiang-Uighur and Taiwan, among others. Likewise, Japan is involved in irredentist claims over the Kurils and Takeshima/Tokdo Islands, with Russia and South Korea, respectively (Hagstrom 2003: 80).

4 The term 'Nansei Shoto', which literally means 'south-western islands', is a geographic reference to 'an arc of islands lying between the southern end of Kyushu and Taiwan … [that] includes, from North to South, the Tokara Islands, the Amami Islands, the Okinawa Islands, and the Yaeyama Islands' (Taira 2004).

5 The official US position is that the Okinawa Reversion Treaty 'does not affect the legal status of those islands at all' and Washington holds a neutral position with regard to the ownership status of the islands (Niksch 1996; Drifte 2003:54).

6 Indeed, most Japanese interviewees opined that 'Senkaku' is a non-issue, and were reluctant to elaborate on questions concerning the sovereignty dispute. For Japan's official position on Senkaku/Diaoyudao, see MOFA's website at http://www.mofa. go.jp/region/asia-paci/senkaku/senkaku.html. Meanwhile, based on the official statements made over the years, Drifte (2008a: 5) observes that the Japanese position has evolved from one of implicitly agreeing to shelving the dispute to a denial of the existence of a territorial dispute.

7 According to Chiu (1999: 9), the PRC initially made a semi-official claim via an article in the *Peking Review* before the Chinese MFA's issuing of a statement of formal legal claim on 30 Dec. 1971.

8 The PLA-Navy also intended to launch a large-scale naval exercise, but was overruled by Deng Xiaoping, a decision ostensibly made in light of the priority given to attaining the much sought after 'anti-hegemony' clause from the Japanese in the PFT (Downs and Saunders 1998–9: 126).

9 According to a *Yomiuri Shimbun* report on 27 Feb. 1992, Deng Xiaoping allegedly told Japanese FM Sonoda Sunao during the 1978 PFT negotiations that 'China tacitly admitted Japan's practical control of the Senkaku Islands' (quoted in Takamine 2005: 454).

10 On 26 Sept. 1996, David Chan, a Hong Kong activist, drowned after reportedly jumping into the water with four other activists when their freighter, *Kien Hwa No.2* was blocked by J-MSA/JCG vessels from landing on Senkaku/Diaoyudao. His death triggered popular demonstrations across Hong Kong and Taiwan, while Chinese authorities scrambled to diffuse anti-Japanese sentiments and curb protest in Mainland China (*SCMP* 10 Oct. 1996; *YS* 7 Oct. 1996).

11 Among the incidents was the landing of Diet-member, Nishimura Shingo on a Senkaku/ Diaoyudao islet in May 1997, which triggered the usual 'reaction–counteraction' dynamic that saw a Chinese diplomatic protest, and Japanese reiteration of their position and denial of official involvement (CNN 6 May 1997). This was followed by clashes between Chinese protesters and the J-MSA/JCG in Sept. 1998 that led to a Chinese boat sinking. See 'Senkaku/Diaoyutai Islands', http://www.globalsecurity. org/military/world/war/senkaku.htm (accessed Aug. 2007). In 2000, a Japanese rightwing group made another landing to build a shrine on one of the islets that brought further diplomatic exchanges (Su 2005: 47).

12 Chinese research vessel incursions into Japanese EEZ rose from 4 in 1997 to 14 in 1998, and 30 in 1999 (*YS* 28 Aug. 2000 cf. Takamine 2005: 454). Drifte (2003: 57) noted the number of incursions at 33 and 24, for 1999 and 2000, respectively. However, there is a categorical difference between the number of Chinese research vessels and warship sightings in Japan's EEZ (see Drifte 2003: 56–8). Regarding the latter, the figure also significantly rose from 2 in 1998, to 27 and 31 in 1999 and 2001 (Drifte 2003: 58; Malik 2000: 22 cf. Roy 2003: 3). A PLA-Navy vessel also successfully circumnavigated the Japanese archipelago in May 2000, an event which heightened Japanese security planners' concerns regarding implications of Chinese incursions on Japan's maritime security (Calder 2001: 108–9).

13 The advanced notification framework agreement signed on 13 Feb. 2001, stipulates the requirement for both sides to provide at least two months advanced notice, including details of the vessel and crew as well as the objective, period and place of research activities (*JT* 14 Feb. 2001).

14 Between 9 and 16 July 2001, the JCG discovered several Chinese ships operating near Senkaku/Diaoyudao in Japan's claimed EEZ without prior notification, which contravened the Feb. 2001 bilateral agreement on advanced notification (Przystup 2001c: 112).

15 Japanese government leasing of the islands began in April 2002 at a cost of JPY22 million annually. The decision was apparently meant to prevent their sale, or block anyone from landing on the islands (BBC 3 Jan. 2003; *JT* 6 Jan. 2003).

16 A Chinese vessel was sighted on 17 Feb. 2004, conducting 'illegal' research activities in Japan's EEZ, prompting the MOFA to call for a cease in Chinese activities on 2–4 March. This was followed by Vice-FM Takeuchi's statement on 8 March 2004, deeming the Chinese activities 'extremely regrettable' in response to the JDA report, citing 11 instances of Chinese illegal and ostensibly military-oriented research activities, since the beginning of the year (Przystup 2004a: 109, 114–15).

17 A resolution aimed at 'preserving [Japan's] territorial integrity' was adopted on 30 March 2004 by the Lower House Security Committee, which requested the Japanese government to 'forcefully promote all sorts of measures, including diplomatic efforts' to defend Japanese territorial sovereignty (Przystup 2004b: 124).

18 The Koizumi administration, represented by CCS Fukuda, reportedly implored the LDP to use non-provocative language in the motion (*DY* 1 April 2004).

19 The disputed oil and natural gas fields include Shirakaba/Chunxiao, Kashi/Tianwaitian, Kusunoki/Duanqiao, Asunaro/Longjing and Kikyo/Lengquan (Drifte 2008b: 39).

20 According to Drifte (2008a/b), Japan has always insisted on settling the demarcation issue as a precondition.

21 The inaugural director-general-level talks took place on 25 Oct. 2004 (Jiji 25 Oct. 2004). There were altogether 11 rounds of 'Japan–China Consultations concerning the ECS and Other Matters' before a breakthrough was achieved with the announcement for joint development on 18 June 2008 (Drifte 2008b: 41).

22 Okinotorishima, the southernmost island of the Japanese archipelago, became a Japanese–Chinese dispute from 2004, following China's contestation of Japan's definition of Okinotorishima as an 'island', which allows the Japanese to establish claim for an extended EEZ, at the expense of Chinese EEZ claims and maritime/geo-strategic interests (Yoshikawa 2007). The Chinese stated that Okinotorishima is more a 'rock' than an 'island', which disqualifies Japanese claims over its EEZ boundary measured from that point (Przystup 2004b: 124). In consequence, China also refuted Japan's allegation of its repeated EEZ violations, notably near Okinotorishima (Drifte 2008a: 20).

23 Under Article 20 of the UNCLOS, a submarine is required to surface and display its national flag while transiting the territorial waters of other foreign countries (cf. Dai 2006: 140 n. 31).

24 The MSDF had apparently detected the submarine days earlier, operating submerged near Japan's maritime border. The JDA was alerted when it trespassed into Japanese waters between the remote southwesterly islands of Tarajima, Miyako and Ishigaki, where it was immediately tracked by two MSDF destroyers and a P-3C aircraft, until it returned to Chinese waters (Curtin 2004b; Ferguson 2004b). MSDF commanders later revealed that the incident could have triggered the first Japanese–Chinese naval battle since the Second World War (*YS* 22 Nov. 2004, cf. Takamine 2005:440).

25 The Chinese confirmed and deemed the incident as 'extremely regrettable' during a meeting between Chinese Vice-FM, Wu Dawei, and the Japanese ambassador, Anami Koreshige, in Beijing (MOFA 2005: 37).

26 Although the joint statement of the 'Two-Plus-Two' talks, officially known as the 'Joint Statement of the US–Japan Security Consultative Committee', generally calls for 'greater collaboration between US and Japanese forces ... in an area stretching from Northeast Asia to South China Sea', the geographical definition also suggests the inclusion of Taiwan and, possibly, the ECS (Klare 2006).

27 METI Minister Nakagawa Shoichi, remarked the possibility of two out of three areas currently developed by China in the ECS extending to the Japanese side of the median line, based on the METI's interim report released on 18 Feb. 2005 (Brooke 2005; Drifte 2008b: 37).

28 The Japanese Ministry of Land, Infrastructure and Transport officially gave Okinotorishima an address (No. 1 Okinotori Island, Ogasawara Village, Tokyo) on 17 June 2005 in an apparent effort to strengthen Japan's expanded EEZ claims from the island's baseline (Liu 2006; Przystup 2005b: 132).

29 Five Chinese warships were reportedly detected in the disputed area in Sept. 2005, prior to the Lower House Elections. A Chinese destroyer apparently targeted its guns on a MSDF P-3C at the vicinity of the Shirakaba/Chunxiao gas field, while Chinese surveillance planes were seen in the area monitoring the operation of Japanese naval ships (Curtin 2005b; Drifte 2008b: 37–8).

30 The SDF, in its 'Security and Guarding Plans', has, for the first time, identified China as a potential threat, and planned for contingencies involving Chinese invasion of Senkaku/Diaoyudao (*IHT* 27 Sept. 2005).

31 Nonetheless, both sides agreed to shelve the EEZ delimitation issue to advance joint development negotiations during the May 2006 talks (Drifte 2008b: 40) while the July round saw a mutual agreement to establish a panel of technical experts to facilitate resolution of, as well as a mechanism to avoid 'contingencies' in the ECS (Fanell 2006).

32 Observers see the Japanese government taking gradual actions since the 'Okinawa reversion' to enhance the degree of 'effective control' over Senkaku/Diaoyudao, such as its gradual and inconspicuous building of structures (i.e. helicopter pads in Uotsuri-shima in 1979) and endorsement of the navigational beacons erected by nationalist groups, like Seirankai and Seinensha (1990) on the islands (Su 2005: 43; Chung 2004: 41–2).

33 According to observers, the stipulation concerning the 'surrounding areas' in the renewed guidelines was taken to mean Taiwan and Senkaku/Diaoyudao (Wu 2000: 299–300).

34 Also in late 2001, a senior Bush administration official indirectly hinted possible US support for Japan in the event of a Chinese attack on Senkaku/Diaoyudao (*KN* 11 Dec. 2001).

35 The Chinese government responded by reiterating its claims to the islands, but stopped short of protesting or criticising Japanese actions with the usual fervent rhetoric (*JT* 24 June 2003).

36 According Urabe's (2004a) comments on the *China Daily* report on the incident, 'the tone of the report is, in relative terms, calm and reasonable', with neither condemnation of the JCG's action, nor the usual 'hysteria' found in Chinese media reporting of Japanese–Chinese issues.

37 Beijing also called for calm, while the Chinese ambassador, Wu Dawei, reportedly 'reminded diplomatically' on China's firm position in his meeting with Vice-FM Takeuchi (*JT* 27 March 2004).

38 Even the popular protest outside the Japanese embassy in Beijing was only made possible with permission from the Chinese government, as reported by the BBC, confirming the conventional wisdom amongst Japanese policy-makers that popular anti-Japanese sentiment are predominantly state-abetted (BBC 25 March 2004).

39 This view is generally acknowledged by the Japanese media. Indeed, it was reported that the police initially preferred the option of prosecuting the activists, but a police official later said that 'At the last minute, politics interfered' (*AS* 29 March 2004). Also, Koizumi reportedly instructed government officials on 'how to handle the issue from a comprehensive viewpoint', and was quoted as saying that the deportation instead of prosecution was 'to avoid hurting bilateral relations with China' (*JT* 27 March 2004).

40 Interviews with a senior official from Foreign Policy Bureau, MOFA, Japan (Tokyo, 27 May 2008), and former Japanese ambassador to China (Tokyo, 9 June 2008).

41 According to Curtin (2004b), Koizumi calmly and carefully addressed Japan's handling of the incident by saying that 'It is unusual, but natural for Japan, a country governed by law and which handles people according to the law … It is necessary for both parties to handle the case in as calm a manner as possible.'

42 Based on Japan's recent and sustained efforts to meet the demands of the security alliance, Japanese policy-makers may have been overly optimistic that the US would reciprocate by meeting its obligation to defend Japan against potential Chinese belligerence in the ECS. Furthermore, the enhanced state of the alliance itself serves as a credible deterrence against any risk-taking by the Chinese to rapidly escalate the dispute, which could compel an alliance response. This is the opinion of many interviewees, including Prof. Mori Kazuko. Interview (Tokyo, 16 May 2008).

43 The deputy spokesperson of the US State Department, Adam Erelli, reiterated the US long-standing stance by telling reporters on 24 March 2004 in the wake of the detention of Chinese activists 'that the US does not take a position on the question of the ultimate sovereignty of the Senkaku-Diaoyu Islands' (quoted in AFP 24 March 2004). Although the US–Japan Security Treaty does cover 'all territories under the administration of Japan', which under the Okinawa Reversion Treaty legally includes Senkaku/Diaoyudao, Washington's reluctance to stand firmly and unequivocally with Japan on the issue, despite Tokyo's efforts to meet the obligations of the US–Japan alliance in Iraq and the Indian Ocean, has certainly disconcerted Japanese policy-makers (Tkacik 2004).

44 On 24 Aug. 2004, Japan's External Trade Organisation (JETRO) announced a record expansion of two-way trade for the first six months of the year, for the fifth consecutive year, and a surplus of imports from China for the first time since 1992 (cf. Przystup 2004c: 123). These encouraging figures would go on to a record high by year's end as China overtook the US for the first time to become Japan's largest trade partner in 2004.

45 Indeed, Japan has, since 1995, strategically utilised ODA as a foreign policy tool towards China in its attempt to put pressure against Chinese military development (Takamine 2005: 440).

46 CCS Fukuda reportedly agreed to the adoption of the resolution, after potentially provocative language that might have antagonised China was removed from the initial draft (Przystup 2004b: 124).

47 Ishihara Nobuteru's nationalist mantle may likely derive from his father, Ishihara Shintaro, the ex-Tokyo governor, and infamous nationalist and anti-China figure.

48 The LDP Working Group on Maritime Interests, chaired by House of Councillors member, Takemi Keizo, was established in 2003, in response to the urgent need for Japan to develop a comprehensive framework for administering its maritime resources. The key impetus was undoubtedly the growing Japanese–Chinese confrontation in the ECS. The Working Group published a report on 11 June 2004, comprising nine proposals to secure Japan's oceanic interests (Shiraishi 2007).

49 The JCG reported as many as 14 cases of Chinese maritime intrusions into Japanese EEZ without prior notification during the first nine months of 2004 (*IHT* 12 Nov. 2004).

50 The LDP secretary-general, Takebe Tsutomu, Shin-Komeito Diet Policy Committee head, Higashi Shunji, and DPJ's president, Okada Katsuya, and shadow Defence Minister, Maehara Seiji, issued statements criticising China for the provocative intrusion and its failure to apologise over the issue (Przystup 2005a: 122; Chan 2004).

51 The *Yomiuri* editorial attacked Tokyo's delayed response as 'untenable', demanding a firmer stand, while *Sankei Shimbun* called the Chinese behaviour on the incident 'unforgivable', and also criticised the Japanese government's initial soft handling, demanding more unspecified 'countermeasures' if China failed to provide an 'honest response' (*DY* 13 Nov. 2004; AFP 13 Nov. 2004).

52 Curtin (2004b) observes that the return of Japan's official delegation and 'fact-finding mission' from North Korea on 13–14 Nov. 2004 would have put the abduction issue back into the limelight and at the top of the nationalist list of preoccupations, thus giving a breather to the comparatively 'mild' submarine problem.

53 Beginning in July 2004, Japan chartered the Norwegian seismic survey ship *Ramform Victory* to survey Japan's side of the line, opposite Shirakaba/Chunxiao, Kashi/Tianwaitian, and Kusunoki/Duanqiao natural gas fields (Harrison 2005: 4).

54 METI chief, Nakagawa Shoichi, expressed to his French counterpart, Herve Gaymard on 13 Jan. 2005 East Asian nations' concern about the prospect of the lifting of China arms embargo (enforced since the 1989 Tiananmen Incident) (*JT* 15 Jan. 2005), while Koizumi reinforced Japanese concerns during his Tokyo meeting with the French President, Jacques Chirac on 27 March (*JT* 28 March 2005).

55 The Tokyo Metropolitan government, formerly led by Ishihara Shintaro, established extensive plans to develop Okinotorishima, while the Japanese government also decided in mid-2005 to build a lighthouse on this 'barren rock' to support its claim to an extended EEZ (*KN* 24 Aug. 2005; BBC 16 May 2005).

56 Besides naval presence and manoeuvring in the ECS vicinity in Sept. 2005, China also announced the formation of the East China Sea naval fleet on 27 Sept. 2005 (*KN* 27 Sept. 2005).

57 The 'safety valve' function of the Joint Statement is commonly acknowledged by observers. Interestingly, the Feb. 2005 situation was somewhat reminiscent of the Hashimoto administration's widely believed effort to place Senkaku/Diaoyudao under the coverage of the revised US–Japan Guidelines, as a 'safety valve' to reduce nationalist-rightwing pressure on the government for a unilateral remilitarisation to defend Japan's territorial integrity, and realise its overall security interests, following the 1996 Senkaku/Diaoyudao dispute (Green 2001: 87–8).

58 An LDP politician, Nakagawa Shoichi is well known for his hawkish and nationalistic disposition, and 'China bashing' remarks (Mori 2007: 59).

59 The Japanese government maintained its assertive stance, declaring on 11 April 2005 that it would proceed with exploration activities despite the massive anti-Japanese demonstration in China (*JT* 12 April 2005). Indeed, after several advanced notifications that failed to elicit Chinese response, Tokyo finally announced on 13 April that it would grant exploratory rights in the ECS to Japanese companies, prompting instantaneous protest and strongly worded warning from Beijing. Nonetheless, Tokyo proceeded with the processing of the application for exploration rights by Teikoku Oil Company on 28 April 2005 (*JT* 15 and 29 April 2005).

60 The DPJ announced its intention to submit a bill to have the JCG protect Japanese companies' test-drilling, or developing maritime resources, and prohibiting resource exploration activities in Japan's EEZ by foreign ships (*DJN* 19 Oct. 2005; Przystup 2006a: 116). Meanwhile, the LDP Working Group on Maritime Interest led by Takemi Keizo, compiled a bill on 1 Dec. 2005 aimed at protecting Japanese vessels engaged in maritime resource and exploration activities within Japan's 200nm EEZ. Specifically, it was meant to support Teikoku Oil's intended test drilling at the disputed waters (*JT* 2 Dec. 2005; Przystup 2006a: 116).

61 DPJ president, Maehara Seiji, raised the 'China threat' notion during his lecture at the Center for Strategic and International Studies (CSIS) in Washington, DC, on 8 Dec. 2005 (Oda 2005). He then told a *Kyodo News* study group on 11 Jan. 2006 that there exist differences of opinion among party ranks regarding the 'China threat' assessment, but he personally would continue perceiving China as an 'actual threat'(cf. Przystup 2006b: 126).

62 Replacing the 'China-bashing' Nakagawa during the cabinet reshuffle in Oct. 2005, Nikai is widely perceived to be a 'pro-China' LDP leader who has developed close contacts with the Chinese political echelon (van Kemenade 2006: 74; *DY* 8 March 2006). A senior METI official interviewed went as far as to call him a 'panda-hugger'. Interview (Tokyo, 28 May 2008). Since taking office, Nikai promoted a moderate, less confrontational approach to resolve the ECS issues, which led to some progress in terms of mutual agreement to shelve the maritime border delimitation impasse and establish a panel of technical experts to facilitate a peaceful resolution during the July 2006 consultations (*PD* 10 July 2006).

63 Interview (Tokyo, 5 June 2008).

64 Interview (Tokyo, 9 June 2008).

65 Such was the opinion of several senior MOFA and METI bureaucrats interviewed during the course of this study.

66 From a rational-choice/economic perspective, both countries are more likely to reach for a mutually equitable settlement and engage in joint development, rather than military confrontation over the ECS gas issue, as the mutual economic benefit

deriving from the former far outweighs the latter strategy. Moreover, both countries have diversified their respective energy sources over the years to enhance energy security, and are, therefore, not over-dependent on the ECS for their energy supply. In fact, the notion of joint development as 'the best way to move forward' (Curtin 2005b) is shared by informed Japanese intellectuals, bureaucrats and political elites interviewed.

67 However, it is also true that Tokyo's so-called 'foot-dragging' over the ECS negotiation was partly caused by the lack of 'driving force', i.e. limited initial interests from Japanese oil companies to invest in the development of the area due to economic and security considerations, apart from the ECS energy resources not being overly important to Japan, considering the low wholesale price of natural gas before 2007. I would like to thank senior METI and MOFA officials for pointing out this observation during our interviews. Interviews with a senior official, Trade Policy Bureau, METI, Japan (Tokyo, 28 May 2008), ex-senior vice-minister, METI, Japan (Tokyo, 5 June 2008), and former Japanese ambassador to China (Tokyo, 9 June 2008).

Conclusion

1 In fact, Abe was the first post-war Japanese premier to choose China as the destination for his first official overseas trip (*PD* 8 Oct. 2006).

Bibliography

Agawa, N. (2004) 'Japan–US relations and the Japanese public', in A. McCreedy *et al., The People vs. Koizumi? Japan–US Relations and Japan's Struggle for National Identity*, Asia Program Special Report, 119, Washington, DC: Woodrow Wilson International Center for Scholars.

Ahn, C. S. (1998) 'Interministry coordination in Japan's foreign policy making', *Pacific Affairs*, 71(1): 41–60.

Anderson, B. (1991) *Imagined Communities: Reflections on the Origins and Spread of Nationalism*, London: Verso.

Anderson, G. E. (2004) 'Lionheart or paper tiger? A first-term Koizumi retrospective', *Asian Perspective*, 28(1): 149–82.

Armitage, R. L., Bob, D. E., Campbell, K. M., Green, M. J., Harrington, K. M., Jannuzi, F., Kelly, J. A., Lincoln, E. J., Manning, R. A., Nealer, K. G., Nye, Jr., J. S., Patterson, T. L., Przystup, J. J., Sakoda, R. H., Wanner, B. P., and Wolfowitz, P. H. (2000) *The United States and Japan: Advancing Toward a Mature Partnership*. Washington, D.C.: Institute of National Strategic Studies, National Defense University, 11 October.

Aron, R. (1966) *Peace and War: A Theory of Peace and War*, tr. R. Howard and A. B. Fox, New York: Doubleday.

Austin, G., and Harris, S. (2001) *Japan and Greater China: Political Economy and Military Power in the Asian Century*, London: Hurst & Co.

Axelrod, R. (1984) *The Evolution of Cooperation*, New York: Basic Books.

Baycroft, T. (1998) *Nationalism in Europe 1789–1945*, Cambridge: Cambridge University Press.

Bedeski, R. E. (1983) *The Fragile Entente: The 1978 Japan–China Peace Treaty in a Global Context*, Boulder, CO: Westview Press.

Befu, H. (1992) 'Symbols of nationalism and Nihonjinron', in R. Goodman and K. Refsing (eds), *Ideology and Practice: Modern Japan*, London: Routledge.

Benfell, S. T. (2002) 'Why can't Japan apologize? Institutions and war memories since 1945', *Harvard Asia Quarterly*, 6(2): <http://www.asiaquarterly.com/content/view/115/> (accessed Oct. 2007).

Berger, T. U. (1996) 'Norms, identity, and national security in Germany and Japan', in P. Katzenstein (ed.), *The Culture of National Security: Norms and Identity in World Politics,* New York: Columbia University Press.

Berger, T. U. (2000) 'Set for stability: prospects for conflict and cooperation in East Asia', *Review of International Studies*, 26(3): 405–28.

Berger, T. U. (2003) 'Power and purpose in Pacific East Asia: a constructivist interpretation', in G. J. Ikenberry and M. Mastanduno (eds), *International Relations Theory and the Asia Pacific*, New York: Columbia University Press.

Berger, T. U. (2007) 'The politics of memory in Japanese foreign relations', in T. U. Berger, M. M. Mochizuki, and J. Tsuchiyama (eds), *Japan in International Politics: The Foreign Policies of an Adaptive State*, Boulder, CO, and London: Lynne Rienner.

Bernstein, R., and Munro, R. H. (1997) *The Coming Conflict with China*, 1st edn, New York: Knopf.

Betts, R. K. (1993–4) 'Wealth, power and instability', *International Security*, 18(3): 34–77.

Bezlova, A. (2001) 'China–Japan: support for action on terror brings rival together', Inter Press Service, 9 Oct.

Billig, M. (1995) *Banal Nationalism*, London: Sage.

Bitzinger, R. A. (2003) 'A paper tiger no more? The US debate over China's military modernization', in S. Limaye (ed.), *Special Assessment: Asia's China Debate*, Honolulu: Asia-Pacific Center for Security Studies.

Bix, H. P. (2001) 'Japan's New Nationalism', *New York Times,* 29 May.

Blanchard, J-M. F. (2000) 'The U.S. role in the Sino–Japanese dispute over the Diaoyu (Senkaku) Islands 1945–1971', *China Quarterly*, 161: 95–123.

Blanchard, J-M. F. (2006) 'China's peaceful rise and Sino–Japanese territorial and maritime tensions', in S. Guo (ed.), *China's 'Peaceful Rise' in the 21st Century: Domestic and International Conditions*, Aldershot: Ashgate.

Bong, Y. D. (2002) *Flashpoint at Sea? Legitimization Strategy and East Asian Island Disputes.* Ph.D. Dissertation, University of Pennsylvania, reproduced by UMI Dissertation Services, Ann Arbor, MI: ProQuest.

Brecher, M. (1972) *The Foreign Policy System of Israel: Setting, Images and Process*, London: Oxford University Press.

Breen, J. (2004) 'The dead and the living in the land of peace: a sociology of the Yasukuni shrine', *Mortality*, 9(1): 76–93.

Breen, J. (ed.) (2007) *Yasukuni: The War Dead and the Struggle for Japan's Past*, London: Hurst & Co.

Breslin, S. (1990) 'The foreign policy bureaucracy', in G. Segal (ed.), *Chinese Politics and Foreign Policy Reform*, London: Routledge.

Brooke, J. (2005) 'Drawing the line on energy', *New York Times,* 29 March: <http://www.nytimes.com/2005/03/29/business/worldbusiness/29joust.html?pagewanted=print&position=> (accessed Oct. 2007).

Brooks, S. G. (1997) 'Duelling realisms', *International Organization*, 51(3): 445–77.

Brown, D. M. (1955) *Nationalism in Japan: An Introductory Historical Analysis*, Berkeley, CA: University of California Press.

Burns, K. G. (2000) 'China and Japan: economic partnership to political ends', in M. Krepon and C. Gagne (eds), *Economic Confidence-Building and Regional Security*, Washington, DC: Henry L. Stimson Center: <http://www.stimson.org/southasia/pdf/burnspdf.pdf> (accessed Feb. 2006).

Calder, K. (2001) 'The new face of Northeast Asia', *Foreign Affairs*, 80(1): 106–12.

Calder, K. (2006) 'China and Japan's simmering rivalry', *Foreign Affairs*, 85(2): 129–39.

Cha, V. D. (2000) 'Abandonment, entrapment, and neoclassical realism in Asia: the United States, Japan, and Korea', *International Studies Quarterly*, 44: 261–91.

Chan, C., and Bridges, B. (2006) 'China, Japan, and the clash of nationalisms', *Asian Perspective*, 30(1): 127–56.

Chan, J. (2004) 'Japan uses submarine incident to whip up anti-Chinese nationalism', *World Socialist Website*, 29 Nov.: <http://www.wsws.org/articles/2004/nov2004/jap-n29.shtml> (accessed Oct. 2007).

Chiu, H. (1999) *An Analysis of the Sino-Japanese Dispute over the T'iaoyutai Islets (Senkaku Gunto)*, Occasional Paper Series in Contemporary Asian Studies, 3(152), Baltimore, MD: University of Maryland.

Choi, W. (2003) 'Persistence and change in Japan–China relationship', *Journal of International and Area Studies*, 10(1): 75–92.

Christensen, T. J. (1996) *Useful Adversaries: Grand Strategy, Domestic Mobilization, and Sino-American Conflict, 1947–1958*, Princeton, NJ: Princeton University Press.

Christensen, T. J. (1999) 'China, the US–Japan alliance, and the security dilemma in East Asia', *International Security*, 23(4): 49–80.

Christensen, T. J. (2005) 'Have old problems trumped new thinking? China's relations with Taiwan, Japan, and North Korea', *China Leadership Monitor*, 14: 1–10.

Chung, C. (2004) *Domestic Politics, International Bargaining and China's Territorial Disputes*, London and New York: RoutledgeCurzon.

Clark, G. (2006) 'Reviving the China threat', *Japan Focus*, 15 Jan.: <http://www.japanfocus.org/article.asp?id=497> (accessed May 2006).

Connor, W. (1994) *Ethnonationalism: The Quest for Understanding*, Princeton, NJ: Princeton University Press.

Conroy, H. (1955) 'Japanese nationalism and expansionism', *American Historical Review*, 60(4): 818–29.

Cooney, K. J. (2007) *Japan's Foreign Policy since 1945*, Armonk, NY: M. E. Sharpe.

Copeland, D. (2000) 'The constructivist challenge to structural realism', *International Security*, 25(2): 187–212.

Cronin, R. P. (2007) 'Abe Shinzo's new nationalism and the future of Sino-Japanese relations', East Asia: Program Publications, Washington, D.C.: Henry L. Stimson Center, article adapted from the 'Afterword' by R. P. Cronin in B. L. Self (2006) *The Dragon's Shadow: The Rise of China and Japan's New Nationalism*, Washington, D.C.: Henry L. Stimson Center. Online: < http://www.stimson.org/images/uploads/research-pdfs/Dragons_Shadow_Afterword_articleJan_2007.pdf> (accessed Aug. 2007).

Curtin, J. S. (2004a) 'Island dispute damages Sino-Japanese relations', *GLOCOM Platform: Debate: Commentary*, 29 March: <http://www.glocom.org/debates/20040329_curtin_island/index.html> (accessed Aug. 2007).

Curtin, J. S. (2004b) 'Submarine incident strains Japan–China ties', *GLOCOM Platform: Debates*, 19 Nov.: <http://www.glocom.org/debates/20041119_curtin_submarine/index.html> (accessed Aug. 2007).

Curtin, J. S. (2005a) 'China–Japan relations under new strain', *GLOCOM Platform*, 26 May: <http://www.glocom.org/debates/20050526_curtin_china/index.html> (accessed June 2007).

Curtin, J. S. (2005b) 'Sea of confrontation: Japan–China territorial and gas dispute intensifies', *Japan Focus*, 19 Oct.: <http://www.japanfocus.org/article.asp?id=426> (accessed June 2006).

Dai, T. J. D. (2006) 'The Diaoyu/Senkaku dispute: bridging the cold divide', *Santa Clara Journal of International Law*, 1: 134–68.

Daniels, P. R. (2004) *Beyond 'Better than Ever': Japanese Independence and the Future of US–Japan Relations*, IIPS Policy Paper, 308E, Tokyo: Institute for International Policy Studies.

Deans, P. (2000) 'Contending nationalisms and the Diaoyutai/Senkaku dispute', *Security Dialogue*, 31(1): 119–31.

Deans, P. (2007) 'Diminishing returns? Prime Minister Koizumi's visits to the Yasukuni shrine in the context of East Asian nationalisms', *East Asia*, 24: 269–94.

Deng, Y. (1997) 'Chinese relations with Japan: implications for Asia-Pacific regionalism', *Pacific Affairs*, 70(3): 373–91.

Desch, M. C. (1998) 'Culture clash: assessing the importance of ideas in security studies', *International Security*, 23(1): 141–70.

Dessler, D. (1989) 'What's at stake in the agent–structure debate?', *International Organization*, 43(3): 441–73.

Dolven, B. (2002) 'Turning a Blind Eye', *Far Eastern Economic Review*, 165(46): 60–1.

Dower, J. W. (1993) 'Peace and democracy in two systems: external policy and internal conflict', in A. Gordon (ed.), *Postwar Japan as History*, Berkeley, CA: University of California Press.

Dower, J. W. (1999) *The Showa Emperor and Japan's Postwar Imperial Democracy*, JPRI Working Paper, 61, Oakland, CA: Japan Policy Research Institute.

Downs, E. S., and Saunders, P. C. (1998-9) 'Legitimacy and the limits of nationalism: China and the Diaoyu Islands', *International Security*, 23(3): 114–46.

Drifte, R. (1990) *Japan's Foreign Policy*, London: Routledge.

Drifte, R. (1996) *Japan's Foreign Policy in the 1990s: From Economic Superpower to What Power?*, New York: St Martin's Press.

Drifte, R. (2002) 'Engagement Japanese style', in M. Soderberg (ed.), *Chinese–Japanese Relations in the Twenty-First Century: Complementarity and Conflict*, London and New York: Routledge.

Drifte, R. (2003) *Japan's Security Relations with China: From Balancing to Bandwagoning?*, London and New York: RoutledgeCurzon.

Drifte, R. (2008a) *Japanese–Chinese Territorial Disputes in the East China Sea: Between Military Confrontation and Economic Cooperation*, working paper, Asia Research Centre, London: London School of Economics and Political Science.

Drifte, R. (2008b) 'From "Sea of Confrontation" to "Sea of Peace, Cooperation and Friendship"? Japan facing China in the East China Sea', *Japan Aktuell*, 3/2008: 27–51.

Druckman, D. (1994) 'Nationalism, patriotism, and group loyalty: a social psychological perspective', *Mershon International Studies Review*, 38: 43–68.

Evangelista, M. (1997) 'Domestic structure and international change', in M. Doyle and G. J. Ikenberry (eds), *New Thinking in International Relations Theory*, Boulder, CO: Westview Press.

Fairbank, J. K. (ed.) (1968) *The Chinese World Order*, Cambridge, MA: Harvard University Press.

Fanell, J. E. (2006) 'China: big troubles on the high seas', *Hoover Digest 2006*, 3: <http://www.hoover.org/publications/digest/4635601.html> (accessed Oct. 2007).

Feaver, P. D., Hellman, G., Schweller, R., Taliaferro, J. W., Wohlforth, W. C., Legro, J. W., and Moravcsik, A. (2000) 'Correspondence: brother, can you spare a paradigm? (Or was anybody ever a realist?)', *International Security*, 25(1): 165–93.

Ferguson, J. (2004a) 'The Diaoyutai-Senkaku Islands dispute reawakened', *China Brief*, 4(3), 4 Feb.: <http://www.jamestown.org/terrorism/news/article.php?articleid=2372861> (accessed Aug. 2007).

Ferguson, J. (2004b) 'Submarine incursion sets Sino-Japanese relations on edge', *China Brief*, 4(23), 24 Nov.: <http://www.jamestown.org/terrorism/news/article.php?articleid=2372934> (accessed Oct. 2007).

Friedberg, A. (1993–4) 'Ripe for rivalry: prospects for peace in a multipolar Asia', *International Security*, 18(3): 5–33.

Fujiwara, K. (2001) 'History and nationalism', *Japan Echo*, 28(4): 36–40.

Fukuda, K., and Yamaori, T. (2004) 'Japanese spirituality and Yasukuni shrine', *Japan Echo*, 31(6): 37–41.

Funabashi, Y. (2000) 'Tokyo's temperance', *Washington Quarterly*, 23(3): 135–44.

Funabashi, Y. (2003) 'The mission of Japan, China are converging', *Asahi Shimbun,* 1 July.

Funabashi, Y. (2005) 'Koizumi landslide: the China factor', *Yale Global Online,* 15 Sept.: <http://yaleglobal.yale.edu/display.article?id=6271> (accessed Sept. 2006).

Gao, B. (1997) *Economic Ideology and Japanese Industrial Policy: Developmentalism from 1931 to 1965*, New York: Cambridge University Press.

Gardner, R. (2002) 'Nationalistic Shinto: a child's guide to Yasukuni shrine', in D. S. Lopez Jr. (ed.), *Religions of Asia in Practice: An Anthology*, Princeton, NJ: Princeton University Press.

Garver, J. W. (1997) *Face Off: China, the United States, and Taiwan's Democratization*, Seattle, WA: University of Washington Press.

Gellner, E. (1983) *Nations and Nationalism*, Oxford: Blackwell.

Gertz, B. (2000) *The China Threat: How the People's Republic Targets America*, Washington, DC: Regnery Publishing Inc.

Glosserman, B. (2003) 'China–Japan perception gap', *Japan Times,* 10 Sept.

Glosserman, B. (2004) 'China's influence soars in Asia', *Japan Times*, 17 May.

Glosserman, B. (2006) 'Deputy and debutante: the new geometry of East Asia', in P. E. Lam (ed.), *Japan's Relations with China: Facing a Rising Power*, London: Routledge.

Gluck, C. (1985) *Japan's Modern Myths: Ideology in the Late Meiji Period*, Princeton, NJ: Princeton University Press.

Goldstein, L., and Murray, W. (2004) 'Undersea dragons: China's maturing submarine force', *International Security*, 28(4): 161–96.

Gong, G. W. (2001a) 'A clash of histories: "remembering and forgetting"'. Issues, structure and strategic implications', in G. W. Gong (ed.) *Memory and History: Issues of Identity in International Relations*, Washington DC: Center for Strategic and International Studies.

Gong, G. W. (2001b) 'The beginning of history: remembering and forgetting as strategic issues', *Washington Quarterly*, 24(2): 45–57.

Green, M. J. (2001) *Japan's Reluctant Realism: Foreign Policy Challenges in an Era of Uncertain Power*, New York: Palgrave.

Green, M. J., and Self, B. L. (1996) 'Japan's China policy: from commercial liberalism to reluctant realism', *Survival*, 38(2): 35–58.

Gries, P. H. (2004) *China's New Nationalism: Pride, Politics, Diplomacy*, Berkeley, CA: University of California Press.

Gries, P. H. (2005a) 'Nationalism, indignation and China's Japan policy', *SAIS Review*, 25(2): 105–14.

Gries, P. H. (2005b) 'China's new thinking on Japan', *China Quarterly*, 184: 831–50.

Guibernau, M. (1996) *Nationalisms: The Nation-State and Nationalism in the Twentieth Century*, New York: Polity Press.

Guzzini, S. (2004) 'The enduring dilemmas of realism in international relations', *European Journal of International Relations*, 10(4): 533–68.

Hagstrom, L. (2003) *Enigmatic Power? Relational Power Analysis and Statecraft in Japan's China Policy*, Stockholm Studies in Politics, 93, Stockholm: Dept of Political Science, Stockholm University.

Hagstrom, L. (2005) 'Quiet power: Japan's China policy in regard to the Pinnacle Islands', *Pacific Review*, 18(2): 159–88.

Harootunian, H. (1999) 'Memory, mourning and national morality', in P. van Der Veer and H. Lehmann (eds), *Nations and Religions: Perspectives on Europe and Asia*, Princeton, NJ: Princeton University Press.

Harrison, S. S. (2005) *Seabed Petroleum in Northeast Asia: Conflict or Cooperation?*, Washington, DC: Woodrow Wilson International Center for Scholars Asia Program.

Hasegawa, M. (1985) 'A postwar view of the Greater East Asia War', *Journal of Historical Review*, 6(4): 451–66.

Hashizume, D. (2001) 'Koizumi and the new nationalism', *Japan Echo*, 28(6): 51–5.

He, Y. (2006) 'National mythmaking and the problems of history in Sino–Japanese relations', in P. E. Lam (ed.) *Japan's Relations with China: Facing a Rising Power*, London: Routledge.

Heazle, M. (2005) *Sino-Japanese Relation and Japan's Emerging Foreign Policy Crisis*, Regional Outlook Paper, 4, Brisbane, Queensland: Griffith Asia Institute.

Heazle, M. (2007) 'Nationalism, security, and prosperity: the three dimensions of Sino–Japan relations', in M. Heazle and N. Knight (eds), *China–Japan Relations in the Twenty-First Century: Creating a Future Past?*, Cheltenham and Northampton, MA: Edward Elgar.

Heginbotham, E., and Samuels, R. J. (1998) 'Mercantile realism and Japanese foreign policy', *International Security*, 22(4): 171–203.

Hilpert, H. G. (2002) 'Cooperation or conflict? What does trade data say?', in H. G. Hilpert and R. Haak (eds), *Japan and China: Cooperation, Competition, and Conflict*, New York: Palgrave Macmillan.

Hilpert, H. G., and Katsuji, N. (2002) 'Economic relations: what can we learn from trade and FDI?', in M. Soderberg (ed.), *Chinese–Japanese Relations in the Twenty-First Century: Complementarity and Conflict*, London and New York: Routledge.

Hiwatari, N. (2005) 'Japan in 2005: Koizumi's finest hour', *Asian Survey*, 46(1): 22–36.

Hobsbawm, E., and Ranger, T. (eds) (1983) *The Invention of Tradition*, Cambridge: Cambridge University Press.

Hood, C. P. (1999) *The Election of Ishihara: A Symbol of Rising Nationalism in Japan?*, Asia Programme Briefing Paper, 7, London: Royal Institute of International Affairs.

Hook, G. D. (2006) 'Building Yellow Sea bridges: Kyushu's role in Japan–China relations', in P. E. Lam (ed.), *Japan's Relations with China: Facing a Rising Power*, London: Routledge.

Hook, G. D., Gilson, J., Hughes, C.W., and Dobson, H. (eds) (2005) *Japan's International Relations: Politics, Economics and Security*, London: Routledge.

Hopf, T. (1998) 'The promise of constructivism in international relations theory', *International Security*, 23(1): 171–200.

Howe, C. (1996) 'China, Japan and economic interdependence in the Asia-Pacific region', in C. Howe (ed.), *China and Japan: History, Trends, and Prospects*, Oxford: Clarendon Press.

Hughes, C. R. (2006) *Chinese Nationalism in the Global Era*, London: Routledge.

Hughes, C. W. (1999) *Japan's Economic Power and Security: Japan and North Korea*, London and New York: Routledge.

Hughes, C. W. (2005) *Japan's Re-emergence as a 'Normal' Military Power*, ADELPHI Paper 368–9, Abingdon: Routledge for the International Institute of Strategic Studies.

Hughes, C. W. (2006) 'Ballistic missile defence and US-Japan, US-UK alliances compared', *GARNET Working Paper*, No. 11/06, December, Coventry: Centre for the Study of Globalisation and Regionalisation, University of Warwick.

Huo, J. (2005) 'Where are Sino–Japanese relations headed?', *Beijing Review*, Oct.: <http:// www.bjreview.com.cn/En-2005/05-44-e/w-3.htm> (accessed Feb. 2006).

Iida, Y. (2003) 'Media politics and reified nation: Japanese culture and politics under information capitalism', *Japanese Studies*, 23(1): 23–42.

Ijiri, H. (1996) 'Sino-Japanese controversy since the 1972 diplomatic normalization', in C. Howe (ed.) *China and Japan: History, Trends, and Prospects*, Oxford: Clarendon Press.

Inayatullah, N., and Blaney, D. L. (1996) 'Knowing encounters: beyond parochialism in international relations theory', in Y. Lapid and F. V. Kratochwil (eds), *The Return of Culture and Identity in IR Theory*, Boulder, CO: Lynne Rienner.

Iriye, A. (1992) *China and Japan in the Global Setting*, Cambridge, MA: Harvard University Press.

Iriye, A. (1996) 'Chinese–Japanese relations, 1945–1990', in C. Howe (ed.), *China and Japan: History, Trends, and Prospects*, Oxford: Clarendon Press.

Itoh, M. (2001) *Japan's Neo-nationalism: The Role of the Hinomaru and Kimigayo Legislation*, JPRI Working Paper, 79, Oakland, CA: Japan Policy Research Institute.

Jain, P. (2000) 'Emerging foreign policy actors: subnational governments and nongovernmental organizations', in T. Inoguchi and P. Jain (eds), *Japanese Foreign Policy Today: A Reader*, New York: Palgrave.

Jain, P. (2006) 'Forging new bilateral relations: Japan–China cooperation at the sub-national level', in P. E. Lam (ed.) *Japan's Relations with China: Facing a Rising Power*, London: Routledge.

Jameson, S. (1997) *Japan's Amoeba Politics*, JPRI Working Paper, 29, Oakland, CA: Japan Policy Research Institute.

Japan Defense Agency (2004) *Defense of Japan 2004*, Tokyo: JDA (English edn).

Japan Defense Agency (2005) *Defense of Japan 2005*, Tokyo: JDA (English edn).

Japan Defense Agency (2006) *Defense of Japan 2006*, Tokyo: JDA (English edn).

Japan Forum on International Relations (1995) *The Policy Recommendations on the Future of China in the Context of Asian Security*, Tokyo: JFIR, Jan.

Jencks, H. W. (1994) 'The PRC's military and security policy in the post-Cold War era', *Issues and Studies*, 30(11): 65–103.

Jervis, R. (1976) *Perception and Misperception in International Politics*, Princeton, NJ: Princeton University Press.

Jin, X. (2002) 'The background and trend of the partnership', in M. Soderberg (ed.), *Chinese–Japanese Relations in the Twenty-First Century: Complementarity and Conflict*, London and New York: Routledge.

Johnson, C. (1995) *Japan: Who Governs? The Rise of the Developmental State*, New York: W. W. Norton.

Johnson, C. (2005) *No Longer the Lone Superpower: Coming to Terms with China*, JPRI Working Paper, 105, Oakland, CA: Japan Policy Research Institute.

Johnston, E. (2007) 'Japan under siege: Japanese media perceptions of China and the two Koreas six decades after World War II', in M. Heazle and N. Knight (eds), *China–Japan Relations in the Twenty-First Century: Creating a Future Past*, Cheltenham and Northampton, MA: Edward Elgar.

Johnstone, C. B. (2000) 'Clinching the giant: Tokyo's China strategy and implications for US–Japan relations', in D. D. Zhang and P. Drysdale (eds), *Japan and China: Rivalry or Cooperation in East Asia?*, Canberra: Asia Pacific Press at Australian National University.

Judt, T. (1994) 'The new old nationalism', *New York Review of Books*, 26 May: 44–51.

Kaneko, M. (2005) 'Lost horizons: the flawed "nationalism" of the Koizumi regime', *Japan Focus*, 12 May: <http://www.japanfocus.org/article.asp?id=279> (accessed June 2006).

Kase, M. (2001) 'Nationalism in moderation is good for Japan', *Daily Yomiuri*, 9 Aug.

Katsumata, H. (2004) 'Govt lax over Senkaku issue/inaction encouraging Chinese to push sovereignty claims', *Daily Yomiuri*, 27 March.

Katzenstein, P. J. (ed.) (1996) *The Culture of National Security: Norms and Identity in World Politics*, New York: Columbia University Press.

Katzenstein, P. J. (2008) *Rethinking Japanese Security: Internal and External Dimensions*, Abingdon and New York: Routledge.

Katzenstein, P. J., and Okawara, N. (2001) 'Japan, Asian-Pacific security, and the case for analytical eclecticism', in P. J. Katzenstein (2008) *Rethinking Japanese Security: Internal and External Dimensions*, Abingdon and New York: Routledge.

Kawashima, S. (2005) 'The history factor in Sino-Japanese ties', *Japan Echo*, 32(5): 16–22.

Kellas, J. (1998) *The Politics of Nationalism and Ethnicity*, 2nd edn, London: Macmillan.

Kemilainen, A. (1964) *Nationalism: Problems Concerning the Word, the Concept and Classification*, Yvaskyla: Kustantajat Publishers.

Keohane, R. O. (1989) 'Neoliberal institutionalism', in R. O. Keohane (ed.), *International Institution and State Power: Essays in International Relations Theory*, Boulder, CO: Westview Press.

Keohane, R. O., and Nye Jr., J. S. (eds) (1977) *Power and Interdependence*, Boston, MA: Little Brown.

Kingston, J. (2004) *Japan's Quiet Transformation: Social Change and Civil Society in the Twenty-First Century*, London: Routledge.

Kingston, J. (2007) 'Japan's war memories, so often misinterpreted', *Japan Times*. 5 Aug.: <http://search.japantimes.co.jp/mail/fb20070805a1.html> (accessed Aug. 2007).

Klare, M. T. (2006) 'Target China: the emerging US–China conflict', *Japan Focus*, 19 April: <http://www.japanfocus.org/article.asp?id=579> (accessed June 2006).

Kliman, D. M. (2006) *Japan's Security Strategy in the Post-9/11 World: Embracing a New Realpolitik*, Washington, DC: CSIS.

Kohn, H. (1965) *Nationalism: Its Meaning and History*, New York and London: D. Van Nostrand.

Koizumi, J., and Shiroyama, S. (2002) 'Battling headwinds to achieve reforms', *Japan Echo*, 29(3): 10–13.

Kojima, T. (2000) 'Japan's China policy', in D. D. Zhang and P. Drysdale (eds), *Japan and China: Rivalry or Cooperation in East Asia?*, Canberra: Asia Pacific Press at Australian National University.

Kokubun, R. (2001) 'Japan–China relations after the Cold War: switching from the "1972 framework', *Japan Echo*, 28(2): 9–14.

Kokubun, R. (2003) 'Beyond normalization: thirty years of Sino–Japanese diplomacy', *Gaiko Forum: Japanese Perspective on Foreign Affairs*, 2(4): 31–9.

Kokubun, R. (2006) 'The shifting nature of Japan–China relations after the Cold War', in P. E. Lam (ed.), *Japan's Relations with China: Facing a Rising Power*, London: Routledge.

Kokubun, R. (2007) 'Changing Japanese strategic thinking toward China', in G. Rozman, K. Togo, and J. P. Ferguson (eds), *Japanese Strategic Thought toward Asia*, London and New York: Palgrave Macmillan.

Konishi, W. S. (2003) '"Double Expectations" in Asia', *GLOCOM Platform: Debate: Commentary*: <http://www.glocom.org/debates/20031208_konishi_double/index.html> (accessed Oct. 2008).

Lakatos, I. (1970) 'Falsification and the methodology of scientific research programmes', in I. Lakatos and A. Musgrave (eds), *Criticism and the Growth of Knowledge*, Cambridge: Cambridge University Press.

Lam, P. E. (2004) *Rise and Fall of China Threat Theory in Japan'*, EAI Background Paper, 208, Singapore: East Asian Institute, National University of Singapore.

Lam, P. E. (2005) 'Japan's deteriorating ties with China: the Koizumi factor', *China: An International Journal*, 3(2): 275–91.

Lam, P. E. (ed.) (2006a) *Japan's Relations with China: Facing a Rising Power*, London: Routledge.

Lam, P. E. (2006b) *Yasukuni Factor in the LDP's Forthcoming Election*, EAI Background Paper, 286, Singapore: East Asian Institute, National University of Singapore.

Lam, P. E. (2006c) *Abe Shinzo's Agenda: A More Assertive and Nationalistic Japan*, EAI Background Paper, 305, Singapore: East Asian Institute, National University of Singapore.

Lapid, Y., and Kratochwil, F. V. (eds) (1996) *The Return of Culture and Identity in IR Theory*, Boulder, CO: Lynne Rienner.

Lee, C. (1976) *Japan Faces China: Political and Economic Relations in the Postwar Era*, Baltimore, MD: Johns Hopkins University Press.

Lee, C. (1984) *China and Japan: New Economic Diplomacy*, Stanford, CA: Hoover Institute Press.

Legro, J. W., and Moravcsik, A. (1999) 'Is anybody still a realist?', *International Security*, 24(2): 5–55.

Liao, X. (2007) 'The petroleum factor in Sino–Japanese relations: beyond energy cooperation', *International Relations of the Asia-Pacific*, 7(1): 23–46.

Lim, R. (2007) 'Lee should avoid Yasukuni', *Japan Times*, 2 June.

Liu, H. C. K. (2006) 'Japan's postwar territorial disputes', in 'China and the US, Part 4, proliferation, imperialism – and the "China threat"', *Asia Times*, 9 Sept.: <http://www.atimes.com/atimes/Korea/HI09Dg01.html> (accessed Oct. 2007).

Lobell, S. E., Ripsman, N. M., and Taliaferro, J. W. (eds) (2009) *Neoclassical Realism, the State, and Foreign Policy*, Cambridge: Cambridge University Press.

Ma, L. (2003) 'New thinking on Sino-Japanese relations', *Japan Echo*, 30(3): 35–40.

McCormack, G. (2000) 'Nationalism and identity in post-cold war Japan', *Pacifica Review*, 12(3): 247–63.

McCormack, G. (2007) *Client State: Japan in the American Embrace*, London and New York: Verso.

McCreedy, A., Agawa, N., Tamamoto, M., Nishi, T. (2004) 'The People vs. Koizumi? Japan-US relations and Japan's struggle for national identity', *Asia Program Special Report*, No.119. Washington D.C.: Woodrow Wilson International Center for Scholars.

McGreevy, A. (2005) 'Arlington National Cemetery and Yasukuni Jinja: history, memory and the sacred', *Japan Focus*, article 359, 10 Aug.: <http://www.japanfocus.org/article.asp?id=359> (accessed May 2006).

McNeill, D. (2001) *Media Intimidation in Japan: A Close Encounter with Hard Japanese Nationalism*, Discussion Paper, 1, *Electronic Journal of Contemporary Japanese Studies (ejcjs)*, 27 March: <http://www.japanesestudies.org.uk/discussionpapers/McNeill.html> (accessed Feb. 2006).

McNeill, D. (2005) *History Redux: Japan's Textbook Battle Reignites,* JPRI Working Paper, 107, Oakland, CA: Japan Policy Research Institute.

McVeigh, B. J. (2001) *Postwar Japan's 'Hard' and 'Soft' Nationalism'*, JPRI Working Paper, 73, Oakland, CA: Japan Policy Research Institute.

McVeigh, B. J. (2004) *Nationalisms of Japan: Managing and Mystifying Identity*, Lanham, MD: Rowman & Littlefield.

Malik, M. (2000) 'Japan wary of assertive China', *Jane's Intelligence Review*, Dec.

Marquand, R. (2005) 'Nationalism drives China, Japan apart', *Christian Science Monitor*, 29 Dec.: <http://www.csmonitor.com/2005/1229/p01s02-woap.htm> (accessed Feb. 2006).

Mastanduno, M., Lake, D., and Ikenberry, G. J. (1989) 'Toward a realist theory of state action', *International Studies Quarterly*, 33(4): 457–74.

Matsumoto, K., Mikuriya, T., and Sakamoto, K. (2005) 'War responsibility and Yasukuni shrine', *Japan Echo*, 32(5): 23–8.

Matsumoto, S. (1971) 'The significance of nationalism in modern Japanese thought: some theoretical problems', *Journal of Asian Studies*, 31(1): 49–56.

Matthews, E. A. (2003) 'Japan's new nationalism', *Foreign Affairs*, 82(6): 74–90.

Mayall, J. (1990) *Nationalism and International Society*, Cambridge: Cambridge University Press.

Mearsheimer, J. J. (1990a) 'Back to the future: instability in Europe after the Cold War', *International Security*, 15(1): 5–56.

Mearsheimer, J. J. (1990b) 'After the Cold War: will we miss it?', *Current*, Nov.: 30–40.

Mearsheimer, J. J. (2001) *The Tragedy of Great Power Politics*, New York: W. W. Norton.

Mendl, W. (1995) *Japan's Asia Policy: Regional Security and Global Interests*, London: Routledge.

Midford, P. (2002) 'The logic of reassurance and Japan's grand strategy', *Security Studies*, 11(3): 1–43.

Miller, J. H. (2000) 'Changing Japanese attitude toward security', in S. Limaye and Y. Matsuda (eds), *Domestic Determinants and Security Policy-Making in East Asia*, Honolulu: National Institute for Defense Studies, Japan and Asia-Pacific Center for Security Studies.

Miller, J. H. (2002) *Japan's Burden of History: Can it Be Lifted?*, APCSS Occasional Paper Series, Honolulu: Asia-Pacific Center for Security Studies.

Miller, J. H. (2005–6) 'Will the real Japan please stand up', *World Policy Journal*, 22(4): 36–46.

Ministry of Foreign Affairs, Japan (2003) *Diplomatic Bluebook 2003*, Tokyo: MOFA.

Ministry of Foreign Affairs, Japan (2005) *Diplomatic Bluebook 2005*, Tokyo: MOFA.

Ministry of Foreign Affairs, Japan (2006) *Diplomatic Bluebook 2006*, Tokyo: MOFA.

Miyashita, A. (2002) 'Japanese foreign policy: the international–domestic nexus', in R. K. Beasley, J. Kaarbo, J. S. Lantis and M. T. Snarr (eds), *Foreign Policy in Comparative Perspective: Domestic and International Influences on State Behaviour*, Washington, DC: CQ Press.

Miyazawa, K. (1997) 'Rethinking the Constitution: a document tested by time', *Japan Quarterly*, 44(3): 10–14.

Mochizuki, M. M. (2007) 'Dealing with a rising China', in T. U. Berger, M. M. Mochizuki and J. Tsuchiyama (eds), *Japan in International Politics: The Foreign Policies of an Adaptive State*, Boulder, CO, and London: Lynne Rienner.

Morgenthau, H. J. (1967) *Politics among Nations: The Struggle for Power and Peace*, 4th edn, New York: Knopf.

Mori, K. (2007) 'New relations between China and Japan: a gloomy, frail rivalry', *Modern Asian Studies Review*, 2: 1–77.

Mulgan, A. G. (2004) 'The leadership role of the prime minister and party', *Policy and Society*, 23(1): 5–20.

Murata, K. (2006) 'Domestic sources of Japanese policy towards China', in P. E. Lam (ed.), *Japan's Relations with China*, London: Routledge.

Muto, Y. (2001) 'Japanese security orientation: a psychological aspect', in G. W. Gong (ed.), *Memory and History in East and Southeast Asia*, Washington, DC: CSIS Press.

Nabeshima, K. (2006) 'Abe off to impressive start', *Japan Times*, 16 Oct.

Nabeshima, K. (2001) 'Cleaning up after Tanaka', *Japan Times*, 14 Aug.

Najita, T. (1980) *Japan: The Intellectual Foundations of Modern Japanese Politics*, Chicago: University of Chicago Press.

Nakanishi, T. (2005) 'China plays its history card', *Japan Echo*, 32(4): 18–23.

Nakata, H. (2007) 'Abe made offering to Yasukuni Shrine instead of visiting', *Japan Times*, 9 May: <http://search.japantimes.co.jp/mail/nn20070509a2.html> (accessed May 2007).

National Institute of Defense Studies (2002) *East Asian Strategic Review 2002*, Tokyo: NIDS.

National Institute of Defense Studies (2003) *East Asian Strategic Review 2003*, Tokyo: NIDS.

Nester, W. (1995) *International Relations: Geopolitical and Geoeconomic Conflict and Cooperation*, New York: Harper Collins.

Newby, L. (1988) *Sino-Japanese Relations: China's Perspective*, London: Routledge.

Niksch, L. (1996) *Senkaku (Diaoyu) Island Dispute: The U.S. Legal Relationship and Obligations*, CRS Report 96-798F, 30 September, Washington D.C.: United States Congressional Research Service.

Nish, I. (2000) 'Nationalism in Japan', in M. Leifer (ed.), *Asian Nationalism*, London: Routledge.

Oda, T. (2005) 'OPINION: Maehara knows threat of China', *Yomiuri Shimbun*, 22 Dec.

Okabe, T. (2001) 'Historical remembering and forgetting in Sino-Japanese relations', in G. W. Gong (ed.), *Memory and History: Issues of Identity in International Relations*, Washington, DC: Center for Strategic and International Studies.

Okazaki, H. (2006) 'Media role helps inflame the Yasukuni issue', *Daily Yomiuri*, 2 Sept.

Okazaki, S. (2005) 'Koizumi uncovered', in S. Okazaki, M. Tamamoto and C. Murphy, 'Behind Japan's foreign policy', *Far Eastern Economic Review*, 168(6): 23–6.

Orr, J. J. (2001) *The Victim as Hero: Ideologies of Peace and National Identity in Postwar Japan*, Honolulu: University of Hawai'i Press.

Ozkirimli, O. (2000) *Theories of Nationalism: A Critical Introduction*, Basingstoke and New York: Palgrave.

Park, C. H. (2001) 'Factional dynamics in Japan's LDP since political reforms: continuity and change', *Asian Survey*, 41(3): 428–61.

Pasic, S. C. (1996) 'Culturing international relations theory: a call for extension', in Y. Lapid and F. V. Kratochwil (eds), *The Return of Culture and Identity in IR Theory*, Boulder, CO: Lynne Rienner.

Pei, M., and Swaine, M. (2005) *Simmering Fire in Asia: Averting Sino-Japanese Strategic Conflict*, Policy Brief, 44, Washington, DC: Carnegie Endowment for International Peace.

Pilling, D. (2002) 'Koizumi to tread a fine line on his visit to North Korea', *Financial Times*, 16 Sept.

Posen, B. (1993) 'Nationalism, the mass army, and military power', *International Security*, 18(2): 80–124.

Prideaux, E. (2006) 'Riding with the rightists', *Japan Times,* 22 Oct.

Przystup, J. (2001a) 'Japan–China relations: the past is always present', *Comparative Connections: A Quarterly e-Journal on East Asian Bilateral Relations*, 3(1): 93–104.

Przystup, J. (2001b) 'Japan–China relations: trouble starts with "T"', *Comparative Connections: A Quarterly e-Journal on East Asian Bilateral Relations*, 3(2): 93–103.

Przystup, J. (2001c) 'Japan–China relations: spiraling downward', *Comparative Connections: A Quarterly e-Journal on East Asian Bilateral Relations*, 3(3): 110–19.

Przystup, J. (2002a) 'Japan–China relations: from precipice to promise', *Comparative Connections: A Quarterly e-Journal on East Asian Bilateral Relations*, 3(4): 89–96.

Przystup, J. (2002b) 'Japan–China relations: smoother sailing across occasional rough seas', *Comparative Connections: A Quarterly e-Journal on East Asian Bilateral Relations*, 4(1): 95–104.

Przystup, J. (2003a) 'Japan–China relations: congratulation, concerns, competition, and cooperation', *Comparative Connections: A Quarterly e-Journal on East Asian Bilateral Relations*, 5(1): 103–11.

Przystup, J. (2003b) 'Japan–China relations: cross currents', *Comparative Connections: A Quarterly e-Journal on East Asian Bilateral Relations*, 5(1): 101–10.

Przystup, J. (2004a) 'Japan–China relations: dialogue of the almost deaf', *Comparative Connections: A Quarterly e-Journal on East Asian Bilateral Relations*, 6(1): 103–15.

Przystup, J (2004b) 'Japan–China relations: not quite all about sovereignty – but close', *Comparative Connections: A Quarterly e-Journal on East Asian Bilateral Relations*, 6(2): 123–34.

Przystup, J. (2004c) 'Japan–China relations: not the best of times', *Comparative Connections: A Quarterly e-Journal on East Asian Bilateral Relations*, 6(3): 117–27.

Przystup, J. (2005a) 'Japan–China relations: a volatile mix: natural gas, a submarine, a shrine, and a visa', *Comparative Connections: A Quarterly e-Journal on East Asian Bilateral Relations*, 6(4): 119–33.

Przystup, J. (2005b) 'Japan–China relations: trying to get behind Yasukuni', *Comparative Connections: A Quarterly e-Journal on East Asian Bilateral Relations*, 7(1): 109–21.

Przystup, J. (2005c) 'Japan–China relations: no end to history', *Comparative Connections: A Quarterly e-Journal on East Asian Bilateral Relations*, 7(2): 119–32.

Przystup, J. (2006a) 'Japan–China relations: Yasukuni stops everything', *Comparative Connections: A Quarterly e-Journal on East Asian Bilateral Relations*, 7(4): 109–22.

Przystup, J. (2006b) 'Japan–China relations: looking beyond Koizumi', *Comparative Connections: A Quarterly e-Journal on East Asian Bilateral Relations*, 8(1): 119–33.

Putnam, R. (1988) 'Diplomacy and domestic politics: the logic of two-level games', *International Organization*, 42(3): 427–60.

Pyle, K. B. (1971) 'Introduction: Some Recent Approaches to Japanese Nationalism', *Journal of Asian Studies*, 31(1): 5–16.

Pyle, K. B. (1996) *The Japanese Question: Power and Purpose in a New Era,* Washington, DC: AEI Press.

Reischauer, E. O. (1977) *The Japanese*, Cambridge, MA: Harvard University Press.

Rice, C. (2000) 'Promoting the National Interest', *Foreign Affairs*, 79(1): 45–62.

Rose, C. (1998) *Interpreting Sino–Japanese Relations: A Case Study in Political Decision-making*, London: Routledge.

Rose, C. (2000) '"Patriotism is not taboo": nationalism in China and Japan and implications for Sino–Japanese relations', *Japan Forum*, 12(2): 169–81.

Rose, C. (2005) *Sino-Japanese Relations: Facing the Past, Looking to the Future?*, Abingdon and New York: RoutledgeCurzon.

Rose, C. (2006) 'The battle for hearts and minds: patriotic education in Japan in the 1990s and beyond', in N. Shimazu (ed.) *Nationalisms in Japan*, London: Routledge.

Rose, C. (2007) 'Stalemate: the Yasukuni Shrine problem in Sino–Japanese relations', in J. Breen (ed.), *Yasukuni: The War Dead and the Struggle for Japan's Past*, London: Hurst & Co.

Rose, G. (1998) 'Neoclassical realism and theories of foreign policy', *World Politics*, 51(1): 144–72.

Rosecrance, R., and Stein, A. A. (eds) (1993) *The Domestic Bases of Grand Strategy*, Ithaca, NY: Cornell University Press.

Roth, A. I. (2006) 'A bold move forward for Neoclassical Realism', *International Studies Review*, 8: 486–8.

Roy, D. (2003) *Stirring Samurai, Disapproving Dragon: Japan's Growing Security Activity and Sino-Japan Relations*, APCSS Occasional Paper Series, Honolulu: Asia-Pacific Center for Security Studies.

Roy, D. (2005) 'The sources and limits of Sino–Japanese relations', *Survival*, 47(2): 191–214.

Rozman, G. (2002) 'China's changing images of Japan, 1989–2001: the struggle to balance partnership and rivalry', *International Relations of the Asia-Pacific*, 2(1): 95–129.

Russett, B. (1993) *Grasping the Democratic Peace: Principles of a Post-Cold War World*, Princeton, NJ: Princeton University Press.

Samuels, R. J. (2007a) 'Securing Japan: the current discourse', *Journal of Japanese Studies*, 33(1): 125–52.

Samuels, R. J. (2007b) *Securing Japan: Tokyo's Grand Strategy and the Future of East Asia*, Ithaca, NY: Cornell University Press.

Samuels, R. J. (2007–8) '"New fighting power!": Japan's growing maritime capabilities and East Asian security', *International Security*, 32(3): 84–112.

Sasada, H. (2006) 'Youth and nationalism in Japan', *SAIS Review*, 26(2): 109–22.

Sasajima, M. (2002) 'Japan's domestic politics and China policymaking', in B. L. Self and J. W. Thompson (eds), *An Alliance for Engagement: Building Cooperation in Security Relations with China*, Washington, DC: Henry L. Stimson Center.

Sasaki, T. (2001) 'A new era of nationalism?', *Journal of Japanese Trade and Industry*, Jan./Feb: 8–11.

Sato, S. (1977) 'The foundations of modern Japanese policy', in R. A. Scalapino (ed.), *The Foreign Policy of Japan*, Berkeley, CA: University of California Press.

Satoh, H. (2006a) *The Odd Couple: Japan and China – the Politics of History and Identity*, JIIA Commentary, 4, Aug., Tokyo: Japan Institute of International Affairs.

Satoh, H. (2006b) *Japan and China: Reaching Reconciliation or Stuck in the Past?*, Asia Programme Briefing Paper, 2, Oct., London: Chatham House.

Schoenbaum, T. J. (2005) 'Resolving the China–Japan dispute over the Senkaku islands', *ZNet/Activism*, 16 Feb.: <http://www.zmag.org/content/print_article.cfm?itemID =7256&secti...> (accessed Aug. 2007).

Schweller, R. L. (2003) 'The progressiveness of neoclassical realism' in C. Elman and M.F. Elman (eds) *Progress in International Relations Theory: Appraising the Field*, Cambridge: MA: MIT Press.

Schweller, R. L. (2004) 'Unanswered threats: a neoclassical realist theory of underbalancing', *International Security*, 29(2): 159–201.

Schweller, R. L. (2006) *Unanswered Threats: Political Constraints on the Balance of Power*, Princeton, NJ: Princeton University Press.

Seaton, P. A. (2007) *Japan's Contested War Memories: The 'Memory Rifts' in Historical Consciousness of WWII*, London: Routledge.

Seckington, I. (2005) 'Nationalism, ideology, and China's "fourth generation" leadership', *Journal of Contemporary China*, 14(42): 23–33.

Self, B. L. (2002) 'China and Japan: a façade of friendship', *Washington Quarterly*, 26(1): 77–88.

Shambaugh, D. (1994) 'The insecurity of security: the PLA's evolving doctrine and threat perceptions towards 2000', *Journal of Northeast Asian Studies*, 13(1): 3–25.

Shambaugh, D. (1996) 'China and Japan towards the twenty-first century: rivals for pre-eminence or complex interdependence?', in C. Howe (ed.), *China and Japan: History, Trends, and Prospects*, Oxford: Clarendon Press.

Shaw, H. (1999) *The Diaoyutai/Senkaku Islands Dispute: Its History and an Analysis of the Ownership Claims of the P.R.C., R.O.C., and Japan*, Occasional Paper/Reprints Series in Contemporary Asian Studies, 152(3), Baltimore, MD: School of Law, University of Maryland.

Shi, Y., 'The China–Japan political relations and the imperative for strategic management', paper presented at international conference on 'The Need for Conflict Prevention and Conflict Management in Sino–Japanese Relations', Tokyo, 8–9 March 2007.

Shibata, Y. (1995) '"Japan passing" could soon replace "Japan bashing"', *Daily Yomiuri*, 19 Sept.

Shibuichi, D. (2005) 'The Yasukuni Shrine dispute and the politics of identity in Japan: why all the fuss?', *Asian Survey*, 45(2): 197–215.

Shimazu, N. (ed.) (2006) *Nationalisms in Japan*, London: Routledge.

Shinoda, T. (2007) *Koizumi's Diplomacy: Japan's Kantei Approach to Foreign and Defence Affairs*, Washington, DC: University of Washington Press.

Shiraishi, T. (2007) 'Japan looks to its ocean', *Japan Echo*, 34(1): 30–1.

Shirk, S. L. (2007) *China: Fragile Superpower*, Oxford and New York: Oxford University Press.

Singer, J. D. (1961) 'The level-of-analysis problem in international relations', *World Politics*, 14(1): 77–92.

Singh, B. (2002) 'Japan's post-cold war security policy: bringing back the normal state', *Contemporary Southeast Asia*, 24(1): 82–105.

Smith, A. D. (1986) *The Ethnic Origins of Nations*, Oxford: Basil Blackwell.

Smith, A. D. (1991) *National Identity*, London: Penguin.

Soderberg, M. (ed.) (2002) *Chinese–Japanese Relations in the Twenty-First Century: Complementarity and Conflict*, London: Routledge.

Soerensen, C. T. N. (2006) 'Strategic "triangularity" in Northeast Asia: the Sino-Japanese security relationship and U.S. policy', *Asian Perspective*, 30(3): 99–128.

Sono, A. (2005) 'I will visit Yasukuni', *Japan Echo*, 32(6): 51–4.

State Council Information Office (SCIO), People's Republic of China (2004) *China's National Defense in 2004*, 27 Dec.: <http://www.china.org.cn/english/2004/Dec/116032.htm> (accessed Nov. 2008).

Sterling-Folker, J. (1997) 'Realist environment, liberal process, and domestic-level variables', *International Studies Quarterly*, 41: 1–25.

Sterling-Folker, J. (2009) 'Neoclassical realism and identity: peril despite profit across the Taiwan Strait', in S. E. Lobell, N. M. Ripsman and J. W. Taliaferro (eds), *Neoclassical Realism, the State, and Foreign Policy*, Cambridge: Cambridge University Press.

Stockwin, J. A. A. (1998) 'The political system: stability and change', in P. Heenan (ed.). *The Japan Handbook*, London: Fitzroy Dearborn.

Stronach, B. (1995) *Beyond the Rising Sun: Nationalism in Contemporary Japan*, Westport, CT: Praeger.

Su, S. W. (2005) 'The territorial dispute over the Tiaoyu/Senkaku Islands: an update', *Ocean Development and International Law*, 36: 45–61.

Suganuma, U. (2000) *Sovereign Rights and Territorial Space in Sino-Japanese Relations: Irredentism and the Diaoyu/Senkaku Islands*, Honolulu: University of Hawai'i Press.

Sutter, R. (2002) 'China and Japan: trouble ahead?', *Washington Quarterly*, 25(4): 37–49.

Taira, K. (2004) 'The China–Japan clash over the Diaoyu/Senkaku Islands', *Japan Focus*: <http://www.japanfocus.org/article.asp?id=157> (accessed May 2006).

Takagi, S. (1999) 'In search of a sustainable equal partnership: Japan–China relations in the post-cold war era', *Japan Review of International Affairs*, 13(1): 17–38.

Takagi, S. (2006) 'The Taiwan factor in Japan–China relations', in P. E. Lam (ed.), *Japan's Relations with China: Facing a Rising Power*, London: Routledge.

Takahara, A. (2004) 'Japan's political response to the rise of China', in R. Kokubun and J. Wang (eds), *The Rise of China and a Changing East Asian Order*, Tokyo and New York: Japan Center for International Exchange.

Takahara, A. (2006) 'Japanese NGOs in China', in P. E. Lam (ed.) *Japan's Relations with China: Facing a Rising Power*, London: Routledge.

Takahara, K. (2007) 'Press clubs: exclusive access to, pipelines for info', *Japan Times,* 30 Jan.

Takahashi, K. (2004) 'Gas and oil rivalry in the East China Sea', *Asia Times,* 27 July: <http://www.atimes.com/atimes/Japan/FG27Dh03.html> (accessed Aug. 2007).

Takamine, T. (2005) 'A new dynamism in Sino-Japanese security relations: Japan's strategic use of foreign aid', *Pacific Review*, 18(4): 439–61.

Takamine, T. (2006) *Japan's Development Aid to China: The Long-Running Foreign Policy of Engagement*, Abingdon and New York: Routledge.

Takashina, S. (2001) 'Yasukuni revisited', *Japan Echo*, 28(6): 48–50.

Taliaferro, J. W. (2006) 'State building for future wars: neoclassical realism and the resource-extractive state', *Security Studies*, 15(3): 464–95.

Tamamoto, M. (2001) 'A land without patriots: the Yasukuni controversy and Japanese nationalism', *World Policy Journal*, 18(3): 33–40.

Tamamoto, M. (2004) 'A nationalist's lament: the slippery slope of Koizumi's foreign policy', in A. McCreedy *et al., The People vs. Koizumi? Japan–US Relations and Japan's Struggle for National Identity*, Asia Program Special Report, 119, Washington, DC: Woodrow Wilson International Center for Scholars.

Tamamoto, M. (2005a) 'After the tsunami, how Japan can lead', *Far Eastern Economic Review*, 168(2): 10–18.

Tamamoto, M. (2005b) 'Sino-Japanese pride and prestige', *Far Eastern Economic Review*, 168(6): 26–9.

Tanaka, A. (1991) *Nitchu kankei 1945–1990*, Tokyo: Tokyo University Press.

Tanaka, A. (2000) 'Domestic politics and foreign policy', in T. Inoguchi and P. Jain (eds), *Japanese Foreign Policy Today: A Reader*, New York: Palgrave.

Tanaka, N. (2003) 'Yasukuni shrine, Japanese nationalism, and the Constitution: prime minister challenged', *ZNet*, 6 Feb.: <http://www.zmag.org/content/print_article.cfm?itemID=2989&sectionID=1> (accessed June 2007).

Tanamichi, K. (2005) 'The youthful face of Japanese nationalism', *Far Eastern Economic Review*, 168(10): 33–6.

Tang, J. (2006) 'Focus: Koizumi shrine visit stirs anger but Asia pins hope on successor Abe', *Kyodo News,* 15 Aug.

Taniguchi, T. (2005) 'A cold peace: the changing security equation in Northeast Asia', *Orbis*, 445–57.

Taylor, R. (1996) *Greater China and Japan: Prospect for an Economic Partnership in East Asia*, London: Routledge.

Terada, T. (2006) 'Forming an East Asian Community: a site for Japan–China power struggle', *Japanese Studies*, 26(1): 5–17.

Tkacik, Jr., J. J. (2004) 'China's new challenge to the U.S.–Japan alliance', *Web Memo*, 533, 13 July, Washington, DC: Heritage Foundation: <http://www.heritage.org/Research/AsiaandthePacific/wm533.cfm?renderforprint=1> (accessed Aug. 2007).

Togo, K. (2006) 'A moratorium on Yasukuni visits', *Far Eastern Economic Review*, 169(5): 5–15.

Tok, S. K. (2005) 'Neither friends nor foes: China's dilemmas in managing its Japan policy', *China: An International Journal*, 3(2): 292–300.

Tokita, H. (2003) 'Eleven questions about Yasukuni shrine', *Japan Echo*, 30(3): 48–9.

Tooze, R. (1996) 'Prologue: states, nationalisms and identities – thinking in IR theory', in J. Krause and N. Renwick (eds), *Identities in International Relations*, London: Macmillan.

Tsang, S. (1999) 'Japan's role in the Asia-Pacific: the views from Greater China', *Security Dialogue*, 30(4): 413–24.

Tsunekawa, K. (2006) *Dependent Nationalism in Contemporary Japan and its Implications for the Regional Order in the Asia-Pacific*, Asia Research Centre Working Paper, 133, Perth: Murdoch University.

Urabe, H. (2004a) 'Activists mark islands' sovereignty – China Daily', *GLOCOM Platform – Media Review*, 186, 19 Jan.: <http://www.glocom.org/mediareviews/nreview/20040119newsreview186/index.html> (accessed Oct. 2007).

Urabe, H (2004b) 'Japan told not to harm Diaoyu Islands activists', *GLOCOM Platform – News Review*, 202, 25 March: <http://www.glocom.org/media_reviews/n_review/20040325_news_r...> (accessed Aug. 2007).

Valencia, M. J. (2007) 'The East China Sea dispute: context, claims, issues, and possible solutions', *Asian Perspective*, 31(1): 127–67.

Van Evera, S. (1994) 'Hypotheses on nationalism and war', *International Security*, 18(4): 5–39.

van Kemenade, W. (2006) *China and Japan: Partners or Permanent Rivals?*, Clingendael Diplomacy Paper, 9, The Hague: Netherlands Institute of International Relations.

van Wolferen, K. (1993) *The Enigma of Japanese Power: People and Power in a Stateless Nation*, Tokyo: Tuttle.

Vasquez, J. A. (1997) 'The realist paradigm and degenerative versus progressive research programs: an appraisal of neotraditional research on Waltz's balancing proposition', *American Political Science Review*, 91: 899–912.

Vogel, E. F. (1986) 'Pax Nipponica?', *Foreign Affairs*, 64(4): 752–67.

Waldron, A. N. (1985) 'Theories of nationalism and historical explanation', *World Politics*, 37(3): 416–33.

Walt, S. M. (1997) 'The progressive power of realism', *American Political Science Review*, 91(4): 931–5.

Waltz, K. N. (1979) *Theory of International Politics*, Reading, MA: Addison-Wesley.

Wan, M. (2006) *Sino-Japanese Relations: Interaction, Logic, and Transformation*, Washington, DC: Woodrow Wilson Center Press.

Wang, J. (2002) 'Adjusting to a "strong-strong relationship": China's calculus of Japan's Asian policy', in T. Inoguchi (ed.) *Japan's Asian Policy: Revival and Response*, New York and Basingstoke: Palgrave Macmillan.

Wang, Q. K. (2000) 'Taiwan in Japan's relations with China and the United States after the Cold War', *Pacific Affairs*, 73(3): 353–73.

Weber, M. (1948) *From Max Weber: Essays in Sociology*, tr. H. H. Gerth and C. Wright-Mills, London: Routledge.

Wendt, A. (1992) 'Anarchy is what states make of it: the social construction of power politics', *International Organization*, 46(2): 391–425.

Wendt, A. (1995) 'Constructing international politics', *International Security*, 20(1): 71–81.

Whiting, A. (1983) 'Assertive nationalism in Chinese foreign policy', *Asian Survey*, 23(8): 913–33.

Whiting, A. (1989) *China Eyes Japan*, Berkeley, CA, and London: University of California Press.

Whiting, A. (1992) 'China and Japan: politics versus economics', *Annals of the American Academy*, 519: 39–51.

Whiting, A. (2000) 'China's Japan policy and domestic politics', in D. D. Zhang and P. Drysdale (eds), *Japan and China: Rivalry or Cooperation in East Asia?*, Canberra: Asia Pacific Press at Australian National University.

Wu, X. (2000) 'The security dimension of Sino–Japanese relations: warily watching one another', *Asian Survey*, 40(2): 296–310.

Yahuda, M. (1996) *The International Politics of the Asia-Pacific, 1945–1995*, London: Routledge.

Yahuda, M. (2006) 'The limits of economic interdependence: Sino-Japanese relations', in A. I. Johnston and R. S. Ross (eds), *New Directions in the Study of China's Foreign Policy*, Stanford, CA: Stanford University Press.

Yamaori, T. (2003) 'The warped wisdom of religious thought in modern Japan', *Japan Echo*, 30(3): 44–7.

Yang, B. (2006) 'Redefining Sino-Japanese relations after Koizumi', *Washington Quarterly*, 29(4): 129–37.

Yang, D. (2002) 'Mirror for the future or the history card? Understanding the "history problem"', in M. Soderberg (ed.), *Chinese-Japanese Relations in the Twenty-First Century: Complementarity and Conflict*, London: Routledge.

Yang, J. (2001) 'Chinese response', in T. Beal, Y. Nozaki and J. Yang, 'Ghost of the past: the Japanese history textbook controversy', *New Zealand Journal of Asian Studies*, 3(2): 177–88.

Yang, J. (2003) 'Sino–Japanese relations: implications for Southeast Asia', *Contemporary Southeast Asia*, 25(2): 306–26.

Yang, J. (2005) 'Two tigers in the same mountain: China's Japan challenge', paper presented at the conference on 'China, Korea, and Japan: The Evolving Relationship', Griffith Asia Institute, Brisbane, 23–24 Nov.

Yoshibumi, W., and Watanabe, T. (2006) 'Yomiuri and Asahi editors call for a national memorial to replace Yasukuni', *Japan Focus*, article 524, 14 Feb.: <http://www.japanfocus.org/article.asp?id=524> (accessed May 2006).

Yoshida, R. (2005) 'Koizumi's shrine trips baffle officials, aides', *Japan Times,* 28 May.

Yoshida, R. (2006) '"Stubborn maverick" makes good on promise', *Japan Times,* 16 Aug.

Yoshida, R., and Terada, S. (2008) 'Japan, China strike deal on gas fields', *Japan Times,* 19 June.

Yoshikawa, Y. (2007) 'The US–Japan–China mistrust spiral and Okinotorishima', *Japan Focus*, 11 Oct.: <http://japanfocus.org/products/details/2541> (accessed Oct. 2007).

Yoshino, K. (1992) *Cultural Nationalism in Contemporary Japan: A Sociological Enquiry*, London: Routledge.

Young, C. (1976) *The Politics of Cultural Pluralism*, Madison, WI: University of Wisconsin Press.

Yu, B. (1999) *Containment by Stealth: Chinese Views of and Policies toward America's Alliances with Japan and Korea After the Cold War*, Stanford, CA: Stanford University, Asia/Pacific Research Center.

Zakaria, F. (1992) 'Realism and domestic politics: a review essay', *International Security*, 17(1): 177–98.

Zakaria, F. (1998) *From Wealth to Power: The Unusual Origins of America's World Role*, Princeton: Princeton University Press.

Zhang, D. D. (2000) 'Managing bilateral economic differences', in D. D. Zhang and P. Drysdale (eds), *Japan and China: Rivalry or Cooperation in East Asia?*, Canberra: Asia Pacific Press at Australian National University.

Zhang, D. D., and Drysdale, P. (2000) 'Uneasy bedfellows in East Asia', in D. D. Zhang and P. Drysdale (eds), *Japan and China: Rivalry or Cooperation in East Asia?*, Canberra: Asia Pacific Press at Australian National University.

Zhao, Q. (1993) *Japanese Policymaking: The Politics behind Politics: Informal Mechanisms and the Making of China Policy*, Westport, CT: Praeger.

Zhao, Q. (1996) *Interpreting Chinese Foreign Policy*, Hong Kong: Oxford University Press.

Zhao, Q. (2002) 'Sino–Japanese relations in the context of the Beijing–Tokyo–Washington triangle', in M. Soderberg (ed.) *Chinese–Japanese Relations in the Twenty-First Century: Complementarity and Conflict*, London: Routledge.

Zhao, S. (1997) *Power Competition in East Asia: From the Old Chinese World Order to Post-Cold War Regional Multipolarity*, London: Macmillan.

Zhao, S. (2000) 'Chinese nationalism and its international orientations', *Political Science Quarterly*, 115(1): 1–33.

Zhao, S. (2005) 'China's pragmatic nationalism: is it manageable?', *Washington Quarterly*, 29(1): 131–44.

Zheng, B. (2005) 'China's "peaceful rise" to great-power status', *Foreign Affairs*, 84(5): 18–24.

Zheng, Y. (1999) *Discovering Chinese Nationalism in China: Modernization, Identity, and International Relations*, Cambridge: Cambridge University Press.

Zhu, J. (2005) 'The real reasons for the anti–Japanese outburst', *Japan Echo*, 32(4): 14–17.

Zoellick, R. (2005) 'Whither China: from membership to responsibility?', speech to the National Committee on US–China Relations, 21 Sept.: <http://www.state.gov/s/d/former/zoellick/rem/53682.htm> (accessed May 2008).

Newswires/news monitoring services/newspapers and internet sources

Agence France-Presse (AFP)
Associated Press (AP)
Asahi Shimbun (*AS*)
British Broadcasting Corporation (BBC)
China Daily (*CD*)
Cable News Network (CNN)
Dow Jones Newswire (DJN)
Guardian

International Herald Tribune (*IHT*)
Japan Times (*JT*)
Jiji Press (Jiji)
Korean Broadcasting System (KBS)
Korea Times (*KT*)
Kyodo News (*KN*)
Mainichi Daily News/Mainichi Shimbun (*MDN/MS*)
New York Times (*NYT*)
Nihon Keizai Shimbun (*Nikkei*)
People's Daily (*PD*)
Reuters
South China Morning Post (*SCMP*)
The Straits Times (*ST*)
Xinhua News Agency (XNA)
Yomiuri Shimbun/Daily Yomiuri (*YS/DY*)
GlobalSecurity.org, 'Senkaku/Diaoyutai Islands': <http://www.globalsecurity.org/military/world/war/senkaku.htm> (accessed Aug. 2007).

Index